CW00321799

An Invitation

TO JOIN THE ROYAL MINT COIN CLUB

In order to satisfy the demands of the modern collector, the Royal Mint has established its own Coin Club to provide its members with the latest information on new coins from both home and abroad. Recognised as the supreme examples of the minter's art, Royal Mint collector coins form a tangible record of our heritage

Some of the benefits of becoming a Coin Club member are:

FREE
Coin Club Membership
No **COMMITMENT**
TO PURCHASE
whatsoever.
ROYAL MINT GUARANTEE
If you're not completely happy,
return your coins within 30 days
for an immediate refund.
FREE
Quarterly
Coin Club Magazine
INTEREST-FREE
Payments on selected
high-value products

ROYAL MINT

ADVANCE NOTIFICATION
of rare and
limited-edition issues.
OPPORTUNITY
to purchase products
which are NOT offered
to the general public.
SPECIAL PRE-ISSUE PRICES
(subject to status)
The confidence that you are
dealing with one of the most
prestigious and reputable
numismatic organisations in the
world with a history
spanning over 1100 years

A TRADITION OF EXCELLENCE

*To receive your free brochure, please telephone 0845 60 88 300
or write to address detailed below, quoting ref. CYB05
Royal Mint Coin Club, FREEPOST, SWC 4207, PO Box 500, Pontyclun CF72 8WP*

Knightsbridge Coins

AUSTRALIAN COINS

Here is a sample of our new 2004 buying prices on scarce
and rare pieces. Prices are in pounds

	F	VF	EF
1930 Penny	£5250	£10250	P.O.R
1923 Halfpenny	£350	£800	£2750
1852 Adelaide Pound Type Two	£2250	£4750	£8000
1919/20 Kookaburra Pattern Id+1/2d from			£5000
Holey Dollar	£11500	£20000	P.O.R
Dump 1813 (fifteen pence)	£3000	£7500	P.O.R
1927 Proof Florin			FDC £2000
1937 Proof Crown			FDC £2000
1938 Proof Crown			FDC £3000

Knightsbridge Coins have just paid a world record price of £93275 for the legendary 1856
Sydney Mint Proof Sovereign and Half. Why risk sending your coins to the other side of the world,
when you can get immediate payment here in the U.K. from the market's No. 1 buyers?!

AMERICAN COINS

Our Buying Prices
For Early US Coins

Half Cents
	F	VF
1793	£1400	£2200
1794	£300	£475
1795	£200	£400
1796	£5000	£8000
1797	£250	£450

Half Dimes
	F	VF
1794/5	£600	£950
1796/7	£600	£950
1800/5	£400	£625

Half Dollars
	F	VF
1794	£950	£600
1795	£400	£850
1796/7		POA

Cents
	F	VF
1793	£1150	£1700
1794	£150	£500
1795	£110	£300
1796	£110	£300
1799	£1250	£2000

Quarters
	F	VF
1796	£2300	£3250
1804	£1100	£1800
1805/7	£200	£450

Dimes
	F	VF
1796	£700	£1200
1797	£700	£950
1798/1807	£300	£450

Dollars
	F	VF
1794	£7500	£12500
1795	£700	£1100
1796/8	£650	£900
1799/1803	£230	£320

Knightsbridge Coins 43 Duke Street, St. James's, London SW1Y 6DD
Tel: (020) 7930 7597/8215/7888   Fax: (020) 7930 8214
Monday to Friday, 10.15am–5.30pm

The only coin dealer with membership of all four Numismatic Organisations

St James's Auctions

Knightsbridge Coins *in association with* **Baldwin's Auctions Ltd**

This is a selection of Coins from our first Auction

We are now accepting **consignments** for Auction 2
which will take place in April / May 2005.
If you have items which you wish to sell,
please contact us at the address below.
Generous advances can be arranged.

Knightsbridge Coins
43 Duke Street
St James's
London SW1Y 6DD
Tel: 020 7930 7597 / 7888 / 8215
Fax: 020 7930 8214

"THE I.A.P.N. dealer, your guide to the world of numismatics"

"More than one hundred of the world's most respected coin dealers are members of the I.A.P.N.
(International Association of Professional Numismatists).
I.A.P.N. members offer the collector an exceptional selection of quality material, expert cataloguing, outstanding service, and realistic pricing.
The I.A.P.N. also maintain the International Bureau for the Suppression of Counterfeit Coins (I.B.S.C.C.) which, for a fee can provide expert opinions on the authenticity of coin submitted to it. A booklet listing the name, address and specialities of all I.A.P.N. members is available without charge by writing to the I.A.P.N. Secretariate". Jean-Luc van der Schueren, 14, Rue de la Bourse, B-1000, Bruxelles.
Tel: +32–2–513 3400   Fax: +32–2–512 2528   E-mail: iapnsecret@compuserve.com   Web site: http://www.iapn-coins.org

ARGENTINA
DERMAN, Alberto José, Avenida Corrientes 368, BUENOS AIRES

AUSTRALIA
NOBLE NUMISMATICS Pty Ltd (Jim Noble), 169 Macquarie Street, SYDNEY NSW 2000

AUSTRIA
HERINEK, Gerhard, Josefstädterstrasse 27, A–1080 WIEN
MOZELT Christine Numismatik, Erich Mozelt, Postfach 19, A–1043 WIEN

BELGIUM
ELSEN, Jean & ses Fils s.a., Avenue de Tervuren 65, B–1040 BRUXELLES
FRANCESCHI & Fils, B, 10, Rue Croix-de-Fer, B–1000 BRUXELLES
VAN DER SCHUEREN, Jean-Luc, 14, Rue de la Bourse, B–1000 BRUXELLES

CANADA
WEIR LTD., Randy, PO Box 64577, UNIONVILLE, Ontario, L3R 0M9

EGYPT
BAJOCCHI, Pietro, 45 Abdel Khalek Sarwat Street, 11511 CAIRO

FRANCE
BOURGEY, Sabine, 7, Rue Drouot, F–75009 PARIS
BURGAN, Claude—Maison Florange, 8, Rue du 4 Septembre, F–75002, PARIS
MAISON PLATT SA, BP 2612, F–75026, Cedex 01, PARIS
NUMISMATIQUE et CHANGE DE PARIS, 3, Rue de la Bourse, F–75002 PARIS
O.G.N., 64, Rue de Richelieu, F–75002 PARIS
A POINSIGNON-NUMISMATIQUE, 4, Rue des Francs Bourgeois, F–67000 STRASBOURG
SILBERSTEIN, Claude, Comptoir de Numismatique, 39, Rue Vivienne, F–75002 PARIS
SPES NUMISMATIQUE WEIL, Alain, 54, Rue de Richelieu, F–75001 PARIS
VINCHON-NUMISMATIQUE, 77, Rue de Richelieu, F–75002 PARIS

GERMANY
DILLER, Johannes, Postfach 70 04 29, D–81304 MÜNCHEN
FRITZ RUDOLF KÜNKER Münzenhandlung, Gutenbergstrasse 23, D–49076 OSNABRÜCK
GARLICH, Kurt B, Albert Schweizer Strasse, 24A, D–63303, DREIEICH-GÖTZENHAIN
GORNY & MOSCH, GIESSENER MÜNZHANDLUNG GmbH, Maximiliansplatz 20, D–80333 MÜNCHEN
HIRSCH, NACHF, Gerhard, Promenadeplatz 10/II, D–80333 MÜNCHEN
JACQUIER, Paul-Francis, Honsellstrasse 8, D–77694 KEHL am RHEIN
KAISER, Rüdiger, Münzfachgeschaft, Mittelweg 54, D–60318 FRANKFURT
KRICHELDORF Nachf., H. H. Günterstalstrasse 16, D–79100 FREIBURG i.Br.
KURPFÄLZISCHE MÜNZENHANDLUNG—KPM, Augusta-Anlage 52, D–68165 MANNHEIM
Leipziger Münzhandlung und Auktion (Heidrun HOHN), Brühl 52, 04109, LEIPZIG
MANFRED OLDING MÜNZENHANDLUNG, Goldbreede 14, D–49078, OSNABRÜCK
MEISTER, MICHAEL, Moltkestrasse 6, D–71634 LUDWIGSBURG
MENZEL, Niels, Dachsteinweg 12, D–12107, BERLIN-MARIENDORF

MÜNZEN-UND MEDAILLENHANDLUG STUTTGART, Charlottenstrasse 4, D–70182 STUTTGART
MÜNZENETAGE-ANTIKE NUMISMATIK (Herrn Dr. M. Brandt), Marktplatz 14, D–70173 ,STUTTGART
NEUMANN GmbH, Ernst, Wetteplatz 6, D–89312, GÜNZBURG
Numismatik LANZ, Luitpoldblock-Maximiliansplatz 10, D–80333 MÜNCHEN
PEUS NACHF, Dr. Busso Bornwiesenweg 34, D–60322 FRANKFURT/M,
Münzhandlung RITTER GmbH Postfach 24 01 26, D–40090 DÜSSELDORF
TIETJEN + CO. Spitalerstrasse 30, D–20095 HAMBURG

WESFÄLISCHE AUKTIONSGESELLSCHAFT oHG, Nordring 22, D–59821, ARNSBERG

HUNGARY
Numismatica Erembolt (Làzló NUDELMAN), Vörösmarty Tèr 6, HG–1051, BUDAPEST

ISRAEL
EIDELSTEIN, Adolfo, PO Box 5135, 31051 HAIFA
QEDAR, Shraga, PO Box 520, IS–91004, JERUSALEM

ITALY
BARANOWSKY s.a.s, Via del Corso 184, I–0187, ROMA
CARLO CRIPPA s.n.c., Via Cavalieri del S. Sepolcro 10, I–20121 MILANO
DE FALCO, Alberto, Corso Umberto 24, I–80138 NAPOLI
FALLANI , Via del Babuino 58a, I–00187, ROMA
GIULIO BERNARDI, Casella Postale 560, I–34 121 TRIESTE
MARCHESI GINO &Figlio (Guiseppe Marchesi), Viale Pietramellara 35, I–40121, BOLOGNA
PAOLUCCI, Raffaele, Via San Francesco 154, I–35121 PADOVA
RINALDI & Figlio, O. Via Cappello 23 (Casa di Giulietta), I–37121 VERONA
VARESI Numismatica s.a.s., Alberto Varesi, Via Robolini 1, I–42–7100, PAVIA

JAPAN
DARUMA INTERNATIONAL GALLERIES, 2–16-32-301, Takanawa, Minato-ku, JP-TOKYO 108-0074
WORLD COINS, 1-15-5, Hamamatsu-cho, Minato-Ku, TOKYO 105-0013

MONACO
GADOURY Editions Victor, 57 rue Grimaldi, "Le Panorama", MC–98000

MOROCCO
RABACOINS Sarl, Lotissement In Chaa Allah, Villa Jacaranda, 10 rue Bienvenue, Youssoufia, RABAT

THE NETHERLANDS
MEVIUS NUMISBOOKS Int. BV Oosteinde 97, NL 7671 VRIEZENVEEN

SCHULMAN BV, Laurens, Brinklaan 84a, NL–1404 GM BUSSUM
VERSCHOOR MUNTHANDEL, Postbus 5803, 3290 AC STRIJEN
WESTERHOF, Jille Binne, Trekpad 38–40, NL–8742 KP, Burgwerd

NORWAY
OSLO MYNTHANDEL AS, (Jan Aamlid) Postboks 355, Sentrum, N–0101, OSLO

PORTUGAL
NUMISPORTO LDA, Mr. Ferreira Leite, Av. Combatentes Grande Guerra 610 LJ6, P–4200-186 PORTO

SINGAPORE
TAISEI STAMPS & COINS (S) PTE LTD, 116 Middle Road, #09–02, ICB Enterprise House, SINGA- 188972

SPAIN
CALICO, X. & F., Plaza del Angel 2, E-08002 BARCELONA

CAYON, Juan R., JANO S.L., Alcala 35, E–28014 MADRID
SEGARA, Fernando P, Plaza Mayor 26, E–28012, MADRID
VICO SA, Jesus, Jorge Juan, 83 Duplicado, E–28009 MADRID

SWEDEN
AHLSTRÖM MYNTHANDEL, AB, Norrmalmstorg 1, 1, PO Box 7662, S–103 94 STOCKHOLM
NORDLINDS MYNTHANDEL AB, Ulf, Karlavagen 46, PO Box 5132, S–102 43 STOCKHOLM

SWITZERLAND
ADOLPH HESS A. G (H. J. Schramm) Postfach 7070, CH–8023, ZÜRICH
FRANK STERNBERG AG, Schanzengasse 10 (Bhf. Stadelhofen), CH–8001 ZÜRICH
HESS—DIVO AG, Postfach 7070, CH–8023, ZÜRICH
LEU NUMISMATIK AG, Postfach 4738, CH–8022 ZÜRICH
MÜNZEN UND MEDAILLEN AG, Postal address: Postfach 3647, CH–4002 BASEL
NUMISMATICA ARS CLASSICA AG, Postfach 2655, CH–8025 ZÜRICH

UNITED KINGDOM
BALDWIN & SONS LTD., A.H. ,11 Adelphi Terrace, LONDON WC2N 6BJ
DAVIES LTD, Paul, PO Box 17, ILKLEY, West Yorkshire LS29 8TZ
CHRISTOPHER EIMER, PO Box 352, LONDON NW11 7RF
FORMAT OF BIRMINGHAM LTD 18 Bennetts Hill, BIRMINGHAM B2 5QJ
KNIGHTSBRIDGE COINS, 43 Duke Street. St. James's, LONDON SW1Y 6DD
LUBBOCK & SON LTD, PO Box 35732, London, W14 7WB
RASMUSSEN Mark, PO Box 42, BETCHWORTH RH3 7YR
RUDD , Chris, PO Box 222. Aylsham, NORFOLK NR11 6TY
SPINK & SON LTD, 69, Southampton Row, Bloomsbury, LONDON WC1B 4ET

UNITED STATES OF AMERICA
BASOK, Alexander, 1954 First Street #186, HIGHLAND PARK, IL 60035
BERK, LTD., Harlan J, 31 North Clark Street, CHICAGO, IL. 60602
BULLOWA, C.E. COINHUNTER, Suite 2112, 1616 Walnut Street, PHILADELPHIA, PA 19103
Classical Numismatic Group Inc (Victor ENGLAND), PO Box 479, LANCASTER, PA 17608
COIN AND CURRENCY INSTITUTE INC, PO Box 1057, CLIFTON, NJ 07014
COIN GALLERIES, 123 West 57 Street, NEW YORK, NY 10019
CRAIG, Freeman, PO Box 4176, SAN RAFAEL, CA 94913
DAVISSON'S LTD, COLD SPRING, MN 56320–1050
DUNIGAN, Mike, 5332 Birchman, Fort Worth, TX 76107
FREEMAN & SEAR, PO Box 641352, LOS ANGELES, CA 90064–6352
FROSETH INC., K.M., PO Box 23116, MINNEAPOLIS, MN 55423
GILLIO Inc., Ronald J., 1103 State Street, SANTA BARBARA, CA 93101
HARVEY, Stephen, PO Box 3778, BEVERLEY HILLS, CA 90212
HINDERLING, Wade, PO Box 606 MANHASSET, NY 11030
KERN, Jonathan K. Co., 441, S. Ashland Avenue, Lexington, KY 40502–2114
KOLBE, George Frederick, PO Drawer 3100, CRESTLINE, CA 92325–3100
KOVACS, Frank L., PO Box 151790, SAN RAFAEL, CA 94915–1790
KREINDLER, Herbert, 236 Altessa Blvd, MELVILLE, NY 11747
MALTER GALLERIES Inc., Joel L., 17003 Ventura Blvd., ENCINO, CA 91316
MARGOLIS, Richard, PO Box 2054, TEANECK, NJ 07666
MARKOV, Dmitry, Coins & Medals, PO Box 950, NEW YORK, NY 10272
MILCAREK, Dr. Ron, PO Box 1028, GREENFIELD, MA 01302
PEGASI Numismatics (Eldert BONTEKOE) PO Box 131040, ANN ARBOR, MI–48113
PONTERIO & ASSOCIATES, Inc, 1818 Robinson Ave., SAN DIEGO, CA 92103
RARCOA INC, 6262 South Route 83, WILLOWBROOK, IL 60527–2998
RARE COIN GALLERIES, Robert van Bebber, PO Box 569, GLENDALE, CA 91209
ROSENBLUM, William M., PO Box 355, EVERGREEN, CO. 80437–0355
RYNEARSON, Dr Paul, PO Box 4009, MALIBU, CA 90264
STACK'S, 123 West 57th Street., NEW YORK, NY 10019
STEPHENS Inc., Karl, PO Box 3038, FALLBROOK, CA 92088
SUBAK Inc., 22 West Monroe Street, Room 1506, CHICAGO, IL 60603
TELLER NUMISMATIC ENTERPRISES 16055 Ventura Blvd., Suite 635, ENCINO, CA 91436
WADDELL, Ltd., Edward J., PO Box 3759, FREDERICK, MD 21705–3759
WORLD-WIDE COINS OF CALIFORNIA, PO Box 3684, SANTA ROSA, CA 95402

VENEZUELA
NUMISMATICA GLOBUS, Apartado de Correos 50418, CARACAS 1050–A

THE
COIN
YEARBOOK
2005

Edited by
James Mackay, MA, DLitt
John W. Mussell, FRGS
and the Editorial Team of COIN NEWS

ISBN 1 870 192 68 0

Published by
TOKEN PUBLISHING LIMITED
Orchard House, Duchy Road, Heathpark, Honiton, EX14 1YD
Telephone: 01404 46972   Fax: 01404 44788
e-mail: info@tokenpublishing.com. Website: http://www.tokenpublishing.com

Printed in Great Britain by J. H. Haynes & Co. Ltd, Sparkford, Yeovil

Contents

Index to advertisers

Foreword

LAST year, as we celebrated our 20th anniversary at Token Publishing, it was an opportunity to wallow in nostalgia and look back over the years. What struck us forcibly were the changes in the trade, both in the dealers and auction houses. It occurs to us that there have probably been more dramatic changes in the trade in the past two decades than in the previous half century, but is this not rather misleading? The names of the businesses may have changed but the personnel have not. Most of the major dealers and auctioneers of the present time have been in the business for many years even if the firms that employed them no longer exist or have moved into other areas. There is, in fact, a very solid core which gives the numismatic industry its stability. It is, by and large, a profession noted for reliability and fair dealing.

Of course, to a certain extent, business practices are governed by legislation designed to protect the customer; much of that either did not exist 40 years ago or was ineffective. Consumer protection and trade description are much more prominent today than they were when we founded Token Publishing, but the trade is much stronger as a result. Despite all the economic vicissitudes of recent years the coin business is in very good shape as can be seen in the quantity and quality of the advertisements in COIN NEWS each month.

All hobbies, and especially those covering collectable subjects, are beset with worries that they are not doing enough to attract youngsters who have so many other alternatives to fill their time. This concern is particularly felt in the sister hobby of philately. But stamp collectors look back to a time when kids all collected stamps and now very few do. Coin collecting was never a mass hobby in the way that philately was and even at the height of the change-checkers' mania as decimalisation approached the ratio of numismatists to philatelists was still fairly small. It is our impression that the number of dealers has steadily increased over the past 20 years. The number of numismatic societies is much the same, but attendance figures appear to have risen steadily and what is perhaps more significant, the number of women taking up the hobby has gone up appreciably.

The market is in good shape. At the top end, each season brings a fresh crop of record prices in the salerooms, but right across the board the market value of coins has risen steadily, year on year. Even allowing for the effects of inflation, coins have gone up in value in real terms. The market continues to expand and diversify, as the never-ending flood of new issues testifies. This is a phenomenon which perpetually intrigues us for it is clear that the gold and silver proof coins that pour from the various mints are ending up in the hands of people who, on the whole, do not fit the profile of the truly committed collectors we meet at coin fairs and club meetings. We hope that the people who invest in such collectables will graduate to mainstream numismatics but more often than not they lose interest and are then bitterly disillusioned when they try to dispose of their holdings and discover that there is no real second market. Of course, these remarks do not apply to the vast majority of people who will be reading these words!

Looking back at the past twelve months we note with satisfaction that the hobby continues to prosper. The coin fairs are as busy as ever and continue to attract newcomers to numismatics. Dealers in general report that their business is in good shape, and it is significant that the pattern of trading has been revolutionised, thanks to the Internet. Not so long ago we remarked on the number of dealers who had acquired websites; now this is commonplace and the fact that a dealer was not dealing on the Net would be cause for comment. The IT Revolution is the greatest and most far-reaching factor governing our lives today and its impact affects us all. As more and more people embrace this technology and get on-line the transformation of coin dealing and auctions will be even greater.

When we reviewed the market in the previous edition the war in Iraq had just ended—or so we imagined. Twelve months later, the situation in that ravaged country appears grimmer than ever and the spectre of global terrorism is omnipresent. Last year the FTSE was struggling to stay above the magic 4000 level. In fact, it was well above that barrier for most of the past year but at the time of writing (mid-August) it has dropped below 4300. The stock markets around the world reflect the uncertainty of the times, property prices have levelled off or are actually beginning to drop and interest rates have risen in a bid to decelerate consumer spending and the appalling level of borrowing which, in the United Kingdom, passed the trillion pound barrier for the first time. The pound continues to be very strong against the US dollar, or perhaps it would be more realistic to say that the dollar is relatively weak against the pound and the Euro. This certainly had a noticeable effect on American bidding at auctions up to the end of 2003 but this has had less impact in the salerooms in the first half of 2004. The overall feeling is that numismatics is a resilient and buoyant business which manages to withstand the ups and downs of the world's money markets and fiscal policies.

When compiling such a publication as COIN YEARBOOK we are inevitably dependent to a large extent on a number of recognised experts in their respective fields, for advice and assistance as well as a precise assessment of current market values. This edition is no exception and we are indebted to our trade colleagues and a number of specialist collectors for their help and co-operation. In particular we would like to thank Royston Norbury of West Essex Coins, Steven Mitchell of Studio Coins (hammered), Chris Rudd (Celtic), Mike Vosper (Roman), Nick Swabey (Maundy), Patrick Mackenzie (decimal) and Chris Denton (Irish) in particular. Many other friends in the trade have helped us in ways too numerous to mention; our grateful and sincere thanks are due to them all for their efforts in helping us to maintain the high standard of presentation and factual accuracy in this latest edition. Our thanks are also due to the various auction houses, mints and dealers who have permitted us to reproduce illustrations from their publications.

The year
at a glance!

An at-a-glance résumé of the main events and occurrences that affected the coin hobby during the past months, as reported in COIN NEWS . . .

June 2003

HRH Prince William of Wales celebrates his 21st birthday on June 21. Alderney, Guernsey and Jersey commission a range of £5 coins from the Royal Mint to mark the occasion.

Brian Watkin, Corbitt's coin specialist and a prominent member of the Tyneside Numismatic Society, dies on June 23.

The Bank of the Netherlands Antilles celebrates its 175th anniversary on June 26.

July 2003

The Bank of Indonesia celebrates its golden jubilee on July 1.

Jean Elsen holds his 75th auction on July 5.

Fenlord Auctions opens in Ely, Cambridgeshire.

A report by the General Accounting Office of the US government reports that almost $2 million worth of coins, banknotes, stamps and other items have been stolen by employees from the US Mint and the Bureau of Engraving and Printing since 1993.

The Royal Mint's annual report, published on July 24, reveals that it made a profit of £1.3 million in 2002–3, compared with a loss of £6.5 million the previous year.

The York Coin & Stamp Fair on July 25–26 attracts a record attendance.

The annual convention of the American Numismatic Association takes place at Baltimore, July 30 to August 2.

August 2003

The Royal Mint strikes the Lord of the Rings coins on behalf of New Zealand where the trilogy was filmed.

Token Publishing celebrates its 20th anniversary with a staff dinner at the Deer Park Hotel, Honiton on August 22.

September 2003

John Rhys-Davies, who played Gimli in the Lord of the Rings trilogy, visits the Pobjoy Mint on September 5 and strikes the first of the coins issued by the Isle of Man depicting scenes and characters from the films.

The 6th annual Collectors Fair in Prague takes place on September 12–14. Now one of the foremost shows in Europe, it attracts a record attendance.

Lisa Camm of Token Publishing marries Rick Keyte on September 27.

The British Museum commissions a medal from the Royal Mint to celebrate its 250th anniversary.

Joe Cribb is appointed Keeper of Coins and Medals at the British Museum in succession to Andrew Burnett who takes up his appointment as Deputy Director of the Museum, and is elected a Fellow of the British Academy.

A Celtic gold stater of the Whaddon Chase type is discovered in the gut of a chicken. This is the second such occurrence, a Whaddon Chase gold stater having been found in the crop of a chicken in 1989.

October 2003

James Brindley, Professor of Geology at University College, Dublin, launches a series of CDs illustrating coin varieties.

The Royal Mint announces new designs for the pound coin, to be released over the next four years.

Richard Lobel of Coincraft celebrates 35 years in the London coin trade by hosting a party attended by over 200 guests

The BNTA holds the 25th annual Coinex at the London Marriott hotel in Grosvenor Square, with a number of invited non-BNTA standholders for the first time.

Concorde makes its last flight on October 24. To mark the passing of the world's only successful supersonic air-liner, the Royal Mint strikes a bimetallic medal showing the aircraft in pure gold against a silver ground.

Dave Greenhalgh, aka Grunal the Moneyer, gives talks and demonstrations at the Bank of England Museum, October 27–31.

The Royal Canadian Mint completely sells out its Natural Wonders holographic coins.

Following the fire that devastated the National Motor Cycle Museum, the Midland Coin Fair moves to a new venue at the Manor Hotel, Meriden while the Museum is being refurbished.

Divers from Odyssey Marine Exploration of Florida discover the wreck of the SS Republic which sank off the Florida coast in 1865 with a cargo that included over $1 million in $20 gold coins.

Wallis & Wallis, the Lewes auction house, celebrates its 75th anniversary.

November 2003

The Royal Mint launches a series of coins with the theme of the history of powered flight, marking the centenary of the first flight by the Wright Brothers.

John Mowbray holds a sale on November 6, consisting of material from the archives of the Reserve Bank of New Zealand, including an Australian holey dollar and two dumps.

The Royal Canadian Mint sells two unique coins on eBay for $55,100 and $62,600 respectively, the proceeds going to Save the Children and the Humane Society of Canada.

A holey dollar, estimated at A$20,000 to A$30,000, sells for A$53,590 (including buyer's premium) at a sale by Noble Numismatic on November 26.

Coin and medal dealer Eddie Smith has part of his stock confiscated by over-zealous German officials after attending the Waffenbourse militaria show in Kassel on November 29, on the grounds that anything depicting the swastika is illegal propaganda. An appeal through his Euro MP is immediately launched. The stock is eventually returned to him intact in June 2004.

December 2003

Wilma, wife of leading coin dealer and fair organiser David Fletcher, dies on December 1.

At the DNW auction on December 9–10 an Australian silver 3d of 1860 fetches £11,270, a world record price.

The Docklands Museum holds a workshop on December 14. Entitled "Token Rights" it gives visitors the chance to strike their own tokens.

An exhibition entitled "Love from the Hermitage" opens in Amsterdam and runs till April 18, 2004. It comprises over 250 items (including coins and medals) from the Hermitage depicting the theme of love.

The Professional Coin Grading Service expands its Set registry to include the Euro coinage.

The Hoffman Mint of California revives an old tradition by striking a calendar medal for 2004.

Colin Cooke sets up a numismatic chat room as part of his website www.colincooke.com

January 2004

The New York International Numismatic Convention takes place at the Waldorf Astoria on January 15–18. A highlight of the convention is the sale of the Chester Krause collection of the coins of Canada and the Maritime Provinces.

The Hong Kong Stamp Expo from January 30 to February 3 included coins, medals and banknotes for the first time.

The World Money Fair takes place at Basle from January 31 to February 1. The Token Publishing team attend the annual event where most of the mints of the world announce their forthcoming programmes.

The Royal Mint celebrates the **bice**ntenary of steam locomotion with a £2 coin depicting Richard Trevithick's locomotive *Penydarran*.

Norway launches a programme of coins to celebrate the centenary of independence in 2005.

The British Museum launches the first major exhibition of British archaeology for over 20 years. 'Buried Treasure: Finding Our Past' runs until March 14 and then goes on tour round leading provincial museums.

Arthur Houghton and Catherine Lorber win the Book of the Year award from the International Association of Professional Numismatis for their two-volume catalogue of Seleucid coins.

February 2004

The Gibraltar government switches from the Pobjoy Mint and awards the contract for its coinage to the Tower Mint. Marketing and distribution will be handed by the Westminster Collection.

The death is announced of Karolyn Hatt, proprietor and publisher of *The Searcher* magazine for metal detecting. She was the widow of Robin Hatt with whom she was associated in the publication of the magazine which was originally produced by Token Publishing in 1985.

The first phase of the annual Trial of the Pyx takes place at the Goldsmiths' Hall, London on February 10.

The Royal Mint launches a 50p coin to celebrate the 50th anniversary of Roger Bannister's first four-minute mile.

The Irish International Coin Fair takes place over the weekend of February 21–22 at the Royal Dublin Society, Ballsbridge.

The Royal Mint launches a series of 18 crown pieces from the Channel Islands to mark the Age of Steam, beginning with Stephenson's Rocket at the Rainhill Trials of 1829.

March 2004

The Asia Money Fair returns to the Raffles City Convention Centre on March 12–14, preceded by a large numismatic sale staged by Mavin International.

The Royal Mint launches an 18-coin series of silver proofs honouring maritime heroes and ships of the Royal Navy. The coins will be released at monthly intervals.

Spink dispose of the Marshall collection formed largely in the 1930s and 1940s.

The Royal Mint strikes a medal to celebrate the England team's victory in the Rugby World Championship in Australia in December.

April 2004

The Congress of the British Association of Numismatic Societies takes place in Chester College over the weekend of April 2–4.

Archaeologist Nick Bendy joins the team of Chris Rudd, the Celtic specialist.

Austria wins the coveted Coin of the Year Award with the 5 Euro coin depicting Schonbrunn Palace. Austria had no fewer than three other winning entries: best gold coin (50 Euro for the religious order of Saints Benedict and Sebastian), best silver coin (Ambras Palace) and most popular coin (Zoo).

The Royal Mint releases a £5 coin to celebrate the centenary of the Entente Cordiale.

May 2004

The Reading Coin Club celebrates its 40th anniversary.

The US Mint announces plans to change the nickel (5c), replacing the reverse showing Jefferson's mansion by a handshake motif symbolising the bicentenary of the purchase of Louisiana from France.

Liberia issues a $10 coin which doubles as a sun-dial. The reverse is divided into hours while a central pin can be removed and inserted into a slot at an angle so that the sun's shadow falls on the appropriate hour.

A hoard of coins discovered in Japan is dated to AD 694—some 15 years earlier than the previously recorded coins, although a document published in 720 refers to coins minted in the 7th century.

The 53rd annual congress of the International Association of Professional Numismatists takes place at Rabat, Morocco.

June 2004

The London Coin Fair takes place on June 5.

The Royal Mint unveils details of its British Military Leaders piedfort collection, commencing with Sir Winston Churchill. The 12 coins, struck in

pure gold, are released at monthly intervals.

Andrew Litherland and Rick Coleman leave Bonhams and join Bloomsbury Auctions, previously a specialist antiquarian book saleroom but now diversifying into numismatics.

Chris Rudd purchases the Silchester Hoard of Celtic coins discovered in 2000. Although declared treasure trove, Hampshire Museum Services withdrew their initial interest in acquiring it.

Greece issues a €2 coin to celebrate the Athens Olympic Games.

To celebrate the 60th anniversary of the D-Day landings, the Royal Mint issues a £5 coin whose action-packed reverse incorporates a poppy picked out in red and black, Britain's first coloured coin.

To mark the commissioning of the liner Queen Mary 2 the Royal Mint, in conjunction with Cunard, produces a commemorative medal, available in silver or nickel-brass.

July 2004

The York Stamp and Coin Fair takes place over the weekend of July 30–31.

Royal Mail launches a collection of silver replicas of stamps issued in the reigns of Edward VII and George V, a follow-up to a previous series featuring the stamps of the Victorian era.

Melbourne firm Downie and Sherwood are appointed official distributor of coins issued to mark the centenary of FIFA, the international football association. Coins from France, Uruguay, Brazil and Switzerland are the first to appear.

August 2004

The World Fair of Money takes place at Pittsburgh, Pennsylvania on August 18–22, the biggest event in the numismatic calendar.

You'll find a veritable treasure trove in every edition

Phone now for a free copy of 'Treasure' on

01376 57 27 55

Pineapple Direct

PO Box 335, Tiptree, Colchester CO5 9WP

Fax orders - (01376) 573 883

Email - pineapple@thecollectoruk.com

Treasure and *The***COLLECTOR** are trading names of Pineapple Direct Ltd.

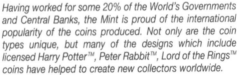

The best and worst of recent coin designs

Sport and colour are the key-words that distinguish the coins released in the latter part of 2003 and the first half of 2004. Football has loomed large because this year not only marks the golden jubilee of UEFA but also the centenary of FIFA, the governing bodies for European and world soccer respectively. Both anniversaries have precipitated a number of coins with predictable designs of footballers in action, assorted trophies and emblems; all very well if you are football daft but not doing anything to advance the frontiers of coin design.

The major sporting event, of course, is the Olympic Games and the fact that the world's greatest sporting contest has returned this year to its roots has not been lost on the artists and engravers of the various mints. Greece pulled out all the stops with its six pairs of silver and gold coins The standard reverse has the 12 European stars enclosing an olive wreath with the Olympic rings and the anthemion emblem of the Greek Mint. The obverses of the six silver €10 coins feature ancient and modern images of the same sports to show the continuity of athletic contests over the millennia, while the gold coins concentrate on historically significant landmarks in Greece. The obverses of the silver coins are completely devoid of inscriptions so that we can savour the sheer beauty of the images without the slightest distraction. The modern image stands out with the ancient image delicately muted and the result is truly sublime.

The Olympic coins from other countries, notably the British Virgin Islands Gibraltar and Sierra Leone, have grappled competently with the classical theme, but that other member of the Pobjoy ensemble, the Isle of Man, has opted for sporting motifs in a modern idiom. This is a country which, in the past, has shown a penchant for incuse inscriptions on raised rims, and this treatment has been adopted in the Olympic series, although segments at the sides or top and bottom rather detract from the overall effect.

Relatively few coins in the period under review deal with royalty, although the celebration of the golden jubilee of the Coronation (a non-event if ever there was one) rumbles on, the pick of the bunch being the coins from Australia, especially the silver 50 cents whose reverse shows a central royal cipher flanked by emblems and neat little inscriptions. A few coins marked Prince William's 21st birthday but on the whole they were rather disappointing, opting for royal arms rather than an up-to-date portrait of the birthday boy himself.

The silver jubilee of Pope John Paul II predictably yielded coins from the Vatican, but the best of them were issued by his native land. Of the coins celebrating the centenary of powered flight the best designs came from the Solomon Islands, struck by the Royal Mint and showing a baker's dozen of aeroplanes from the Curtiss Jenny to Concorde. It is rather surprising that the disappearance of the latter from the skies has not inspired more coins showing this highly distinctive aircraft.

Many of the coins produced each year are predictable and obviously market-led, catering to the most popular themes. Harry Potter and the Lord of the Rings are prime examples of this, with the Isle of Man getting in on both acts. Appropriately, New Zealand, where the Peter Jackson trilogy was filmed in about 150 different locations, produced a superb set, struck by the Royal Mint.

The Lord of the Rings trilogy set consists of six cupro-nickel coins issued by New Zealand.

23

For collectors looking for unusual subjects there were two this year with a mathematical theme. From Hungary came a silver 5000 forint coin celebrating the birth centenary of the mathematician Janos Neumann whose bust appears on the reverse, but the obverse has the inscription and value surrounded by binary numbers. But it's back to Australia, to the Perth Mint this time, for the 2004 Kookaburra 10 ounce coin featuring a wide range of mathematical symbols and numbers, continuing the theme of Evolution of recent years.

Every year we look at the list of the coins which earned the prestigious Coin of the Year Awards and often wonder at how the judges reached their decision. To be sure, there is a largely subjective element in deciding what constitutes the world's most popular coin and some of the other categories are also a matter of individual taste. But for once we are inclined to agree with the judges that the overall winner should be the €10 coin released by Austria to publicise the Imperial Palace of Schönbrunn, now a UNESCO World Heritage Site. Fortunately both obverse and reverse were devoted to it, thus giving the engraver more scope than usual; but the image of the central façade with one of the great baroque fountains in the foreground is a masterpiece by any standard, while the reverse, showing the Palm House, the largest steel and glass greenhouse in Europe, provides a pleasing contrast of architectural styles that complement each other.

Austria has an impressive track record for fine coin design and the fact that it took no fewer than four of this year's awards is testimony to the remarkably high standard of technical excellence and superb design bordering on genius. Our favourite series is the set of eight coins which have been illustrating different periods in Austria's history, the glories of the Biedermeier period contrasting with the last coin in the set, symbolising the postwar period by showing a jeep containing military policemen of the four occupying powers. Incidentally, a nice touch for collectors of Americana (apart from the "snowdrop" in the jeep) is the initials ERP on a wall in the background, referring to the European Recovery Program, better known as the Marshall Plan.

These Austrian coins manage to cram in a lot of detail without conveying the impression of clutter or fussiness. Neighbouring Switzerland, on the other hand, seems to be going through a minimalist

Canada Day "Bundle". The bundle is a promotional package of water bottle, T-shirt and post-card as well as the coin.

phase, recent coins having a new reverse in which the Swiss cross is reduced almost to vanishing point, while the Latin name for the Confederation is deliberately misaligned, although why this was considered desirable is baffling.

Canada has struck some beautiful coins over the years and the new series featuring lighthouses is well up to the mark; but coin design has been uneven at times and this year produced an oddity. Its theme is a Canada Day Bundle and a casual glance certainly conveys the impression of some sort of baggage. In fact the bundle is a promotional package containing a water-bottle a T-shirt and a postcard as well as the 25c coin. If it were not for the press release we would never have guessed that the image on the reverse was a cartoon rendering of a moose.

There have been no technical innovations this year, although we have noted a spectacular upsurge in the use of contrasting metals, colours and holographic effects.

Not so long ago coloured coins were regarded as a gimmick and purists felt that this aspect detracted from the sheer beauty of the actual metal, in gold, silver or bronze. Now colour techniques are becoming more widespread and also much more subtle than they were a few years ago, and the examples over the past year make a very pleasing group.

Colour lends itself beautifully to portraiture. Traditionally, most coins preferred a profile in low relief and by and large attempts at full-face portraits were not successful. Thanks to the advent of multicolour techniques, however, full face portraits are not only more practical but also much more realistic. Excellent examples of this are provided by the Cook Islands which, in deference to Australia, launched a series last year featuring notorious bushrangers. While the obverse continues to bear the profile of the Queen, the reverse of these coins portray Ned Kelly, Ben Hall, Mad Dan Morgan and Captain Thunderbolt, using genuine sepia photographs enhanced by subtle flesh tones.

It seems strange that any country should want to celebrate the lives of murderers and thieves, but Ned Kelly and his contemporaries have long since passed into the realms of folk hero. Still, we await the day when the Royal Mint strikes coins in honour of Robin Hood, the man who robbed the rich to help the poor. A previous set from the Cook Islands celebrated great railways of the world and had the principal motifs delicately enhanced with

Australian, Sydney to Athens—Olympic Games 2004 coins.

subtle
background tints.

The Royal Australian **Mint** itself, which **has** produced a number of fine bimetallic coins in recent years, has not been slow to embrace the latest technology, as the coins for the Olympic Games testify. Among the latest coins from Australia are gold and silver coins marking the transition of the Olympiad from Sydney to Athens, with the Australian flag and Olympic rings picked out in full colour. It is highly probable that other coloured coins will appear later this year in connection with the Olympics in Athens

The rival Perth Mint has also produced some excellent examples of coloured coins, notably the bullion silver piece celebrating the 50th anniversary of Australian Antarctic Territory with subtle colours suggesting the characteristic blue of the polar ice. The most dramatic effect is imparted by the new holographic dollar coin with its multicolour rendering of kangaroos.

Israel has also jumped on the colour bandwagon with 1, 2 and 10 sheqel coins celebrating the genius of the country's contribution to architecture and applied design. The obverses have geometric shapes creating the letter aleph, while the reverses have coloured shapes below the inscriptions. A singular feature of these coins, however, is the overall jet-black appearance against which the coloured elements are contrasted.

Among other colourful coins noted recently are the 15,000 kip silver coin from Laos showing the flower horn fish in all its ruddy glory and coins marking Poland's entry into the European Union with the EU and Polish flags side by side. Gold and silver coins from the People's Republic of China celebrating the Lantern Festival and showing a child and lantern in full colour, while coins celebrating the Lunar New Year have reverse motifs showing monkeys in full natural colour.

Our own Royal Mint has embraced the new technology although keeping it well within bounds. A £5 piece commemorating the 60th

anniversary of D-Day shows troops going ashore on the Normandy beaches, with aircraft overhead and warships in the background, but a subtle and poignant touch is created by the inclusion of a single Haig poppy, in red with a black button centre at the foot of the reverse.

Sadly this coin will not be available from banks and post offices in the UK as it was produced by the Mint for the Bailiwick of Guernsey. The emotive design by David Cornell pays tribute to the courage and determination of Allied troops who triumphed in adversity and against all the odds to secure the freedom which so many of us take for granted. For Guernsey it has even greater poignancy, for the D-Day invasion nearby bypassed the Channel Islands which had to endure Nazi domination for a further eleven months before they were liberated. Although the coin is now available at banks in Guernsey, for every coin sold a donation is being made to the Royal British Legion.

The exact technique used to produce coloured coins is a closely guarded secret but it is believed to involve a process akin to silk-screen printing. The secret seems to be to make the colour stick but then again, it is unlikely that any of these costly confections will ever pass from hand to hand in everyday circulation.

The Pobjoy Mint by no means has the monopoly in creating coloured coins which rely on the secondary metal for this effect. A silver 25 Euro coin from Austria, celebrating the 150th anniversary of the Semmering Railway has a green centre, struck in niobium—believed to be the first time this metal has been applied to coinage. Meanwhile bimetallic and trimetallic coins continue to pour forth from the world's mints, with noteworthy examples of the latter from Gibraltar and, of course, Royal Mint's new £2 coin for the bicentenary of steam locomotion. When it comes to the downright bizarre, Slovakia can teach other countries a thing or two, for its latest coins, ranging from 20 to 5000 Slovak crowns, are rectangular and in fact reproduce the obverse designs of the current banknotes, with the central motifs picked out in contrasting metals.

£5 piece commemorating the 60th anniversary of D-Day.

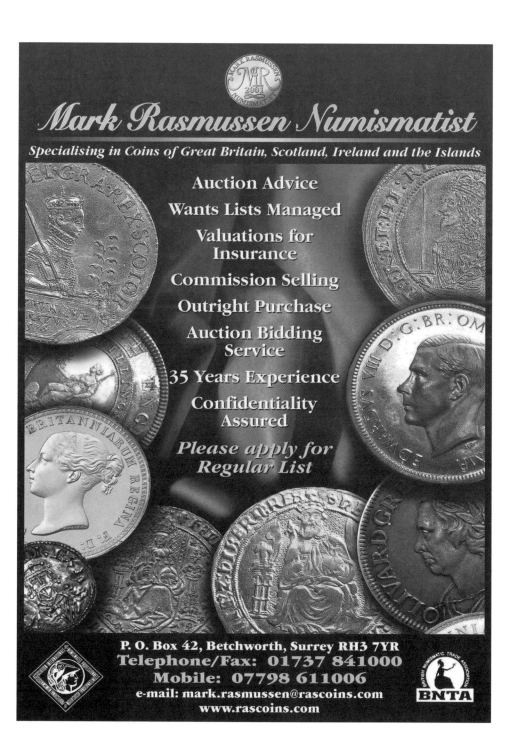
27

Books
of the year

Every coin collector knows that knowledge is the key to forming a good collection and each year new books or new editions of older works, as well as standard reference works, are up-dated by dedicated specialists. Here we list the most important numismatic titles that have appeared during the past year. Most have been reviewed in COIN NEWS.

COINS OF ENGLAND & THE UNITED KINGDOM. Xvi, 531pp. Illustrated throughout. Laminated card covers. Spink, £18.

Originally published by Seaby in 1929 and by Spink in more recent years, this is the standard catalogue for those who like to see coins arranged chronologically by reign. It features every major coin type from the Celtic era to the present day. Valuations are given for every coin type listed in two grades for hammered and three for milled coins.

EURO COINS AND NOTES. 192pp, Card covers. Cheveau-légers, €6.96

This catalogue in full colour details all the notes and coins of the Euro zone with details of mintmarks, secret ciphers and serials, including errors and die variants both commemorative and general circulating items.

EXPLORING PREHISTORIC AND ROMAN ENGLAND, by Barry Marsden. Card covers. Illustrated in colour throughout. Greenlight Publishing, £15.

This provides a detailed survey of archaeological sites in England covering the period down to the 5th century, with inventories of finds, including coin hoards. Rich in background detail, it places Celtic Britain in its proper context as well as the Roman province down to the beginning of the so-called Dark Ages.

FOR WANT OF GOOD MONEY: the story of Ireland's Coinage, by Edward Colgan. 205pp. Casebound. Wordwell, £21. *Available from Token Publishing Ltd.*

The author is well-known as a regular contributor to COIN NEWS and has been studying the coins of Ireland for more than 30 years. The treatment is chronological, successive chapters dealing with the earliest pennies struck by the Norsemen between 997 and 1150 in imitation of English sterlings, right down to the coinage of the Irish Free State and the Republic, including the adoption of the Euro. This is an indispensable reference work for all students of Irish coinage.

GAULISH AND EARLY BRITISH GOLD COINAGE, by John Sills. xii, 554pp, 17 plates, 40 maps, 123 figures, 39 tables. Spink, £95.

This stupendous volume has been a labour of love for many years. It is unsurpassed for sheer scholarly detail and will be the last word on the subject for many years to come, a 10-year distillation of research at the Oxford Celtic Coin Index.

IRISH SMALL SILVER, JOHN–EDWARD VI,
by Paul and Bente Withers. Xxx pp. Card covers.
Galata, £12.
The latest in the 'Small Change' series, this little book covers the Anglo-Irish coinage from Prince John in the late 12th century to Edward VI in the mid-15th century. Crammed with detail and exceptionally well inustrated.

MONEY GALORE,
the Story of the Welsh
Pound, by Ivor Wynne
Jones. 112pp illustrated
throughout, plus 1pp of
coloured illustrations.
Paperback. Landmark
Publishing, £9.95.

This is the fascinating story of Richard Williams, a former bank clerk and entrepreneur who fooled the government into endorsing his privately produced Welsh banknotes. This audacious escapade back in 1969 was short-lived but the notes from 1 to 1 million punt captured the imagination and are avidly collected to this day.

NORSKE
PENGESEDLER, 1695-
2003, by Karl Saethre
and Hans Gunnar
Eldorsen. 298pp.
Paperback. Bergens
Coin & Banknote
Company, 350 kroner.

This is the 18th edition of a very comprehensive handbook devoted to the paper money of Norway but it has been expanded to almost twice the size of previous editions. Not only has there been a wholesale revision of the text from the last edition, but a major addition this time details the paper money and scrip used at the various Norwegian, Swedish, American and Russian mining facilities in Spitsbergen and Bear Island. At the other end of the time scale the extremely rare and little known issued from Norway produced between 1695 and 1877 have now been listed and priced for the first time. The book is beautifully illustrated in colour

and encompasses all notes down to the latest 100kr with security foil strip introduced in 2003. Notes are priced in up to seven grades, and the text is in English as well as Norwegian.

ROMAN COIN PRICE YEARBOOK, by Morten
Eske Mortensen. Available from the author
at Drejogade 26 F 501, DK-2100, Copenhagen,
Denmark, or email mem@image.dk

This book lists the prices realised at auction for all Roman republican and imperial coins throughout the world during the years 2001-2. Over 9,000 republican and 25,000 imperial coins are listed, providing a realistic guide to their values.

STANDARD CATALOG OF WORLD COINS,
1601-1700, by Chester L. Krause and Cliford
Mishler. 1,392pp. Illustrated with 18,500 black
and white images throughout. Softbound.
Krause Publications, £45.

This is undoubtedly the most detailed catalogue of world coins of the 17th century. In this edition the coins of several German states are admitted for the first time, while the listings of several countries, including Britain, have been extensively revised.

STANDARD CATALOG OF WORLD
COINS, 1901-2004, by Chester L. Krause and
Clifford Mishler. 2,300pp. Softbound. Krause
Publications, £40.

The 32nd edition of this very popular catalogue deals with the 20th century and beyond, including all the commemorative pieces as well as circulating coinage, with prices fully updated.

STANDARD CATALOG
OF WORLD GOLD
COINS, by Chester L.
Krause and Clifford
Mishler. 1,100pp.
Softbound. Krause
Publications, £59.95.

This is the fourth edition of the catalogue embracing gold coins of the world of all periods, the prices being updated right across the board.
Available from Token Publishing Ltd.

A THOUSAND GUINEAS: a Checklist of Imitation Guineas and their Fractions, by W. Bryce Neilson. 68 A4pp. Paperback. Galata, £15.

Imitation guinea counters were produced from the 1760s for use at the card table, and the various manufacturers were not slow to produce base-metal imitations of the spade guinea on its inception in 1787. The advent of the sovereign in 1816 led in due course to gaming counters based on it as well, notably the Cumberland Jacks and Prince of Wales model half-sovereigns, but these imitations were frowned upon by the authorities and as a result there was a resurgence of the imitation spade guineas 'in memory of the good old days' in the 1860s. Many of these latter-day imitations served as advertisements for the Birmingham firms that manufactured them. The number of different imitations is truly mind-boggling, this book being the fruit of over 30 years research.

TOKENS AND TALLIES THROUGH THE AGES, by Edward Fletcher. 96pp. Softbound. Profusely illustrated in colour. Greenlight Publishing, £15.

This is a remarkably comprehensive survey of the tokens and tallies used in Britain from medieval times to the 19th century, together with a detailed list of books for further reading on specific aspects of the subject.

All
Shapes
and sizes

An interesting and inexpensive way for the beginner to approach the formation of a coin collection might well be that known as thematic collecting. Natural history (flora and fauna), famous buildings and other landmarks, transport, sporting events, etc., have all been depicted on coins and tokens, but a more basic idea, as DENZIL WEBB explains, is not so concerned with what is depicted on the piece, but its shape.

It has been suggested that the only reason the vast majority of coins are round is because that in ancient times it was found that a globule of hot metal struck with a hammer flattened into a roughly circular shape.

1 anna from India and the 12-sided Canada 5 cents.

One of the most fascinating innovations of the ancient world was the production of "domed" or saucer-shaped coins from a pair of dies, one convex, the other concave. Such coins were minted by the Byzantines in the 11th century. The only modern production of such pieces, which are known as scyphates, are in-store 1/2d and 1d checks issued by many tradesmen in the 1920s and 1930s, designed to prevent their improper use in vending and gaming machines. In passing, it is worth noting that coins which could only be used at the premises of the issuer are frequently referred to as tokens, but should rightly be called checks. True tokens, issued during times of a chronic shortage of small change, were minted to be used anywhere.

It is often said that necessity is the mother of invention, and the underlying reason for the introduction of coins in varying formats was to enable coins to be produced that contrasted with existing circulating coinage. If, for example, the

50p piece, introduced in the autumn of 1969, was not to be confused with florins (two shillings) or halfcrowns (two shillings and sixpence), the ideal solution was to design a piece of a different shape. The only alternative would have been to introduce a much larger coin. When considering the possible formats that the new coin might adopt, it was also necessary to take into account the requirements of the vending and gaming industries. Thankfully, the 50p and 20p coins have not caused any problems. There was also a sound economic reason for the introduction of the 50p coin rather than a banknote of the same value. Paper money has a life of only six months, and the cost of distribution and withdrawal is high. On the other hand, although the initial costs of coin production are much higher, a life-span of some fifty years ensures that in the medium to longer terms, substantial savings would be made. The technical name for the world's first seven-sided coin is "equilateral curve heptagon".

Apart from a few high value issues, such as the eight-sided (octagon) $50 commemorative of 1915 issued in the United States, the majority of unusual-shaped issues are of low face value, and are easily obtained from dealers' oddments trays for a very modest outlay. They are also frequently available at flea-markets and car boot sales. There is ample scope to form a substantial collection, especially so if tradesmens' checks are taken into consideration. Surprisingly triangular-shaped coins are quite hard to find, although a pair of checks in this format were issued by Newcastle-upon-Tyne Co-operative Society. These are pre-payment checks for doorstep milk delivery, and are valued at one third and one half pint respectively. As far as

Square one cent from the Straits Settlements.

checks are concerned, perhaps the most unusual shape is a half-circle or pieces that are somewhat over half.

Collectors should bear in mind that monarchs and heads of state change over the years. For example, the Iraqi ten fils with a scalloped edge occurs in five types—kings Faisal I, Ghazi I, Faisal II young head, Faisal II old head, and the Republic. Scalloped edged coins are in fact more common than one might suspect. Another four may be obtained from Paraguay, namely 10, 15, 25 and 50 cents.

It is interesting to note that the majority of these off-beat coins are from countries of the former British Empire (now Commonwealth), the Middle-East and Africa. The only item from

Europe that comes to mind is a square 5 cents in zinc from Holland, which circulated during World War II.

The beginner can get off to a good start by obtaining specimens of all the available United Kingdom issues. There are two sizes of the 50p piece, and some special issues, i.e. the centenary of public libraries, the EEC and NHS. There are two types of the twelve-sided brass threepence piece, namely that depicting a thrift plant, and the portcullis issue. And don't forget the 20p!

Prior to commencing this article, I did a rough check of known "shaped" issues, and found that the greatest number are scalloped edge types—27 from 17 countries. The next highest score was square types—14 from eight countries. Six, eight, ten and twelve-sided pieces occur to a lesser extent. I must stress, however, that this is only a rough guide, and should not therefore be regarded as in any way complete. India may be compared to Iraq: "shaped" coins often occurring in every reign from Edward VII till the establishment of the Republic. Looking for specimens from small island communities such as Fiji, Seychelles, Maldive Islands and Surinam, is most rewarding.

The internet

an alternative place to sell, or buy, numismatic items

Collector WILLIAM McCREATH is an avid user of the internet and in this short article introduces us to the vagaries of trading "on-line". It is assumed that readers are UK-based, have some knowledge of eBay and can navigate the site effectively.

Online auctions are becoming increasingly popular amongst the coin collecting fraternity, with such names as Speedbid, bidwyze and bid2u, although admittedly they are dominated by eBay, to the same degree that Microsoft dominates operating systems for computers. It is the largest auction site on the internet and for English speakers it can be found at www.ebay.com or www.ebay.co.uk. At any one time these two sites between them have around 8,000 British coins and a similar number of British banknotes on offer. They also have categories for tokens and medals. The numismatic items being offered range from the extremely common to, very occasionally, unique. Additionally they have a vast range of other collectable items to choose from. The value of individual lots can range from close to zero to many thousands or even tens of thousands of pounds. Searching the sites will usually give a hit (be successful), no matter how obscure the item is—if not this week, then probably next. To give an example, I found a book on eBay within two weeks that an Uncle of mine had been looking for for several years.

Sellers on eBay range from well known dealers to those that seem, from their listings, to have no knowledge at all of the items they offer. The lack of knowledge is on occasion quite breathtaking—cupro-nickel coins are often described as being silver and Churchill crowns as "rare" or even "stunning". In my experience very few items described on-line as "stunning" actually are.

If you have an item that you are not sure about selling, search the "completed items" to check whether listing it would be worth while. If a similar item has previously sold well, then get listing. If you are going to sell on eBay ensure that you list the item in the correct category to help

achieve the maximum exposure to prospective bidders. It may be worth the small extra fee to list in two categories, for example a golfing medal in the medal section could also be listed in the golf section to give it extra exposure. Use as much of the title space as possible; the maximum allowed is 55 characters but I have seen "COIN" as the only word present—this does not encourage browsers to click on your auction lot. The denomination, date and grade would be a good start, with any other information that can be squeezed in. Some collectors will search only the auction titles and exclude the longer description, hoping to reduce the number of hits to home-in on—this is another good reason to include as much of the essential information in the 55 character auction title as possible. A short but accurate description should be aimed at—some sellers have a screen full of terms and conditions but precious little about the item they have on offer. Fancy graphics are a turn off for many people, they are irritating and increase the download time considerably. One USA-based seller often has nice UK coins for sale but when their name appears I stop the download to avoid the music and over-the-top graphics that include a bird flapping its wings. How many bids do they miss out on because of this nonsense?

Another certain way of reducing the number of bids you get is to have some of these in your auction title, "look", "l@@k", "must see" or a row of symbols like "+++++++" or "!!!!!!!!!!!!". Some buyers do searches that exclude items with "look" or "l@@k" in the title. Using these in the title gives the impression to many that the seller must be an idiot. The repeated use of poor spelling or grammar will also put prospective bidders off. Common errors are, "sort after" for "sought after", "very rarer" and "commemative" for "commemorative". Some sellers have the same error in every auction they list, sometimes dozens of them, this does not inspire confidence. Listing in ALL CAPITALS will reduce the number of bids as many eBay buyers will not read a listing in ALL CAPITALS as it is difficult to read.

Always give a full description of a coin, including the size. Don't assume that everybody knows the size of the coin on offer. Many youngsters, even in the UK, have no idea of the size of a halfcrown and as many prospective bidders live overseas, it is better to mention the size every time.

A clear picture of the item being sold is essential as many bidders have the rule, "no pic equals no bid" as they think that the seller has something to hide. Try to keep the file size below 100k as if it is too big, and therefore takes too long, many potential bidders will stop the download part of the way through. As coins are small this is less of a problem. Computer monitors draw the screen at around 72 dots per inch so a scan done at 600 dpi is a waste of time and will result in a very large file size. I would recommend scanning coins at around 200 dpi as this will give a larger than life screen image but isn't so big that minor blemishes will look the size of the grand canyon.

It is better to start off selling low value items and move on to the more expensive once you have built up a good reputation and have several positive feedbacks under your belt. Buyers are reluctant to buy high value items from new members as they fear being scammed. It is not unknown for a scammer to "borrow" a picture from another web site and pretend that they have an expensive coin for sale. One eBay seller did something even stranger: he offered a "proof Gothic crown" and, strangely, he had recently bought a modern copy of a Gothic crown on eBay. The picture he used for his selling auction was the identical picture used by the seller of the copy coin. I asked him, by email, if the coin he was selling was the copy he had bought recently for £15.49. He replied that it was not and the coin he was selling was genuine. He expected bidders to believe that he was selling a genuine coin worth a few thousand pounds but using a picture of a copy coin! The copy coin eventually "sold" for £150.

Giving advice on selling on eBay is easy but buying is a lot more complicated as there are many pitfalls. The biggest problem on eBay is the gross overgrading of coins. It is common to see coins less than fine being described as "good very fine". You may find this hard to believe if you have never visited eBay, but some sellers grossly overgrade every coin they sell and they have hundreds of happy buyers. The experienced

collector will not be taken in but new buyers are fooled every day—they will get a nasty shock if they try to sell these worn and often cleaned coins they have bought to a reputable dealer.

Surprisingly junk seems to sell better than quality items. Low-grade material often sells for above the true value and high-grade items sometimes sell for below market price, although there are always exceptions of course.

eBay has a feedback system where a satisfied buyer can give a positive feedback thus increasing the seller's feedback total by one. Unsatisfied buyers can give a negative report, decreasing the seller's score by one or if they are unsure they can give a neutral, which has no effect on the seller's feedback total. Some unhappy buyers are reluctant to give a bad seller a negative feedback as they fear a retaliatory negative. Giving a negative when deserved may help prevent others having a bad buying experience.

If a seller has less than 100% perfect feedback it is essential to read the feedback before bidding and if the rating is below 99% think carefully before bidding. Reading the feedback left by sellers below 100% can be most enlightening. If they insult the giver of a justified negative then don't bid on any of their auctions. Keep a "do not bid on" list of sellers and stick to it, a leopard will not change its spots.

If an eBay seller lists only uncirculated coins or notes ask yourself the question: how many well established dealers do you know that sell only uncirculated notes or coins? The answer, of course, will be none. How can a seller only have uncirculated coins or notes for sale, unless they overgrade? With coins the grade can be seen from the picture, but with notes it is very difficult or even impossible to grade from an image on a screen so you have to rely on the sellers' description being accurate—but very often it's not. I have seen coins in less than fine condition described as having "slight ware (sic)". I would recommend only buying uncirculated notes of recent vintage as older ones are likely to be overgraded or pressed, or both. Recently one buyer bought a number of notes at a major auction, the same notes were then sold on eBay at higher grades, after they had been ironed. This was obvious because the serial numbers of some of the notes matched the notes illustrated in the auction catalogue. The seller now has two negatives and he responded to them by calling the unhappy buyers rude names, this shows him up in his true colours.

A seller that describes every note and coin that he has up for auction as "rare" or "very rare" should be avoided as they are untrustworthy, in my experience items described as "rare" are often very common low grade items. The truly rare coins or notes are sometimes sold by people that have no idea of the rarity of the item they have for sale—this is when a bargain may be had.

Some regular sellers of numismatic items very often only give vague grading descriptions like "very nice collectable condition". In my mind I see this as an attempt to reduce the likelihood of them getting an item returned for being overgraded. I would avoid bidding on items offered by this type of seller. It is common for bad sellers with many negatives to reappear under a new selling name—it's fortunate that the bad sellers are often not very bright and continue with their previous listing style or text and colours used so they can be easily identified.

eBay insist that they are only a venue and can not be held responsible for the selling of fakes and the actions of scammers. I would accept this, because of the millions of items for sale at any one time they can't be expected to vet all items and sellers. The worst scamming appears in the "antiquities" section. Have a look at the Chinese items listed and you will see "silver", "jade" and "amber" items allegedly centuries old selling for very low prices, with usually a very high delivery cost—£58 seems to be a popular amount to charge. The sellers are usually based in China and the listings are often accompanied by far too many pictures of the item. The items being sold as "antiquities" are modern tourist souvenirs and the bad feedback that they eventually get is often very amusing as is their reply to it.

This is only my opinion of buying and selling on eBay and other people's experiences may vary. However, I would encourage collectors to visit the auction sites, but be careful. I welcome correspondence on the subject of eBay or other online numismatic activities and I can be contacted at william.mccreath@ntlworld.com.

Talking

Tokens

Strictly speaking, a token is any piece of money whose intrinsic value is less than its face value. In that sense, therefore, all modern coins are mere tokens, because their metallic worth is invariably less than their nominal, legal tender value. Until the 19th century, however, most countries issued coins which contained metal up to the value at which they circulated. This applied mainly to gold and silver coins, but it should be noted that Britain's first copper penny and twopence (1797) were so cumbersome because they contained one and two ounces of metal respectively, copper being then valued at a penny an ounce.

The desire for parity between intrinsic and nominal value led to copper coins containing a small plug of silver to bring them up to their full value. The UK abandoned full value in 1816; as a result of the recoinage of that year the gold sovereign became the absolute standard and all silver and copper coins became mere tokens. The difference between real and nominal value widened in subsequent years with the debasement of silver coins and finally the replacement of silver altogether by cupro-nickel and other base alloys. Oddly enough, there have been many instances of small copper or bronze coins in recent years which had a greater intrinsic value than their face value and actually cost twice as much to produce as they were worth in circulation.

A token is an outward sign or pledge, something given or shown as a guarantee of authority or good faith. The word comes from German *zeichen* and Old English *tacen*, meaning a sign or mark. From this developed the notion of a promise, symbol or keepsake. In the numismatic sense, however, the term is restricted to any coinlike object, either issued by a body other than a government, or something which is used in place of money and can be exchanged for specified goods and services. Broadly speaking, tokens include any unofficial coins supplied by local bodies or occasionally even private individuals and tolerated in general circulation at times of shortage of government issues of small change.

Tokens go back a surprisingly long way. The earliest issues in base metal with limited local validity were produced by Sicily in the middle of

the fifth century BC, the bronze litra being easier to handle than its tiny silver counterpart. Himera was one of the first towns to issue such tokens, but by the end of the century many Sicilian towns had adopted small bronze pieces as token currency, the intrinsic value of which was considerably below the circulating value placed on them by the issuing authorities.

This concept gradually spread to all other parts of the Greek world. Under the Roman Empire, base-metal tokens were issued from the time of Augustus to the late third century AD. Sometimes referred to quasi-autonomous coinage, these pieces were struck mostly in bronze with the nominal value of drachmae or sestertii, and have portraits of local deities instead of the Roman emperor and members of his family. These tokens were struck by every town and city and their range and variety is enormous.

This concept survived the fall of the Roman Empire and many towns in medieval Europe continued to strike small base-metal pieces for use as local currency. They were usually accorded a measure of legality because they were authorised by the royal or imperial government, even if their actual design and metal content were decided by the municipal authorities. In addition to the tokens which served as small change there are other categories of coinlike material which deserve comment.

Jetons (from French *jeter*, to throw) originated in medieval France as counters used on the chequerboard by merchants and bankers as well as royal treasurers to do their monetary calculations. These pieces spread rapidly all over Europe, but found their greatest expression at Nuremberg where, in the hands of Hans Krauwinckel (flourished 1580–1620), they attained the status of an art form and were often produced in thematic sets.

While many jetons were struck in gold or silver and were eventually used (especially in France) as a form of New Year bonus to servants, the vast majority of them were struck in debased silver alloys (billon) or in copper, bronze, brass or pewter. Base-metal Nuremberg jetons, in fact, often circulated as small change in countries where there was a shortage of total lack of government issues of small change. This situation arose in England early in the 14th century, Nuremberg jetons circulating freely until 1335 when they were banned by statute.

English tokens

The first indigenous tokens in England were cast or struck in lead and have been recorded as circulating in 1404. For many years these local farthings and half-farthings were tolerated but had no official sanction. They were certainly well-established in Tudor times and it was not until 1598 that any attempt was made to regulate them. Queen Elizabeth then licensed Bristol to issue lead tokens, to be valid within a ten-mile radius of the city. At the same time, private tokens were expressly forbidden, so that the municipal tokens were given a monopoly. By the end of the Civil War (1649) there was an acute shortage of small change, and illicit tokens, mainly in lead and including pewter, brass, copper or even leather pieces, were revived in England and Wales.

Almost 4,000 types of token were issued in London alone, by tradesmen and shopkeepers of all kinds, and often circulating no farther than the end of the street. As the vast majority were produced before the Great Fire of 1666 they form an invaluable record of London streets and their occupants from this period. Following the introduction of regal copper farthings and halfpence in 1672 these tradesmen's tokens were banned, but they continued in some parts of England until 1674, and survived in Ireland until 1679. By contrast there was virtually no need for tokens in 17th century Scotland because of an abundant supply of copper coinage, and only two Scottish tokens (c. 1668) have so far been recorded.

In many ways tokens benefited the poor, who were no longer compelled to purchase more than they actually required because the smallest coin available was a penny. Tokens were also used as alms, as people would gladly give a farthing but would think twice about giving a halfpenny or penny. For this reason many tokens of the 17th century were inscribed "Remember the Poore",

17th century tokens come in a variety of shapes and sizes.

"For the Poore's Advantage" or "For Change & Charitie" or some other pious slogan.

There were even tokens inscribed in verse: "To supply the poore's need is charitie indeed". Other poetic inscriptions include "When you please, I'll change thee", "Although but brass, yet let me pass", "Welcome you be to trade with me" or "Take these that will, I'll change them still".

Eighteenth century tokens

Tokens were revived in the British Isles in 1787 to fill a gap in the regal coinage. Silver pennies for general circulation were only sporadically produced in the reign of George III and none at all were minted after 1786. The dearth of copper halfpence and farthings was even greater as none was minted after 1775. On this occasion the way was led by the Angelsey Copper Mining Company which began striking pennies with the effigy of a Druid on the obverse. This triggered off an immense deluge of token pennies, halfpennies and farthings. The range was not as great as it had been in the 17th century as fewer individual shopkeepers now issued them.

There was a greater concentration of tokens issued by municipal authorities and the more important merchant companies. On the other hand, the quality of design and execution improved beyond all recognition and latterly they were aimed at the contemporary collector market, with emphasis on heraldry, landmarks, scenery, historic events and portraits of local and national celebrities. These tokens enjoyed a decade of use before they

The prolific issues of 18th century tokens such as this one were banned on the introduction of the "Cartwheel" coinage in 1797.

were banned following the introduction of the "Cartwheel" coinage in 1797.

Nineteenth century tokens

Silver tokens were issued between 1804 and 1816 as a result of a continuing shortage of silver coins. At first countermarked Spanish dollars and half-dollars were issued but in 1811–12 the Bank of England released silver pieces inscribed BANK TOKEN on the reverse, with the value and date below. The obverse portrayed George III and had his name and titles round the circumference like the proper silver coins. Denominations of 1s6d and 3s were issued; though 9d pieces exist they were only patterns. The Bank of Ireland had silver tokens in the same period, but denominated in a decimal system of 5, 10 and 30 pence, as well as 6 shillings. Many private silver tokens were issued in 1811–12 in denominations from 3d to 5s, mainly by private banks, local authorities and large companies.

Copper or bronze tokens were again issued in the British Isles from 1811 to the 1830s. As no copper subsidiary coins were issued between 1807 and 1821 (no halfpence or pennies until 1825–26) the range of tokens in this period was far greater than ever. Significantly a high proportion of these tokens were now issued by banks rather than by private individuals.

Other types of tokens

Tokens have been produced in most countries at some time or another. Very extensive series, for example, were produced in Canada and Australia before these countries introduced subsidiary coinage. They were also produced on a number of occasions in the USA, from the revolutionary period onwards, and notably during the Hard Times (1834–44) during a shortage of copper cents and half-cents. There was a further spate of local tokens during the Civil War (1861–65), often with patriotic motifs and having a propaganda purpose as well as filling the gap in the coinage. Many countries issued tokens during and after the First World War, every type of material from pasteboard and wood to leather and even rubber being pressed into service. A special category consists of trade dollars issued all over Canada. These are often commemorative or intended as tourist mementoes, but they have a nominal value, redeemable for cash within a certain area and over a fixed period, usually twelve months. They are immensely popular and now have a wide following in North America.

In Britain from the 18th century onwards tokens were often issued by textile mills, collieries, iron foundries and other industrial undertakings in exchange for a day's work. These tokens could only be used to obtain goods from the company stores, and were eventually outlawed by the Truck Act in 1844. Nevertheless they survived in various parts of Britain, often in specific forms of labour. A very prolific series, for example, consists of hop-pickers' tokens, associated mainly with the hopfields of Kent and Sussex. In Scotland, however, fruit-pickers' tokens were also issued by many of the farms in the Clyde Valley and the fruit-growing areas of Perthshire and Angus.

The Parys Mines of Anglesey produced vast numbers of "Druid's Head" tokens.

Hop pickers were usually paid in tokens which are highly collected today.

Another vast area consists of the checks and tokens issued by co-operative societies, often in proportion to the money spent by the member in the societies' stores, as a form of dividend. When a certain quantity of checks had been accumulated they could be exchanged for goods or services. The same concept underlay the discount schemes, premium giveaways and trading stamps of more recent items.

Tokens of metal, pasteboard or even plastic have been used as a method of controlling the use of public transport by employees of companies, the Post Office or local authorities, being given out whenever it was necessary for an employee to travel on official business. Such tokens were produced by local authorities or the private companies operating buses, ferries, trams and other services. At the other end of the spectrum are the tokens and passes, often in silver or even gold, or ivory, which were issued to directors of the railway companies to enable them to travel free of charge. Tokens in the same materials, and for the same purpose, were produced for the use of the directors and shareholders of theatres and other places of entertainment, and were often highly ornate in design.

Gaming tokens

This is another vast field, ranging from the brass halfpenny and penny tokens issued by many pubs and taverns in the 19th century for use in games of chance, to the modern tokens, often in cupro-nickel, bronze or aluminium-bronze, used in one-armed bandits and fruit machines. These tokens range from the fairly utilitarian designs showing perhaps a company name and a unit of value only, to the very elaborate tokens used by casinos and gaming clubs, often with special security features built into their design and composition. Many of the gaming tokens of more recent years have a quasi-commemorative or publicity character.

Richard Orchard's Sawbridgeworth token sold for the world record price of £24,400 in 1998.

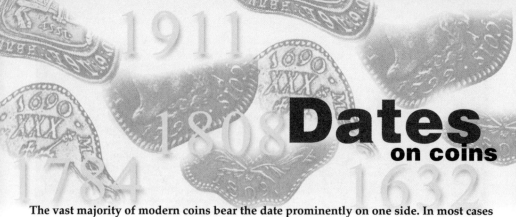

Dates on coins

The vast majority of modern coins bear the date prominently on one side. In most cases dates are expressed in modified Arabic numerals according to the Christian calendar and present no problem in identification. There have been a few notable exceptions to this general rule, however. Morocco, for example, has used European numerals to express dates according to the Moslem calendar, so that a coin dated 1321 actually signifies 1903. Dates are almost invariably written from left to right—even in Arabic script which writes words from right to left. An exception, however, occurred in the Philippines quarto of 1822 where the date appeared as 2281, and the "2s" back to front for good measure.

	ARABIC-TURKISH	CHINESE, JAPANESE KOREAN, ANNAMESE (ORDINARY)	CHINESE, JAPANESE KOREAN, ANNAMESE (OFFICIAL)	INDIAN	SIAMESE	BURMESE
1	١	一	壹	९	๑	၁
2	٢	二	貳	٢	๒	၂
3	٣	三	叁	३	๓	၃
4	٤	四	肆	୪	๔	၄
5	٥	五	伍	५	๕	၅
6	٦	六	陸	६	๖	၆
7	٧	七	柒	७	๗	၇
8	٨	八	捌	८	๘	၈
9	٩	九	玖	९	๙	၉
0	٠			٥	๐	၀
10	١٠	十	拾		๑๐	
100	١٠٠	百			๑๐๐	
1000	١٠٠٠	千				

Dates in Roman numerals have been used since 1234 when this practice was adopted by the Danish town of Roskilde. Such Roman numerals were used sporadically throughout the Middle Ages and in later centuries and survive fitfully to this day. This was the system used in England for the first dated coins, the gold half-sovereigns of Edward VI struck at Durham House in 1548 (MDXLVIII). This continued till 1550 (MDL) but thereafter Arabic numerals were used, beginning with the half-crown of 1551. Notable exceptions of more recent times include the Gothic coinage of Queen Victoria (1847–87).

The first coin with the date in European numerals was a plappart of St Gallen, Switzerland dated 1424, but this was an isolated case. In 1477 Maria of Burgundy issued a guldiner which bore a date on the reverse, in the form of two pairs of digits flanking the crown at the top. The numerals in this instance were true Gothic, an interesting transition between true Arabic numerals and the modified Arabic figures now used in Europe. The Tyrolese guldengroschen of 1484–6 were the first coins to be regularly dated in European numerals and thereafter this custom spread rapidly.

For the numismatist, the problem arises when coins bear a date in the numerals of a different alphabet or computed according to a different era. Opposite is a table showing the basic numerals used in different scripts. The various eras which may be found in coin dates are as listed and explained opposite.

Hijra

The era used on Moslem coins dates from the flight of Mohammed from Mecca to Medina on July 15, 622 and is often expressed as digits followed by AH (*Anno Hegirae*). Moslems employ a lunar calendar of twelve months comprising 354 11/30 days. Tipu Sultan of Mysore in 1201 AH (the fifth year of his reign)introduced a new era dating from the birth of Mohammed in AD 570 and using a luni-solar system. Tipu also adopted the Hindu cycle of sixty years (the Tamil Brihaspate Cycle), but changed this two or three years later, from Hijra to Muludi.

Afghan coins used the lunar calendar until 1920 and during 1929–31, but at other times have used the solar calendar. Thus the Democratic Republic began issuing its coins in SH 1358 (1979).

To convert an AH date to the Christian calendar you must translate the Arabic into European numerals. Taking an Arabic coin dated 1320, for example, first deduct 3% (to convert from the Moslem lunar year to our solar year). This gives 39.6 which, rounded up to the nearest whole number, is 40. Deduct 40 from 1320 (1280), then add 622. The answer is 1902.

There have been a few notable exceptions. Thus the Khanian era of Ilkhan Ghazan Mahmud began on 1st Rajab 701 AH (1301). This era used a solar calendar, but was shortlived, being confined to coins of Mahmud and his nephew Abu Said down to year 34 (1333).

The era of Tarikh Ilahi was adopted by the Mughal emperor Akbar in the thirteenth year of his reign (922 AH). This era dated from his accession on 5th Rabi al-Sani 963 AH (February 19, 1556). The calendar had solar months and days but no weeks, so each day of the month had a different name. This system was used by Akbar, Jahangir and Shah Jahan, often with a Hijra date as well.

Saphar

The era of the Caesars began on January 1, 38 BC and dated from the conquest of Spain by Augustus. Its use on coinage, however, seems to have been confined to the marabotins of Alfonso VIII of Castile and was expressed in both Latin and Arabic.

Samvat

The era of Vikramaditya began in 57 BC and was a luni-solar system used in some Indian states. Coins may be found with both Samvat and Hijra dates. Conversion to the Christian date is simple; merely subtract 57 from the Samvat to arrive at the AD date.

Saka

This originated in the southwestern district of Northern India and began in AD 78. As it used the luni-solar system it converts easily by adding 78 to the Saka date.

Nepal

Nepalese coins have used four different date systems. All coins of the Malla kings were dated in Nepal Samvat (NS) era, year 1 beginning in 881. This system was also used briefly by the state of Cooch Behar. Until 1888 all coins of the Gurkha dynasty were dated in the Saka era (SE) which began in AD 78. After 1888 most copper coins were dated in the Vikram Samvat (VS) era from 57 BC. With the exception of some gold coins struck in 1890 and 1892, silver and gold coins only changed to the VS era in 1911, but now this system is used for all coins struck in Nepal. Finally, dates in the Christian era have appeared on some commemorative coins of recent years.

Ethiopian

This era dates from August AD 7, so that EE 1885 is AD 1892. Ethiopian dates are expressed in five digits using Amharic numerals. The first two are the digits of the centuries, the third is the character for 100, while the fourth and fifth are the digits representing the decade and year. On modern coins dates are rendered in Amharic numerals using the Christian era.

Thailand

Thai coins mainly use the Buddhist era (BE) which dates from 543 BC, but some coins have used dates from the Chula-Sakarat calendar (CS) which began in AD 638, while others use a Ratanakosind Sok (RS) date from the foundation of the Chakri dynasty in AD 1781.

Hebrew

The coins of Israel use the Jewish calendar dating from the beginning of the world (Adam and Eve in the Garden of Eden) in 3760 BC. Thus the year 1993 is rendered as 5753. The five millennia are assumed in dates, so that only the last three digits are expressed. 735 therefore equates with AD 1975. Dates are written in Hebrew letters, reading from right to left. The first two characters signify 400 and 300 respectively, totalling 700. The third letter denotes the decades (*lamedh* = 30) and the fourth letter, following the separation mark (") represents the final digit (*heh* = 5). The Jewish year runs from September or October in the Christian calendar.

Dates from the creation of the world

This system was also used in Russia under Ivan IV. The dating system *Anno Mundi* (AM) was established by the Council of Constantinople in AD 680 which determined that the birth of Christ had occurred in 5508 AM. Ivan's coins expressed the date as 7055 (1447).

Dynastic dates

The system of dating coinage according to regnal years is a feature of Chinese and Japanese coins. Chinese coins normally have an inscription stating that they are coins of such and such a reign period (not the emperor's name), and during the Southern Sung dynasty this was joined by the numeral of the year of the reign. This system was continued under the republic and survives in Taiwan to this day, although the coins of the Chinese Peoples Republic are dated in western numerals using the Christian calendar.

Early Japanese coins bore a reference to the era (the title assumed by each emperor on his accession) but, like Chinese coins, could not be dated accurately. From the beginning of the Meiji era (1867), however, coins have included a regnal number. The Showa era, beginning in 1926 with the accession of Hirohito, eventually ran to sixty-three (expressed in western numerals on some denominations, in Japanese ideograms on others) to denote 1988, although the rest of the inscription was in Japanese characters.

Dynastic dates were used on Korean milled coins introduced in 1888. These bore two characters at the top *Kae Kuk* (founding of the dynasty) followed by quantitative numerals. The system dated from the founding of the Yi dynasty in 1392. Curiously enough, some Korean banknotes have borne dates from the foundation of the first dynasty in 2333 BC.

Iran adopted a similar system in 1975, celebrating the 15th anniversary of the Pahlavi regime by harking back to the glories of Darius. The new calendar dated from the foundation of the Persian Empire 2535 years earlier, but was abolished only three years later when the Shah was overthrown.

Political eras

France adopted a republican calendar in 1793 when the monarchy was abolished. Coins were then inscribed L'AN (the year) followed by Roman numerals, but later Arabic numerals were substituted. This continued to the year 14 (1806) but in that year the Emperor Napoleon restored the Christian calendar. The French system was emulated by Haiti whose coins dated from the revolution of 1803. The date appeared as AN followed by a number until AN 31 (1834) on some coins; others had both the evolutionary year and the Christian date from 1828 until 1850 (AN 47). Coins with a date in the Christian calendar appeared only in 1807–9 and then from 1850 onwards.

Mussolini introduced the Fascist calendar to Italy, dating from the seizure of power in October 1922. This system was widely employed on documents and memorials, but was first used on silver 20 lire coins of 1927 and then only in addition to the Christian date and appearing discreetly as Roman numerals. Subsequently it was extended to gold 50 lire and 100 lire coins in 1931 and the subsidiary coinage in 1936, being last used in the year XXI (1943).

Let Coincraft help you in three ways...

Publishers of the Standard Catalogues

Coincraft are the publishers of the Standard Catalogues of English, Scottish and Irish coins and other numismatic books.

We always need to buy

Coincraft needs to buy: single items to entire collections, dealers inventories, hoards, accumulations, you name it and we will make you an offer. Over 90% of our offers are accepted. Sell where the dealers sell.

If you like numbers:

Coincraft has 2 buildings, 25 staff, in the past 5 years we have spent over £900,000 on advertising and added over 52,000 collectors to our mailing list. We are listed in the Guinness Book of Records for buying the largest, heaviest, and most expensive lot of banknotes ever sold.

In person

Call in person at either of our two shops at 44 & 45 Great Russell Street, just across from the British Museum. Open Monday to Friday 9.30 to 5.00 and Saturday from 10.00 till 2.30.

Friendly, personal service and an interesting display of coins, banknotes, medallions, ancient coins and antiquities, to tempt and delight you.

By post

Coincraft publishes Britain's only coin newspaper, The Phoenix, published every three weeks. It contains 24 tabloid sized pages of special offers and rare items, many not available anywhere else.

You can't buy a subscription, but you can get a complimentary copy free, just for the asking.

On the internet

Our website, www.coincraft.com is available 24 hours a day. There are many interesting features including a comprehensive numismatic glossary.

Keep looking, more is being added every day.

Coincraft
FRIENDLY PROFESSIONAL SERVICE SINCE 1955

44 & 45 Great Russell Street, London WC1B 3LU
(opposite the British Museum)

Tel 020 7636 1188 and 020 7637 8785
Fax 020 7323 2860 and 020 7637 7635
Web www.coincraft.com Email info@coincraft.com

Find out why collectors say;
Coincraft, nice people to do business with.

Around the *World*

Listed here are the names of all the coins of the world, many of which have been around for hundreds of years, others are no longer in use. Some of the denominations have been introduced only recently, whilst others are familiar household words. A number of the names are shared by different countries and a few have even been used by different civilisations.

Abazi   Caucusus
Abbasi, Abbassi   Afghanistan, Georgia, Persia
Ackey   Gold Coast
Adli Altin   Ottoman Empire
Afghani   Afghanistan
Agnel   France
Agora (ot)   Israel
Ahmadi   Mysore, Yemen
Akce   Turkey
Akcheh   Turkestan
Albertusdaler   Denmark
Albus   German States, Swiss Cantons
Altin, Altun   Egypt, Turkey
Altinlik   Turkey
Altyn, Altynnik   Russia
Amani   Afghanistan
Amman Cash   Mewar Udaipur, Pudukota,   India
Angel   England, Scotland, Isle of Man

Angel

Angelet   France
Angelot   France
Angster   Lucerne
Anna   Burma, India, Pakistan, Kenya, Muscat & Oman
Antoninianus   Rome
Ardite   Navarre
Argentino   Argentina
Ariary   Malagasy Republic
As   Rome
Asarfi   Nepal

Ashrafi   Afghanistan, Awadh, Bahawalpur, Egypt,   Hyderabad
Asper   Algeria, Egypt, Libya, Trebizond, Tunisia,   Turkey
Asses   Luxembourg
At   Laos
Atia   Portuguese India
Atribuo   Frankfurt
Att   Cambodia, Laos, Siam (Thailand)
August d'Or   Saxony
Augustale   Sicily
Aurar (plural **Eyrir**)   Iceland
Austral   Argentina
Avo   Macau, Timor
Bagarone   Bologna
Bagattino   Venice
Baggliangster   Lucerne
Baht   Thailand
Baiocco (plural **Baiocchi**)   Papal States
Baisa   Oman
Baiza   Kuwait
Baizah   Muscat & Oman
Balboa   Panama
Ban (plural **Bani** or **Banu**)   Roumania
Banica   Croatia
Barbarina   Mantua
Barbonaccio   Lucca
Barbone   Lucca
Barbuda   Portugal
Barilla   Philippines
Batzen   German States, Swiss Cantons
Bawbee   Scotland
Bazaruco   Portuguese India
Bazaruk   Dutch Settlements in India
Belga   Belgium
Benduqi   Morocco
Besa (plural **Bese**)   Ethiopia, Somalia
Beshlik   Soviet Central Asia
Bezant   Byzantine Empire, Cyprus, Jerusalem
Bezzo   Italian States

Bianco (plural **Bianchi**)   Bologna, Papal States
Biche   French Indian Settlements
Binio   Roman Empire
Bipkwele   Equatorial Guinea
Bir (r)   Ethiopia
Bisti   Caucasia
Bit   Guyana, West Indies
Bitt   Danish Virgin Islands
Black Dog   Nevis
Blaffert   Switzerland
Blanc   France
Blodsklipping   Sweden
Bluzger   Swiss Cantons
Bodle   Scotland
Bogach   Yemen
Bolivar   Venezuela
Boliviano   Bolivia
Bolognino   Papal States
Bonk   Ceylon, Dutch East Indies
Bonnet   Scotland
Boo   Japan
Braspenning   Flanders
Broad   England
Bu   Japan
Budju   Algeria
Buqsha   Yemen Arab Republic
Burbe(ns)   Tunisia
Butut   Gambia
Cache   French Indian Settlements
Cagliareso   Italian States
Calderilla   Spain
Candareen   China
Carbovanetz   Ukraine
Carlin   Sicily
Carlino   Papal States
Carolin   Austria,German States, Sweden
Cash   China, Hong Kong, India, Mysore,
   Travancore, Turkestan, Vietnam
Cassathaler   German States
Cauri   Guinea
Ceitil   Portugal
Cent   Australia, Bahamas, Barbados, Belize,
   Bermuda, Botswana, British East Caribbean
   Territories, British Honduras, British North
   Borneo, British Virgin Islands, Brunei,
   Canada, Cayman Island, Ceylon, China,
   Cochin China, Cocos (Keeling) Islands,
   Cook Islands, Curacao, Cyprus, Danish
   West Indies, East Africa, Ethiopia, Fiji,
   French Indochina, Gilbert and Ellice Islands,
   Guyana, Hawaii, Hong Kong, Indonesia,
   Jamaica, Kenya, Kiao Chau (Kiatschau),
   Kiribati, Laos, Liberia, Malaya, Malaysia,
   Malta, Mauritius, Netherlands, Netherlands
   Antilles, Netherlands Indies, New Zealand,
   Nova Scotia, Panama, Prince Edward Island,
   Sarawak, Seychelles, Sierra Leone, Singapore,

   Solomon Islands, South Africa, Sri Lanka,
   Straits Settlements, Suriname, Swaziland,
   Tanzania, Trinidad and Tobago, Tuvalu,
   Uganda, United States of America, Virgin
   Islands, Zanzibar, Zimbabwe
Centas (plural **Centa, Centu**)   Lithuania
Centavo   Angola, Argentina, Bolivia, Brazil,
   Cape Verde Islands, Chile, Colombia, Costa
   Rica, Cuba, Dominican Republic, Ecuador,
   El Salvador, Guatemala, Guinea-Bissau,
   Honduras, Mexico, Mozambique, Nicaragua,
   Paraguay, Peru, Philippines, Portugal,
   Portuguese Guinea, Portuguese India, Puerto
   Rico, St Thomas and Prince Islands, Timor,
   Venezuela
Centecimo   Bolivia
Cententionalis   Roman Empire
Centesimo   Bolivia, Chile, Dominican Republic,
   Ethiopia, Italian East Africa, Italy, Panama,
   Paraguay, San Marino, Somalia, Uruguay,
   Vatican
Centime   Algeria, Antwerp, Belgian Congo,
   Belgium, Cambodia, Cameroon, Cochin
   China, Comoro Islands, Djibouti, France,
   French Equatorial Africa, French Guiana,
   French Indochina, French Oceania, French
   Polynesia, French Somali Coast, French West
   Africa, Guadeloupe, Guinea, Haiti, Laos,
   Monaco, Morocco, New Caledonia, Reunion,
   Senegal, Switzerland, Togo, Tunisia, Vietnam,
   Westphalia, Yugoslavia, Zaire
Centimo   Costa Rica, Mozambique, Paraguay,
   Peru, Philippines, Puerto Rico, St Thomas and
   Prince Islands, Spain, Venezuela
Centu   Lithuania
Chaise   Antwerp, Bavaria, France
Chervonetz (plural **Chervontzy**)   Russia
Chetrum   Bhutan
Cheun   South Korea
Chiao   China, Formosa, Manchukuo
Chi'en   China
Chio   China
Cho-gin   Japan

Chomseh   Yemen
Chon   Korea
Christian d'Or   Denmark
Chuckram   Travancore
Colon   Costa Rica, El Salvador
Condor   Chile, Colombia, Ecuador
Cordoba   Nicaragua
Cornado   Spain
Cornuto   Savoy
Coroa de Prata   Portugal
Coroin   Eire
Corona   Austrian provinces of Italy, Naples
Coronato   Castile, Naples
Couronne d'Or   France
Crocione   Italian States
Crossazzo   Genoa
Crown   Ascension, Australia, Bermuda, England, Ghana, Gibraltar, Ireland, Isle of Man, Jamaica, Jersey, Malawi, New Zealand, Nigeria, Rhodesia, Rhodesia and Nyasaland, St Helena, Scotland, Southern Rhodesia, Tristan da Cunha, Turks and Caicos Islands

Cruzadinho   Brazil, Portugal
Cruzado   Brazil, Portugal
Cruzeiro   Brazil
Cuartillo, Cuartino   Mexico
Cuarto   Bolivia, Spain
Daalder   Netherlands
DakBler   Danish West Indies, Denmark, Sweden
Dam   Afghanistan, India, Nepal
Daric   Persia
Dauphin   France
Decime   France
Decimo   Argentina, Chile, Colombia, Ecuador, Galapagos
Decussis   Roman Republic
Dekadrachm   Syracuse, Hellenistic kingdoms
Dekanummion   Byzantine Empire
Dekobolon   Greece
Demareteion   Syracuse
Demer   France

Demy   Scotland
Denar   Hungary
Denarius   Rome
Denaro   Italian States
Denga   Russia
Dengi   Roumania
Denier   France and colonies, Haiti, Swiss Cantons
Denning   Denmark
Deut   Rhineland, Westphalia
Deutschemark   Germany
Dhofari Riyal   Yemen
Diamante   Ferrara
Diamantino   Ferrara
Dicken   Swiss Cantons
Didrachm   Greece
Dime   Canada, Hawaii, USA
Dinar   Afghanistan, Algeria, Bahrain, Hejaz, Iraq, Kuwait, Morocco, Persia, Saudi Arabia, Serbia, Tunisia, Turkey, Yugoslavia
Diner   Andorra
Dinero   Peru, Spain
Diobol   Greece
Dirham   Jordan, Libya, Morocco, United Arab Emirates
Dirhem   Dubai, Iraq, Morocco, Qatar
Dio, Diu   Portuguese India
Disme   USA
Dobla   Genoa, Naples and Sicily
Doblado   Spanish colonies
Doblenca, Doblenga   Aragon, Barcelona
Dobler   Mallorca
Doblon   Chile, Spain, Urugay
Dobra   St Thomas and Prince
Dodekadrachm   Carthage
Doit   Netherlands, Netherlands Indies, Indonesia
Dokdo   Junagadh, Kutch, Nawanagar (Indian States)
Dollar   Anguilla, Antigua and Barbuda, Australia, Bahamas, Belize, Bermuda, Canada, Cayman Islands, China, Cocos (Keeling) Islands, Cook Islands, East Caribbean Territories, Fiji, Great Britain, Grenada, Guyana, Hawaii, Hong Kong, Indonesia, Jamaica, Japan, Kiribati, Liberia, Malaysia, Mauritius, Montserrat, Newfoundland, New Zealand, Panama, St Kitts-Nevis, St Lucia, St Vincent, Scotland, Sierra Leone, Singapore, Solomin Islands, Straits Settlements, Trinidad and Tobago, Tuvalu, USA, Virgin Islands, Western Samoa, Zimbabwe
Dolya   Russia
Dong   Annam, Vietnam
Doppia   Italian States
Doppietta   Sardinia
Double   Guernsey

Dou Dou French Indochina
Douzain France
Drachma Crete, Greece
Dram Armenia
Dreibatzner Austria, German States
Dreigroscher Lithuania, Prussia
Dreiling German States
Dub Hyderabad, India
Dubbeltje Holland
Ducat Austria, Austrian States, Courland,
  Czechoslovakia, Denmark, German States,
  Hungary, Italian States, Liechtenstein, Liege,
  Netherlands,Poland, Roumania, Sweden,
  Swiss Cantons, Russia, Yugoslavia
Ducaton Belgium, Netherlands
Ducatone Italian States
Dudu India
Duetto Italian States
Duit Ceylon, German States, Netherlands,
  Netherlands Indies
Dukat Czechoslovakia, German States,
  Hungary, Poland, Sweden, Yugoslavia
Duplone Swiss Cantons
Duro Spain
Dyak Nepal
Ecu Belgium, Bosnia, France, Gibraltar
Ekuele Equatorial Guinea
Elisabeth d'Or Russia
Emalangeni Swaziland
Escalin Belgium, Guadeloupe, Haiti, Liege,
  Martinique
Escudillo Spain
Escudo Angola, Argentina, Azores, Bolivia,
  Cape Verde Islands, Central American
  Republic, Chile, Colombia, Costa Rica,
  Ecuador, Guadeloupe, Guatemala, Guinea-
  Bissau, Madeira, Mexico, Mozambique,
  Peru, Portugal, Portuguese Guinea/India, St
  Thomas and Prince Islands, Spain, Timor
Espadin Portugal
Esphera Goa
Euro Austria, Belgium, Finland, France,
  Germany, Greece, Ireland, Italy, Luxembourg,
  Monaco, The Netherlands, Portugal, San
  Marino, Spain, The Vatican
Excelente Spain
Eyrir (singular **Aurar**) Iceland
Fals Iraq
Faluce Ceylon
Falus Afghanistan, China, India, Iran, Morocco,
  Turkestan
Fanam Ceylon, Dutch East Indies, Travancore
Fano Tranquebar (Danish Indian Settlements)
Fanon French Indian Settlements
Farthing Antigua, Ceylon, Great Britain, Isle of
  Man, Jamaica, Malta, Scotland, South Africa
Fels Algeria

Fen People's Republic of China, Manchukuo
Fenig (ow) Poland
Feoirling Eire
Ferding Courland, Livonia
Filiberto Savoy
Filippo Italian States
Filler Hungary
Fils Bahrain, Iraq, Jordan, Kuwait, South
  Arabia, United Arab Emirates, Yemen
Fiorino Italian States
Flitter South German States
Floirin Eire
Florin Australia, Austria, East Africa, Fiji,
  Great Britain, Hungary, Ireland, Malawi, New
  Zealand, Rhodesia and Nyasaland, South
  Africa, Swiss Cantons
Follis Rome, Byzantine Empire
Forint Hungary

Franc Algeria, Belgian Congo, Belgium,
  Burundi, Cambodia, Cameroon, Central
  African Republic, Chad, Comoro Islands,
  Congo, Danish West Indies, Djibouti,
  Dominican Republic, Ecuador,
  France, French colonies, Gabon, Guadeloupe,
  Guinea, Ivory Coast, Katanga, Luxembourg,
  Madagascar, Malagasy Republic, Mali,
  Martinique, Mauretania, Monaco, Morocco,
  New Caledonia, New Hebrides, Reunion,
  Ruanda-Urundi, Rwanda, St Pierre and
  Miquelon, Senegal, Switzerland, Togo,
  Tunisia, West African States
Francescone Italian States
Franchi Switzerland
Franco Dominican Republic, Ecuador, Italian
  States, Swiss Cantons
Frang Luxembourg
Frank(en) Belgium, Liechtenstein, Saar,
  Switzerland, Westphalia
Franka Ara Albania
Frederik d'Or Denmark
Friedrich d'Or German States
Fyrk Sweden
Gabellone Papal States

Gayah   Sumatra
Gazetta   Venice
Genovino   Genoa, Florence, Venice
Genevoise   Geneva
George Noble   England
Georgstaler   German States
Gersh   Ethiopia
Gigliato   Hungary, Naples, Rhodes
Gigot   Brabant, Flanders
Gin   Japan
Giorgino   Ferrara, Modena
Giovannino   Genoa
Girsh   Hejaz, Nejd, Saudi Arabia, Sudan
Giulio   Italian States
Golde   Sierra Leone
Goldgulden   German States, Swiss Cantons
Goldpfennig   German States
Goryoban   Japan
Gourde   Haiti
Gourmier   Morocco
Gram   Afghanistan
Gramme   Burma
Gramo   Bolivia, Tierra del Fuego
Grana   Italian States
Grano   Italian States, Mexico,
   Sovereign Order of Malta
Grenadino   Colombia, New Granada
Greschl   Roumania, Transylvania
Grivenka   Russia
Grivennik   Russia
Grivna (plural **Grivny**)   Ukraine
Groat   Great Britain
Groeschl   Bohemia
Groot   Netherlands
Gros   France
Groschel   German States
Groschen   Austria, German States, Poland,
   Swiss Cantons
Groshen   Austria, German States
Grossetto   Dalmatia, Illyria, Venice
Grosso   Italian States
Grossone   Italian States
Grosspfennig   Pomerania, Rhineland
Grossus   Courland, Poland
Grosz (plural **Grosze** or **Groszy**)   Poland
Grote   German States
Grush   Albania
Guarani   Paraguay
Guerche   Egypt, Saudi Arabia
Guinea   Great Britain, Saudi Arabia
Gulden   Austria, Curacao, German States,
   Netherlands, Netherlands Indies, Swiss
   Cantons
Guldiner   Austria, South German States, Swiss
   Cantons
Gutegroschen   North and Central German
   States

Guterpfennig   German States
Habibi   Afghanistan
Halala   Saudi Arabia, Yemen
Halbag   Frankfurt
Haler (plural **Halere, Haleru**)   Czechoslovakia,
   Czech Republic
Halierov   Slovakia
Haller   Swiss Cantons
Hao   China, Vietnam
Hapalua   Hawaii
Hardhead   Scotland
Hardi   France, Turin
Hau   Tonga
Hayrir Altin   Iraq, Turkey
Hekte   Lesbos, Mytilene
Heller   Austria, German States, German East
   Africa
Helm   England
Henri d'Or   France
Hryvnia   Ukraine
Hsien   China
Hvid   Denmark
Hwan   Korea
Hyperpyron   Byzantine Empire
Ichibu-gin   Japan
Ikilik   Russia
Imadi   Yemen
Imami   Mysore
Imperial   Russia
Isabella   Spain
Ischal   Russia
Ishu Gin   Japan
Jacondale   France
Jawa   Nepal
Jeon   Korea
Jerome d'Or   Westphalia
Jiao   People's Republic of China
Jedid   Egypt
Jefimok (plural **Jefimki**)   Russia
Joachimico   Italy
Joachimik   Poland
Joachimstaler   Bohemia
Joao   Portugal
Johanna   Portugal
Johannes   Portugal
Jokoh   Kelantan, Malaysia
Judenpfennig   Frankfurt
Justo   Portugal
Kapang   Sarawak
Kapeikas   Latvia, Belarus
Karolin   German States
Kas   Danish Indian Settlements
Kasu   Mysore
Kazbeg   Caucasia, Safavid Persia
Khayriya   Egypt
Khoum   Mauretania
Kin   Japan

Kina   Papua New Guinea
Kip   Laos
Koban   Japan
Kobo   Nigeria
Kopec   Poland
Kopejek   Outer Mongolia (Tannu Tuva)
Kopek   Russia
Kori   Kutch**Korona**   Bohemia and Moravia, Hungary, Slovakia
Kortling   German States
Korun(a) (plural **Koruny** or **Koruncic**) Czechoslo-vakia
Koula   Tonga
Krajczar   Hungary
Kran   Iran, Persia
Kreu(t)zer   Austria, Austrian States, Czechoslovakia, German States, Hungary, Liechtenstein, Poland, Roumania, Swiss Cantons
Krona (plural **Kronor** or **Kronur**)   Iceland, Sweden
Krona (plural **Kroner** or **Kronen**)   Austria, Denmark, German States, Greenland, Liechtenstein, Norway
Kroon(i)   Estonia
Krugerrand   South Africa
Kuna (plural **Kune**)   Croatia
Kupang   Malaysia, Thailand
Kurus   Turkey
Kuta   Congo-Kinshasa, Zaire
Kwacha   Malawi, Zambia
Kwanza   Angola
Kwartnik   Poland
Kyat   Burma, Myanmar
Kyrmis   Russia
Lang   Annam
Laree, Lari, Lariat or Larin   Maldive Islands
Lati, Lats   Latvia
Laurel   England
Lei   Roumania
Lek (plural **Leke** or **Leku**)   Albania
Lempira   Honduras
Leone   Sierra Leone
Leopard   England
Lepton (plural **Lepta**)   Crete, Greece, Ionian Islands
Leu (plural **Lei**)   Roumania
Lev(a)   Bulgaria
Li   Manchukuo
Liang   China, Laos
Liard   Belgium, France, Luxembourg
Libra   Peru
Licente   Lesotho
Likuta   Zaire
Lilangeni   Swaziland
Lion   Scotland
Lion d'Or   Austrian Netherlands

Lira (plural **Lire**)   Eritrea, Italian East Africa, Italy, San Marino, Syria, Turkey, Vatican
Lira (plural **Lirot**)   Israel
Lisente   Lesotho
Litas (plural **Litai** or **Litu**)   Lithuania

Litra   Sicily, Syracuse
Livre   France, Guadeloupe, Lebanon, Martinique, Mauritius, Reunion
Louis d'Argent   France
Louis d'Or   France
Luhlanga   Swaziland
Lumma   Armenia
Lweis   Angola
Mace   China
Macuta   Angola
Magdalon d'Or   Aix-en-Provence, Tarascon
Mahalek   Ethiopia
Mahallak   Harar
Mahbub   Egypt, Ottoman Empire
Mahmudi   Saudi Arabia
Makuta   Zaire
Maloti   Lesotho
Manat   Azerbaijan
Manghir   Crimea
Marabotin   Moorish kingdoms, Southern Spain
Maravedi   Spain
Marchetto   Italian States
Marck   German States
Marengo   France
Mariengroschen   German States
Mark   Germany, German States, German New Guinea, Norway, Poland, Sweden
Marka   Estonia
Markka(a)   Finland
Mas   Malaysia
Masriya   Egypt
Masson   Lorraine and Bar
Mat   Burma
Matapan   Venice
Mathbu   Morocco
Maticaes   Mozambique
Matona   Ethiopia
Mattier   German States
Maximilian d'Or   German States

Mazuna   Morocco
Medin   Egypt
Mehmudiye Altin   Ottoman Empire
Meinhard   Austria, German States
Melgarejo   Bosnia
Merk   Scotland
Metica   Mozambique
Meung   Japan
Mil   Cyprus, Hong Kong, Israel, Malta, Palestine
Milan d'Or   Serbia
Miliarense   Byzantine Empire
Milesima   Spain
Millieme   Egypt, Libya
Millime   Tunisia
Milreis   Brazil
Miscals   China
Mohar   Nepal
Mohur   Afghanistan, Bikanir, Cooch Behar,
   Gwalior, Hyderabad, India (Mughal Empire),
   Maldive Islands, Netherlands Indies, Rajkot
Moidore (Moeda de ouro)   Portugal
Momme   Japan
Mon   Japan, Ryukyu Islands
Mongo   Mongolia
Mouton d'Or   France
Mu   Burma
Mun   Korea
Mung   Mongolia
Munzgulden   Swiss Cantons
Muzuna   Algeria
Naira   Nigeria
Nami-sen   Japan
Napoleon   France
Naya Paisa   Bhutan, India
Negotiepenning   Netherlands
Neugroschen   German States
New Pence   Gibraltar, Great Britain, Guernsey,
   Isle of Man, Jersey
Ngultrum   Bhutan
Ngwee   Zambia
Nisar   Afghanistan, India
Nisfiya   Egypt
Noble   Austria,England, Scotland, Isle of Man
Nomisma   Byzantine Empire
Nonsunt   Scotland
Nummion (plural Nummia)   Byzantine Empire
Oban   Japan
Obol   Greece, Ionian Islands
Ochavo   Spain
Octavo   Mexico, Philippines
Omani   Oman
Onca   Mozambique
Oncia   Italian States
Onlik   Crimea
Onluk   Turkey
Onza   Bolivia, Chile, Costa Rica, Mexico
Or   Sweden

Ore   Denmark, Faroe Islands, Greenland,
   Norway, Sweden
Ort(e)   Poland, Prussia
Ortug (plural Ortugar)   Sweden
Ouguiya   Mauretania
Pa'anga   Tonga
Pagoda   India (Madras)
Pahlavi   Iran
Pai   India, Siam (Thailand)
Paisa   Afghanistan, Bhutan, India, Nepal,
   Pakistan
Panchia   India
Pano   Portuguese Africa
Paoli   Italian States
Papetto   Papal States
Para (plural Paras or Parades)   Crimea, Egypt,
   Greece, Iraq, Libya, Nejd, Roumania,
   Saudi Arabia, Serbia, Sudan, Syria, Turkey,
   Walachia, Yugoslavia
Pardao   Portuguese India
Parisis d'Or   France
Pataca   Macau
Pataco   Portugal
Patagon   Belgium
Patrick   Ireland
Pavillon d'Or   France
Pe   Burma, Cambodia
Peca   Portugal
Pengo   Hungary
Penni(a)   Finland
Penning(ar)   Denmark, Sweden
Penny (plural Pence)   Australia, Bahamas,
   Barbados, Bermuda, Biafra, British Guiana,
   British East Africa British West Africa,
   Canada, Ceylon, Falkland Islands, Fiji,
   Gambia, Ghana, Gibraltar, Gold Coast,
   Great Britain, Guernsey, Ireland, Isle of Man,
   Jamaica, Jersey, Malawi, Montserrat, New
   Guinea, New Zealand, Nigeria, Rhodesia
   and Nyasaland, St Helena, St Kitts-Nevis,
   South Africa, Southern Rhodesia, Trinidad &
   Tobago, Tristan da Cunha, Zambia
Pentekontalitron   Sicily
Pentekontedrachm   Hellenistic kingdoms
Pentenummion   Byzantine Empire
Perper(a)   Montenegro
Pesa   German East Africa
Peseta   Andorra, Equatorial Guinea, Peru,
   Spain
Pesewa   Ghana
Peso   Argentina, Bolivia, Cambodia, Chile,
   Colombia, Costa Rica, Cuba, Dominican
   Republic, El Salvador, Guatemala, Guinea-
   Bissau, Honduras, Mexico, Netherlands
   Antilles, Nicaragua, Paraguay, Peru,
   Philippines, Puerto Rico, Uruguay, Venezuela
Pessa   Yemen (Lahej), Zanzibar

Around the world

Petermannchen Trier
Pfennig(e) Austria, Bohemia, Germany, German
  States, Poland, Swiss Cantons
Pfenning Austrian States, German States
Philippeioi Macedon
Phoenix Greece
Piastra Italian States
Piastre Annam, Cambodia, Cochin China,
  Cyprus, Denmark, Egypt, French Indochina,
  Hejaz, Iraq, Khmer, Lebanon, Libya, Nejd,
  Saudi Arabia, Syria, Sudan, Tonkin, Tunisia,
  Turkey, Vietnam, Yemen
Piataltynny Russia
Picciolo Sovereign Order of Malta
Piccolo Italian States
Pice Bhutan, Ceylon, East Africa, India, Kenya,
  Malaysia
Pinto Portugal
Piso Philippines
Pistole France, German States, Ireland,
  Scotland, Swiss Cantons
Pitis Brunei, Java, Sumatra, Siam
Plack Scotland
Plappart Switzerland
Poisha Bangladesh
Poltina Russia
Poltura Hungary, Roumania
Poludenga Russia
Polupoltinnik Russia
Polushka Russia
Pond Transvaal
Pound Ascension, Australia, Biafra, Cyprus,
  Egypt, Falkland Islands, Ghana, Gibraltar,
  Great Britain, Guernsey, Iran, Isle of Man,
  Israel, Jersey, Malta, Nigeria, Rhodesia, St
  Helena, South Arabia, South Africa, Sudan,
  Syria
Protea South Africa
Pruta(ot) Israel
Puffin Lundy
Pul Afghanistan, China, Turkestan
Pula Botswana
Puli Caucasia
Pultorak Poland
Pya(t) Burma
Pysa Zanzibar
Qindar(ka) Albania
Qiran Afghanistan
Qirsh Egypt
Quadrans Roman Republic
Quan Annam
Quart Gibraltar, Swiss Cantons
Quart d'Ecu France
Quartenses Silesia
Quartillo Spain
Quartinho Portugal
Quarto Ecuador, Mexico, Philippines, Spain

Quartuncia Rome
Quaternio Rome
Quattrino Italian States
Qepiq Azerbaijan
Quetzal Guatemala
Quinarius Rome
Quint USA
Quinto di Scudo Papal States
Rand South Africa
Rappen Switzerland
Rasi Netherlands Indies
Reaal Curacao
Real(es) Argentina, Bolivia, Central American
  Republic, Chile, Colombia, Costa Rica,
  Dominican Republic, Ecuador, El Salvador,
  Venezuela
Real Batu Indonesia
Reichsmark Germany
Reichspfennig Germany
Reichsthaler Germany
Reis Angola, Azores, Brazil, Madeira,
  Mozambique, Portugal, Portuguese India
Reisedaler Denmark
Rentenmark Germany
Rentenpfennig Germany
Reul Eire
Rial Iran, Morocco, Muscat and Oman, Oman,
  Persia, Yemen Arab Republic
Rider Scotland
Riel Kampuchea
Rigsbankdaler Denmark
Rigsbankskilling Denmark
Rigsdaler, Denmark, Norway
Rigsmontskilling Denmark
Rijder Friesland, Guelderland, United Provinces
Rijksdaalder Netherlands
Riksdaler Sweden
Riksdaler Riksmynt Sweden
Riksdaler Specie Sweden
Rin Japan
Ringgit Malaysia
Rio Japan
Rixdollar Ceylon
Riyal Iran, Iraq, Saudi Arabia, United Arab
  Emirates, Yemen Arab Republic
Rose Noble England
Rouble Russia, USSR
Royal d'Or France
Royalin(er) Tranquebar, Danish Indian
  Settlements
Rub Ethiopia
Rubel German occupation of Russia
Rubiya Egypt
Ruble Poland, Transnistria
Rublis Latvia
Rufiyaa Maldive Islands
Rumi Altin Ottoman Empire

Rupee Afghanistan, Andaman Islands, Bhutan, Burma, China, Cocos Keeling Islands, India, Iran, Kenya, Mauritius, Nepal, Pakistan, Saudi Arabia, Seychelles, Sri Lanka, Tanzania, Tibet, United Arab Emirates, Yemen

Rupia Portuguese India, Somalia

Rupiah Indonesia

Rupie German East Africa

Ruspone Italian States

Ryal England, Hejaz, Iran, Muscat and Oman, Nejd, Oman, Persia, Quaiti State, Saudi Arabia, Yemen, Zanzibar

Ryo Japan

Rytterpenning Denmark, Hanseatic League

Saidi Oman

Saiga Merovingian Empire

Salung Siam (Thailand)

Salut d'Or France

Sampietrino Papal States

Sanar Afghanistan

Sanese Siena

Santa Croce Italian States

Santim(at) Morocco

Santims (plural **Santimi** or **Santimu**) Latvia

Sapeque Annam, Cochin China, French Indochina

Sar Sinkiang

Sarrazzino Crusader kingdoms

Satang Siam (Thailand)

Sceat Anglo-Saxon England

Scellino Somalia

Schilling Austria, German States, Poland, Swiss Cantons

Schoter Breslau, Silesia

Schwaren German States

Scilling Eire

Scudo Bolivia, Italian States, Mexico, Malta, Papal States, Peru, San Marino

Sechsling German States

Semis Rome

Semuncia Rome

Sen Brunei, Cambodia, Indonesia, Irian Barat, Japan, Kampuchea, Malaysia, Riau Lingga, West New Guinea

Sene Samoa

Sengi Zaire

Seniti Tonga

Sent Estonia

Sente Lesotho

Senti Estonia, Somalia, Tanzania

Sentimo Philippines

Serebrnik Bulgaria

Sertum Bhutan

Sesena Spain

Sesino Italian States

Sestertius Rome

Sestino Italian States

Shahi Afghanistan, Iran, Turkestan

Sheqal(im) Israel

Shilingi Tanzania

Shilling Australia, Biafra, British West Africa, Canada, Cyprus, East Africa, Fiji, Gambia, Ghana, Great Britain, Grenada, Guernsey, Ireland, Isle of Man, Jamaica, Jersey, Kenya, Malawi, Malta, New Guinea, New Zealand, Nigeria, Scotland, Somalia, South Africa, Trinidad and Tobago, Uganda, Zambia

Sho Nepal, Tibet

Shokang Tibet

Shu Japan

Siglos Achaemenid Empire

Sik Siam (Thailand)

Silbergroschen German States, Luxembourg

Silbergulden South Germany

Sizain France

Skar Tibet

Skilling Danish West Indies, Denmark, Norway, Sweden

Skillingrigsmont Denmark

Skot Prussia, Silesia

Sol(es) Argentina, Belgium, Bolivia, France, Haiti, Luxembourg, Mauritius, Peru, Reunion, Switzerland, Windward Islands

Soldo (plural **Soldi**) Italian States, Swiss Cantons, Papal States, Yugoslavia

Solidus Argentina, Bolivia, Peru, Rome

Solot Siam

Som Kyrgyzstan

Somalo Somalia

Sosling Denmark

Sou Canada, French colonies, Guadeloupe, Mauritius, Reunion, Spain

Souverain d'Or Austrian Netherlands

Sovereign Australia, Canada, England, Falkland Islands, India, Isle of Man, Saudi Arabia, South Africa, United Kingdom

Sovrano Italian States

Speciedaler Denmark, Norway

Species Ducat Denmark

Srang Tibet

Stater Greece

Stella USA

Stiver British Guiana, Ceylon, Demerara and Essequibo, Dutch East Indies, Netherlands

Stotinka Bulgaria

Stuber German States

Stuiver   Curacao, Dutch East Indies,
   Netherlands, Netherlands Antilles
Styca   Northumbria
Styver   Sweden
Su   South Vietnam
Sucre   Ecuador, Galapagos
Sueldo   Bolivia, Spain
Sukus   Indonesia
Sultani   Algeria, Libya, Tunisia
Surre Altin   Ottoman Empire
Syli   Guinea
Tackoe   Gold Coast
Tael   China, Laos
Taka   Bangladesh
Tala   Samoa, Tokelau
Talar(a)   Poland
Talaro   Ethiopia
Taler   German States, Poland, Swiss Cantons
Talirion   Greece
Tallero   Ethiopia, Italian States, Ragusa
Tambac-tron   Annam
Tambala   Malawi
Tamlung   Siam
Tanga   Portuguese India
Tangka   Tibet
Tanka   Nepal
Tankah   Burma
Tarin   Naples, Sicily
Taro (plural Tari)   Italian States, Malta
Tek Altin   Ottoman Empire
Tenga   China, Bokhara, Turkestan
Ternar   Poland
Tester   England
Testern   British East Indies
Testone   Italian States
Testoon   England
Tetartemorion   Greece
Tetarteron   Byzantine Empire
Tetradrachm   Greece
Tetrobol   Greece
Thaler   Austria, Austrian States, Courland,
   Czechoslovakia, German States, Hungary,
   Liechtenstein, Poland, Roumania, Switzerland
Thebe   Botswana
Theler   Frankfurt
Thistle Crown   England
Thistle Merk   Scotland
Thistle Noble   Scotland
Thrymsa   Anglo-Saxon England
Tical   Cambodia, Thailand
Tien   Annam, Vietnam
Tilla   Afghanistan, Sinkiang, Turkestan
Timasha   Afghanistan
Tostao   Portugal

Toea   Papua New Guinea
Tola   India, Nepal
Tolar   Slovenia
Toman   Iran, Persia, Azerbaijan
Tornese   Italian States
Tournois   France
Trade Dollar   Great Britain, Japan, USA
Trah   Malaysia
Tremissis   Rome, Byzantine Empire, Franks,
   Lombards, Visigoths
Tressis   Rome
Triens   Rome
Trihemiobol   Greece
Triobol   Greece
Tritartemorion   Greece
Tughrik   Mongolia
Turner   Scotland
Tympf   Poland
Tyyn   Kyrgyzstan
Unghero   Italian States
Unicorn   Scotland
Unit   Scotland, French West Africa
Unite   England
Van   Vietnam
Vatu   Vanuatu
Veld Pond   South African Republic
Venezolano   Venezuela
Vereinstaler   Austria-Hungary, German States
Victoriate   Rome
Vierer   Swiss Cantons
Vintem   Portugal
Wan   Korea
Wark   Ethiopia
Warn   Korean
Wen   China
Whan   Korea
Won   South Korea
Xerafim   Portuguese India
Xu   Vietnam
Yang   Korea
Yarim   Turkey
Yen   Japan
Yirmilik   Ottoman Empire
Yuan   China
Yuzluk   Ottoman Empire
Zaire   Zaire
Zalat   Yemen Arab Republic
Zecchino   Italian States, Malta
Zelagh   Morocco
Zeri Mahbub   Egypt, Libya, Turkey
Zloty (plural Zlote or Zlotych)   Poland
Zolota   Turkey
Zolotnik   Russia
Zolotoj   Russia

Glossary of
coin terms

In this section we list all the terms commonly encountered in numismatics or in the production of coins.

Abbey Coins Medieval coins struck in the abbeys, convents and other great religious houses which were granted coinage rights. These coins were often used also by pilgrims journeying from one monastery to another.

Abschlag (German for "discount") A *restrike* from an original die.

Accolated Synonym for *conjoined* or *jugate* and signifying two or more profiles overlapping.

Acmonital Acronym from *Aciaio Monetario Italiano*, a stainless steel alloy used for Italian coins since 1939.

Adjustment Reduction of metal in a *flan* or *blank* to the specified weight prior to striking, accomplished by filing down the face. Such file marks often survived the coining process and are occasionally met with in coins, especially of the 18th century.

Ae Abbreviation for the Latin *Aes* (bronze), used for coins made of brass, bronze or other copper alloys.

Aes Grave (Latin for heavy bronze) Heavy circular coins first minted at Rome in 269 BC.

Aes Rude (Latin for rough bronze) Irregular lumps of bronze which gradually developed into ingots of uniform shape and were the precursors of coins in Rome.

Aes Signatum (Latin for signed bronze) Bronze ingots of regular size and weight, bearing marks of authority to guarantee their weight (289–269 BC).

Agonistic (Greek) Term for coins issued to commemorate, or pertaining to, sporting events.

Alliance Coinage struck by two or more states acting together and having common features of design or inscription.

Alloy Coinage metal composed of two or more metallic elements.

Altered Deliberately changed, usually unofficially, with the aim of increasing the numismatic value of a coin, medal or note. This applies particularly to dates, where a common date may be altered to a rare date by filing or re-engraving one of the digits.

Aluminium (American *Aluminum*) Silvery lightweight metal, developed commercially in the late 19th century for commemorative medals, but used for tokens and emergency money during the First World War and since 1940 widely used in subsidiary coinage.

Aluminium-bronze Alloy of aluminium and copper. Hard-wearing and gold-coloured, it is now widely used in tokens and subsidiary coinage.

Amulet Coin or medal believed to have talismanic qualities, such as warding off disease and bad luck. Many Chinese and Korean pieces come into this category. See also *Touchpiece*.

Androcephalous Heraldic term for creatures with a human head.

Anepigraphic Coins or medals without a legend.

Annealing Process of heating and cooling applied to metal to relieve stresses and prepare it for striking into coins.

Annulet Small circle often used as an ornament or spacing device in coin inscriptions.

Antimony Brittle white metal, chemical symbol *Sb*, virtually impractical as a coinage metal but used for the Chinese 10 cents of Kweichow, 1931. Alloyed with tin, copper or lead, it produces the white metal popular as a medallic medium.

Antoniniani Silver coins minted in Imperial Rome. The name derives from the Emperor Caracalla (Marcus Aurelius Antoninus) in whose reign they were first struck. The silver content was progressively reduced and by the last issue (AD 295) they were reduced to *billon*.

Ar Abbreviation for Latin *Argentum* (silver), used for coins struck in this metal.

Assay Mark Mark applied to a medal struck in precious metal by an assayer or assay office as a guarantee of the fineness of the metal.

Assignat Type of paper money used in France

1789–96, representing the land assigned to the holders.

Attribution   Identification of a coin by characteristics such as issuing authority, date or reign, mint, denomination, metal, and by a standard reference.

Au   Abbreviation for *aurum* (Latin for gold), denoting coins of this metal.

AU   Abbreviation for "About Uncirculated", often found in catalogues and dealers' lists to describe the condition of a numismatic piece.

Autodollar   Name given to the silver yuan issued by Kweichow, 1928, and having a contemporary motor car as the obverse motif.

Auxiliary Payment Certificate   Form of paper money intended for use by American military personnel stationed in overseas countries. See also *Baf* and *Scrip*.

Babel Note   Nickname given to the paper money of the Russian Socialist Federated Soviet Republic (1919) because it bore the slogan "workers of the world unite" in seven languages, a reference to the biblical tower of Babel.

Baf   Acronym from British Armed Forces, the popular name for the vouchers which could only be exchanged for goods in service canteens from 1945 onwards.

Bag Mark   Minor scratch or abrasion on an otherwise uncirculated coin, caused by coins in mint bags knocking together.

Banknote   Form of paper money issued by banks and usually promising to pay the bearer on demand in coin of the realm.

Barbarous   Imitation of Greek or Roman coins by the Celtic and Germanic tribes who lived beyond the frontiers of the civilised world.

Base   Non-precious metals or alloys.

Bath Metal   Inferior bronze alloy, named after the English city where it was used for casting cannon. Used by William Wood of Bristol for Irish and American tokens and by Amos Topping for Manx coins of 1733/4.

Beading   Ornamental border found on the raised rim of a coin.

Behalfszahlungsmittel   German term for auxiliary payment certificates used in occupied Europe from 1939 to 1945.

Bell Metal   Alloy of copper and tin normally used for casting bells, but employed for the subsidiary coinage of the French Revolutionary period.

Billon   Silver alloy containing less than 50 per cent fine silver, usually mixed with copper. In Spain this alloy was known as *vellon*.

Bi-metallic   Coins struck in two separate metals or alloys. Patterns for such coins exist from the 19th century but actual coins with a centre of one metal surrounded by a ring of another did not appear till 1982 (Italy, San Marino and Vatican). Canada introduced coins with a tiny plaque inset in a second metal (1990). See also *Clad, Plugged* and *Sandwich*.

Bi-metallism   Monetary system in which two metals are in simultaneous use and equally available as legal tender, implying a definite ratio between the two. A double standard of gold and silver, with a ratio of 16:1, existed till the mid-19th century.

Bingle   American term for a trade token, more specifically the US government issue of tokens for the Matacuska, Alaska colonization project, 1935.

Birthday Coins   Coins celebrating the birthday of a ruler originated in Roman Imperial times, notably the reigns of Maximianus (286–305) and Constantinus I (307–37). Birthday talers were issued by many German states, and among recent examples may be cited coins marking the 70th, 80th and 90th birthdays of Gustaf Adolf VI of Sweden, 80th and 90th birthday coins from the British Commonwealth for the Queen Mother, and coins honouring Queen Elizabeth, the Duke of Edinburgh and the Prince of Wales.

Bit   Term denoting fragments of large silver coins, cut up and circulating as fractional values. Spanish dollars were frequently broken up for circulation in the American colonies and the West indies. Long bits and short bits circulated at 15 and 10 cents respectively, but the term came to be equated with the Spanish real or eighth peso, hence the American colloquialism "two-bit" signifying a quarter dollar.

Black Money   English term for the debased silver deniers minted in France which circulated freely in England until they were banned by government decree in 1351.

Blank   Piece of metal, cut or punched out of a roller bar or strip, and prepared for striking to produce coins. Alternate terms are *flan* and *planchet*.

Blundered Inscription   Legend in which the lettering is jumbled or meaningless, indicating

"Breeches" money, so-called from the reverse design!

A "Cartwheel" penny, so called because of its cumbersome size.

the illiteracy of the tribes who copied Greek and Roman coins.

Bonnet Piece Scottish gold coin, minted in 1539–40. The name is derived from the obverse portraying King James V in a large, flat bonnet.

Bon Pour French for "good for", inscribed on Chamber of Commerce brass tokens issued in 1920–7 during a shortage of legal tender coinage.

Bouquet Sou Canadian copper token halfpenny of 1837 deriving its name from the nosegay of heraldic flowers on the obverse.

Box Coin Small container formed by *obverse* and *reverse* of two coins, hollowed out and screwed together.

Bracteate (Latin *bractea*, a thin piece of metal) Coins struck on blanks so thin that the image applied to one side appears in reverse on the other. First minted in Erfurt and Thuringia in the 12th century, and later produced elsewhere in Germany, Switzerland and Poland till the 14th century.

Brass Alloy of copper and zinc, widely used for subsidiary coinage. The term was also formerly used for bronze Roman coins, known numismatically as first, second or third brass.

Breeches Money Derisive term given by the Royalists to the coinage of the Commonwealth, 1651, the conjoined elongated oval shields on the reverse resembling a pair of breeches.

Brockage Mis-struck coin with only one design, normal on one side and *incuse* on the other. This occurs when a coin previously struck adheres to the die and strikes the next blank to pass through the press.

Broken Bank-note Note issued by a bank which has failed, but often applied more generally to banknotes which have been demonetised.

Bronze Alloy of copper and tin, first used as a coinage metal by the Chinese c. 1000 BC. Often used synonymously with copper, though it

should be noted that bronze only superseded copper as the constituent of the base metal British coins in 1860.

Bull Neck Popular term for the coins of King George III, 1816–17.

Bullet Money Pieces of silver, *globular* in shape, bearing various *countermarks* and used as coins in Siam (Thailand) in the 18th and 19th centuries.

Bullion Precious metal in bars, ingots, strip or scrap (i.e. broken jewellery mounts, watch-cases and plate), its weight reckoned solely by weight and fineness, before being converted into coin.

Bullion Coin A coin struck in platinum, gold or silver, whose value is determined solely by the prevailing market price for the metal as a commodity. Such coins do not generally have a nominal face value, but include in their inscriptions their weight and fineness. Good examples of recent times include the Krugerrand (South Africa), the Britannia (UK), the Maple Leaf (Canada), Libertad (Mexico), the Nugget (Australia) and the Eagle (USA).

Bun Coinage British coins of 1860–94 showing Queen Victoria with her hair in a bun.

Bungtown Coppers Derisive term (from Anglo-American slang *bung*, to swindle or bribe) for halfpence of English or Irish origin, often counterfeit, which circulated in North America towards the end of the colonial period.

Carat (American *Karat*) Originally a unit of weight for precious stones, based on carob seeds (ceratia), it also denotes the fineness or purity of gold, being 1/24th part of the whole. Thus 9 carat gold is .375 fine and 22 carat, the English sovereign standard, is .916 fine. Abbreviated as ct or kt.

Cartwheel Popular term for the large and cumbersome penny and twopenny pieces of 1797 weighing one and two ounces, struck by Matthew Boulton at the Soho Mint, Birmingham.

Cased Set Set of coins in mint condition, housed in the official case issued by the mint. Formerly leather cases with blue plush or velvet lining were used, but nowadays many sets are encapsulated in plastic to facilitate handling.

Cash (from Portuguese *caixa*, Hindi *kasu*). Round piece of bronze or brass with a square hole in the centre, used as subsidiary coinage in China for almost 2000 years, till the early 12th century. In Chinese these pieces were known as *Ch'ien* or *Li* and strung together in groups of 1000 were equivalent to a silver tael.

Cast Coins Coins cast from molten metals in moulds. This technique, widespread in the case of early commemorative medals, has been used infrequently in coins, the vast majority of which are struck from *dies*. Examples of cast coins include the Chinese cash and the Manx coins of 1709.

Check A form of *token* given as a means of identification, or issued for small amounts of money or for services of a specific nature.

Cheque (American *Check*) A written order directing a bank to pay money.

Chop (Hindi, to seal). Countermark, usually consisting of a single character, applied by Chinese merchants to precious metal coins and ingots as a guarantee of their weight and fineness. Coins may be found with a wide variety of chop marks and the presence of several different marks on the same coin considerably enhances its interest and value. See also *Shroff mark*.

Christmas Coins issued as Christmas gifts date from the Middle Ages when the Venetian Doges struck *Osselle* as presents for their courtiers. In modern times, however, the custom has developed only since the late 1970s, several countries having issued attractive coins at Christmas since then.

Cistophori (Greek for chest bearing) a generic term for the coins of Pergamum with an obverse motif of a chest showing a serpent crawling out of the half-opened lid. Cistophori became very popular all over Asia Minor in the 3rd and 2nd centuries BC and were struck also at mints in Ionia, Phrygia, Lydia and Mysia.

Clad Coins Coins with a core of one alloy, covered with a layer or coating of another. US half dollars from 1965 to 1970, for example, had a core of 21 per cent silver and 79 per cent copper, bonded to outer layers of 80 per cent silver and 20 per cent copper. More recently, however, coins usually have a body in a cheap alloy, with only a thin cladding of a more expensive material, such as the British 1p and 2p coins of stainless steel with a copper cladding, introduced late in 1992.

Clash Marks Mirror image traces found on a coin which has been struck from a pair of dies, themselves damaged by having been struck together without a blank between.

Clipped Coins Precious metal coins from which small amounts have been removed by clipping the edges. It was to prevent this that *graining* and *edge inscriptions* were adopted.

Cob Crude, irregularly shaped silver piece, often with little more than a vestige of die impressions, produced in the Spanish American mints in the 16th–18th centuries.

Coin Piece of metal, marked with a device, issued by government authority and intended for use as money.

Collar Retaining ring within which the *dies* for the *obverse* and *reverse* operate. When the *blank* is struck under high pressure between the dies the metal flows sideways and is formed by the collar, taking up the impression of *reeding* or *edge inscription* from it.

Commemorative Coin, medal, token or paper note issued to celebrate a current event or the anniversary of a historic event or personality.

Communion Token Token, cast in lead, but later struck in pewter, brass, bronze or white metal, issued to members of a congregation to permit them to partake of the annual communion service in the Calvinist and Presbyterian churches. John Calvin himself is said to have invented the communion token in 1561 but they were actually referred to in the minutes of the Scottish General Assembly in 1560. Later they were adopted by the Reformed churches in many parts of Europe. They survived in Scotland till the early years of this century. Each parish had its own tokens, often bearing the names or initials of individual ministers, with dates, symbols and biblical texts.

Conjoined Term denoting overlapped profiles of two or more rulers (e.g. William and Mary).

Contorniate (from Italian *contorno*, edge). Late 4th and 5th century Roman bronze piece whose name alludes to the characteristic grooving on the edges.

Contribution Coins Coins struck by Bamberg, Eichstatt, Fulda and other German cities in the 1790s during the First Coalition War against the French Republic. The name alludes to the fact that the bullion used to produce the coins necessary to pay troops was raised by contribution from the Church and the public.

Convention Money Any system of coinage agreed by neighbouring countries for mutual acceptance and interchange. Examples include the Amphictyonic coins of ancient Greece, and the Austrian and Bavarian talers and gulden of 1753–1857 which were copied by other south German states and paved the way for the German Monetary union.

Copper Metallic element, chemical symbol *Cu*, widely used as a coinage medium for 2,500 years. Pure or almost pure copper was used

A typical communion token from Canada.

for subsidiary coinage in many countries till the mid-19th century, but has since been superseded by copper alloys which are cheaper and more durable: *bronze* (copper and tin), *brass* (copper and zinc), *Bath metal* or *bell metal* (low-grade copper and tin), *aluminium-bronze* (copper and aluminium), *potin* (copper, tin, lead and silver) or *cupro-nickel* (copper and nickel). Copper is also alloyed with gold to give it its reddish hue, and is normally alloyed with silver in coinage metals. When the copper exceeds the silver content the alloy is known as *billon*.

Copperhead Popular term for a copper *token* about the size and weight of an American cent which circulated in the USA during the Civil War (1861–65) during a shortage of subsidiary coinage. Many different types were produced, often of a political or patriotic nature.

Coppernose Popular name for the debased silver shillings of Henry VIII. Many of them were struck in copper with little more than a silver wash which tended to wear off at the highest point of the obverse, the nose on the full-face portrait of the king.

Counter A piece resembling a coin but intended for use on a medieval accountancy board or in gambling. See also *jeton*.

Counterfeit Imitation of a coin, token or banknote intended for circulation to deceive the public and defraud the state.

Countermark Punch mark applied to a coin some time after its original issue, either to alter its nominal value, or to authorise its circulation in some other country.

Cowrie Small shell (*Cypraea moneta*) circulating as a form of primitive currency from 1000 BC (China) to the present century (East and West Africa) and also used in the islands of the Indian and Pacific Oceans.

Crockard Debased silver imitation of English pennies produced in the Netherlands and imported into England in the late 13th century. Edward I tried to prevent their import then, in 1299, allowed them to pass current as halfpennies. As they contained more than a halfpennyworth of silver this encouraged their trading in to be melted down and they disappeared from circulation within a year. Sometimes known as *pollards*. See also *Lushbourne*.

Crown Gold Gold of 22 carat (.916) fineness, so called on account of its adoption in 1526 for the English gold crown. It has remained the British standard gold fineness ever since.

Cumberland Jack Popular name for a counter or medalet of sovereign size, struck unofficially in 1837 in brass. The figure of St George was replaced by the Duke of Cumberland on horseback with the inscription "To Hanover" a reference to the unpopular Duke of Cumberland, uncle of Queen Victoria, who succeeded to the Hanoverian throne since Victoria, as a female, was debarred by Salic law from inheritance.

Cupellation (Latin *cupella*, a little cup). Process by which gold and silver were separated from lead and other impurities in their ores. A cupel is a shallow cup of bone-ash or other absorbent material which, when hot, absorbs any molten material that wets its surface. Lead melts and oxidises with impurities into the cupel, whereas gold and silver remain on the cupel. Cupellation is also used in assaying the fineness of these precious metals.

Cupro-nickel Coinage alloy of 75 per cent copper and 25 per cent nickel, now widely used as a base metal substitute for silver. A small amount of zinc is added to the alloy in modern Russian coins.

Currency Coins, tokens, paper notes and other articles intended to pass current in general circulation as money.

Current Coins and paper money still in circulation.

Cut Money Coins cut into smaller pieces to provide correspondingly smaller denominations. The cross on many medieval coins assisted the division of silver pennies into halfpence and farthings. Spanish dollars were frequently divided into *bits* which themselves became units of currency in America and the West Indies.

Darlehnskassen (German for "state loan notes"). Paper money issued during the First World War in an abortive bid to fill the shortage of coinage in circulation. These low-denomination notes failed to meet demand and were superseded by local issues of small *Notgeld* in 1916.

Debasement The reduction in the precious metal content of the coinage, widely practised since time immemorial by governments for economic reasons. British coins, for example, were debased from sterling (.925 fine) silver to .500 in 1920 and from silver to cupro-nickel in 1947.

Decimalisation A currency system in which the principal unit is subdivided into ten, a hundred, or a thousand fractions. Russia was the first country to decimalise, in 1534 when the rouble of 100 kopeks was introduced, but it was not till 1792 that France adopted the franc of 100 centimes and 1793 when the USA introduced the dollar of 100 cents. Most European countries decimalised their currency in the 19th century. Britain toyed with the idea, introducing the florin or tenth of a pound in 1849 as the first step, but did not complete the process till 1971. The last countries to decimalise were Malta and Nigeria, in 1972 and 1973 respectively.

Demidiated Heraldic term to describe the junction of two armorial devices, in which only half of each is shown.

Demonetisation The withdrawal of coins or paper money from circulation and declaring them to be worthless.

Device Heraldic term for the pattern or emblem on coins or paper notes.

Die Hardened piece of metal bearing a mirror image of the device to be struck on one side of a coin or medal.

Die Proof An impression, usually pulled on soft carton or India paper, of an *intaglio* engraving of a banknote, usually taken during the progress of the engraving to check the detail. Banknote proofs of this nature usually consist of the portrait or some detail of the design, such as the border, rather than the complete motif.

Dodecagonal Twelve-sided, a term applied to the nickel-brass threepence of Great Britain, 1937–67.

Dump Any primitive coin struck on a very thick *flan*, but more specifically applied to the circular pieces cut from the centre of Spanish dollars, countermarked with the name of the colony, a crown and the value, and circulated in New South Wales at 15 pence in 1813. See *Holey Dollar*.

Duodecimal Currency system based on units of twelve, i.e. medieval money of account (12 denarii = 1 soldo) which survived in Britain as 12 pence to the shilling as late as 1971.

Ecclesiastical Coins Coins struck by a religious authority, such as an archbishop, bishop, abbot, prior or the canons of a religious order. Such coins were common in medieval times but survived as late as the early 19th century, the bishops of Breslau (1817) and Gurk (1823) being the last prelates to exercise coinage rights. Coins were struck by authority of the Pope at Rome till 1870 but since 1929 coinage has been struck at the Italian state mint on behalf of the Vatican.

Edge Inscription Lettering on the edge of a coin or medal to prevent clipping. Alluding to this, the Latin motto *Decus et Tutamen* (an ornament and a safeguard) was applied to the edge of English milled coins in the reign of Charles II.

Edge Ornament An elaboration of the *graining* found on many milled coins to prevent clipping, taking the form of tiny leaves, florets, interlocking rings, pellets and zigzag patterns. In some cases the ornament appears between layers of more conventional reeding.

EF Abbreviation for Extremely Fine.

Effigy An image or representation of a person, normally the head of state, a historical personage, or an allegorical figure, usually on the *obverse* or "heads" side of a coin or medal.

Electrotype A reproduction of a coin or medal made by an electrolytic process.

Electrum Alloy of gold and silver, sometimes called white gold, used for minting the staters of Lydia, 7th century BC, and other early European coins.

Elongated Coin An oval *medalet* created by passing a coin, such as an American cent, between rollers under pressure with the effect of squeezing it out and impressing on it a souvenir or commemorative motif.

Emergency Money Any form of money used in times of economic and political upheaval, when traditional kinds of currency are not available. Examples include the comparatively crude silver coins issued by the Royalists during the *Civil War* (1642–49), *obsidional* money, issued in time of siege, from Tyre (1122) to Mafeking (1900), the *Notgeld* issued by many German towns (1916–23), *encased money, fractional currency, guerrilla notes, invasion, liberation* and *occupation money* from the two World Wars and minor campaigns. Among the more recent examples may be cited the use of sweets and cheques in Italy (1976–77) and the issue of coupons and vouchers in many of the countries of the former Soviet Union pending the introduction of their own distinctive coins and notes.

Enamelled Coins Coins decorated by enamelling the obverse and reverse motifs in contrasting colours was an art practised by many jewellers in Birmingham and Paris in the 19th century, and revived in Europe and America in the 1970s.

Encased Money Postage and revenue stamps enclosed in small metal and mica-faced discs, circulated as small change in times of emergency. The practice was invented by John Gault, a Boston sewing-machine salesman, during the American Civil War (1862). The face of the stamp was visible through the transparent window, while the back of the disc was embossed with firms' advertisements. This practice was revived during and after the First World War when there was again a shortage of small coins. Encased stamps have also been recorded from France, Austria, Norway, Germany and Monaco. See also under *Stamp Money*.

Engrailing Technical term for the close serrations or vertical bars round the edge of a coin, applied as a security device.

Engraving The art of cutting lines or grooves in plates, blocks or dies. Numismatically this takes the form of engraving images into the face of the dies used in striking coins, a process which has now been almost completely superseded by *hubbing* and the use of *reducing machinery*. In the production of paper money, *intaglio* engraving is still commonly practised. In this process the engraver cuts the design into a steel die and the printing ink lies in the grooves. The paper is forced under great pressure into the grooves and picks up the ink, and this gives banknotes their characteristic ridged feeling to the touch. Nowadays many banknotes combine traditional intaglio engraving with multicolour lithography or photogravure to defeat the would-be counterfeiter.

Epigraphy The study of inscriptions, involving the classification and interpretation of coin legends, an invaluable adjunct to the study of a coin series, particularly the classical and medieval coins which, in the absence of dates and mintmarks, would otherwise be difficult to arrange in chronological sequence.

Erasion The removal of the title or effigy of a ruler from the coinage issued after his or her death. This process was practised in imperial Rome, and applied to the coins of Caligula, Nero and Geta, as part of the more general practice of *damnatio memoriae* (damnation of the memory) ordered by the Senate.

Error Mistakes on coins and paper money may be either caused at the design or engraving stage, or as a result of a fault in the production processes. In the first category come mis-spellings in legends causing, in extreme cases, *blundered inscriptions*, or anachronisms or inaccuracies in details of the design. In the second, the most glaring error is the mule caused by marrying the wrong dies. Faulty alignment of dies can cause obverse and reverse to be out of true. Although many coins are issued with obverse and reverse upside down in relation to each other, this can also occur as an error in coins where both sides should normally be facing the same way up. Other errors caused at the production stage include striking coins in the wrong metal or with the wrong *collar* thus creating a different edge from the normal.

Essay (From the French *essai*, a trial piece). The term is applied to any piece struck for the purposes of examination, by parliamentary or financial bodies, prior to the authorisation of an issue of coins or paper money. The official nature of these items distinguishes them from *patterns*, which denote trial pieces often produced by mints or even private individuals bidding for coinage contracts.

Evasion Close copy or imitation of a coin, with sufficient deliberate differences in the design or inscription to avoid infringing counterfeit legislation. A good example is the imitation of Sumatran coins by European merchants, inscribed SULTANA instead of SUMATRA.

Exergue Lower segment of a coin or medal, usually divided from the rest of the *field* by a horizontal line, and often containing the date, value, ornament or identification symbols.

Exonumia Generic term for numismatic items not authorised by a government, e.g. *patterns, tokens, medalets* or *model coins.*

F Fine

Face The surface of a coin, medal or token, referred to as the *obverse* or the *reverse*. The corresponding faces of a paper note are more correctly termed *verso* and *recto*, but the coin terms are often used instead.

An example of a "Facing" portrait on the obverse of a medallion of Henry Simms, 1901. Actual size 360mm.

Facing Term for the portrait, usually on the obverse, which faces to the front instead of to the side (profile).

Fantasy Piece of metal purporting to be the coinage of a country which does not exist. Recent examples include the money of Atlantis and the Hutt River Province which declared its independence of Western Australia.

FDC Abbreviation for *Fleur de Coin*, a term denoting the finest possible condition of a coin.

Fiat Money Paper notes issued by a government but not redeemable in coin or bullion.

Field Flat part of the surface of a coin or medal, between the *legend*, the *effigy* and other raised parts of the design.

Fillet Heraldic term for the ribbon or headband on the effigy of a ruler or allegorical figure.

Find Term applied to an archaeological discovery of one or more coins. A large quantity of such material is described as a *hoard*.

Flan Alternative name for *blank* or *planchet*, the piece of metal struck between dies to produce a coin or medal.

Forgery An unauthorised copy or imitation, made with the intention of deceiving collectors. Forgeries intended to pass current for real coins or notes are more properly called *counterfeits*.

Fractional Currency Emergency issue of small-denomonation notes by the USA in 1863–5, following a shortage of coins caused by the Civil War. This issue superseded the *Postage Currency* notes, but bore the inscription "Receivable for all US stamps", alluding to the most popular medium of small change at that time. Denominations ranged from 3c to 50c.

Franklinium Cupro-nickel alloy developed by the Franklin Mint of Philadelphia and used for coins, medals and gaming tokens since 1967.

Freak An *error* or *variety* of a non-recurring type, usually caused accidentally during production.

Frosting Matt surface used for the high relief areas of many proof coins and medals, for greater contrast with the mirrored surface of the field.

Funeral Money Imitations of banknotes, used in China and Latin America in funeral ceremonies.

Geat (Git) Channel through which molten metal is ducted to the mould. Cast coins and medals often show tiny protrusions known as geat marks.

Ghost Faint image of the design on one side of a coin visible on the other. Good examples were the British penny and halfpenny of George V, 1911–27, the ghosting being eliminated by the introduction of a smaller effigy in 1928.

Globular Coins struck on very thick *dumps* with convex faces. The term is applied to some Byzantine coins, and also the *bullet money* of Siam (Thailand).

Godless (or *Graceless*) Epithet applied to any coin which omits the traditional reference to the deity, e.g. the British florin of 1849 which omitted D.G. (*Dei Gratia*, "by the Grace of God").

Gold Precious metal, chemical symbol and numismatic abbreviation *Au*, from the *Latin Aurum*, used as a coinage medium from the 7th century BC till the present day. The purity of gold is reckoned in *carats* or a decimal system. Thus British gold sovereigns are 22 carat or .916 fine. Medieval coins were 23.5 carat or .995 fine, and some modern bullion coins are virtually pure gold, denoted by the inscription .999. Canadian maple leaves are now struck in "four nines" gold and bear the inscription .9999.

Goodfor Popular name for token coins and *emergency money* made of paper or card, from the inscription "Good for" or its equivalent in other languages (e.g. French *Bon pour* or Dutch *Goed voor*) followed by a monetary value. They have been recorded from Europe, Africa and America

during times of economic crises or shortage of more traditional coinage.

Gothic Crown Popular name for the silver crown issued by the United Kingdom (1847–53), so-called on account of its script (more properly Old English, rather than Gothic).

Grain The weight of a single grain of wheat was taken as the smallest unit of weight in England. The troy grain was 1/5760 of a pound, while the avoirdupois grain was 1/7000 pound, the former being used in the weighing of precious metals and thus employed by numismatists in weighing coins. A grain is 1/480 troy ounce or 0.066 gram in the metric system.

Graining Term sometimes used as a synonym for the *reeding* on the edge of milled coins.

Gripped Edge Pattern of indentations found on the majority of American cents of 1797, caused by the milling process. Coins of the same date with a plain edge are rather scarcer.

Guerrilla Money Money issued in areas under the control of guerrillas and partisans during wartime range from the *veld ponds* of the Boers (1900–2) to the notes issued by the Garibaldi Brigade in Italy and the anti-fascist notes of Tito's forces in Yugoslavia. The most prolific issues were those produced in Luzon, Mindanao and Negros Occidental by the Filipino resistance during the Japanese occupation (1942–5).

Guilloche French term signifying the intricate pattern of curved lines produced by the rose engine and used as a security feature in the production of banknote, cheques, stocks and share certificates.

Gun Money Emergency coinage of Ireland (1689–91) minted from gunmetal, a type of bronze used in the casting of cannon. All denominations of James II, from the sixpence to the crown, normally struck in silver, were produced in this base metal.

Gutschein German word for voucher or coupon, denoting the paper money used aboard ships of the Imperial Navy during the First World War. The last issue was made at Scapa Flow, 1918–19, during the internment of the High Seas Fleet.

Hammered Term denoting coins produce by the traditional method of striking a *flan* laid on an anvil with a hammer. A characteristic of hammered coins is their uneven shape which tended to encourage *clipping*. This abuse was gradually eliminated by the introduction of the screw press in the 15th century and the mechanisation of coining processes in the course of the 16th and 17th centuries.

Hard Times Token Copper piece the size of the large cent, issued in the USA, 1834–44, during a shortage of coins caused by the collapse of

"Hard Times" tokens issued by the New York and Harlem Railroad Company.

the Bank of the United States, the panic of 1837 and the economic crisis of 1839, the landmarks in the period known as the Hard Times. Banks suspended *specie* payments and the shortage of coinage was filled by tradesmen's tokens. Many of these were more in the nature of satirical *medalets* than circulating pieces.

Hat Piece Alternative name for the *bonnet piece* of James VI of Scotland, 1591.

Hell Notes Imitation paper money used in Chinese funeral ceremonies and buried with the dead to pay for services in the next world.

Hoard Accumulation of coins concealed in times of economic or political upheaval and discovered, often centuries later. Under English common law, such hoards are subject to th law of *treasure trove* if they contain precious metal.

Hog Money Popular name for the early coinage of Bermuda, issued about 1616. The coins were minted in brass with a silver wash and circulated at various values from twopence to a shilling. They derived their name from the hog depicted on the obverse, an allusion to the pigs introduced to the island in 1515 by Juan Bermudez.

Holed Term denoting two different categories: (a) coins which have been pierced for suspension as a form of jewellery or talisman, and (b) coins which have a hole as part of their design. In the latter category come the Chinese *cash* with a square hole, and numerous issues of the 19th and 20th centuries from many countries, with the object of reducing weight and metal without sacrificing overall diameter.

Holey Dollar Spanish silver peso of 8 reales with the centre removed. The resultant ring was counter-marked "New South Wales" and dated 1813, with "Five Shillings" on the reverse, and placed into circulation during a shortage of British coin. The centre, known as a *dump*, was circulated at 15 pence.

Hub Heavy circular piece of steel on which the *die* for a coin or medal is engraved. The process of cutting the die and transferring the master die, by means of intermediary *punches*, to the die from which the coins will be struck, is known as hubbing. Soft steel is used in the preliminary process, and after the design has been transferred, the hub is hardened by chemical action.

Hybrid Alternative name for a *mule*.

Imitation Money Also known as play money or toy money, it consists of coins and notes produced for games of chance (like Monopoly), children's toy shops and post offices, as tourist souvenirs, or for political satire (e.g. the shrinking pound or dollar). See also *funeral money*, *hell notes*, *model coins* and *skit notes*.

Imprint Inscription on a paper note giving the name of the printer.

Incuse Impression which cuts into the surface of a coin or medal, as opposed to the more usual raised relief. Many of the earliest coins, especially those with a device on one side only, bear an incuse impression often in a geometric pattern. An incuse impression appears on one side of the coins, reflecting the image on the other side. Few modern coins have had an incuse design, notable examples being the American half and quarter eagle gold coins of 1908–29 designed by Bela Pratt. Incuse inscriptions on a raised rim, however, are more common, and include the British *Cartwheel* coins of 1797 and the 20p coins since 1982.

Inflation Money Coins produced as a result of inflation date back to Roman times when bronze minimi, little bigger than a pinhead, circulated as denarii. Nearer the present day inflation has had devastating effects on the coinge and banknotes of Germany (1921–3), Austria (1923), Poland (1923), Hungary (1945–6), Greece (1946) and many Latin American countries since the 1980s. Hungary holds the record for the highest value of any note ever issued — one thousand million adopengos, which is written as 20,000,0 00,000,000,000,000,000,000,000 pengos.

Ingot Piece of precious metal, usually cast in a mould, and stamped with the weight and fineness. though mainly used as a convenient method of storing bullion, ingots have been used as currency in many countries, notably Russia and Japan.

Inlay Insertion into the surface of a coin or medal of another substance for decorative effect. e.g. Poland Amber Trade Routes 20zl (amber), Isle of Man Queen Mother centenery (pearl) and various coins incorporating rubies or diamonds.

Intaglio Form of *engraving* in which lines are cut into a steel die for the recess-printing of banknotes.

Intrinsic The net metallic value of a coin, as distinguished from the nominal or face value.

Iron Metal, chemical symbol *Fe* (from Latin

Ferrum), used as a primitive form of currency from classical times onwards. Iron spits (obeliskoi) preceded the obol as the lowest unit of Greek coinage, a handful of six spits being worth a drachma (from *drassomai*, "I grasp"). Cast iron coins were issued in China as a substitute for copper *cash*. Many of the emergency token issues of Germany during the First World War were struck in iron. Iron coins were issued by Bulgaria in 1943. See also *Steel*.

Ithyphallic (Greek for "erect penis"). Term descriptive of coins of classical Greece showing a satyr.

Janiform Double profiles back to back, after the Roman god Janus.

Jeton (From French *jeter*, to throw). Alternative term for *counter*, and used originally on the chequerboard employed by medieval accountants. Nuremberg was the most important centre for the production of medieval jetons, often issued in lengthy portrait series. In modern parlance the term is often synonymous with *token*, though more specifically confined to pieces used in vending equipment, parking meters, laundromats, telephones and urban transport systems in many European countries. Apart from security, removing the temptation of vandals to break into the receptacles, the main advantage of such pieces is that they can be retariffed as charges increase, without any alteration in their design or composition, a method that is far cheaper than altering costly equipment to take larger coins.

Jubilee Head The effigy of Queen Victoria by Joseph Boehm adopted for British coinage after the 1887 Golden Jubilee.

Jugate (From Latin *jugum*, a yoke). Alternative to *accolated* or *conjoined* to denote overlapping profiles of rulers.

Key Date Term describing the rarest in a long-running series of coins with the dates changed at annual intervals.

Kipperzeit German term meaning the time of clipped money, denoting the period during and after the Thirty Years War (1618–48) in which debased and clipped money was in circulation.

Klippe Rectangular or square pieces of metal bearing the impression of a coin. Coins of this type were first struck in Sweden in the 16th century and were subsequently produced in many of the German states. The idea has been revived in recent years as a medium for striking commemorative pieces.

Knife Money Cast bronze pieces, with an elongated blade and a ring at one end to facilitate stringing together in bunches, were used as currency in China from the 9th century BC until the 19th century.

Kreditivsedlar (Swedish for "credit notes"). The name given to the first issue of paper money made in the western world. Paper money of this type was the brainchild of Johan Palmstruch at Riga in 1652, but nine years elapsed before it was implemented by the Stockholm Bank. The notes were redeemable in copper *platmynt*.

Laureate Heraldic term for a laurel wreath, often framing a state emblem or shown, in the Roman fashion, as a crown on the ruler's forehead.

Leather Money Pieces of leather embossed with an official device have been used as money on various occasions, including the sieges of Faenza and Leiden and in the Isle of Man in the 15th and 16th centuries. Several towns in Austria and Germany produced leather tokens during and after the First World War.

Legal Tender Coins or paper money which are declared by law to be current money and which tradesmen and shopkeers are obliged to accept in payment for goods or services. (See *Money and the Law*).

Legend The inscription on a coin or medal.

Liberation Money Paper money prepared for use in parts of Europe and Asia, formerly under Axis occupation. Liberation notes were used in France, Belgium and the Netherlands in 1944–5, while various Japanese and Chinese notes were overprinted for use in Hong Kong when it was liberated in 1945. Indian notes overprinted for use in Burma were issued in 1945–6 when that country was freed from Japanese occupation.

Ligature (From Latin *ligatus*, bound together). Term denoting the linking of two letters in a *legend*, e.g. Æ and Œ.

Long Cross Coinage Type of coinage introduced by King Henry III in 1247, deriving its name from the reverse which bore a cross whose arms extended right to the edge to help safeguard the coins against *clipping*. This remained the style of the silver penny, its fractions and multiples, till the reign of Henry VII, and vestiges of the long cross theme can be seen in the silver coins throughout the remaining years of the Tudor period.

Love Token A coin which has been altered by smoothing one or both surfaces and engraving initials, dates, scenes, symbols of affection and messages thereon.

Lushbourne English word for base pennies of inferior silver, said to have emanated from Luxembourg, from which the name derived. These coins were first minted under John the Blind who adopted the curious spelling of his name EIWANES in the hope that illiterate English merchants might confuse it with EDWARDVS and thus be accepted as coin issued in the name of Edward III. Lushbournes were also minted by Robert of Bethune, William I of Namur and the bishops of Toul during the mid-14th century.

Lustre The sheen or bloom on the surface of an uncirculated coin resulting from the centrifugal flow of metal caused by striking.

Magnimat Trade name used by VDM (*Verein Deutscher Metallwerke*) for a high-security alloy containing copper, nickel and magnetised steel. First used for the 5 deutschemark coin of 1975, it has since been adopted for other high-value coins in Germany and other countries.

Manilla Copper, bronze or brass rings, sometimes shaped like horseshoes and sometimes open, with flattened terminals, used as currency in West Africa until recent years.

Matrix Secondary die for a coin or medal, produced from the master die by means of an intermediate punch. In this way dies can be duplicated from the original cut on the reducing machine.

Matt or Matte Finely granulated surface or overall satin finish to proof coins, a style which was briefly fashionable at the turn of the century. The Edward VII proof set of 1902 is a notable example. In more recent years many issues produced by the Franklin Mint have been issued with this finish.

Maundy Money Set of small silver coins, in denominations of 1, 2, 3 and 4 pence, distributed by the reigning British monarch to the poor and needy on Maundy Thursday. The custom dates back to the Middle Ages, but in its present form, of distributing pence to as many men and women as the years in the monarch's age, it dates from 1666. At first ordinary silver pennies and multiples were used but after they went out of everyday use distinctive silver coins were produced specifically for the purpose from the reign of George II (1727–60) onwards. For centuries the ceremony took place in Westminster Abbey but since 1955 other venues have been used in alternate years.

Medal (French *medaille*, Italian *medaglia*, from Latin *metallum*). A piece of metal bearing devices and legends commemorating an event or person, or given as an award. Military medals date from the 16th and 17th centuries, but were not generally awarded to all ranks till the 19th century. Commemora-tive medals can be traced back to Roman times, but in their present form they date from the Italian Renaissance when there was a fashion for large cast portrait medals.

Medalet A small medal, generally 25mm or less in diameter.

Medallion Synonym for medal, but usually confined to those with a diameter of 50mm or more.

Milling Process denoting the mechanical production of coins, as opposed to the handmade technique implied in *hammering*. It alludes to the use of watermills to drive the machinery of the screw presses and blank rollers developed in the 16th century. As the even thickness and diameter of milled coins permitted a security edge, the term milling is popularly, though erroneously, used as a synonym for *graining* or *reeding*.

Mint The place in which coins and medals are produced. Mint condition is a term sometimes used to denote pieces in an uncirculated state.

Mint Set A set of coins or medals in the package or case issued by the mint. See also *year set*.

Mintmark A device appearing on a coin to denote the place of minting. Athenian coins of classical times have been recorded with up to 40 different marks, denoting individual workshops. In the 4th century AD the Romans adopted this system to identify coins struck in provincial mints. This system was widely used in the Middle Ages and survives in France and Germany to this day. Initials and symbols are also used to identify mints, especially where the production of a coin is shared between several different mints. From 1351 onwards symbols were adopted in England to denote periods between trials of the *Pyx*, and thus assist the proper chronological sequence of coins, in an era prior to the adoption of dating. These mintmarks continued into the 17th century, but gradually died out as the use of dates became more widespread. See also *countermark* and *privy mark*.

Mionnet Scale Scale of nineteen diameters covering all sizes of coins belonging to the classical period, devised by the French numismatist, Theodore-Edme Mionnet (1770–1842) during the compilation of his fifteen-volume catalogue of the numismatic collection in the Bibliotheque Nationale in Paris.

Mirror Finish The highly polished surface of proof coins.

Misstrike A coin or medal on which the impression has been struck off-centre.

Model Coin Tiny pieces of metal, either reproducing the designs of existing coins (used as play money by children) or, more specifically, denoting patterns produced by Joseph Moore and Hyam Hyams in their attempts to promote an improved subsidiary coinage in 19th century Britain. These small coins were struck in bronze with a brass or silver centre and were designed to reduce the size of the existing cumbersome range of pence, halfpence and farthings.

Modified Effigy   Any coin in which the profile on the obverse has been subtly altered. Examples include minor changes in the Victorian Young Head and Old Head effigies and the George V profile by Sir Bertram Mackennal.

Money Order   Certificate for a specified amount of money, which may be transmitted by post and encashed at a money order office or post office. This system was pioneered by Britain and the United States in the early 19th century and is now virtually worldwide. The term is now confined to certificates above a certain value, the terms *postal order* and *postal note* being used for similar certificates covering small amounts.

Mule   Coin whose obverse is not matched with its official or regular reverse. Mules include the erroneous combination of dies from different reigns, but in recent years such hybrids have arisen in mints where coins for several countries are struck. Examples include the Coronation Anniversary crowns combining Ascension and Isle of Man dies and the 2 cent coins with Bahamas and New Zealand dies. *Restrikes* of rare American coins have been detected in which the dated die has been paired with the wrong reverse die, e.g. the 1860 restrike of the rare 1804 large cent.

Mute   An *anepigraphic* coin, identifiable only by the devices struck on it.

Nail Mark   Small indentation on ancient coins. The earliest coins of Asia Minor developed from the electrum *dumps* which merchants marked with a broken nail as their personal guarantee of value, the ancient counterpart of the *chop* marks used in China and Japan.

NCLT Coins   Abbreviation for "Non Circulating Legal Tender", a term devised by modern coin catalogues to denote coins which, though declared *legal tender*, are not intended for general circulation on account of their precious metal content or superior finish.

Nicked Coin   Coin bearing a tiny cut or nick in its edge. Silver coins were tested by this method, especially in the reign of Henry I (1100–35) when so many base silver pennies were in circulation. Eventually people refused to accept these nicked coins a problem which was only overcome when the state decreed that all coins should have a nick in them.

Nickel   Metallic element, chemical symbol *Ni*, a hard white metal relatively resistant to tarnish, and extensively used as a cheap substitute for silver. It was first used for the American 5 cent coin in 1866, hence its popular name which has stuck ever since, although nowadays the higher denominations are minted in an alloy of copper and nickel. Although best known as a silver substitute, nickel was widely used in Jamaica (1869–1969) for halfpence and pennies and in British West Africa for the tiny 1/10th pennies (1908–57). Pure nickel was used for French francs and German marks, but usually it is alloyed with copper or zinc to produce *cupro-nickel* or nickel brass.

Notaphily   Hybrid word from Latin *nota* (note) and Greek philos (love), coined about 1970 to denote the branch of numismatics devoted to the study of paper money.

Notgeld   German word meaning emergency money, applied to the *tokens*, in metals, wood, leather and even ceramic materials, issued during the First World War when coinage disappeared from circulation. These tokens were soon superseded by low-denomination paper money issued by shops and businessmen in denominations from 10 to 50 pfennige and known as *kleine Notgeld* (small emergency money). These notes were prohibited in September 1922 but by that time some 50,000 varieties are thought to have been issued. Inflation raced out of control and the government permitted a second issue of local notes, known as *large Notgeld*, as the denominations were in thousands, and latterly millions, of marks. Some 3,600 types appeared in 1922 and over 60,000 in 1923 alone. These mementoes of the German hyperinflation ceased to circulate in 1924 when the currency was reformed.

Numismatics   The study of coins, medals and other related fields, a term derived from the Latin *numisma* and Greek *nomisma* (money).

Obsidional Currency   (From Latin *obsidium*, a siege). Term for *emergency money* produced by the defenders of besieged towns and cities. These usually took the form of pieces of silver plate, commandeered for the purpose, crudely marked with an official device and the value. Instances of such seige coinage have been recorded from the 12th to the 19th centuries.

Obverse   The "heads" side of a coin or medal, generally bearing the effigy of the head of state or an allegorical figure.

Off Metal   Term denoting a piece struck in a metal other than the officially authorisied or issued alloy. This originally applied to *patterns* which were often struck in lead or copper instead of gold and silver as trial pieces or to test the dies; but in recent years it has applied to collectors' versions, e.g. proofs in platinum, gold or silver of coins normally issued in bronze or cupro-nickel.

Overdate   One or more digits in a date altered by superimposing another figure. Alterations of this kind, by means of small hand punches, were made to dated dies so that they could be used in years other than that of the original manufacture. Coins with overdates invariably show traces of the original digit.

Overstrike   Coin, token or medal produced by using a previously struck pieces as a flan. The Bank of England dollar of 1804 was overstruck on Spanish pieces of eight, and examples showing traces of the original coins are worth a good premium.

Paduan   Name given to imitations of medals and bogus coins produced in Italy in the 16th century, and deriving from the city of Padua where forgeries of bronze sculpture were produced for the antique market.

Patina   Oxidation forming on the surface of metallic objects. So far as coins and medals are concerned, this applies mainly to silver, brass, bronze and copper pieces which may acquire oxidation from the atmosphere, or spectacular patination from salts in the ground in which they have been buried. In extreme forms patina leads to verdigris and other forms of rust which corrode the surface, but in uncirculated coins it may be little more than a mellowing of the original *lustre*. Coins preserved in blue velvet presentation cases often acquire a subtle toning from the dyes in the material.

Pattern   Piece resembling a coin or medal, prepared by the mint to the specifications or on the authorisation of the coin-issuing authority, but also applied to pieces produced by mints when tendering for coinage or medal contracts. Patterns may differ from the final coins as issued in the type of alloy used (*off metal*) but more often they differ in details of the design.

Pellet   Raised circular ornament used as a spacing device between words and abbreviations in the *legend* of coins and medals. Groups of pellets were also used as ornaments in the angles of the cross on the reverse of English silver pennies.

Piece de Plaisir   (French for "fancy piece"). Term given to coins struck in a superior precious metal, or to a superior finish, or on a much thicker flan than usual. See *off metal*, *piedfort* and *proof*.

A piedfort £1 coin compared to one of a normal flan.

Piedfort (Piefort)   Piece struck with coinage dies on a *flan* of much more than normal thickness. This practice originated in France in the late 16th century and continues to the present day. In recent years it has been adopted by mints in Britain and other countries as a medium for collectors' pieces.

Pile   Lower die incorporating the obverse motif, used in striking coins and medals. See also *trussel*.

Planchet   French term used as an alternative for *blank* or *flan*.

Plaque or **Plaquette**   Terms sometimes used for medals struck on a square or rectangular flan.

Plaster   Cast taken from the original model for a coin or medal sculpted by an artist, and used in modern reducing machines in the manufacture of the master *die*.

Plated Coins   Coins stuck in base metal but given a wash of silver or some other precious metal. This expedient was adopted in inflationary times, from the Roman Republic (91 BC) till the Tudor period. American cents of 1943 were struck in steel with a zinc coating, and more recently *clad* coins have produced similar results.

Platinum   The noblest of all precious metals, platinum has a higher specific gravity than gold and a harder, brighter surface than silver. Until an industrial application was discovered in the mid-19th century, it was regarded as of little value, and was popular with counterfeiters as a cheap substitute for gold in their forgeries which, with a light gold wash, could be passed off as genuine. It was first used for circulating coins in Russia (the chief source of the metal since 1819) and 3, 6 and 12 rouble coins were mined at various times between 1828 and 1845. In recent years platinum has been a popular metal for limited-edition proof coins.

Platmynt   (Swedish for "plate money"). Large copper plates bearing royal cyphers and values from half to ten dalers produced in Sweden between 1643 and 1768. They represented laudable attempts by a country rich in copper to produce a coinage in terms of its silver value, but the net result was far too cumbersome to be practical. The weight of the daler plate, for example, ranged from 766 grams to 1.1kg, and special carts had to be devised to transport them!

Plugged Coins   Coins struck predominantly in one metal, but containing a small plug of another. This curious practice may be found in the farthings of Charles II (1684–85) and the halfpence or farthings of James II (1685–87), which were struck in tin, with a copper plug, to defeat forgers.

Pollard   Alternative name for *crockard*.

Porcelain Money   Tokens made of porcelain circulated in Thailand from the late 18th century till 1868. The Meissen pottery struck tokens in 1920–22 as a form of small *Notgeld*, using reddish-brown Bottger stoneware and white *bisque* porcelain. These ceramic tokens circulated in various towns of Saxony.

Postage Currency Small paper notes in denominations of 5, 10, 25 and 50 cents, issued by the US federal government in 1862–63, were thus inscribed and had reproductions of postage stamps engraved on them — five 5c stamps on the 25c and five 10c stamps on the 50c notes. The earliest issue even had perforations in the manner of stamps, but this unnecessary device was soon done away with. See also *stamp money*.

Postal Notes or Orders Low-value notes intended for transmission by post and encashable at post offices. Introduced by Britain in 1883, they were an extension of the earlier *money order* system, and are now issued by virtually every country.

Potin (French for pewter). Alloy of copper, tin, lead and silver used as a coinage metal by the Celtic tribes of eastern Gaul at the beginning of the Christian era.

Privy Mark Secret mark incorporated in the design of a coin or medal to identify the minter, or even the particular die used. The term is also used more loosely to denote any small symbol or initials appearing on a coin other than a *mint mark*, and is sometimes applied to the symbols associated with the trial of the *Pyx* found on English coins.

Prize Coins Coins of large size and value struck primarily as prizes in sporting contests. this principle dates from the late 5th century BC when Syracuse minted decadrachms as prizes in the Demareteian Games. The most notable example in modern times is the lengthy series of talers and five-franc coins issued by the Swiss cantons since 1842 as prizes in the annual shooting festivals, the last of which honoured the Lucerne contest of 1939.

Profile A side view of the human face, widely used as a coinage effigy.

Proof Originally a trial strike testing the *dies*, but now denoting a special collectors' version struck with dies that have been specially polished on *flans* with a mirror finish. Presses operating at a very slow speed, or multi-striking processes, are also used.

Propaganda Notes Paper money containing a political slogan or a didactic element. During the Second World War forgeries of German and Japanese notes were produced by the Allies and additionally inscribed or overprinted with slogans such as "Co-Prosperity Sphere—What is it worth?" (a reference to the Japanese occupied areas of SE Asia). Forged dollars with anti-

American propaganda were airdropped over Sicily by the Germans in 1943 and counterfeit pounds with Arabic propaganda over Egypt in 1942–43. Various anti-communist organisations liberated propaganda forgeries of paper money by balloon over Eastern Europe during the Cold War period.

Provenance Mark Form of *privy mark* denoting the source of the metal used in coins. Examples include the plumes or roses on English coins denoting silver from Welsh or West of England mines, and the elephant or elephant and castle on gold coins denoting bullion imported by the African Company. Coins inscribed VIGO (1702–03) or LIMA (1745–46) denote bullion seized from the Spaniards by Anglo-Dutch privateers and Admiral Anson respectively. Other provenance marks on English coins include the letters EIC and SSC, denoting bullion imported by the East India Company or the South Sea Company.

Pseudo Coins Derisory term coined in recent years to signify pieces of precious metal, often struck in *proof* versions only, aimed at the international investment market. Many of these pieces, though bearing a nominal face value, are not *legal tender* in the countries purporting to issue them and in many cases they go straight from the overseas mint where they are produced to coin dealers in America and western Europe, without ever appearing in the so-called country of origin. See also *NCLT coins*.

Punch or Puncheon Intermediate *die* whereby working dies can be duplicated from the master die, prior to the striking of coins and medals.

Pyx Box in which a specimen from every 15 pounds troy weight of gold and every 60 pounds of silver minted in England is kept for annual trial by weight and assay. Many of the *mintmarks* on English coins of the 14th–17th centuries were in use from one trial to the next and still exist today and can therefore be used to date them.

Reducing Machinery Equipment designed on the pantographic principle for transferring the image from a *plaster* to a *hub* and reducing it to the size of the actual coin or medal. The image is transferred by means of a stylus operating rather like a gramophone needle, but working from the centre to the outer edge.

Reeding Security edging on coins, consisting of close vertical ridges. As a rule, this appears all round the edge but some coins, e.g. New Zealand's 50c (1967) and the Isle of Man's £1 (1978) have segments of reeding alternating with a plain edge, to help blind and partially sighted persons to identify these coins.

Re-issue A coin or note issued again after an extended lapse of time.

Relief Raised parts of the *obverse* and *reverse* of coins and medals, the opposite of *incuse*.

Remainder A note from a bank or issuing authority which has never been circulated, due to inflation, political changes or bank failure. Such notes, some-times in partial or unfinished state (e.g. missing serial numbers or signatures), are generally unloaded on to the numismatic market at a nominal sum and provide a good source of inexpensive material for the beginner.

Restrike Coin, medal or token produced from *dies* subsequent to the original use. Usually restrikes are made long after the original and can often be identified by marks caused by damage, pitting or corrosion of the dies after they were taken out of service.

Retrograde Term describing inscriptions running from right to left, or with the letters in a mirror image, thought to arise from unskilled die-cutters failing to realise that inscriptions have to be engraved in negative form to achieve a positive impression. Retrograde inscriptions are common on ancient Greek coins, but also found on Roman and Byzantine coins.

Reverse The side of a coin or medal regarded as of lesser importance; in colloquial parlance, the "tails" side.

Saltire Heraldic term for a cross in the shape of an X.

Sandwich Coin *blank* consisting of thin outer layers in one alloy bonded to a core in another. See *clad coins*.

Sceat (Anglo-Saxon for "treasure", or German *Schatz*). Money of account in Kent early in the 7th century as the twelfth part of a shilling or Merovingian gold tremissis. As a silver coin, it dates from about AD 680–700 and weighed about 20 grains, putting it on par with the Merovingian denier or penny. Sceats spread to other parts of England in the 8th century but tended to decline in weight and value, but from about 760 it was gradually superseded by the silver penny minted under Offa and his successors.

Scissel The clippings of metal left after a *blank* has been cut. Occasionally one of these clippings accidentally adheres to the blank during the striking process, producing characteristic crescent-shaped flaws on the finished coin.

Scrip Paper money of restricted validity or circulation, e.g. *Bafs* and other military scrip used in canteens and post exchanges.

Scyphate (Greek *scypha*, a skiff or small boat). Byzantine coin with a concave *flan*.

Sede Vacante (Latin for "Vacant See"). Coins struck at *ecclesiastical mints* between the death of a prelate and the election of his successor are often thus inscribed. This practice originated at Rome in the 13th century and spread to every part of Europe.

Seignorage or Seigneurage Royalty or percentage paid by persons bringing *bullion* to a mint for conversion into coin, but nowadays synonymous with the royalty paid by mints in respect of the precious metal versions of coins sold direct to collectors. It arises from the medieval right of the king to a small portion of the proceeds of a mint, and amounted to a tax on moneying. It has also been applied to the money accruing to the state when the coinage is re-issued in an alloy of lesser fineness, as, for example, the debased sovereigns of Henry VIII in 20 instead of 23 carat gold, the king's treasury collecting the difference.

Series Term applied to sets of medals of a thematic character, which first became fashionable in the early 18th century. Jean Dassier pioneered the medallic series in the 1720s with his set of 72 medals portraying the rulers of France till Louis XV. The idea was developed by J. Kirk, Sir Edward Thomason, J. Mudie and A. J. Stothard in Britain, and by Moritz Fuerst and Amedee Durand in Europe. The fashion died out in the 19th century, but has been revived in America and Europe since 1964.

Serrated Having a notched or toothed edge, rather like a cogwheel. Coins of this type, struck in *electrum*, an alloy of silver and gold, are known from Carthage in the 2nd century BC, and some silver denarii of Rome in the 2nd century AD also come into this category.

Sexagesimal System Monetary system in which the principal unit is divided into 60 parts. The oldest system in the Western world was based on the gold talent of 60 minae and the mina of 60 shekels. In medieval Europe 60 groschen were worth a fine mark; in England from 1551, the silver coinage was based on the crown of 60 pence, and in the south German states till 1873 the gulden was worth 60 kreuzers.

Shin Plasters Derisory term originally applied to the Continental currency notes issued during the American War of Independence, the fractional currency of the Civil War period and also the low-denomination notes of Canada between 1870 and 1935, but often applied indiscriminately to any other low-denomination, small-format notes.

Short Cross Coinage Term for the silver coinage introduced by Henry II in 1180 and minted till 1247 at which time it was replaced by the *Long Cross* type. The termination of the arms of the cross on the reverse well within the circumference encouraged the dishonest practice of *clipping*.

Shroff Mark A *countermark* applied by Indian

bankers or merchants to attest the full weight and purity of coins. See also *chop*.

Siege Money See *Obsidional Currency*

Silver Precious metal, chemical symbol *Ag*, numismatic abbreviation *Ar*, from Latin *Argentum*, widely used as a coinage metal from the 6th century BC to the present day.

Sterling silver denotes an alloy of .925 fine silver with .075 copper. Fine silver alloys used over the past 2,500 years have ranged from .880 to .960 fine, but base silver has also been all too common. British coins from 1920 to 1946 were struck in .500 fine silver, while alloys of lesser fineness are known as *billon* or *vellon*. Silver alloyed with gold produces a metal called *electrum*, used for the earliest coinage of the western world, the staters of Lydia in the 7th century BC. Since 1970 silver as a medium for circulating coinage has almost virtually disappeared, yet the volume of silver coins for sale to collectors has risen considerably in recent years.

Skit Note Piece of paper masquerading as a banknote. It differs from a *counterfeit* in that its design parodies that of a genuine note, often for political, satirical or advertising reasons. Others were produced as April Fools' Day jokes or a form of Valentine (e.g. the Bank of Lovers). In recent years they have been produced as advertising gimmicks, or as coupons permitting a discount off the list price of goods.

Slug Popular name for the $50 gold pieces produced by private mints in California in the mid-19th century. The term is also applied nowadays to *tokens* intended for use in gaming machines.

Spade Guinea Name given to the guineas of George III issued between 1787 and 1799 because the shield on the reverse design resembled the shape of a spade. In Victorian times the spade guinea was extensively copied in brass for gaming counters.

Spade Money Cast bronze pieces resembling miniature spades and other agricultural implements, used as money and derived from the actual implements which had previously been used in barter. Often referred to as *Pu* or *Boo* money.

Specie Financial term denoting money in the form of precious metals (silver and gold), usually struck as coin, as opposed to money in the form of paper notes and bills of exchange. It occurs in the name of some European coins (e.g. *speciedaler*, *speciestaler* and *speciesducat*) to denote the use of fine silver or gold.

Specimen Generally used to denote a single piece, but more specifically applying to a coin in a special finish, less than *proof* in quality but superior to the general circulating version. It also denotes paper notes intended for circulation between banks or for press publicity and distinguished from the generally issued version by zero serial numbers, punch holes or a security endorsement.

Spintriae Metal tokens produced in Roman imperial times, with erotic motifs, thought to have been tickets of admission to brothels.

Spit Copper or iron rod used as a primitive form of currency in the Mediterranean area. The Greek word *belos* meant a spit, dart or bolt, and from this came the word *obolos* used for a coin worth a 6th of a drachma.

Stamp Money Both postage and revenue (fiscal) stamps have circulated as money during shortages of coins, from the American Civil War onwards. *Encased postage stamps* were used in the USA, 1861–62, before they were superseded by *Postage Currency* notes, but the same expedient was adopted by many countries during and immediately after the First World War. Stamps affixed to special cards have circulated as money in Rhodesia (now Zimbabwe) in 1900, the French colonies and Turkey during the First World War, in Spain during the Civil War (1936–39) and the Philippines during the Second World War. Stamps printed on thick card, with an inscription on the reverse signifying their parity with silver coins, were issued in Russia (1917–18) and also in Armenia, the Crimea and the Ukraine (1918–20). During the Second World War Ceylon (now Sri Lanka) and several Indian states issued small money cards with contemporary stamps printed on them.

Steel Refined and tempered from *iron*, and used in chromed or stainless versions as a coinage metal in the 20th century. Zinc-coated steel cents were issued by the USA (1943) but in the form known as *acmonital* (nickel steel) it has been extensively used by Italy since 1939. Other alloys of nickel and steel have been used for coins of the Philippines (1944–45) and Roumania since 1963. Chrome steel was used by France for 5 centime coins in 1961–64. Copper-clad steel is now extensively used for subsidiary coins formerly struck in bronze.

Sterling Word of uncertain origin denoting money of a standard weight and fineness, and hence the more general meaning of recognised worth. The traditionally accepted derivation from the Easterlings, north German merchants who settled in London in the 13th century and produced silver pennies of uniform fineness, is unlikely as the term has been found in documents a century earlier. A more plausible explanation is from Old English *steorling* ("little coin with a star"), alluding to Viking pennies with this device, or even as a diminutive of *stater*. Sterling silver denotes silver of .925 fineness.

Stone Money Primitive currency in the form of large stone discs, used in West Africa in the pre-colonial period, and in the Pacific island of Yap (now Micronesia) as recently as 1940.

Striation A pattern of alternate light and dark parallel marks or minute grooves on the surface of a coin or medal. In the latter case it is sometimes done for textural effect, but in coins it may result from faulty *annealing*. Deliberate ridging of the surface, however, was a distinctive feature of Japanese *koban* and *goryoban* coins of 1736–1862.

Styca Name given to the debased silver *sceats* of Northumbria in the 8th century.

Tael Chinese unit of weight corresponding to the European ounce and sometimes referred to as a liang. It was a measure of silver varying between 32 and 39 grams. In the 19th century it served as *money of account*, 100 British or Mexican trade dollars being worth 72 tael. The term has also been loosely applied to the Chinese silver yuan, although this was worth only .72 tael, or 7 mace and 2 candareens (10 candareens = 1 mace; 10 mace = 1 tael).

Thrymsa Early Anglo-Saxon gold coin based on the Merovingian tremissis or third-solidus, current in Kent, London and York about AD 63–75.

Tical Unit of weight in Thailand, first appearing as coins in the form of crudely shaped *bullet money* current from the 14th till the late 19th centuries. When European-style coins were introduced in 1860 the word was retained as a denomination (32 solot = 16 atts = 8 peinung or sio = 4 songpy or sik = 2 fuang= 1 salung or quarter-tical. The currency was decimalised in 1909 (100 satangs = 1 tical), and the tical was superseded by the baht about 1950.

Tin Metallic element, chemical symbol Sn (from Latin *Stannum*). Because of its unstable nature and tendency to oxidise badly when exposed to the atmosphere, it is unsatisfactory as a coinage metal, but has been used on several occasions, notably in Malaya, Thailand and the East Indies. In was also used for British halfpence and farthings, 1672–92.

Token Any piece of money whose nominal value is greater than its intrinsic value is, strictly speaking, a token or promise. Thus most of the coins issued since 1964 can be regarded in this light, but numismatists reserve the term for a piece of limited validity and circulation, produced by tradesmen, chambers of commerce and other organisations during times of a shortage of government coinage. The term is also loosely applied to metal tickets of admission, such as *communion tokens*, or *jetons* and *counters* intended for games of chance. Tokens with a nominal value may be produced for security reasons to lessen the possibility of theft from milk bottles, vending machines, telephones, parking meters and transport facilities. Tokens exchangeable for goods have been issued by co-operative societies and used in prisons and internment camps in wartime. In addition to the traditional coinage alloys, tokens have been produced in ceramics, plastics, wood, stout card, leather and even rubber, in circular, square or polygonal shapes.

Tombac Type of brass alloy with a high copper content, used in coinage requiring a rich golden colour. It is, in fact, a modern version of the *aurichalcum* used by the Romans. It was used for the Canadian 5-cent coins of 1942–43, while 5- and 10-pfennig coins of Germany have a tombac cladding on a steel core.

Touchpiece Coin kept as a lucky charm, but more specifically the medieval gold angel of England which was worn round the neck as an antidote to scrofula, otherwise known as king's evil, from the belief that the reigning monarch possessed the power of healing by touch. The ceremony of touching for king's evil involved the suspension of an angel round the victim's neck, hence the prevalence of these coins pierced for suspension.

Trade Coins Coins widely used as a medium of international trade, often far beyond the boundaries of the country issuing them. The earliest examples were the Aiginetan turtles and Athenian tetrdrachms of the classical period. In the Middle Ages the English *sterling* was widely prized on account of its silver purity. Arab dinars and Italian florins were popular as gold coins in late-medieval times, while the British gold sovereign has been the preferred gold coin of modern times. The Maria Theresa silver thaler of Austria, with its date frozen at 1782, has been minted widely down to the present time for circulation in the Near and Middle East as a trade coin. Trade dollars were minted by Britain, the USA, the Netherlands and Japan to compete with the Spanish, and later the Mexican, peso or 8-reales coins as a trading medium in the Far East.

Transport Tokens Coin-like pieces of metal, plastic or card, issued by companies and corporations to employees and exchangeable for rides on municipal transport systems, date from the mid-19th century. In more recent times similar tokens have been used in many countries to activate turnstiles in buses, trams and rapid-transit railway systems.

Treasury Note   Paper money worth 10 shillings or one pound, issued by the British Treasury on the outbreak of the First World War when *specie* payments were suspended, and continuing till 1928 when the Bank of England took over responsibility for note-issuing.

Treasure Trove   Articles of precious metal concealed in times of economic or political upheaval and discovered years (often centuries) later are deemed by law to be treasure trove (from the French word *trouve*, found). For further details see *Money and the Law*.

Trial Plate   Plate of the same metal as the current coinage against which the fineness and quality of the coins produced are compared and tested.

Troy Weight   System of weights derived from the French town of Troyes whose standard pound was adopted in England in 1526. It continued in Britain till 1879 when it was abolished, with the exception of the troy ounce and its decimal parts and multiples, which were retained for gold, silver, platinum and precious stones. The troy ounce of 480 grains is used by numismatists for weighing coins.

Truncation   Stylised cut at the base of a coinage effigy, sometimes containing a die number, engraver's initials or *mintmark*.

Trussel   Reverse die in *hammered* coinage, the opposite of the *pile*.

Type   Principal motif on a coin or medal, enabling numismatists to identify the issue.

Type Set   A set of coins comprising one of each coin in a particular series, regardless of the actual date of issue.

Uncirculated   Term used in grading coins to denote specimens in perfect condition, with original mint lustre. In recent years the term "Brilliant Uncirculated" has been adopted (abbreviated as BUnc or BU).

Uniface   Coin, medal or token with a device on one side only.

Variety   Variation in, or modification of type, effigy, motif or inscription.

Vecture   Term (mainly US) for a *transport token*.

Veiled Head   The effigy of Queen Victoria by Thomas Brock adopted for British coinage after 1893—often referred to as the "Old Head" coinage.

The Veld Pond   (Dutch for "field pound"). Gold coin struck by the Boer guerrillas at Pilgrims Rest in 1902, in imitation of the British sovereign.

Vellon   Spanish form of *billon*.

VF   Abbreviation for Very Fine, used to describe the state of a coin or medal.

VG   Abbreviation for Very Good.

Vignette   Strictly speaking the pictorial element of a paper note shading off into the surrounding unprinted paper rather than having a clearly defined border or frame; but nowadays applied generally to the picture portion of a banknote, as opposed to portrait, armorial or numeral elements.

Vis-à-Vis   (French for "face to face"). Term describing coins with double portraits of rulers, their profiles or busts facing each other. A good example is the English coinage of Philip and Mary, 1554–58.

Wampum   Barter currency of the North American Indians, composed of shells of *Venus mercenaria* strung together to form belts or "fathoms" worth 5 shillings. Wampum were tariffed variously from three to six to the English penny in the American colonies till 1704.

White Gold   Alternative term for *electrum*.

Wire Money   Primitive currency of the Maldive Islands in the form of lengths of silver wire known as lari, from which the modern currency unit *laree* is derived. The term was also applied to English coins of the 18th century in which the numerals of value were exceptionally thin, resembling wire.

Wooden Coins   Thin pieces of wood used as tokens are known from many parts of China and Africa, and as small *Notgeld* from Austria and Germany during the First World War. Wooden nickels is the somewhat contradictory name given to tokens of a commemorative nature, widely popular in the USA since 1930.

Year set.   A set of coins issued annually by a mint. It often contains specimens not generally released for circulation in that year.

Young Head   Profile of Queen Victoria sculpted by William Wyon for the Guildhall Medal of 1837 and subsequently utilised for British coins struck from 1837 to 1860 (copper) and 1887 (silver and gold).

Zinc   Metallic element, chemical symbol Zn, widely used, with copper, as a constituent of brass. Alloyed with copper to form *tombac*, it was used for Canadian 5-cent coins (1942–43) and, coated on steel, it was used for American cents (1943). Zinc was used for *emergency coinage* in Austria, Belgium, Luxembourg and Germany (1915–18) and in Germany and German-occupied countries during the Second World War. Since then alloys of copper, nickel and zinc have been used for coinage in Eastern Europe, and an alloy of zinc with titanium has been developed in the 1970s as a potential substitute for *bronze* in subsidiary coinage.

Mintmarks
of the world

The following is a list of the initials and symbols denoting mints. In many cases, notably the Royal Mint, no mintmark was used on either British coins or those struck on behalf of other countries. Conversely many countries have only used one mintmark, that of one or other of the leading private mints.

It should be noted that the mintmarks of the main private mints have been recorded on the coins of the following countries:

H (Heaton, later the Birmingham Mint):
Australia, Bolivia, British Honduras, British North Borneo, British West Africa, Bulgaria, Canada, Ceylon, Chile, Colombia, Costa Rica, Cyprus, Dominican Republic, East Africa, Ecuador, Egypt, El Salvador, Finland, French Indochina, Great Britain, Greece, Guatemala, Guernsey, Haiti, Hong Kong, Iran, Israel, Italy, Jamaica, Jersey, Liberia, Malaya and British Borneo, Mauritius, Mombasa, Mozambique, Newfoundland, Nicaragua, Poland, Roumania, Sarawak, Serbia, Siam, Straits Settlements, Uruguay and Venezuela.

FM (Franklin Mint, Philadelphia): Bahamas, Belize, British Virgin Islands, Cayman Islands, Cook Islands, Guyana, Jamaica, Liberia, Malaysia, Malta, Panama, Papua New Guinea, Philippines, Solomon Islands, Trinidad and Tobago.

PM (Pobjoy Mint, Sutton, Surrey): Ascension, Bosnia, Cook Islands, Gibraltar, Isle of Man, Liberia, Macau, Niue, Philippines, St Helena, Senegal, Seychelles, Tonga and Tristan da Cunha.

ALBANIA
L	London
R	Rome
V	Valona

ARGENTINA
BA	Buenos Aires
Bs	Buenos Aires
B.AS	Buenos Aires
JPP	Jose Policarpo Patino
M	Mendoza
PNP	Pedro Nolasco Pizarro
PP	Pedro Nolasco Pizarro
PTS	Potosi
R	Rioja
RA	Rioja
SE	Santiago del Estero
SoEo	Santiago del Estero
TN	Tucuman

AUSTRALIA
A	Perth
D	Denver
H	Heaton (1912–16)
I	Bombay (1942–43)
I	Calcutta (1916–18)
M	Melbourne
P	Perth
PL	Royal Mint, London
S	Sydney
S	San Francisco (1942–43)
Dot before and after PENNY and I on obverse	Bombay (1942–43)
Dot before and after HALFPENNY and I on obverse	Bombay (1942–43)
Dot before and after PENNY	Bombay (1942–43)
Dot after HALFPENNY	Perth
Dot before SHILLING	Perth (1946)
Dot above scroll on reverse	Sydney (1920)
Dot below scroll on reverse	Melbourne (1919–20)
Dot between designer's initials KG	Perth (1940–41)
Dot after AUSTRALIA	Perth (1952–53)

AUSTRIA
A	Vienna (1765–1872)
AH–AG	Carlsburg, Transylvania (1765–76)
AH–GS	Carlsburg (1776–80)
A–S	Hall, Tyrol (1765–74)
AS–IE	Vienna (1745)
AW	Vienna (1764, 1768)
B	Kremnitz (1765–1857)
B–L	Nagybanya (1765–71)

B–V	Nagybanya (1772–80)
C	Carlsburg (1762–64)
C	Prague (1766–1855)
C–A	Carlsburg (1746–66)
C–A	Vienna (1774–80)
CG–AK	Graz (1767–72)
CG–AR	Graz (1767)
C–K	Vienna (1765–73)
CM	Kremnitz (1779)
CVG–AK	Graz (1767–72)
CVG–AR	Graz (1767)
D	Graz (1765–72), Salzburg (1800–09)
E	Carlsburg (1765–1867)
EC–SK	Vienna (1766)
EvM–D	Kremnitz (1765–74)
EvS–AS	Prague (1765–73)
EvS–IK	Prague (1774–80)
F	Hall (1765–1807)
FH	Hall
G	Graz (1761–63)
G	Gunzburg (1764–79)
G	Nagybanya (1766–1851)
G–K	Graz (1767–72)
G–R	Graz (1746–67)
GTK	Vienna (1761)
H	Hall (1760–80)
H	Gunzburg (1765–1805)
H–A	Hall (1746–65)
H–G	Carlsburg (1765–77)
H–S	Carlsburg (1777–80)
IB–FL	Nagybanya (1765–71)
IB–IV	Nagybanya (1772–80)
IC–FA	Vienna (1774–80)
IC–IA	Vienna (1780)
IC–SK	Vienna (1765–73)
I–K	Graz (1765-67)
I–K	Vienna (1767)
IZV	Vienna (1763–65)
K	Kremnitz (1760–63)
K–B	Kremnitz (1619–1765)
K–D	Kremnitz (1765)
K–M	Kremnitz (1763–65)
M	Milan (1780–1859)
N	Nagybanya (1780)
N–B	Nagybanya (1630–1777, 1849)
O	Oravicza (1783–1816)
P	Prague (1760–63)
P–R	Prague (1746–67)
PS–IK	Prague (1774–80)
S	Hall (1765–80), Schmollnitz (1763–1816)
S–C	Gunzburg (1765–74)
SC–G	Gunzburg (1765)
S–F	Gunzburg (1775–80)
S–G	Gunzburg (1764–65)
S–IE	Vienna (1745)
SK–PD	Kremnitz (1774–80)
TS	Gunzburg (1762–88)

V	Venice (1805–66)
VC–S	Hall (1774–80)
VS–K	Prague (1774–80)
VS–S	Prague (1765–73)
W	Vienna (1748–63)
W–I	Vienna (1746–71)

BAHAMAS

FM	Franklin Mint
JP	John Pinches

BELGIUM

A	Vienna
B	Kremnitz
C	Prague
E	Carlsburg
F	Hall
G	Nagybanya
H	Gunzburg
hand	Antwerp
lion	Bruges

BELIZE (British Honduras)

FM	Franklin Mint
H	Heaton (1912–16)

BOLIVIA

H	Heaton (1892–1953)
P, PTR, PTS	Potosi

BRAZIL

A	Berlin (1913)
B	Bahia (1714–1831)
C	Cuiaba (1823–33)
G	Goias (1823–33)
M	Minas Gerais (1823–28)
P	Pernambuco
R	Rio de Janeiro (1703–1834)
RS	Rio de Janeiro (1869)
SP	Sao Paulo (1825–32)

BRITISH NORTH BORNEO (Sabah)

H	Heaton (1882–1941)

BRITISH WEST AFRICA

G	JR Gaunt, Birmingham
H	Heaton, Birmingham (1911–57)
K	King's Norton
KN	King's Norton
SA	Pretoria

BULGARIA

A	Berlin
BP	Budapest
Heaton	Heaton, Birmingham (1881–1923)
KB	Kormoczbanya
cornucopia	Paris
thunderbolt	Poissy

CANADA

C	Ottawa
H	Heaton (1871–1907)
maple leaf	Ottawa (on coins struck after the year inscribed on them)

CENTRAL AMERICAN REPUBLIC

CR	San Jose (Costa Rica)
G	Guatemala
NG	Guatemala
T	Tegucigalpa (Honduras)

CEYLON

H	Heaton (1912)

CHILE

A	Agustin de Infante y Prado (1768–72)
AJ	The above and Jose Maria de Bobadilla (1800–01)
D	Domingo Eizaguirre
DA	Domingo Eizaguirre and Agustin de Infante (1772–99)
BFF	Francisco Rodriguez Brochero
FJJF	Brochero and Jose Maria de Bobadilla (1803–17)
H	Heaton (1851)
J	Jose Larraneta (1749–67)
So	Santiago
VA	Val Distra

COLOMBIA

A	Paris
B	Bogota
BA	Bogota
B.B	Bogota
H	Heaton (1912)
M	Medellin
NR	Nuevo Reino
NoRo	Nuevo Reino
P	Popayan
PN, Pn	Popayan
SM	Santa Marta

COSTA RICA

CR	San Jose (1825–1947)
HBM	Heaton (1889–93)
S	San Domingo
SD	San Domingo

COURLAND

ICS	Justin Carl Schroder
IFS	Johan Friedrich Schmickert

CYPRUS

H	Heaton (1881–2)

DENMARK

FF	Altona
KM	Copenhagen Altona (1842)
crown	Copenhagen
heart	Copenhagen
orb	Altona (1839–48)

Other letters are the initials of mintmasters and moneyers

DOMINICAN REPUBLIC

HH	Heaton (1888–1919)

EAST AFRICA

A	Ackroyd & Best, Morley
H	Heaton (1910–64)
I	Bombay
K	Kynoch (IMI)
KN	King's Norton
SA	Pretoria

ECUADOR

BIRM^MH	Heaton (1915)
BIRMING- HAM	Heaton (1899–1900, 1928)
D	Denver
H	Heaton (1890, 1909, 1924–5)
HEATON BIRMING- HAM	Heaton (1872–95)
HF	Le Locle
LIMA	Lima
Mo	Mexico
PHILA	Philadelphia
QUITO	Quito
SANTIAGO	Santiago de Chile

EGYPT

H	Heaton (1904–37)

EL SALVADOR

CAM	Central American Mint, San Salvador
H	Heaton (1889–1913)
Mo	Mexico
S	San Francisco

FIJI

S	San Francisco

FINLAND

H	Heaton (1921)
heart	Copenhagen (1922). Since then coins have been struck at Helsinki without a mintmark.

Initials of mintmasters:

S	August Soldan (1864–85)
L	Johan Lihr (1885–1912)
S	Isaac Sundell (1915–47)

L	V. U. Liuhto (1948)
H	Uolevi Helle (1948–58)
S	Allan Soiniemi (1958–75)
SH	Soiniemi & Heikki Halvaoja (1967–71)
K	Timo Koivuranta (1977, 1979)
KN	Koivuranta and Antti Neuvonen (1978)
KT	Koivuranta and Erja Tielinen (1982)
KM	Koivuranta and Pertti Makinen (1983)
N	Reino Nevalainen (1983)

FRANCE

A	Paris (1768)
AA	Metz (1775–98)
B	Rouen (1786–1857)
B	Beaumont le Roger (1943–58)
BB	Strasbourg (1743–1870)
C	Castelsarrasin (1914, 1942–46)
CC	Genoa (1805)
CL	Genoa (1813–14)
D	Lyons (1771–1857)
G	Geneva (1796–1805)
H	La Rochelle (1770–1837)
L	Limoges (1766–1837)
K	Bordeaux (1759–1878)
L	Bayonne (1761–1837)
M	Toulouse (1766–1837)
MA	Marseilles (1787–1857)
N	Montpellier (1766–93)
O	Riom
P	Dijon
Q	Perpignan (1777–1837)
R	Royal Mint, London (1815)
R	Orleans (1780–92)
T	Nantes (1739–1835)
U	Turin (1814)
V	Troyes
W	Lille (1759–1857)
X	Amiens (1740)
&	Aix en Provence (1775)
9	Rennes
cow	Pau (1746–93)
flag	Utrecht (1811–14)
crowned R	Rome (1811–14)
thunderbolt	Poissy (1922-24)
star	Madrid (1916)

In addition, French coins include symbols denoting the privy marks of Engravers General (Chief Engravers since 1880) and Mint Directors.

GERMANY
The first name gives the location of the mint, and the second the name of the country or state issuing the coins.

A	Amberg, Bavaria (1763–94)
A	Berlin (1850)
A	Clausthal, Hannover (1832–49)
AE	Breslau, Silesia (1743–51)

AGP	Cleve, Rhineland (1742–43)
AK	Dusseldorf, Julich-Berg (1749–66)
ALS	Berlin (1749)
B	Bayreuth, Franconia (1796–1804)
B	Breslau, Silesia (1750–1826)
B	Brunswick, Brunswick (1850–60)
B	Brunswick, Westphalia (1809–13)
B	Dresden, Saxony (1861–72)
B	Hannover, Brunswick (1860–71)
B	Hannover, East Friesland (1823–25)
B	Hannover, Hannover (1821–66)
B	Hannover, Germany (1866–78)
B	Regensburg, Regensburg (1809)
B	Vienna, Germany (1938–45)
BH	Frankfurt (1808)
B–H	Regensburg, Rhenish Confederation (1802–12)
C	Cassel, Westphalia (1810–13)
C	Clausthal, Brunswick
C	Clausthal, Westphalia (1810–11)
C	Dresden, Saxony (1779–1804)
C	Frankfurt, Germany (1866–79)
CHI	Berlin (1749–63)
CLS	Dusseldorf, Julich-Berg (1767–70)
D	Aurich, East Friesland (1750–1806)
D	Dusseldorf, Rhineland (1816–48)
D	Munich, Germany (1872)
E	Dresden, Germany (1872–87)
E	Koenigberg, East Prussia (1750–98)
E	Muldenhutte, Germany (1887–1953)
EC	Leipzig, Saxony (1753–63)
EGN	Berlin (1725–49)
F	Dresden, Saxony (1845–58)
F	Magdeburg, Lower Saxony (1740–1806)
F	Cassel, Hesse-Cassel (1803–07)
F	Stuttgart, Germany (1872)
FW	Dresden, Saxony (1734–63)
G	Dresden, Saxony (1833–44, 1850–54)
G	Glatz, Silesia (1807–09)
G	Karlsruhe, Germany (1872)
G	Stettin, Pomerania (1750–1806)
GK	Cleve (1740–55)
GN	Bamberg, Bamberg
H	Darmstadt, Germany (1872–82)
H	Dresden, Saxony (1804–12)
HK	Rostock, Rostock (1862–64)
I	Hamburg, Germany (1872)
IDB	Dresden, Prussian occupation (1756–59)
IEC	Dresden, Saxony (1779–1804)
IF	Leipzig, Saxony (1763–65)
IGG	Leipzig, Saxony (1716–34, 1813–32)
J	Hamburg, Germany (1873)
J	Paris, Westphalia (1808–09)
L	Leipzig, Saxony (1761–62)
MC	Brunswick, Brunswick (1813–14, 1820)
PM	Dusseldorf, Julich-Berg (1771–83)
PR	Dusseldorf, Julich-Berg (1783–1804)

S	Dresden, Saxony (1813–32)
S	Hannover, Hannover (1839–44)
S	Schwabach, Franconia (1792–94)
SGH	Dresden, Saxony (1804–12)
ST	Strickling, Blomberg (1820–40)

GREAT BRITAIN

A	Ashby (1645)
B	Nicolas Briot (1631–39)
B	Bridgnorth (1646)
B	Bristol (1696)
Br	Bristol (1643–45)
C	Chester (1696)
CARL	Carlisle (1644–45)
CC	Corfe Castle (1644)
CHST	Chester (1644)
CR	Chester (1644)
E	Southwark (1547–49)
E	Exeter (1696)
E	Edinburgh (1707–13)
E*	Edinburgh (1707–09)
H	Heaton, Birmingham (1874–1919)
HC	Hartlebury Castle (1646)
K	London (1547–49)
KN	King's Norton
N	Norwich (1696)
OX	Oxford (1644–45)
OXON	Oxford (1644)
PC	Pontefract (1648–49)
SC	Scarborough (1644–45)
SOHO	Birmingham (1797–1806)
T	Canterbury (1549)
TC	Bristol (1549)
WS	Bristol (1547–49)
Y	Southwark (1551)
boar	Shrewsbury (1643–44)
book	Aberystwyth (1638–42)
bow	Durham House (1548–49)
castle	Exeter (1644–45)
crown	Aberystwyth Furnace (1648–49)
plume	Shrewsbury (1642)
plume	Oxford (1642–46)
plume	Bristol (1643–46)

Other symbols and marks on the hammered coins of Great Britain are usually referred to as Initial Marks. Complete listings of these marks appear in a number of specialist publications.

GREECE

A	Paris
B	Vienna
BB	Strasbourg
H	Heaton (1921)
K	Bordeaux
KN	King's Norton
owl	Aegina (1828–32)
owl	Athens (1838–55)
thunderbolt	Poissy

GUATEMALA

CG	Guatemala City (1733-76)
G	Guatemala City (1776)
H	Heaton (1894–1901)
NG	Nueva Guatemala (1777)

GUERNSEY

H	Heaton (1855–1949)

HAITI

A	Paris
HEATON	Heaton (1863)

HONDURAS

A	Paris (1869–71)
T	Tegucigalpa (1825–62)

HONG KONG

H	Heaton (1872–1971)
KN	King's Norton

HUNGARY

A	Vienna
B	Kremnitz
BP	Budapest
CA	Vienna
G	Nagybanya
GN	Nagybanya
GYF	Carlsburg
HA	Hall
K	Kremnitz
KB	Kremnitz
NB	Nagybanya
S	Schmollnitz
WI	Vienna

INDIA

B	Bombay (1835-1947)
C	Calcutta (1835-1947)
I	Bombay (1918)
L	Lahore (1943-45)
M	Madras (1869)
P	Pretoria (1943-44)
diamond	Bombay
dot in diamond	Hyderabad
split diamond	Hyderabad
star	Hyderabad

IRAN

H	Heaton (1928–29)

IRAQ

I	Bombay

ISRAEL

H	Heaton (1951–52)
star of David	Jerusalem

ITALY AND STATES
B	Bologna
B/I	Birmingham (1893–4)
FIRENZE	Florence
H	Heaton (1866–67)
KB	Berlin
M	Milan
N	Naples
OM	Strasbourg
R	Rome
T	Turin
V	Venice
ZV	Venice
anchor	Genoa
eagle head	Turin

JAMAICA
C	Ottawa
FM	Franklin Mint
H	Heaton (1882–1916)

JERSEY
H	Heaton (1877)

KENYA
C/M	Calcutta
H	Heaton (1911–64)

LIBERIA
B	Berne
FM	Franklin Mint
H	Heaton (1896–1906)
PM	Pobjoy Mint

LIECHTENSTEIN
A	Vienna
B	Berne
M	Munich

LUXEMBOURG
A	Paris
H	Gunzburg
anchor	Paris
angel	Brussels
caduceus	Utrecht
double eagle	Brussels
sword	Utrecht

MALAYSIA
B	Bombay
FM	Franklin Mint
H	Heaton (1955–61)
I	Calcutta (1941)
I	Bombay (1945)
KN	King's Norton
W	James Watt, Birmingham

MAURITIUS
H	Heaton (1877–90)
SA	Pretoria

MEXICO
A, As	Alamos
C, CN	Culiacan
CA, CH	Chihuahua
Ce	Real del Catorce
D, Do	Durango
Eo	Tlalpam
GA	Guadalajara
GC	Guadelupe y Calvo
Go	Guanajuato
Ho	Hermosillo
M, Mo	Mexico City
Mo	Morelos
MX	Mexico City
O, OA, OKA	Oaxaca
Pi	San Luis Potosi
SLPi	San Luis Potosi
TC	Tierra Caliente
Z, Zs	Zacatecas

MONACO
A	Paris
M	Monte Carlo
clasped hands	Cabanis
thunderbolt	Poissy

MOZAMBIQUE
H	Heaton (1894)
R	Rio

NETHERLANDS AND COLONIES
Austrian Netherlands (1700-93)
H	Amsterdam
S	Utrecht
W	Vienna
hand	Antwerp
head	Brussels
lion	Bruges

Kingdom of the Netherlands
B	Brussels (1821–30)
D	Denver (1943–45)
P	Philadelphia (1941–45)
S	Utrecht (1816–36)
S	San Francisco (1944–45)
Sa	Surabaya
caduceus	Utrecht

NICARAGUA
H	Heaton (1880–1916)
NR	Leon de Nicaragua

NORWAY
hammers	Kongsberg

PANAMA

CHI	Valcambi
FM	Franklin Mint

PERU

AREQ, AREQUIPA	Arequipa
AYACUCHO	Ayacucho
CUZCO, Co	Cuzco
L, LM, LR	Lima
LIMAE	Lima
PASCO	Pasco
Paz, Po	Pasco
P	Lima (1568-70)
P	Philadelphia
S	San Francisco

PHILIPPINES

BSP	Bangko Sentral Pilipinas
D	Denver (1944–45)
FM	Franklin Mint
M, MA	Manila
PM	Pobjoy Mint
S	San Francisco (1903–47)
5 point star	Manila

POLAND

AP	Warsaw (1772–74)
CI	Cracow (1765–68)
EB	Warsaw (1774–92)
EC	Leipzig (1758–63)
FF	Stuttgart (1916–17)
FH	Warsaw (1815–27)
FS	Warsaw (1765–68)
FWoF	Dresden (1734–64)
G	Cracow (1765–72)
H	Heaton (1924)
IB	Warsaw (1811–27)
IGS	Dresden (1716–34)
IP	Warsaw (1834–43)
IS	Warsaw (1768–74)
JGG	Leipzig (1750–53)
JS	Warsaw (1810–11)
KG	Warsaw (1829–34)
MV, MW	Warsaw
arrow	Warsaw (1925–39)
Dot after date	Royal Mint (1925)
8 torches	Paris (1924)

ROUMANIA

B	Bucharest (1879–85)
C	Bucharest (1886)
H	Heaton (1867–1930)
HUGUENIN	Le Locle
J	Hamburg
KN	King's Norton
V	Vienna

W	Watt, Birmingham
thunderbolt	Poissy

RUSSIA

AM	Annensk (1762–96)
BM	Warsaw (1825–55)
bM	St Petersburg (1796)
C–M	Sestroretsk (1762–96)
CM	Souzan (1825–55)
E–M	Ekaterinburg (1762–1810)
KM	Kolpina (1810)
K–M	Kolyvan (1762–1810)
MM, M–M	Moscow (1730–96)
MMD	Moscow (1730–96)
MW	Warsaw (1842–54)
NM	Izhorsk (1811–21)
SP	St Petersburg (1798–1800)
SPB	St Petersburg (1724–1915)
SPM	St Petersburg (1825–55)
T–M	Feodosia (1762–96)

SAN MARINO

M	Milan
R	Rome

SIAM

(Thailand)	H Heaton (1898)

SOUTH AFRICA

SA	Pretoria

SPAIN

B	Burgos
B, BA	Barcelona
Bo	Bilbao
C	Catalonia
C	Cuenca
C	Reus
CA	Zaragoza
G	Granada
GNA	Gerona
LD	Lerida
J, JA	Jubia
M, MD	Madrid
P	Palma de Majorca
PpP, PL, PA	Pamplona
S, S/L	Seville
Sr	Santander
T, To, Tole	Toledo
TOR:SA	Tortosa
V, VA, VAL	Valencia
crowned C	Cadiz
crowned M	Madrid
aqueduct	Segovia
crowned shield	Tarragona
pomegranate	Granada
quartered shield	Palma
scallop	Coruna

SPAIN *continued*

stars:

3 points	Segovia
4 points	Jubia
5 points	Manila
6 points	Madrid
7 points	Seville (1833)
8 points	Barcelona (1838)
wavy lines	Valladolid

SURINAM

P	Philadelphia
S	Sydney
caduceus	Utrecht

SWITZERLAND

A	Paris
AB	Strasbourg
B	Berne
B	Brussels (1874)
BA	Basle
BB	Strasbourg
S	Solothurn

URUGUAY

H	Heaton (1869)

UNITED STATES OF AMERICA

C	Charlotte, North Carolina
Cc	Carson City, Nevada
D	Dahlonega, Georgia (1838–61)
D	Denver, Colorado (1906)
O	New Orleans
P	Philadelphia
S	San Francisco
W	West Point

VENEZUELA

A	Paris
H	Heaton (1852)
HEATON	Heaton (1852–63)

YUGOSLAVIA (including former Serbia)

A	Paris
H	Heaton (1883–84)
KOBHNUA, A.D.	Kovnica
V	Vienna
thunderbolt	Poissy

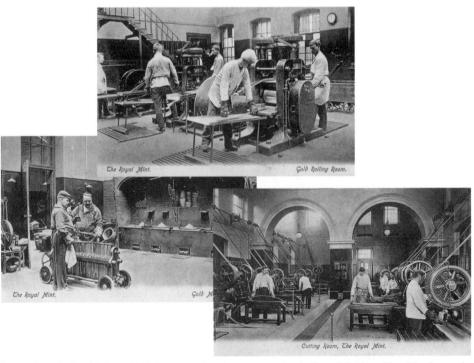

Images from the Royal Mint c. 1900 from a set of contemporary postcards. From left: The gold melting house; the gold rolling room and the cutting room.

Coin
inscriptions

This alphabetical listing is confined to inscriptions found on coins, mainly in the form of mottoes or of a commemorative nature. Names of rulers are, for the most part, excluded. Where the inscription is in a language other than English a translation is given, followed by the name of the issuing country or authority in parentheses.

A Deo et Caesare From God and the Emperor (Frankfurt).

A Domino Factum est Istud et est Mirabile in Oculis Nostris This is the Lord's doing and it is marvellous in our eyes (England, Mary).

A Solo Iehova Sapientia From God alone comes true wisdom (Wittgenstein).

Ab Inimicis Meis Libera Me Deus Free me from enemies (Burgundy).

Ad Legem Conventionis According to the law of the Convention (Furstenberg).

Ad Normam Conventionis According to the standard of the Convention (Prussia).

Ad Palmam Pressa Laeturo Resurgo Pressed to the palm I rise more joyfully (Wittgenstein).

Ad Usam Luxemburgi CC Vallati For the use of the besieged Luxembourgers (Luxembourg siege coins).

Adiuva Nos Deus Salutaris Noster Help us, O God, our Saviour (Lorraine).

Adventus Optimi Principis The coming of the noblest prince (Papacy).

Aes Usibus Aptius Auro Bronze in its uses is more suitable than gold (Brazil).

Aeternum Meditans Decus An ornament intended for all time (Alencon).

Aliis Inserviendo Consumor I spend my life devoted to others (Brunswick-Wolfenbuttel).

Alles Mit Bedacht All with reflection (Brunswick).

Amor Populi Praesidium Regis The love of the people is the king's protection (England, Charles I).

Ang Fra Dom Hib & Aquit (King) of England and France, Lord of Ireland and Aquitaine (England, Edward III).

Anno Regni Primo In the first year of the reign (Britain, edge inscription on crowns).

Apres les Tenebres la Lumiere After the shadows, the light (Geneva).

Archangelus Michael Archangel Michael (Italy, Grimoald IV).

Ardua ad Gloriam Via Struggles are the way to glory (Waldeck).

Arte Mea Bis Iustus Moneta Lud Iust By my art I am twice the just coin of King Louis (France, 1641).

Aspera Oblectant Wild places delight (Nassau-Weilburg).

Aspice Pisas Sup Omnes Specio Behold the coin of Pisa, superior to all (Pisa).

Audiatur Altera Pars Let the other part be heard (Stavelot).

Auf Gott Trawe Ich In God I trust (Brunswick).

Ausen Gefaesen der Kirchen und Burger From the vessels of the Church and citizens (Frankfurt siege, 1796).

Auspicio Regis et Senatus Angliae By authority of the king and parliament of England (East India Company).

Auxilio fortissimo Dei With the strongest help of God (Mecklenburg).

Auxilium de Sanctio Aid from the sanctuary (Papacy).

Auxilium Meum a Dno Qui Fecit Celum e Terram My help comes from God who made heaven and earth (Portugal).

Beata Tranquillatis Blessed tranquillity (Rome, Licinius II).

Beatus Qui Speravit in dom Blessed is he who has hoped in the Lord (Mansfeld).

Benedic Haereditati Tuae Blessings on your inheritance (Savoy).

Benedicta Sit Sancta Trinitas Blessed be the Holy Trinity (Albon).

Benedictio Domini Divites Facit The blessing of the Lord makes the rich (Teschen).

Benedictus Qui Venit in Nomine Domini Blessed is he who comes in the name of the Lord (Flanders).

Beschaw das Ziel Sage Nicht Viel Consider the matter but say little (Quedlinburg).

Besser Land und Lud Verloren als ein Falscher Aid Geschworn Better to lose land and wealth than swear a false oath (Hesse).

Bey Gott ist Rath und That With God is counsel and deed (Mansfeld).

Britanniarum Regina Queen of the Britains (Britain, Victoria).

Britt Omn Rex King of all the Britains (i.e. Britain and the overseas dominions) (Britain, 1902–52).

Cal et Car Com de Fugger in Zin et Norn Sen & Adm Fam Cajetan and Carl, Counts of Fugger in Zinnenberg and Nordendorf, Lords and Administrators of the Family (Empire, Fugger).

Candide et Constanter Sincerely and steadfastly (Hesse-Cassel).

Candide sed Provide Clearly but cautiously (Osterwitz).

Candore et Amore With sincerity and love (Fulda).

Candore et Constantia With sincerity and constancy (Bavaria).

Capit Cath Ecclesia Monasteriensis Chapter of the Cathedral Church of Munster (Munster).

Capit Eccle Metropolit Colon Chapter of the Metropolitan Church of Cologne (Cologne).

Capitulum Regnans Sede Vacante Chapter governing, the See being vacant (Eichstadt).

Carola Magna Ducissa Feliciter Regnante Grand Duchess Charlotte, happily reigning (Luxembourg).

Carolus a Carolo Charles (I) to Charles (II) (England).

Cedunt Prementi Fata The fates yield to him who presses (Ploen, Hese-Cassel).

Charitate et Candore With charity and sincerity (East Frisia).

Charta Magna Bavariae The Great Charter of Bavaria (Bavaria).

Christo Auspice Regno I reign under the auspices of Christ (England, Charles I).

Christus Spes Una Salutis Christ is our one hope of salvation (Cleve).

Chur Mainz Electoral Principality of Mainz (Mainz).

Circumeundo Servat et Ornat It serves and decorates by going around (Sweden).

Civibus Quorum Pietas Coniuratione Die III Mai MDCCXCI Obrutam et Deletam Libertate Polona Tueri Conabatur Respublica Resurgens To the citizens whose piety the resurgent commonwealth tried to protect Poland overturned and deprived of liberty by the conspiracy of the third day of May 1791 (Poland).

Civitas Lucemborgiensis Millesimum Ovans Expletannum Completing the celebration of a thousand years of the city of Luxembourg (Luxembourg).

Civium Industria Floret Civitas By the industry of its people the state flourishes (Festival of Britain crown, 1951).

Cluniaco Cenobio Petrus et Paulus Peter and Paul from the Abbey of Cluny (Cluny).

Comes Provincie Fili Regis Francie Court of Provence and son of the King of France (Provence).

Communitas et Senatus Bonon City and senate of Bologna (Bologna).

Concordia Fratrum The harmony of the brothers (Iever).

Concordia Patriae Nutrix Peace, the nurse of the fatherland (Waldeck).

Concordia Res Parvae Crescunt Little things increase through harmony (Batavian Republic).

Concordia Res Parvae Crescunt, Discordia Dilabuntur By harmony little things increase, by discord they fall apart (Lowenstein-Wertheim-Virneburg).

Concordia Stabili With lasting peace (Hildesheim).

Confidens Dno Non Movetur He who trusts in God is unmoved (Spanish Netherlands).

Confidentia in Deo et Vigilantia Trust in God and vigilance (Prussian Asiatic Company).

Confoederato Helvetica Swiss Confederation (Switzerland)

Conjuncto Felix Fortunate in his connections (Solms).

Conservator Urbis Suae Saviour of his city (Rome, 4th century).

Consilio et Aequitate With deliberation and justice (Fulda).

Consilio et Virtutis With deliberation and valour (Hesse-Cassel).

Constanter et Sincere Steadfastly and sincerely (Lautern).

Crescite et Multiplicamini Increase and multiply (Maryland).

Cristiana Religio Christian religion (Germany, 11th century).

Crux Benedicat May the cross bless you (Oldenburg).

Cuius Cruore Sanati Sumus By His sacrifice are we healed (Reggio).

Cultores Sui Deus Protegit God protects His followers (England, Charles I).

Cum Deo et Die (Jure) With God and the day (Wurttemberg).

Cum Deo et Jure With God and the law (Wurttemberg).

Cum Deo et Labore With God and work (Wittgenstein).

Cum His Qui Orderant Pacem Eram Pacificus With those who order peace I was peaceful (Zug).

Curie Bonthon to so Doulo Protect his servant, o Lord (Byzantine Empire).

Custos Regni Deus God is the guardian of the kingdom (Naples and Sicily).

Da Gloriam Deo et Eius Genitrici Marie Give glory to God and His mother Mary (Wurttemberg).

Da Mihi Virtutem Contra Hostes Tuos Give me

valour against mine enemies (Netherlands, Charles V).

Dat Wort is Fleis Gworden The word is made flesh (Muster).

Date Caesaris Caesari et Quae Sunt Dei Deo Render unto Caesar the things that are Caesar's and unto God the things that are God's (Stralsund).

De Oficina . . . From the mint of . . . (France, medieval).

Decreto Reipublicae Nexu Confoederationis Iunctae Die V Xbris MDCCXCII Stanislao Augusto Regnante By decree of the state in conjunction with the joint federation on the fifth day of December 1792, Stanislaus Augustus ruling (Poland).

Decus et Tutamen An ornament and a safeguard (Britain, pound).

Deducet Nos Mirabiliter Dextera Tua Thy right hand will guide us miraculously (Savoy).

Denarium Terrae Mariae Penny of Maryland (Maryland).

Deo Conservatori Pacis To God, preserver of peace (Brandenburg-Ansbach).

Deo OM Auspice Suaviter et Fortiter sed Luste nec Sibi sed Suis Under the auspices of God, greatest and best, pleasantly and bravely but justly, not for himself but for his people (Speyer).

Deo Patriae et Subditio For God, fatherland and neighbourhood (Mainz).

Der Recht Glaubt In Ewig Lebt Who believes in right will live in eternity (Linange-Westerburg).

Der Rhein ist Deutschlands Strom Nicht Deutschlands Grenze The Rhine is Germany's River not Germany's Frontier.

Deum Solum Adorabis You will venerate God alone (Hesse).

Deus Constituit Regna God establishes kingdoms (Ni jmegen).

Deus Dat Qui Vult God gives to him who wishes (Hanau-Munzenberg).

Deus et Dominus God and Lord (Rome, 3rd century).

Deus in Adiutorium Meum Intende God stretch out in my assistance (France).

Deus Providebit God will provide (Lowenstein-Wertheim-Virneburg).

Deus Refugium Meum God is my refuge (Cleve).

Deus Solatium Meum God is my comfort (Sweden).

Dextera Domini Exaltavit Me The right hand of God has raised me up (Modena, Spain).

Dextra Dei Exalta Me The right hand of God exalts me (Denmark).

Dieu et Mon Droit God and my right (Britain, George IV).

Dilexit Dns Andream The Lord delights in St Andrew (Holstein).

Dilexit Dominus Decorem Iustitiae The Lord is pleased with the beauty of justice (Unterwalden).

Dirige Deus Gressus Meos O God, direct my steps (Tuscany, Britain, Una £5).

Discerne Causam Meam Distinguish my cause (Savoy).

Divina Benedictiae et Caesarea Iustitia Sacrifice of blessings and imperial justice (Coblenz).

Dn Ihs Chs Rex Regnantium Lord Jesus Christ, King of Kings (Rome, Justinian II).

Dns Ptetor Ms Z Lib'ator Ms The Lord is my protector and liberator (Scotland, David II).

Dominabitur Gentium et Ipse He himself will also be lord of the nations (Austrian Netherlands).

Domine Conserva Nos in Pace O Lord preserve us in peace (Basle, Mulhausen).

Domine Elegisti Lilium Tibi O Lord Thou hast chosen the lily for Thyself (France, Louis XIV).

Domine ne in Furore Tuo Arguas Me O Lord rebuke me not in Thine anger (England, Edward III).

Domine Probasti Me et Congnovisti Me O Lord Thou hast tested me and recognised me (Mantua).

Domini est Regnum The Kingdom is the Lord's (Austrian Netherlands).

Dominus Deus Omnipotens Rex Lord God, almighty King (Viking coins).

Dominus Mihi Adiutor The Lord is my helper (Spanish Netherlands).

Dominus Providebit The Lord will provide (Berne).

Dominus Spes Populi Sui The Lord is the hope of his people (Lucerne).

Donum Dei ex Fodinis Vilmariens A gift of God from the Vilmar mines (Coblenz).

Duce Deo Fide et Justicia By faith and justice lead us to God (Ragusa).

Dum Praemor Amplior I increase while I die prematurely (Savoy).

Dum Spiro Spero While I live, I hope (Pontefract siege coins).

Dum Totum Compleat Orbem Until it fills the world (France, Henri II).

Dura Pati Virtus Valour endures hardships (Saxe-Lauenburg).

Durae Necessitatis Through force of necessity (Bommel siege, 1599).

Durum Telum Necessitas Hardship is a weapon of necessity (Minden).

Dux et Gubernatores Reip Genu Duke and governors of the republic of Genoa (Genoa).

E Pluribus Unum One out of more (USA).

Eccl S. Barbarae Patronae Fodin Kuttenbergensium Duo Flor Arg Puri The church of St Barbara, patron of the Kuttensberg mines, two florins of pure silver (Hungary).

Een en Ondelbaer Sterk One and indivisible (Batavian Republic).

Eendracht Mag Macht Unity makes strength (Belgium, South African Republic).

Einigkeit Recht und Freiheit   Union, right and freedom (Germany).

Electorus Saxoniae Administrator   Elector and administrator of Saxony (Saxony).

Elimosina   Alms (France, Pepin).

Ep Fris & Ratisb Ad Prum Pp Coad Aug   Bishop of Freising and Regensburg, administrator of Pruem, prince-provost, co-adjutant bishop of Augsburg (Trier).

Equa Libertas Deo Gratia Frat Pax in Virtute Tua et in Domino Confido   I believe in equal liberty by the grace of God, brotherly love in Thy valour and in the Lord (Burgundy).

Equitas Iudicia Tua Dom   Equity and Thy judgments O Lord (Gelderland).

Espoir Me Conforte   Hope comforts me (Mansfeld).

Espreuve Faicto Par Lexpres Commandement du Roy   Proof made by the express commandment of the King (France, piedforts).

Et in Minimis Integer   Faithful even in the smallest things (Olmutz).

Ex Auro Argentes Resurgit   From gold it arises, silver again (Sicily).

Ex Auro Sinico   From Chinese gold (Denmark).

Ex Flammis Orior   I arise from the flames (Hohenlohe-Neuenstein-Ohringen).

Ex Fodinis Bipontio Seelbergensibus   From the Seelberg mines of Zweibrucken (Pfalz-Birkenfeld).

Ex Metallo Novo   From new metal (Spain).

Ex Uno Omnis Nostra Salus   From one is all our salvation (Eichstadt, Mulhouse).

Ex Vasis Argent Cleri Mogunt Pro Aris et Focis   From the silver vessels of the clergy of Mainz for altars and for hearths (Mainz).

Ex Visceribus Fodinse Bieber   From the bowels of the Bieber mine (Hanau-Munzenberg).

Exaltabitur in Gloria   He shall be exalted in glory (England, quarter nobles).

Exemplum Probati Numismatis   An example of a proof coin (France, Louis XIII piedforts).

Exemtae Eccle Passau Episc et SRI Princ   Prince Bishop of the freed church of Passau, prince of the Holy Roman Empire (Passau).

Expectate Veni   Come, o expected one (Roman Britain, Carausius).

Extremum Subidium Campen   Kampen under extreme siege (Kampen, 1578).

Exurgat Deus et Dissipentur Inimici Eius   Let God arise and let His enemies be scattered (England, James I).

Faciam Eos in Gentem Unam   I will make them one nation (England, unites and laurels).

Faith and Truth I will Bear unto You   (UK £5, 1993).

Fata Consiliis Potiora   The fates are more powerful than councils (Hesse-Cassel).

Fata Viam Invenient   The fates will find a way (Gelderland).

Fecit Potentiam in Brachio Suo   He put power in your forearm (Lorraine).

Fecunditas   Fertility (Naples and Sicily).

Fel Temp Reparatio   The restoration of lucky times (Rome, AD 348).

Felicitas Perpetua   Everlasting good fortune (Rome, Constantius II).

Felix coniunctio   Happy Union (Brandenburg-Ansbach).

Fiat Misericordia Tua Dne   Let Thy mercy be O Lord (Gelderland).

Fiat Voluntas Domini Perpetuo   Let the goodwill of the Lord last for ever (Fulda).

Fidei Defensor   Defender of the Faith (Britain).

Fidelitate et Fortitudine   With fidelity and fortitude (Batthanyi).

Fideliter et Constanter   Faithfully and steadfastly (Saxe-Coburg-Gotha).

Fidem Servando Patriam Tuendo   By keeping faith and protecting the fatherland (Savoy).

Filius Augustorum   Son of emperors (Rome, 4th century).

Fisci Iudaici Calumnia Sublata   The false accusation of the Jewish tax lifted (Rome, Nerva).

Florent Concordia Regna   Through harmony kingdoms flourish (England, Charles I and II).

Fortitudo et Laus Mea Dominu   Fortitude and my praise in the Lord (Sardinia).

Free Trade to Africa by Act of Parliment *(Sic)* (Gold Coast).

Friedt Ernehrt Unfriedt Verzehrt   Peace nourishes, unrest wastes (Brunswick).

Fulgent Sic Littora Rheni   Thus shine the banks of the Rhine (Mannheim).

Fundator Pacis   Founder of peace (Rome, Severus).

Gaudium Populi Romani   The joy of the Roman people (Rome, 4th century).

Gen C Mar VI Dim Col USC & RAMAI Cons & S Conf M   General field marshal, colonel of the only dragoon regiment, present privy councillor of both their sacred imperial and royal apostolic majesties, and state conference minister (Batthanyi).

Gerecht und Beharrlich   Just and steadfast (Bavaria).

Germ Hun Boh Rex AAD Loth Ven Sal   King of Germany, Hungary and Bohemia, Archduke of Austria, Duke of Lorraine, Venice and Salzburg (Austria).

Germ Jero Rex Loth Bar Mag Het Dux   King of Germany, Jerusalem, Lorraine and Bar, Grand Duke of Tuscany (Austrian Netherlands).

Germania Voti Compos   Germany sharing the vows (Brandenburg-Ansbach).

Gloria ex Amore Patriae   Glory from love of country (Denmark).

Gloria in Excelsis Deo   Glory to God in the highest (France, Sweden).

Gloria Novi Saeculi   The glory of a new century (Rome, Gratian).

God With Us (England, Commonwealth).

Godt Met Ons God with us (Oudewater).

Gottes Freundt der Pfaffen Feindt God's friend, the Pope's enemy (Brunswick, Christian).

Gratia Dei Sum Id Quod Sum By the grace of God, I am what I am (Navarre).

Gratia Di Rex By the grace of God, king (France, 8th century).

Gratitudo Concivibus Exemplum Posteritati Gratitude to fellow Citizens, an example to posterity (Poland).

Gud och Folket God and the people (Sweden).

Hac Nitimur Hanc Tuemur With this we strive, this we shall defend (Batavian Republic).

Hac Sub Tutela Under this protection (Eichstadt).

Haec Sunt Munera Minerae S Antony Eremitae These are the rewards of the mine of St Antony the hermit (Hildesheim).

Hanc Deus Dedit God has given this (Pontefract siege coins).

Hanc Tuemur Hac Nitimur This we defend, by this we strive (Batavian Republic).

Has Nisi Periturus Mihi Adimat Nemo Let no one remove these (Letters) from me under penalty of death (Commonwealth, edge inscription).

Henricus Rosas Regna Jacobus Henry (united) the roses, James the kingdoms (England and Scotland, James VI and I).

Herculeo Vincta Nodo Bound by a Herculean fetter (Savoy).

Herr Nach Deinem Willen O Lord Thy will be done (Palatinate, Erbach).

Herre Gott Verleich Uns Gnade Lord God grant us grace (Brunswick).

Hic Est Qui Multum Orat Pro Populo Here is he who prays a lot for the people (Paderborn).

Hir Steid te Biscop Here is represented the bishop (Gittelde).

His Ventis Vela Levantur By these winds the sails are raised up (Hesse-Cassel).

Hispaniarum Infans Infante of Spain and its dominions (Spain).

Hispaniarum et Ind Rex King of Spain and the Indies.

Hispaniarum Rex King of Spain (Spain).

Hoc Signo Victor Eris With this sign you will be victor (Rome, Vetranio).

Honeste et Decenter Honestly and decently (Nassau-Idstein).

Honi Soit Qui Mal y Pense Evil to him who evil thinks (Britain, George III).

Honni Soit Qui Mal y Pense (Hesse-Cassel).

Hospitalis et S Sepul Hierusal Hospital and Holy Sepulchre of Jerusalem (Malta).

Hun Boh Gal Rex AA Lo Wi et in Fr Dux King of Hungary, Bohemia and Galicia, Archduke of Austria, Dalmatia, Lodomeria, Wurzburg and Duke in Franconia (Austria).

Hung Boh Lomb et Ven Gal Lod III Rex Aa King of Hungary, Bohemia, Lombardo-Venezia, Galicia, Lodomeria and Illyria, Archduke of Austria (Austria).

Ich Dien I serve (Aberystwyth 2d, UK 2p).

Ich Getrawe Got in Aller Noth I trust in God in all my needs (Hesse-Marburg).

Ich Habe Nur Ein Vaterland und das Heisst Deutschland I have only one fatherland and that is called Germany (Germany).

Ielithes Penniae Penny of Gittelde (Gittelde, 11th century).

Iesus Autem Transiens Per Medium Illorum Ibat But Jesus, passing through the midst of them, went His way (England, Scotland, Anglo-Gallic).

Iesus Rex Noster et Deus Noster Jesus is our king and our God (Florence).

Ihs Xs Rex Regnantium Jesus Christ, King of Kings (Byzantine Empire).

Ihsus Xristus Basileu Baslie Jesus Christ, King of Kings (Byzantine Empire).

Imago Sanch Regis Illustris Castelle Legionis e Toleto The image of Sancho the illustrious king of Castile, Leon and Toledo.

In Casus Per Vigil Omnes In all seasons through vigil (Wertheim).

In Deo Meo Transgrediar Murum In my God I shall pass through walls (Teschen).

In Deo Spes Mea In God is my hope (Gelderland).

In Domino Fiducia Nostra In the Lord is our trust (Iever).

In Equitate Tua Vivificasti Me In thy equity Thou hast vivified me (Gelderland).

In God We Trust (USA).

In Hoc Signo Vinces In this sign shalt thou conquer (Portugal).

In Honore Sci Mavrici Marti In honour of the martyr St Maurice (St Maurice, 8th century).

In Manibus Domini sortes Meae In the hands of the Lord are my fates (Mainz siege, 1688–9).

In Memor Vindicatae Libere ac Relig In memory of the establishment of freedom and religion (Sweden).

In Memoriam Conjunctionis Utriusque Burgraviatus Norice In memory of the union of both burgraviates in peace (Brandenburg-Ansbach).

In Memorian Connub Feliciaes Inter Princ Her Frider Carol et Dub Sax August Louis Frider Rodas D 28 Nov 1780 Celebrati In memory of the most happy marriage between the hereditary prince Friedrich Karl and the Duchess of Saxony Augusta Louisa Frederika, celebrated on 28 Nov 1780 (Schwarzburg-Rudolstadt).

In Memorian Felicisssimi Matrimonii In memory of the most happy marriage (Wied).

In Memoriam Pacis Teschinensis Commemorating the Treaty of Teschen (Brandenburg-Ansbach).

In Nomine Domini Amen In the name of the Lord amen (Zaltbommel).

In Omnem Terram Sonus Eorum In to all the land

their shall go sound (Chateau Renault, Papal States).

In Silencio et Spe Fortitudo Mea In silence and hope is my fortitude (Brandenburg-Kustrin).

In Spe et Silentio Fortitudo Mea In hope and silence is my fortitude (Vianen).

In Te Domine Confido In you O Lord I place my trust (Hesse).

In Te Domine Speravi In You, O Lord, I have hoped (Gurk).

In Terra Pax Peace in the land (Papacy).

In Via Virtuti Nulla Via There is no way for virtue on the way. (Veldenz).

Ind Imp, Indiae Imperator, Imperatrix Emperor (Empress) of India (Britain).

India Tibi Cessit India has yielded to thee (Portuguese India).

Infestus Infestis Hostile to the troublesome (Savoy).

Inimicos Eius Induam Confusione As for his enemies, I shall clothe them in shame (Sardinia, England, Edward VI).

Insignia Capituli Brixensis The badge of the chapter of Brixen (Brixen).

Isti Sunt Patres Tui Verique Pastores These are your fathers and true shepherds (Papacy).

Iudicium Melius Posteritatis Erit Posterity's judgment will be better (Paderborn).

Iure et Tempore By right and time (Groningen).

Iusques a Sa Plenitude As far as your plenitude (France, Henri II).

Iuste et Constanter Justly and constantly (Paderborn).

Iustirt Adjusted (Hesse-Cassel).

Iustitia et Concordia Justice and harmony (Zurich).

Iustitia et Mansuetudine By justice and mildness (Bavaria, Cologne).

Iustitia Regnorum Fundamentum Justice is the foundation of kingdoms (Austria).

Iustitia Thronum Firmat Justice strengthens the throne (England, Charles I).

Iustus Non Derelinquitur The just person is not deserted (Brandenburg-Calenberg).

Iustus Ut Palma Florebit The just will flourish like the palm (Portugal).

L Mun Planco Rauracorum Illustratori Vetustissimo To L Municius Plancus the most ancient and celebrated of the Rauraci (Basle).

Landgr in Cleggov Com in Sulz Dux Crum Landgrave of Klettgau, count of Sulz, duke of Krumlau (Schwarzburg-Sonderhausen).

Latina Emeri Munita Latin money of Merida (Suevi).

Lege et Fide By law and faith (Austria).

Lex Tua Veritas Thy law is the truth (Tuscany).

Liberta Eguaglianza Freedom and equality (Venice).

Libertad en la Ley Freedom within the law (Mexico).

Libertas Carior Auro Freedom is dearer than gold (St Gall).

Libertas Vita Carior Freedom is dearer than life (Kulenberg).

Libertas Xpo Firmata Freedom strengthened by Christ (Genoa).

Liberte, Egalite, Fraternite Liberty, equality, fraternity (France).

Lucerna Pedibus Meis Verbum Est Thy word is a lamp unto mine feet (England, Edward VI).

Lumen ad Revelationem Gentium Light to enlighten the nations (Papacy).

L'Union Fait la Force The union makes strength (Belgium)

Macula Non Est in Te There is no sin in Thee (Essen).

Magnus ab Integro Saeculorum Nascitur Ordo The great order of the centuries is born anew (Bavaria).

Mandavit Dominus Palatie hanc Monetam Fiert The lord of the Palatine ordained this coin to be made (Balath).

Manibus Ne Laedar Avaris Lest I be injured by greedy hands (Sweden).

Mar Bran Sac Rom Imp Arcam et Elec Sup Dux Siles Margrave of Brandenburg, archchamberlain of the Holy Roman Empire and elector, senior duke of Silesia (Prussia).

Maria Mater Domini Xpi Mary mother of Christ the Lord (Teutonic Knights).

Maria Unxit Pedes Xpisti Mary washes the feet of Christ (France, Rene d'Anjou).

Mater Castrorum Mother of fortresses (Rome, Marcus Aurelius).

Matrimonio Conjuncti Joined in wedlock (Austria).

Me Coniunctio Servat Dum Scinditur Frangor The relationship serves me while I am being torn to pieces (Lowenstein-Wertheim).

Mediolani Dux Duke of Milan (Milan).

Mediolani et Man Duke of Mantua and Milan (Milan).

Memor Ero Tui Iustina Virgo I shall remember you, o maiden Justina (Venice).

Merces Laborum Wages of work (Wurzburg).

Mirabilia Fecit He wrought marvels (Viking coinage).

Misericordia Di Rex King by the mercy of God (France, Louis II).

Mo Arg Ord Foe Belg D Gel & CZ Silver coin of the order of the Belgian Federation, duchy of Guelder-land, county of Zutphen (Guelderland).

Moneta Abbatis Coin of the abbey (German ecclesiastical coins, 13th–14th centuries).

Moneta Argentiae Ord Foed Belgii Holl Silver coin of the federated union of Belgium and Holland (Batavian Republic).

Mo No Arg Con Foe Belg Pro Hol New silver coin of the Belgian Federation, province of Holland (Holland).

Mo No Arg Pro Confoe Belg Trai Holl   New silver coin of the confederated Belgian provinces, Utrecht and Holland (Batavian Republic).

Mon Lib Reip Bremens   Coin of the free state of Bremen (Bremen).

Mon Nova Arg Duc Curl Ad Norma Tal Alb   New silver coin of the duchy of Courland, according to the standard of the Albert thaler (Courland).

Mon Nov Castri Imp   New coin of the Imperial free city of . . . (Friedberg).

Moneta Bipont   Coin of Zweibrucken (Pfalz-Birkenfeld-Zweibrucken).

Monet Capit Cathedr Fuld Sede Vacante   Coin of the cathedral chapter of Fulda, the see being vacant (Fulda).

Moneta in Obsidione Tornacensi Cusa   Coin struck during the siege of Tournai (Tournai, 1709).

Moneta Livosesthonica   Coin of Livonia (Estonia).

Moneta Nov Arg Regis Daniae   New silver coin of the king of Denmark (Denmark).

Moneta Nova Ad Norman Conventionis   New coin according to the Convention standard (Orsini-Rosenberg).

Moneta Nova Domini Imperatoris   New coin of the lord emperor (Brunswick, 13th century).

Moneta Nova Lubecensis   New coin of Lubeck.

Moneta Nova Reipublicae Halae Suevicae   New coin of the republic of Hall in Swabia.

Moneta Reipublicae Ratisbonensis   Coin of the republic of Regensburg.

Nach Alt Reichs Schrot und Korn   According to the old empire's grits and grain (Hesse).

Nach dem Conventions Fusse   According to the Convention's basis (German Conventionsthalers).

Nach dem Frankf Schlus   According to the Frankfurt standard (Solms).

Nach dem Schlus der V Staend   According to the standard of the union (Hesse).

Navigare Necesse Est   It is necessary to navigate (Germany).

Nec Aspera Terrent   Nor do difficulties terrify (Brunswick).

Nec Cito Nec Temere   Neither hastily nor rashlly (Cambrai).

Nec Numina Desunt   Nor is the divine will absent (Savoy).

Nec Temere Nec Timide   Neither rashly nor timidly (Danzig, Lippe).

Necessitas Legem Non Habet   Necessity has no law (Magdeburg).

Nemo Me Impune Lacessit   No one touches me with impunity (UK, Scottish pound edge inscription).

Nihil Restat Reliqui   No relic remains (Ypres).

Nil Ultra Aras   Nothing beyond the rocks (Franque-mont).

No Nobis Dne Sed Noi Tuo Da Gloriam   Not to us, o Lord but to Thy name be glory given (France, Francis I).

Nobilissimum Dom Ac Com in Lipp & St   Most noble lord and count in Lippe and Sternberg (Schaumburg-Lippe).

Nomen Domini Turris Fortissima   The name of the Lord is the strongest tower (Frankfurt).

Non Aes Sed Fides   Not bronze but trust (Malta).

Non Est Mortale Quod Opto   What I desire is not mortal. (Mecklenburg).

Non Mihi Sed Populo   Not to me but to the people (Bavaria).

Non Relinquam Vos Orphanos   I shall not leave you as orphans (Papacy).

Non Surrexit Major   None greater has arisen (Genoa, Malta).

Nullum Simulatum Diuturnum Tandem   Nothing that is feigned lasts long (Wittgenstein).

Nummorum Famulus   The servant of the coinage (England, tin halfpence and farthings).

Nunquam Retrorsum   Never backwards (Brunswick-Wolfenbuttel).

O Crux Ave Spes Unica   Hail, o Cross, our only hope (England half-angels, France, Rene d'Anjou).

O Maria Ora Pro Me   O Mary pray for me (Bavaria).

Ob Cives Servatos   On account of the rescued citizens (Rome, Augustus).

Oculi Domini Super Iustos   The eyes of the Lord look down on the just (Neuchatel).

Omnia Auxiliante Maria   Mary helping everything (Schwyz).

Omnia Cum Deo   Everything with God (Reuss-Greiz).

Omnia cum Deo et Nihil Sine Eo   Everthing with God and nothing without Him (Erbach).

Omnis Potestas a Deo Est   All power comes from God (Sweden).

Opp & Carn Dux Comm Rittb SCM Cons Int & Compi Mareschal   Duke of Troppau and Carniola, count of Rietberg, privy councillor of his sacred imperial majesty, field marshal (Liechtenstein).

Opp & Carn . . . Aur Velleris Eques   Duke of Troppau . . . knight of the Golden Fleece (Liechtenstein).

Opportune   Conveniently (Savoy).

Optimus Princeps   Best prince (Rome, Trajan).

Opulentia Salerno   Wealthy Salerno (Siculo-Norman kingdom).

Pace et Iustitia   With peace and justice (Spanish Netherlands).

Pacator Orbis   Pacifier of the world (Rome, Aurelian).

Palma Sub Pondere Crescit   The palm grows under its weight (Waldeck).

Pater Noster   Our Father (Flanders, 14th century).

Pater Patriae   Farther of his country (Rome, Caligula).

Patria Si Dreptul Meu   The country and my right (Roumania).

Patrimon Henr Frid Sorte Divisum   The heritage of Heinrich Friedrich divided by lot (Hohenlohe-Langenberg).

Patrimonia Beati Petri   The inheritance of the blessed Peter (Papacy).

Patrona Franconiae   Patron of Franconia (Wurzburg).

Pax Aeterna   Eternal peace (Rome, Marcus Aurelius).

Pax et Abundantia   Peace and plenty (Burgundy, Gelderland).

Pax Missa Per Orbem   Peace sent throughout the world (England, Anne).

Pax Petrus   Peace Peter (Trier, 10th century).

Pax Praevalet Armis   May peace prevail by force of arms (Mainz).

Pax Quaeritur Bello   Peace is sought by war (Commonwealth, Cromwell).

Pecunia Totum Circumit Orbem   Money goes round the whole world (Brazil).

Per Aspera Ad Astra   Through difficulties to the stars (Mecklenburg-Schwerin).

Per Angusta ad Augusta   Through precarious times to the majestic (Solms-Roedelheim, a pun on the name of the ruler Johan August).

Per Crucem Tuam Salva Nos Christe Redemptor   By Thy cross save us, O Christ our Redeemer (England, angels).

Per Crucem Tuam Salva Nos Xpe Redemt   By Thy cross save us, O Christ our Redeemer (Portugal, 15th century).

Perdam Babillonis Nomen   May the name of Babylon perish (Naples).

Perennitati Iustissimi Regis   For the duration of the most just being (France, Louis XIII).

Perennitati Principis Galliae Restitutionis   For the duration of the restoration of the prince of the Gauls (France, Henri IV).

Perfer et Obdura Bruxella   Carry on and stick it out, Brussels (Brussels siege, 1579–80).

Perpetuus in Nemet Vivar   Hereditary count in Nemt-Ujvar (Batthanyi).

Pietate et Constantia   By piety and constancy (Fulda).

Pietate et Iustitia   By piety and justice (Denmark).

Plebei Urbanae Frumento Constituto   Free distribu-tion of grain to the urban working-class established (Rome, Nerva).

Pleidio Wyf Im Gwlad   True am I to my country (UK, Welsh pound edge inscription).

Plus Ultra   Beyond (the Pillars of Hercules) (Spanish America).

Point du Couronne sans Peine   Point of the crown without penalty (Coburg).

Pons Civit Castellana   The bridge of the town of Castellana (Papacy).

Populus et Senatus Bonon   The people and senate of Bologna (Bologna).

Post Mortem Patris Pro Filio   For the son after his father's death (Pontefract siege coins).

Post Tenebras Lux   After darkness light (Geneva).

Post Tenebras Spero Lucem   After darkness I hope for light (Geneva).

Posui Deum Adiutorem Meum   I have made God my helper (England, Ireland, 1351–1603).

Praesidium et Decus   Protection and ornament (Bologna).

Prima Sedes Galliarum   First see of the Gauls (Lyon).

Primitiae Fodin Kuttenb ab Aerari Iterum Susceptarum   First results dug from the Kuttenberg mines in a renewed undertaking (Austria).

Princps Iuventutis   Prince of youth (Roman Empire).

Pro Defensione Urbis et Patriae   For the defence of city and country (France, Louis XIV).

Pro Deo et Patria   For God and the fatherland (Fulda).

Pro Deo et Populo   For God and the people (Bavaria).

Pro Ecclesia et Pro Patria   For the church and the fatherland (Constance).

Pro Fausio PP Reitur VS   For happy returns of the princes of the Two Sicilies (Naples and Sicily).

Pro Lege et Grege   For law and the flock (Fulda).

Pro maximo Dei Gloria et Bono Publico   For the greatest glory of God and the good of the people (Wurttemberg).

Pro Patria   For the fatherland (Wurzburg).

Propitio Deo Secura Ago   With God's favour I lead a secure life. (Saxe-Lauenburg).

Protector Literis Literae Nummis Corona et Salus   A protection to the letters (on the face of the coin), the letters (on the edge) are a garland and a safeguard to the coinage (Commonwealth, Cromwell broad).

Protege Virgo Pisas   Protect Pisa, O Virgin (Pisa).

Provide et Constanter   Wisely and firmly (Wurttem-berg).

Providentia et Pactis   Through foresight and pacts (Brandenburg-Ansbach).

Providentia Optimi Principis   With the foresight of the best prince (Naples and Sicily).

Proxima Fisica Finis   Nearest to natural end (Orciano).

Proxima Soli   Nearest to the sun (Modena).

Pulcra Virtutis Imago   The beautiful image of virtue (Genoa).

Pupillum et Viduam Suscipiat   May he support the orphan and the widow (Savoy).

Quae Deus Conjunxit Nemo Separet   What God hath joined let no man put asunder (England, James I).

Quem Quadragesies et Semel Patriae Natum Esse Gratulamur   Whom we congratulate for the forty-first time for being born for the fatherland (Lippe-Detmold).

Qui Dat Pauperi Non Indigebit   Who gives to the poor will never be in need (Munster).

Quid Non Cogit Necessitas   To what does Necessity not drive. (Ypres).

Quin Matrimonii Lustrum Celebrant   They celebrate their silver wedding (Austria, 1879).

Quocunque Gesseris (Jeceris) Stabit   Whichever way you throw it it will stand (Isle of Man).

Quod Deus Vult Hoc Semper Fit   What God wishes always occurs. (Saxe-Weimar).

Reconduntur non Retonduntur   They are laid up in store, not thundered back (Savoy).

Recta Tueri   Defend the right (Austria).

Recte Constanter et Fortiter   Rightly, constantly and bravely (Bavaria).

Recte Faciendo Neminem Timeas   May you fear no one in doing right. (Solms-Laubach).

Rector Orbis   Ruler of the world (Rome, Didius Julianus).

Rectus et Immotus   Right and immovable (Hesse).

Redde Cuique Quod Suum Est   Render to each that which is his own (England, Henry VIII).

Redeunt antiqui Gaudia Moris   There return the joys of ancient custom (Regensburg).

Reg Pr Pol et Lith Saxon Dux   Royal prince of Poland and Lithuania and duke of Saxony (Trier).

Regia Boruss Societas Asiat Embdae   Royal Prussian Asiatic Society of Emden (Prussia).

Regier Mich Her Nach Deinen Wort   Govern me here according to Thy word (Palatinate).

Regnans Capitulum Ecclesiae Cathedralis Ratisbonensis Sede Vacante   Administering the chapter of the cathedral church at Regensburg, the see being vacant (Regensburg).

Regni Utr Sic et Hier   Of the kingdom of the Two Sicilies and of Jerusalem (Naples and Sicily).

Religio Protestantium Leges Angliae Libertas Parliamenti   The religion of the Protestants, the laws of England and the freedom of Parliament (England, Royalists, 1642).

Relinquo Vos Liberos ab Utroque Homine   I leave you as children of each man (San Marino).

Restauracao da Independencia   Restoration of inde-pendence (Portugal, 1990).

Restitutor Exercitus   Restorer of the army (Rome, Aurelian).

Restitutor Galliarum   Restorer of the Gauls (Rome, Gallienus).

Restitutor Generis Humani   Restorer of mankind (Rome, Valerian).

Restitutor Libertatis   Restorer of freedom (Rome, Constantine).

Restitutor Orbis   Restorer of the world (Rome, Valerian).

Restitutor Orientis   Restorer of the east (Rome, Valerian).

Restitutor Saeculi   Restorer of the century (Rome, Valerian).

Restitutor Urbis   Restorer of the city (Rome, Severus).

Rosa Americana Utile Dulci   The American rose, useful and sweet (American colonies).

Rosa Sine Spina   A rose without a thorn (England, Tudor coins).

Rutilans Rosa Sine Spina   A dazzling rose without a thorn (England, Tudor gold coins).

S Annae Fundgruben Ausb Tha in N Oe   Mining thaler of the St Anne mine in Lower Austria (Austria).

S Ap S Leg Nat Germ Primas   Legate of the Holy Apostolic See, born Primate of Germany (Salzburg).

S Carolus Magnus Fundator   Charlemagne founder (Munster).

S. Gertrudis Virgo Prudens Niviella   St Gertrude the wise virgin of Nivelles (Nivelles).

SI Aul Reg Her & P Ge H Post Mag   General hereditary postmaster, supreme of the imperial court of the hereditary kingdom and provinces (Paar).

S. Ian Bapt F. Zachari   St John the Baptist, son of Zachary (Florence).

S. Kilianus Cum Sociis Francorum Apostoli   St Kilian and his companions, apostles to the Franks (Wurzburg).

S. Lambertus Patronus Leodiensis   St Lambert, patron of Liege (Liege).

Sac Nupt Celeb Berol   For the holy matrimony celebrated at Berlin (Brandenburg-Ansbach).

Sac Rom Imp   Holy Roman Empire (German states).

Sac Rom Imp Provisor Iterum   Administrator of the Holy Roman Empire for the second time (Saxony).

Salus Generis Humani   Safety of mankind (Rome, Vindex).

Salus Patriae   Safety of the fatherland (Italy).

Salus Populi   The safety of the people (Spain).

Salus Provinciarum   Safety of the provinces (Rome, Postumus).

Salus Publica Salus Mea   Public safety is my safety (Sweden).

Salus Reipublicae   The safety of the republic (Rome, Theodosius II).

Salus Reipublicae Suprema Lex   The safety of the republic is the supreme law (Poland).

Salvam Fac Rempublicam Tuam   Make your state safe (San Marino).

Sanctus Iohannes Innoce   St John the harmless (Gandersheim).

Sans Changer   Without changing (Isle of Man).

Sans Eclat   Without pomp (Bouchain siege, 1711).

Sapiente Diffidentia   Wise distrust (Teschen).

Scutum Fidei Proteget Eum / Eam   The shield of faith shall protect him / her (England, Edward VI and Elizabeth I).

Secundum Voluntatem Tuam Domine   Your favourable will o Lord (Hesse).

Securitati Publicae   For the public safety (Brandenburg-Ansbach).

Sede Vacante   The see being vacant (Papal states, Vatican and ecclesiastical coinage).

Sena Vetus Alpha et W Principum et Finis Old Siena alpha and omega, the beginning and the end (Siena).

Senatus Populus QR Senate and people of Rome (Rome, 1188).

Si Deus Nobiscum Quis Contra Nos If God is with us who can oppose us (Hesse).

Si Deus Pro Nobis Quis Contra Nos If God is for us who can oppose us (Roemhild).

Sieh Deine Seeligkeit Steht Fest Ins Vaters Liebe Behold thy salvation stands surely in thy Father's love (Gotha).

Signis Receptis When the standards had been recovered (Rome, Augustus).

Signum Crucis The sign of the cross (Groningen).

Sincere et Constanter Truthfully and steadfastly (Hesse-Darmstadt).

Sit Nomen Domini Benedictum Blessed be the name of the Lord (Burgundy, Strasbourg).

St T X Adiuto Reg Iste Domba Let it be to you, o Christ, the assistant to the king of Dombes (Dombes).

Sit Tibi Xpe Dat q'tu Regis Iste Ducat May this duchy which Thou rulest be given to Thee, O Christ (Venice, ducat).

Sit Unio Haec Perennis May this union last for ever (Hohenlohe-Langenberg).

Sola Bona Quae Honesta The only good things are those which are honest (Brunswick).

Sola Facta Deum Sequor Through deeds alone I strive to follow God (Milan).

Soli Deo Honor et Gloria To God alone be honour and glory (Nassau).

Soli Reduci To him, the only one restored (Naples and Sicily).

Solius Virtutis Flos Perpetuus The flower of Virtue alone is perpetual (Strasbourg).

Spes Confisa Deo Nunquam Confusa Recedit Hope entrusted in God never retreats in a disorderly fashion (Lippe).

Spes Nr Deus God is our hope (Oudenarde siege, 1582).

Spes Rei Publicae The hope of the republic (Rome, Valens).

Strena ex Argyrocopeo Vallis S Christoph A New Year's gift from the silver-bearing valley of St Christopher (Wurttemberg, 1625).

Sub His Secura Spes Clupeus Omnibus in Te Sperantibus Under these hope is safe, a shield for all who reside hope in Thee (Bavaria).

Sub Pondere Under weight (Fulda).

Sub Protectione Caesarea Under imperial protection (Soragna).

Sub Tuum Praesidium Confug We flee to Thy protection (Salzburg).

Sub Umbra Alarum Tuarum Under the shadow of Thy wings (Iever, Scotland, James V).

Subditorum Salus Felicitas Summa The safety of the subjects is the highest happiness (Lubeck).

Sufficit Mihi Gratia Tua Domine Sufficient to me is Thy grace, o Lord (Ploen).

Supra Firmam Petram Upon a firm rock (Papacy).

Susceptor Noster Deus God is our defence (Tuscany).

Sydera Favent Industriae The stars favour industry (Furstenberg).

Sylvarum Culturae Praemium Prize for the culture of the forest (Brandenburg-Ansbach).

Tali Dicata Signo Mens Fluctuari Nequit Consecrated by such a sign the mind cannot waver (England, Henry VIII George noble).

Tandem Bona Caus Triumphat A good cause eventually triumphs (Dillenburg).

Tandem Fortuna Obstetrice With good luck ultimately as the midwife (Wittgenstein).

Te Stante Virebo With you at my side I shall be strong (Moravia).

Tene Mensuram et Respice Finem Hold the measure and look to the end (Burgundy).

Tert Ducat Secular Tercentenary of the duchy (Wurttemberg).

Thu Recht Schev Niemand Go with right and fear no one (Saxe-Lauenburg).

Tibi Laus et Gloria To Thee be praise and glory (Venice).

Timor Domini Fons Vitae The fear of the Lord is a fountain of life (England, Edward VI shillings).

Tout Avec Dieu Everything with God (Brunswick, 1626).

Traiectum ad Mosam The crossing of the Maas (Maastricht).

Transvolat Nubila Virtus Marriageable virtue soon flies past (Grueyeres).

Travail, Famille, Patrie Work, family, country (Vichy France).

Triumphator Gent Barb Victor over the barbarian people (Byzantine Empire, Arcadius).

Tueatur Unita Deus May God guard these united (Kingdoms) (England, James I; Britain, 1847).

Turck Blegert Wien Vienna besieged by the Turks (Vienna, 1531).

Tut Mar Gab Pr Vid de Lobk Nat Pr Sab Car et Aug Pr de Lobk Regency of Maria Gabriela, widow of the prince of Lobkowitz, born princess of Savoy-Carignan, and August prince of Lobkowitz (Lobkowitz).

Tutela Italiae The guardianship of Italy (Rome, Nerva).

Ubi Vult Spirat He breathes where he will (Papacy).

Ubique Pax Peace everywhere (Rome, Gallienus).

Union et Force Union and strength (France).

Urbe Obsessa The city under siege (Maastricht).

Urbem Virgo Tuam Serva Protects thy city o virgin (Mary) (Strasbourg).

USC & RAM Cons Int Gen C Mar & Nob Praet H Turmae Capit Privy councillor of both their holy imperial and royal apostolic majesties, general field marshal and captain of the noble praetorian Hungarian squadrons (Eszterhazy).

Vculis Aulae Argenteis Patriae Indigenti Ministravit Auxilia   With the silver vessels of the court aid was brought to the needy fatherland (Eichstadt, 1796).

Veni Luumen Cordium   Come light of hearts (Vatican).

Veni Sancte Spiritus   Come Holy Ghost (Vatican).

Verbum Domini Manet in Aeternum   The word of the Lord abides forever (Hesse-Darmstadt, Veldenz).

Veritas Lex Tua   The truth is your law (Salzburg).

Veritas Temporis Filia   Truth is the daughter of time (England and Ireland, Mary Tudor).

Veritate et Labore   By truth and work (Wittgenstein).

Veritate et Iustitia   By truth and justice (German states).

Victoria Principum   The victory of princes (Ostrogoths).

Videant Pauperes et Laetentur   Let the poor see and rejoice (Tuscany).

Virgo Maria Protege Civitatem Savonae   Virgin Mary Protect the city of Savona (Savona).

Viribus Unitis   With united strength (Austria).

Virtute et Fidelitate   By virtue and faithfulness (Hesse-Cassel).

Virtute et Prudentia   With virtue and prudence (Auersperg).

Virtute Viam Dimetiar   I shall mark the way with valour (Waldeck).

Virtutis Gloria Merces   Glory is the reward of valour (Holstein-Gottorp).

Vis Unita Concordia Fratrum Fortior   United power is the stronger harmony of brothers (Mansfeld).

Visitavit Nos Oriens ex Alto   He has visited us arising on high (Luneburg).

Vivit Post Funera   He lives after death (Bremen).

Von Gottes Gn Iohan Bischof Zu Strasburg Landtgraf in Elsass   By God's grace John, Bishop of Strasbourg, Landgrave in Alsace (Strasbourg).

Vota Optata Romae Fel   Vows taken for the luck of Rome (Rome, Maxentius).

Vox de Throno   A voice from the throne (Papacy).

Was Got Beschert Bleibet Unerwert   What God hath endowed leave undisturbed

Wider macht und List Mein Fels Gott Ist   Against might and trickery God is my rock (Hesse-Cassel).

Xpc Vincit Xpc Regnat   Christ conquers, Christ reigns (Scotland, Spain).

Xpc Vivet Xpc Regnat Xpc Impat   Christ lives, Christ reigns, Christ commands (Cambrai).

Xpe Resurescit   Christ lives again (Venice).

Xpistiana Religio   Christian religion (Carolingian Empire).

Xps Ihs Elegit me Regem Populo   Jesus Christ chose me as king to the people (Norway).

Zelator Fidei Usque ad Montem   An upholder of the faith through and through (Portugal).

Zum Besten des Vaterlands   To the best of the fatherland (Bamberg).

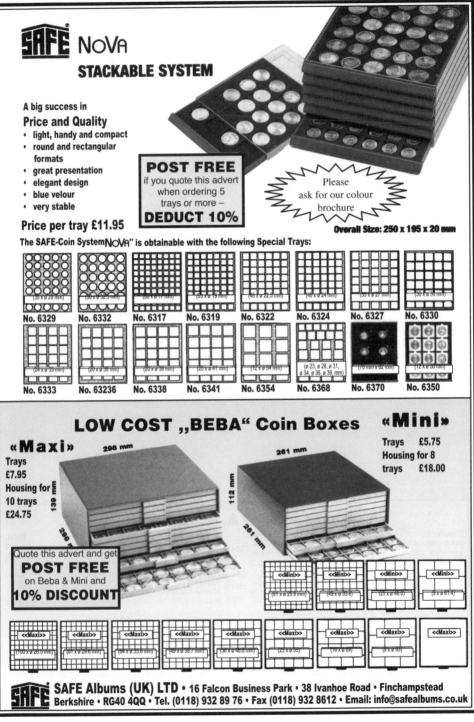

Care
of coins

There is no point in going to a great deal of trouble and expense in selecting the best coins you can afford, only to let them deteriorate in value by neglect and mishandling. Unless you give some thought to the proper care of your coins, your collection is unlikely to make a profit for you if and when you come to sell it. Housing your coins is the biggest problem of all, so it is important to give a lot of attention to this.

Storage

The ideal, but admittedly the most expensive, method is the coin cabinet, constructed of air-dried mahogany, walnut or rosewood (*never* oak, cedar or any highly resinous timber likely to cause chemical tarnish). These cabinets have banks of shallow drawers containing trays made of the same wood, with half-drilled holes of various sizes to accommodate the different denominations of coins. Such cabinets are handsome pieces of furniture but, being largely handmade, tend to be rather expensive. Occasionally good specimens can be picked up in secondhand furniture shops, or at the dispersal of house contents by auction, but the best bet is still to purchase a new cabinet, tailored to your own requirements.

Peter Nichols of 3 Norman Road, St Leonards-on-Sea, East Sussex TN37 6NH (telephone 01424 436682) is a specialist manufacturer of display and storage systems who has also been producing coin and medal cabinets to suit every need for more than a quarter of a century. He can produce a cabinet to fit into a wall safe or some other form of security box. He can match existing work, and thus replicate cabinets which you may already be using, or even produce designs to suit your specific requirements. The only proviso is that the cabinets are made in only one timber—Brazilian mahogany, for reason of chemical balance. A nice touch is that all the products in the Nichols repertoire take their names from Elizabethan mint-marks.

Nichols also offers a custom drilling service for coin trays, either all of the same diameter or in mixed sizes, depending on what you require. Drilling templates are also available on request. Apart from coin cabinets, Peter Nichols manufactures *medal* cabinets in two basic types, the seven-tray Pheon and the fourteen-tray Crozier. The cases for

these cabinets are similar in all respects to the coin cabinets, but medal trays are twice the thickness of coin trays. Each tray is made up from solid mahogany mouldings, base and polished mahogany front edges and trimmed with two turned brass knobs. The base of each tray is trimmed with a red felt pad.

The 4-tray Martlet — the smallest in an extensive range from Peter Nichols.

The Crozier — a cabinet for the connoisseur.

The Mini-Porter, smallest of Abafil's plush Diplomat range.

Nichols produces a wide range of cabinets from the seven-tray Pheon all the way up to the massive 40-tray specials designed for the British Museum. All cabinets are fitted with double doors. Nichols also produces the glass-topped Crown display case and the Sceptre display case, fitted with a glazed lid and containing a single tray. The Orb range of display cases are intended for wall mounting and are ideal for a display of campaign medals and decorations.

Prices start at around £30 for a four-tray Martlet coin cabinet and go all the way to the Coronet thirty-tray version at about £300. They are not cheap, but you have the satisfaction of acquiring exquisite examples of the cabinetmaker's craft which would be an elegant addition to any lounge or study.

An excellent compromise is provided by firms such as Abafil of Italy and Lindner of Germany who manufacture coin trays in durable, felt-lined materials with shallow compartments to suit the various sizes of coins. These trays interlock so that they build up into a cabinet of the desired size, and there are also versions designed as carrying cases, which are ideal for transporting coins.

Collectors Gallery of 24 The Parade, St Mary's Place, Shrewsbury, SY1 1DL (telephone: 01743 272140, fax: 01743 366041) is the UK agent and distributor for the Abafil series manufactured in Milan. These cases are of stout wooden construction covered with simulated leather and lined with red plush. The Diplomat range is designed primarily for secure transportation, but the Mini-diplomat, at around £40, makes a good static cabinet, and can take up to three standard trays holding a maximum of 241 coins, while the Custom case holds 14 de luxe or 20 standard trays and will house up to 1,500 coins. Even cheaper is the Mignon case holding up to 105 coins, ideally suited for carrying in a briefcase or travel bag.

Lindner Publications of 3A Hayle Industrial Park, Hayle, Cornwall TR27 5JR (telephone 01736 751914) are well-known for their wide range of philatelic and numismatic accessories, but these include a full array of coin boxes, capsules, carrying cases and trays. The basic Lindner coin box is, in fact, a shallow tray available in a standard version or a smoked glass version. These trays have a crystal clear frame, red felt inserts and holes for various diameters of coins and medals. A novel feature of these trays is the rounded insert which facilitates the removal of coins from their spaces with the minimum of handling. These boxes are designed in such a manner that they interlock and can be built up into banks of trays, each fitted with a draw-handle and sliding in and out easily. Various types of chemically inert plastic capsules and envelopes have been designed for use in combination with plain shallow trays, without holes drilled. Lindner also manufacture a range of luxury cases lined in velvet and Atlas silk with padded covers and gold embossing on the spines, producing a most tasteful and elegant appearance.

Safe Albums of 16 Falcon Business Park, 38 Ivanhoe Road, Finchampstead, Berkshire RG40 4QQ (telephone 0118 932 8976) are the UK agents for the German Stapel-Element, a drawer-stacking system with clear plasticiser-free trays that fit into standard bookshelves. The sliding coin compartments, lined with blue velvet, can be angled for display to best advantage. Stackable drawers cost around £15 each, and can be built up to any height desired. A wide range of drawer sizes is available, with compartments suitable for the smallest coins right up to four-compartment trays designed for very large artefacts such as card-cases or cigarette cases. The Mobel-Element cabinet is a superb specialised cabinet constructed of the finest timber with a steel frame and steel grip bars which can be securely locked. It thus combines elegance with security and is the ideal medium for the most valuable coins and medals.

There are also various storage systems, such as

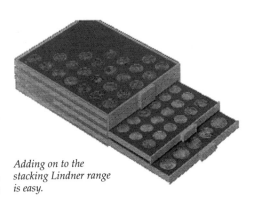

Adding on to the stacking Lindner range is easy.

Coindex, which operate on the principle of narrow drawers in which the coins are stored in envelopes of chemically-inert plastic. A strip across the top holds a little slip giving a brief description, catalogue number and the price of each coin.

Kwikseal of the USA produce cards with a plastic window: these cards are especially suitable for slabbing coins. The traditional method used by many collectors was to house coins in small, air-dried manila envelopes that could be stored upright in narrow wooden or stout card boxes—knife-boxes were highly regarded as being the right width and depth. The Sydney Museum in Australia, for example, keeps its coins in manila envelopes stored in plastic lunch-boxes which seemed to do the job pretty well!

Albums can be carried around easily

Safe's cabinet combines elegance with security.

Coin Albums

When coin collecting became a popular hobby in the 1960s, several firms marketed ranges of coin albums. They had clear plastic sleeves divided into tiny compartments of various sizes and had the merit of being cheap and taking up little room on a bookshelf.

They had several drawbacks, however, not the least being the tendency of the pages to sag with the weight of the coins, or even, in extreme cases, to pull away from the pegs or rings holding them on to the spine. They required very careful handling as the coins could easily fall out of the top row as the pages were turned. The more expensive albums had little flaps that folded over the top of the coin to overcome this problem.

Arguably the worst aspect of these albums was the use of polyvinyl chloride (PVC) in the construction of the sleeves. Collectors soon discovered to their horror that this reacted chemically with their coins, especially those made of silver, causing a rather disgusting yellow slime to adhere to the coins' surface. I shudder to think how many fine collections were ruined as a result, or of the countless coins that required highly expert treatment in a bid to restore them to as near the original condition as possible.

Fortunately the lesson has been learned and the coin albums now on the market are quite safe. Lindner offer a wide range of albums designed to house coins, medals or banknotes. The old problem about sagging pages is overcome by the use of a multi-ring binding welded to a very stout spine, while the sleeves contain neither Styrol nor PVC and will not affect any metals at all. In addition to pages with pockets of uniform size, the Karat range of albums operates on a slide principle which enables the user to insert vertical strips of different sizes on the same page, so that the coins of one country or series, or perhaps a thematic display of coins from different countries, can be displayed side by side.

Safe Albums offer a wide range of albums in the Coinholder System and Coin-Combi ranges. These, too, offer the choice of fixed pages with uniform-sized pockets, or interchangeable sliding inserts for different sizes side by side.

Cleaning Coins

This is like matrimony—it should not be embarked on lightly. Indeed, the advice given by the magazine *Punch* in regard to marriage is equally sound in this case—don't do it! It is far better to have a dirty coin than an irretrievably damaged one. Every dealer has horror stories of handling coins that previous owners have cleaned, to their detriment. The worst example I ever saw was a display of coins found by a metal detectorist who "improved" his finds by abrading them in the kind of rotary drum used by lapidarists to polish gemstones. If you really must remove the dirt and grease from coins, it is advisable to practise on coins of little value.

Warm water containing a mild household detergent or washing-up liquid will work wonders in removing surface dirt and grease from most coins, but silver is best washed in a weak solution of ammonia and warm water—one part ammonia to ten parts water. Gold coins can be cleaned with diluted citric acid, such as lemon juice. Copper or bronze coins present more of a problem, but patches of verdigris can usually be removed by careful washing in a 20 per cent solution of sodium sesquicarbonate. Wartime coins made of tin, zinc, iron or steel can be cleaned in a 5 per cent solution of caustic soda containing some aluminium or zinc foil or filings, but they must be rinsed afterwards in clean water and carefully dried. Cotton buds are ideal for gently prising dirt out of coin legends and crevices in the designs. Soft brushes (with animal bristles—*never* nylon or other artificial bristles)

designed for cleaning silver are most suitable for gently cleaning coins.

Coins recovered from the soil or the sea bed present special problems, due to chemical reaction between the metals and the salts in the earth or sea water. In such cases, the best advice is to take them to the nearest museum and let the professional experts decide on what can or should be done.

Both Lindner and Safe Albums offer a range of coin-cleaning kits and materials suitable for gold, silver, copper and other base alloys respectively. Safe (living up to their name) also provide a stern warning that rubber gloves should be worn and care taken to avoid breathing fumes or getting splashes of liquid in your eyes or on your skin. Obviously, the whole business of cleaning is a matter that should not be entered into without the utmost care and forethought.

POLISHING: A WARNING

If cleaning should only be approached with the greatest trepidation, polishing is definitely *out!* Beginners sometimes fall into the appalling error of thinking that a smart rub with metal polish might improve the appearance of their coins. Short of actually punching a hole through it, there can hardly be a more destructive act. Polishing a coin may improve its superficial appearance for a few days, but such abrasive action will destroy the patina and reduce the fineness of the high points of the surface. Even if a coin is only polished once, it will never be quite the same again, and an expert can tell this a mile off.

Celtic
coinage of Britain

Celtic coins were the first coins made in Britain. They were issued for a century and a half before the Roman invasion, and possibly a little later in some areas. They were issued by 11 tribal groups or administrative authorities situated southeast of a line from the Humber to the Severn. In this short article Celtic specialist CHRIS RUDD introduces this increasingly popular area.

The earliest coins were uninscribed and often abstract in design. Later ones carried the names of local leaders and tribal centres, and in the southeast became increasingly Roman in style, sometimes copying classical images quite closely.

Most Celtic coins were struck between two dies on flans of gold, silver, billion and bronze. Some were cast in strip moulds in tin-rich bronze alloy called "potin".

Because the Celts wrote no books and left no written records of their activities, little is known about the people and places behind their coins. Who made them? When? Where? And why? These are questions that are still largely unanswered, except in the very vaguest terms. Celtic cataloguers talk about gold quarters, silver units and silver minims. But the truth is we don't even know what the Celts themselves called their coins.

British Celtic coins are among the most fascinating ever fashioned and perhaps the least familiar to the average collector because of their rarity. Like the Celts themselves, Celtic coin designs are wild, free flowing, flamboyant and full of fun. Yes, Celtic moneyers had a great sense of humour!

Celtic coins bear a vast variety of gods and goddesses, armed warriors, chariot wheels, hidden faces, decapitated heads, suns, moons, stars, thunderbolts, floral motifs, magic signs and phallic symbols. Plus a menagerie of antelopes, bears, boars, bulls, cocks, crabs, cranes, dogs, dolphins, ducks, eagles, hares, all kinds of horses (some with wings, some with human heads, many with three tails, a few breathing fire), goats, lions, lizards, owls, rams, rats, ravens, snakes, stags, starfish, worms and wolves. Not to mention dragons, griffins, hippocamps, sphinxes and ram-horned serpents.

Ask any metal detectorist how many Celtic coins he or she has found and you will immediately realise they are rarer than Roman coins in this country—at least a thousand times rarer on average. This is because far fewer Celtic coins were minted, in smaller runs, over a much shorter time span. Though some may have been made as early as 80 BC, the majority of British Celtic coins were struck from 54 BC to AD 43; barely 100 years of production, and most of that seems to have been sporadic.

However, the greater rarity of Celtic coins doesn't mean they are necessarily more costly than other ancient coins: in fact, they are often cheaper. You see, in the coin market, demand determines price. The more collectors that want a coin, the higher its price.

A recent survey revealed "worldwide there may be no more than 150 regular private collectors of

Method that may have been used for striking Celtic coins (drawing by Simon Pressey).

103

Celtic coins, buying on average one or more coins per month". Whereas there are literally thousands of people collecting the other major series of ancient and medieval coins. That is why Celtic coins are still comparatively less costly than Greek, Anglo-Saxon and English hammered coins. The Celtic market is smaller, though expanding. For example a very fine Celtic gold stater typically costs half the price of a Greek gold stater or an English gold noble of comparable quality and rarity. The price differential

can be even more dramatic at major international auctions. But the disparity is diminishing as more and more collectors are beginning to appreciate the hitherto unrecognised beauty, scarcity and good value of British Celtic coins. So now could be a good time to start collecting Celtic coins, before their prices begin climbing more steeply.

Thirty years ago collecting British Celtic coins was a rich man's hobby and understanding them was the lonely pursuit of a few scholarly

Celtic hoards
100+ coins in italics

1 Alfriston	22 Farnham	43 Sherborne
2 Alresford	23 Field Baulk	44 Snettisham
3 Ashdown Forest	24 Folkestone	45 South Ferriby
4 Badbury	25 Freckenham	46 Timsbury
5 Birchington	26 Hengistbury	47 Waltham St Lawrence
6 Birling	27 High Wycombe	48 Wanborough
7 Bognor	28 Hod Hill	49 Westerham
8 Brentford	29 Holdenhurst	50 Weston
9 Brettenham	30 Honingham	51 Whaddon Chase
10 Cheriton	31 Honley	52 Wimblington
11 Chippenham	32 Joist Fen	53 Winterborne Monkton
12 Chirton	33 Lancing Down	54 Wonersh
13 Chute	34 Lenham Heath	55 Yarmouth
14 Clacton	35 Lightcliffe	56 Sunbury on Thames
15 Corfe Common	36 Mount Batten	57 Lakenheath
16 Danebury	37 Nunney	58 Thurrock
17 Donhead St Mary	38 Portsmouth	59 Pershore
18 Epping Forest	39 Ringwood	60 Eriswell
19 Essendon	40 Santon Downham	61 Scole
20 Farley Heath	41 Savernake	62 Fring
21 Farnborough	42 Selsey	63 Alton

Coin-using tribes in late Iron Age Britain

● Possible mint site
□ Tribal centre
---- Approximate tribal boundary

© CHRIS RUDD 1998

Eleven tribal groups minted coins in late Iron Age Britain, c. 80 BC–AD 45. The boundaries shown here are guesstimates, not actual, and often follow rivers, many of which are still known by their Celtic names.

Silver unit attributed to King Esuprastus of the Eceni, whose death resulted in the revolt of Queen Boudica, AD 60 (drawn four times actual size by Susan White).

numismatists. Today, thanks to the popularity of metal detecting, Celtic coins are more plentiful and almost everyone can afford to collect them. Most ancient coin dealers sell Celtic coins, some for as little as £20 each, and you will always find a few trays of them at every coin fair.

British Celtic coins are also easier to study today, thanks to the publication of some excellent books on the subject. The Celtic collector's bible is *Celtic Coinage of Britain* by Robert D. Van Arsdell (Spink, 1989)—well researched, well written, well illustrated, always quoted in dealers' catalogues, often controversial when dates are discussed and hopefully to be republished soon in a revised edition. For the dedicated Celtic devotee *British Iron Age Coins in the British Museum* by Richard Hobbs (British Museum Press, 1996) is an invaluable companion volume to Van Arsdell—more cautious, less speculative.

By far the best introductory book is *Celtic Coinage in Britain* by Dr Philip de Jersey (Shire Archaeology, 1996) who manages the Celtic Coin Index, a photographic record of over 31,000 British coins at the Institute of Archaeology, Oxford. In plain language Dr Philip de Jersey explains how Celtic coins and the images they carry can reveal information on the political, economic and social life of the Celts. *Celtic Coinage in Britain* contains clear twice-size photos of over a hundred Celtic

coins, some of them rarely seen before. It gives the names, addresses and phone numbers of the museums in England, Scotland and Wales with the best and most accessible collections of Celtic coins.

In short, if you want to know more about British Celtic coins, *Celtic Coinage in Britain* is where you start reading and keep reading. This is the best little book ever written about British Celtic coins and outstanding value for money at £4.99.

How should you start collecting British Celtic coins? First, get a few of the commoner uninscribed types from each of the 11 tribal areas, aiming for the highest grade you can comfortably afford. Then you may wish to get an inscribed coin of each of the main rulers. You would also be well advised to acquire some Gaulish coins at the same time, because many British coins were influenced by Gallic prototypes.

How much do British Celtic coins cost? Very little, considering how scarce they are. Types with legends usually cost more than those without and top quality bronze is frequently more pricey than top quality silver (which may surprise you) because silver is commoner and generally survives better after two-thousand years underground.

Chris Rudd is a well-known dealer who specialises in Celtic coins.

Collecting

Ancient coins

Ancient coins differ from most other series which are collected in Britain in that every piece has spent the major part of the last two thousand years in the ground. As JOHN CUMMINGS, dealer in ancient coins and antiquities explains here, the effect that burial has had on the surface of the coin determines more than anything else the value of a particular piece. With more modern coins, the only things which affect price are rarity and grade. There may be a premium for coins exhibiting particularly fine tone, or with outstanding pedigrees, but an 1887 crown in "extremely fine" condition has virtually the same value as every other piece with the same grade and of the same date. With ancient coins the story is very different.

A large number of different criteria affect the price of an ancient coin. Factors affecting prices can be broken down into several categories:

Condition

The most important factor by far in determining price. Ancient coins were struck by hand and can exhibit striking faults. Value suffers if the coin is struck with the designs off-centre, is weakly struck, or if the flan is irregular in shape. Many of the Celtic tribes issued coins of varying fineness and those made from low quality gold or silver are worth less than similar specimens where the metal quality is better. Conversely, coins on exceptional flans, particularly well struck, or with fine patinas command a premium.

Many ancient coins have suffered during their stay in the ground. It must be borne in mind that the prices given in the price guide are for uncorroded, undamaged examples. A Roman denarius should be graded using the same criteria as those used for grading modern coins. The surfaces must be good, and the coin intact. The fact that the coin is 2,000 years old is irrelevant as far as grading is concerned. Coins which are not perfectly preserved are not without value but the value for a given grade decreases with the degree of fault.

Rarity

As with all other series, rare coins usually command higher prices than common ones

although this is not written in stone. A unique variety of a small fourth century Roman bronze coin, even in perfect condition, can be worth much less than a more worn and common piece from an earlier part of the empire. In the Celtic series, there is an almost infinite variety of minor types and a unique variety of an uninscribed type will rarely outbid an inscribed issue of a known king.

Historical and local significance

Types which have historical or local interest can command a price far above their scarcity value. Denarii of the emperor Tiberius are believed to have been referred to in the New Testament and command a far higher price than a less interesting piece of similar rarity. Similarly, pieces which have British reverse types such as the "VICT BRIT" reverse of the third century AD are more expensive than their scarcity would indicate. The 12 Caesars are ever popular especially in the American market and this affects prices throughout the world. In the Celtic series, coins of Cunobelin or Boudicca are far more popular than pieces which have no historical interest but which are far scarcer.

Reverse types

All Roman emperors who survived for a reasonable time issued coins with many different reverse types. The most common of these usually show various Roman gods. When a coin has an unusual reverse it always enhances the value.

Particularly popular are architectural scenes, animals, references to Judaism, and legionary types.

Artistic merit

The Roman coinage is blessed with a large number of bust varieties and these can have a startling effect on price. For example, a common coin with the bust facing left instead of right can be worth several times the price of a normal specimen. Like many of the emperors, the coinage of Hadrian has a large number of bust varieties, some of which are extremely artistic and these, too, can command a premium.

The coinage used in Britain from the time of the invasion in AD 43 was the same as that intro-duced throughout the Empire by the emperor Augustus around 20 BC. The simple divisions of 2 asses equal to one dupondius, 2 dupondii equal to 1 sestertius, 4 sestertii equal to one denarius and 25 denarii equal to one aureus continued in use until the reformation of the coin-age by Caracalla in AD 214.

Aureus (gold)

Denarius (silver)

Sestertius (bronze)

Dupondius (copper)

As (copper)

Introducing

Hammered coinage

The hammered currency of medieval Britain is among some of the most interesting coinage in the world. The turbulent history of these islands is reflected in the fascinating changes in size, design, fineness and workmanship, culminating in the many strange examples that emanated from the strife of the Civil War.

The Norman Conquest of England in 1066 and succeeding years had far-reaching effects on all aspects of life. Surprisingly, however, it had little impact on the coinage. William the Conqueror was anxious to emphasise the continuity of his reign, so far as the ordinary people were concerned, and therefore he retained the fabric, size and general design pattern of the silver penny. Almost 70 mints were in operation during this reign, but by the middle of the 12th century the number was reduced to 55 and under Henry II (1154–89) it fell to 30 and latterly to only eleven. By the early 14th century the production of coins had been centralised on London and Canterbury, together with the ecclesiastical mints at York and Canterbury. The silver penny was the principal denomination throughout the Norman period, pieces cut along the lines of the cross on the reverse continuing to serve as halfpence and farthings.

Eight types of penny were struck under William I and five under his son William Rufus, both profiles (left and right) and facing portraits being used in both reigns allied to crosses of various types. Fifteen types were minted under Henry I (1100–35), portraiture having now degenerated to crude caricature, the lines engraved on the coinage dies being built up by means of various punches. Halfpence modelled on the same pattern were also struck, but very sparingly and are very rare.

On Henry's death the succession was contested by his daughter Matilda and his nephew Stephen of Blois. Civil war broke out in 1138 and continued till 1153. Stephen controlled London and its mint, but Matilda and her supporters occupied the West Country and struck their own coins at Bristol. Several of the powerful barons struck their own coins, and there were distinct regional variants of the regal coinage. Of particular interest are the coins struck

Silver pennies of, from left to right, William I, William Rufus, Henry I and Stephen.

from obverse dies with Stephen's portrait erased or defaced, believed to date from 1148 when the usurper was under papal interdict.

Peace was restored in 1153 when it was agreed that Matilda's son Henry should succeed Stephen. On the latter's death the following year, Henry II ascended the throne. Coins of Stephen's last type continued to be minted till 1158, but Henry then took the opportunity to overhaul the coinage which had become irregular and substandard during the civil war. The new "Cross Crosslet" coins, usually known as the Tealby coinage (from the hoard of over 5,000 pennies found at Tealby, Lincolnshire in 1807), were produced at 30 mints, but when the recoinage was completed this number was reduced to a dozen. The design of Henry's coins remained virtually the same throughout more than two decades, apart from minor variants. Then, in 1180, a new type, known as the Short Cross coinage, was introduced. This was a vast improvement over the poorly struck Cross Crosslet coins and continued without alteration, not only to the end of the reign of Henry II in 1189, but throughout the reigns of his sons Richard (1189–99) and John (1199–1216) and the first half of the reign of his grandson Henry III (1216–46). Throughout that 66 year period, however, there were minor variations in portraits and lettering which enable numismatists to attribute the HENRICUS coins to specific reigns and periods.

"Tealby" type penny, left, and "Short Cross" penny of Henry II.

The style and workmanship of the Short Cross coinage deteriorated in the reign of Henry III. By the 1220s coin production was confined to the regal mints at London and Canterbury, the sole exception being the ecclesiastical mint maintained by the Abbot of Bury St Edmunds.

Halfpence and farthings were briefly struck in 1221–30, though halfpence are now extremely rare and so far only a solitary farthing has been discovered.

By the middle of this reign the coinage was in a deplorable state, being poorly struck, badly worn and often ruthlessly clipped. In 1247 Henry ordered a new coinage and in this the arms of the cross on the reverse were extended to the rim as a safeguard against clipping. This established a pattern of facing portrait and long cross on obverse and reverse respectively that was to continue till the beginning of the 16th century. Several provincial mints were re-activated to assist with the recoinage but they were all closed down again by 1250, only the regal mints at London and Canterbury and the ecclesiastical mints at Durham and Bury St Edmunds remaining active.

"Long Cross" pennies of Henry III, left, and Edward I.

In 1257 Henry tentatively introduced a gold penny (worth 20 silver pence and twice the weight of a silver penny). The coin was undervalued and soon disappeared from circulation.

The Long Cross coinage of Henry III continued under Edward I till 1279 when the king introduced a new coinage in his own name. The penny continued the style of its predecessors, though much better designed and executed; but new denominations were now added. Henceforward halfpence and farthings became a regular issue and, at the same time, a fourpenny coin known as the groat (from French *gros*) was briefly introduced (minting ceased in 1282 and was not revived till 1351). Due to the centralisation of coin production the name of the moneyer was now generally dropped, although it lingered on a few years at Bury St Edmunds. The provincial mints were again revived in 1299–1302 to recoin the lightweight foreign imitations of pennies which had flooded in from the Continent.

The coinage of Edward II (1307–27) differed only in minor respects from that of his father, and a similar pattern prevailed in the first years of Edward III. In 1335 halfpence and farthings below the sterling fineness were struck. More importantly, further attempts were made to introduce gold coins. In 1344 the florin or double

Pre-Treaty Noble of Edward III which contained reference to France in the legend.

leopard of six shillings was introduced, along with its half and quarter. This coinage was not successful and was soon replaced by a heavier series based on the noble of 80 pence (6s. 8d.), half a mark or one third of a pound. The noble originally weighed 138.5 grains but it was successively reduced to120 grains, at which weight it continued from 1351. During this reign the protracted conflict with France known as the Hundred Years' War erupted. Edward III, through his mother, claimed the French throne and inscribed this title on his coins. By the Treaty of Bretigny (1361) Edward temporarily gave up his claim and the reference to France

Noble of Edward IV, issued before he was forced to abandon the throne of England.

was dropped from the coins, but when war was renewed in 1369 the title was resumed, and remained on many English coins until the end of the 18th century. The silver coinage followed the pattern of the previous reign, but in 1351 the groat was re-introduced and with it came the twopence or half-groat. Another innovation was the use of mintmarks at the beginning of the inscriptions. Seven types of cross and one crown were employed from 1334 onwards and their sequence enables numismatists to date coins fairly accurately.

The full range of gold (noble, half-noble and quarter-noble) and silver (groat, half-groat, penny, halfpenny and farthing) continued under Richard II (1377–99). Little attempt was made to alter the facing portrait on the silver coins, by now little more than a stylised caricature anyway.

Noble of Henry IV which was reduced in weight due to the shortage of gold.

Under Henry IV (1399–1413) the pattern of previous reigns prevailed, but in 1412 the weights of the coinage were reduced due to a shortage of bullion. The noble was reduced to 108 grains and its sub-divisions lightened proportionately. The penny was reduced by 3 grains, and its multiples and sub-divisions correspondingly reduced. One interesting change was the reduction of the fleur de lis of France from four to three in the heraldic shield on the reverse of the noble; this change corresponded with the alteration in the arms used in France itself. The Calais mint, opened by Edward III in 1363, was closed in 1411. There was no change in the designs used for the coins of Henry V (1413–22) but greater use was now made of mintmarks to distinguish the various periods of production. Coins were by now produced mainly at London, although the episcopal mints at Durham and York were permitted to strike pennies.

The supply of gold dwindled early in the reign of Henry VI and few nobles were struck after 1426. The Calais mint was re-opened in 1424 and struck a large amount of gold before closing finally in 1440. A regal mint briefly operated at York in 1423–24. Mintmarks were now much more widely used and tended to correspond more closely to the annual trials of the Pyx. The series of civil upheavals known as the Wars of the Roses erupted in this period.

In 1461 Henry VI was deposed by the Yorkist Earl of March after he defeated the Lancastrians at Mortimer's Cross. The Yorkists advanced on London where the victor was crowned Edward IV. At first he continued the gold series of his predecessor, issuing nobles and quarter-nobles, but in 1464 the weight of the penny was reduced to 12 grains and the value of the noble was raised to 100 pence (8s. 4d.). The ryal or rose-

Groat of Richard III (1483–85).

noble of 120 grains, together with its half and quarter, was introduced in 1465 and tariffed at ten shillings or half a pound. The need for a coin worth a third of a pound, however, led to the issue of the angel of 80 grains, worth 6s. 8d., but this was initially unsuccessful and very few examples are now extant. The angel derived its name from the figure of the Archangel Michael on the obverse; a cross surmounting a shield appeared on the reverse.

In 1470 Edward was forced to flee to Holland and Henry VI was briefly restored. During this brief period (to April 1471) the ryal was discontinued but a substantial issue of angels and half-angels was made both at London and Bristol. Silver coins were struck at York as well as London and Bristol, the issues of the provincial mints being identified by the initials B or E (Eboracum, Latin for York). Edward defeated the Lancastrians at Tewkesbury and deposed the luckless Henry once more. In his second reign

Edward struck only angels and half-angels as well as silver from the groat to halfpenny. In addition to the three existing mints, silver coins were struck at Canterbury, Durham and the archiepiscopal mint at York. Mintmarks were now much more frequent and varied. Coins with a mark of a halved sun and rose are usually assigned to the reign of Edward IV, but they were probably also struck in the nominal reign of Edward V, the twelve-year-old prince held in the Tower of London under the protection of his uncle Richard, Duke of Gloucester. Coins with this mark on the reverse had an obverse mark of a boar's head, Richard's personal emblem. The brief reign of Richard III (1483–5) came to an end with his defeat at Bosworth and the relatively scarce coins of this period followed the pattern of the previous reigns, distinguished by the sequence of mint marks and the inscription RICAD or RICARD.

In the early years of Henry VII's reign the coinage likewise followed the previous patterns, but in 1489 the first of several radical changes was effected, with the introduction of the gold sovereign of 20 shillings showing a full-length portrait of the monarch seated on an elaborate throne. For reverse, this coin depicted a Tudor rose surmounted by a heraldic shield. A similar reverse appeared on the ryal of 10 shillings, but the angel and angelet retained previous motifs. The silver coins at first adhered to the medieval pattern, with the stylised facing portrait and long cross, but at the beginning of the 16th century a large silver coin, the testoon or shilling of 12 pence, was introduced and adopted a realistic profile of the king, allied to a reverse showing a cross surmounted by the royal arms. The same design was also used for the later issue of groat and half groat.

First coinage Angel of Henry VIII which retained the traditional 23.5 carat fineness.

111

This established a pattern which was to continue till the reign of Charles I. In the reign of Henry VIII, however, the coinage was subject to considerable debasement. This led to the eventual introduction of 22 carat (.916 fine) gold for the crown while the traditional 23 H carat gold was retained for the angel and ryal. This dual system continued until the angel was discontinued at the outset of the Civil War in 1642; latterly it had been associated with the ceremony of touching for "King's Evil" or scrofula, a ritual used by the early Stuart monarchs to bolster their belief in the divine right of kings.

Under the Tudors and Stuarts the range and complexity of the gold coinage increased, but it was not until the reign of Edward VI that the silver series was expanded. In 1551 he introduced the silver crown of five shillings, the first English coin to bear a clear date on the obverse. Under Mary dates were extended to the shilling and sixpence.

The mixture of dated and undated coins continued under Elizabeth I, a reign remarkable for the range of denominations—nine gold and

The magnificent Rose-Ryal of James I.

eight silver. The latter included the sixpence, threepence, threehalfpence and threefarthings, distinguished by the rose which appeared behind the Queen's head.

The coinage of James I was even more complex, reflecting the king's attempts to unite his dominions. The first issue bore the legend ANG:SCO (England and Scotland), but from 1604 this was altered to MAG: BRIT (Great Britain). This period witnessed new denominations, such as the rose-ryal and spur-ryal, the unite, the Britain crown and the thistle crown, and finally the laurel of 20 shillings and its sub-divisions.

In the reign of Elizabeth experiments began with milled coinage under Eloi Mestrell. These continued sporadically in the 17th century, culminating in the beautiful coins struck by Nicholas Briot (1631–39). A branch mint was established at Aberystwyth in 1637 to refine and coin silver from the Welsh mines. Relations between King and Parliament deteriorated in the reign of Charles I and led to the Civil War (1642). Parliament controlled London but continued to strike coins in the King's name. The Royalists struck coins, both in pre-war and new types, at Shrewsbury, Oxford, Bristol, Worcester, Exeter, Chester, Hereford and other Royalist strongholds, while curious siege pieces were pressed into service at Newark, Pontefract and Scarborough.

After the execution of Charles I in 1649 the Commonwealth was proclaimed under Oliver Cromwell. Gold and silver coins were now inscribed in English instead of Latin. Patterns portraying Cromwell and a crowned shield restored Latin in 1656. Plans for milled coinage were already being considered before the Restoration of the monarchy in 1660. Hammered coinage appeared initially, resuming the style of coins under Charles I, but in 1662 the hand-hammering of coins was abandoned in favour of coins struck on the mill and screw press. The hammered coins of 1660–62 were undated and bore a crown mintmark, the last vestiges of medievalism in British coinage.

A SIMPLIFIED PRICE GUIDE
TO
ANCIENT COINS
USED IN BRITAIN

Coins illustrated in the following listings are indicated with an asterisk (*)

PART I

CELTIC

The prices given in this section are those that you would expect to pay from a reputable dealer and not the prices at which you could expect to sell coins.

The list below contains most of the commonly available types: a full comprehensive guide is beyond the scope of this book. Prices are for coins with good surfaces which are not weakly struck or struck from worn dies. Examples which are struck from worn or damaged dies can be worth considerably less. Particularly attractive examples of bronze Celtic coins command a very high premium. Where a price is given for an issue of which there are many varieties, the price is for the most common type.

The illustrations are representative examples only and are indicated by an asterisk (*) in the listings.

	F	VF	EF
UNINSCRIBED COINAGE			
GOLD STATERS			
Gallo-Belgic A	£650	£1500	£5500
Gallo-Belgic E (Ambiani)	£150	£250	£450
Chute type	£150	£275	£450
Cheriton type			
normally rather "brassy" metal	£200	£400	£850
Corieltauvi (various types)	£150	£350	£550
Norfolk "wolf" type			
fine gold	£200	£400	£750
brassy gold	£125	£250	£450
very debased	£85	£175	£375
*Whaddon Chase types	£200	£400	£850
Wonersh type	£200	£400	£850
Eceni (various types)	£250	£450	£850
Remic type	£200	£350	£575
Dobunni	£250	£450	£850
GOLD QUARTER STATERS			
North Thames types	£155	£250	£450
North Kent types	£155	£250	£450
Eceni	£145	£200	£375
Sussex types	£100	£175	£325
Dobunni	£150	£250	£500
SILVER COINAGE			
North Thames types	£85	£155	£300
South Thames types	£85	£155	£300
Durotriges full stater			
fine silver	£65	£155	£275
*base silver	£40	£85	£180
Durotriges small silver	£35	£85	£175

Uninscribed Whaddon Chase type gold stater

Uninscribed Durotriges base silver stater

	F	VF	EF
Dobunni	£50	£100	£250

(Note—Most examples are base in appearance. Prices for examples with fine surfaces are appreciably higher)

	F	VF	EF
Corieltauvi	£45	£100	£200
Eceni ("crescent" types)	£30	£75	£150
Eceni ("Norfolk god" types)	£50	£100	£250
Armorican Billon staters	£75	£150	£400

POTIN COINAGE

	F	VF	EF
Kent	£20	£50	£100

BRONZE COINAGE

	F	VF	EF
Durotriges debased stater	£25	£55	£100
*Durotriges cast bronzes	£60	£120	£200
North Thames types. Various issues from:	£40	£100	£400

INSCRIBED CELTIC COINAGE

Durotriges cast bronze

ATTREBATES & REGNI

	F	VF	EF
*Commios			
stater	£550	£1500	£2850
silver unit	£75	£150	£300
silver minim	£60	£120	£250
Tincomarus			
stater	£420	£850	£2000
quarter stater	£145	£250	£450
silver unit	£75	£140	£275
silver minim	£155	£285	£550
Eppillus			
quarter stater	£145	£235	£425
silver unit	£75	£145	£300
bronze			Rare
Verica			
stater	£255	£550	£1000
quarter stater	£155	£275	£425
silver unit	£55	£150	£250
Epaticcus			
stater	£1000	£2000	£4000
*silver unit	£50	£100	£265
silver minim	£55	£110	£275
Caratacos			
silver unit	£165	£320	£465
silver minim	£110	£220	£325

Commios stater

CANTIACI

	F	VF	EF
Dubnovellaunos			
stater	£280	£565	£900
silver unit	£130	£210	£500
bronze unit	£55	£150	£350
Vosenos			
stater	£1000	£2500	£5000
quarter stater	£275	£585	£1200
silver unit	£135	£285	£650
bronze unit	£110	£215	£550
Sam			
silver unit	£175	£350	£750
bronze unit	£100	£250	£500
Eppillus			
stater	£1000	£2000	£4250
quarter stater	£145	£255	£500
silver unit	£65	£145	£350
bronze unit	£55	£125	£450
Amminus			
silver unit	£155	£320	£650
silver minim	£110	£215	£450
bronze unit	£80	£155	£500

Epaticcus silver unit

	F	VF	EF
Solidu			
silver unit...	£500	£1000	£2250
silver minim......................................	£500	£1000	£1500

DUROTRIGES
Crab

	F	VF	EF
silver...	£155	£320	£650
silver minim......................................	£100	£250	£400

TRINOVANTES
Addedomaros

	F	VF	EF
stater...	£265	£500	£800
quarter stater	£155	£320	£550

Dubnovellaunos

	F	VF	EF
stater...	£255	£455	£775
quarter stater	£155	£310	£550
*bronze unit......................................	£55	£130	£450

Dubnovellaunos bronze unit

CATUVELLAUNI
Tasciovanos

	F	VF	EF
*stater...	£225	£425	£1000
quarter stater	£130	£235	£450
silver unit...	£80	£165	£375
bronze unit	£55	£135	£350
bronze half unit	£55	£135	£275

Sego

	F	VF	EF
stater...	£1000	£3000	£4000
quarter stater	£600	£1750	£3000
silver unit...	£250	£500	£1000
bronze unit	£80	£200	£400

Dias

	F	VF	EF
silver unit...	£100	£200	£400
bronze unit	£50	£150	£400

Rues

	F	VF	EF
bronze unit	£50	£150	£400

Andoco

	F	VF	EF
stater...	£510	£1250	£2750
quarter stater	£210	£420	£755
silver unit...	£155	£400	£750
bronze..	£85	£215	£355

Cunobelin

	F	VF	EF
*stater...	£200	£455	£1000
quarter stater	£145	£265	£420
silver unit...	£85	£165	£360
bronze unit	£65	£145	£320

Tasciovanos stater

AGR

	F	VF	EF
quarter stater	£600	£1500	£3000
silver unit...	£500	£1000	£2000

DOBUNNI
Anted

	F	VF	EF
stater...	£325	£650	£1350
silver unit...	£55	£120	£300

Eisu

	F	VF	EF
stater...	£450	£750	£1500
silver unit...	£55	£125	£325

Catti

	F	VF	EF
stater...	£255	£525	£1250

Comux

	F	VF	EF
stater...	£800	£1650	£3250

Corio

	F	VF	EF
stater...	£265	£525	£1000
quarter stater	£200	£355	£625

Boduoc

	F	VF	EF
stater...	£1000	£2250	£3550
silver unit...	£200	£500	£850

Cunobelin stater

ECENI	F	VF	EF
Duro Cam			
silver unit...	£110	£265	£550
Anted			
stater..	£425	£1000	£2500
silver unit...	£35	£65	£185
silver half unit...................................	£45	£95	£200
Ecen			
silver unit...	£40	£75	£185
silver half unit...................................	£45	£95	£200
Saenu			
silver unit...	£65	£125	£285
Aesu			
silver unit...	£65	£125	£285
Esuprastus			
silver unit...	£420	£1,000	£1850
Ale Scavo			
silver unit...	£355	£765	£1550

Vep Corf silver unit

CORIELTAUVI			
Cat			
silver unit...	£400	£1000	£2000
Vep			
stater..	£400	£1000	£2500
silver unit...	£75	£150	£300
Aunt Cost			
stater..	£255	£565	£1000
silver unit...	£85	£185	£315
silver half unit...................................	£85	£160	£300
Esuprasu			
stater..	£330	£675	£1250
silver unit...	£155	£310	£550
Vep Corf			
stater..	£410	£1000	£2150
*silver unit	£80	£185	£300
silver half unit...................................	£100	£215	£450
Dumno Tigir Seno			
stater..	£755	£1850	£3150
silver unit...	£100	£185	£500
Volisios Dumnocoveros			
*stater..	£310	£725	£1550
silver unit...	£100	£185	£475
silver half unit...................................	£100	£185	£450
Volisios Dumnovellaunos			
stater..	£300	£675	£1250
silver half unit...................................	£150	£335	£655
Volisios Cartivellaunos			
stater	£1000	£2000	£4000
silver half unit...................................	£300	£620	£1150
Latios Ison			
stater..	£1000	£2000	£4000
silver unit...	£155	£420	£1150

Volisios Dumnocoveros stater

Illustrations by courtesy of
Chris Rudd.

A SIMPLIFIED PRICE GUIDE
TO
ANCIENT COINS USED IN BRITAIN

PART II
ROMAN BRITAIN

In certain cases, especially with large bronze coins, the price for coins in extremely fine condition are _much_ higher than the price for the same coin in very fine condition as early bronze coins are seldom found in hoards and perfect undamaged examples are rarely available.

The illustrations provided are a representative guide to assist with identification only and are indicated by an asterisk (*) in the listings.

	F	VF	EF
Republican			
denarius (Roma/Biga) ....from	£18	£45	£145
denarius (other types)	£20	£50	£165
as..	£50	£150	—
Sextus Pompey			
denarius (his bust)	£200	£600	£1,500
denarius (other types)......................	£100	£325	£800
Julius Caesar			
aureus	£375	£900	£1850
denarius ("elephant" type)	£65	£160	£395
denarius (Ceasar portrait)	£220	£600	£1500
denarius (heads of godesses)	£50	£125	£275
Brutus			
denarius (his portrait)......................	£7000	£22000	£60000
denarius (others).............................	£100	£300	£900
Mark Antony			
denarius ("Galley" type)	£45	£120	£300
denarius (with portrait)	£95	£275	£675
AR quinarius	£35	£100	£260
Mark Antony & Octavian			
AR denarius	£125	£375	£875
Octavian			
gold aureus......................................	£900	£2300	£5500
denarius...	£90	£225	£575
Augustus			
gold aureus (Caius & Lucius Caesar)	£495	£1300	£2900
denarius (Caius & Lucius Caesar).....	£45	£125	£340
*other types.....................................	£60	£175	£400
dupondius or as (large SC)	£45	£110	£300
quadrans..	£14	£35	£95

Augustus

Germanicus

Caligula

119

	F	VF	EF
Livia			
sestertius or dupondius	£125	£375	£1500
Tiberius			
aureus (Tribute penny)	£400	£1250	£2650
denarius (Tribute penny)	£65	£175	£425
sestertius	£130	£425	£1800
as	£50	£160	£475
Drusus			
as	£60	£180	£465
Caligula			
denarius (rev. his portrait)	£360	£1100	£2700
sestertius	£275	£775	£3100
as...	£70	£260	£775
Germanicus			
*as	£65	£175	£440
Agrippa			
as...	£60	£160	£500
Agrippina Senior			
sestertius	£350	£1100	£4500
Claudius			
aureus ("DE BRITANN" type)	£850	£2200	£5300
denarius as above..............................	£300	£800	£2100
didrachm as above	£250	£750	£1800
denarius other types	£250	£625	£1600
sestertius	£135	£425	£1600
as	£40	£125	£395
quadrans	£13	£40	£110
Irregular British as............................	£20	£65	£185
Antonia			
dupondius	£100	£295	£950
Nero			
aureus..	£475	£1250	£2800
denarius	£85	£250	£650
sestertius	£140	£400	£1800
as	£40	£130	£375
Civil War			
denarius	£165	£450	£1100
Galba			
denarius	£90	£325	£875
*sestertius	£195	£600	£2600
as	£75	£225	£775
Otho			
denarius	£185	£550	£1600
Vitellius			
denarius	£90	£280	£850
sestertius	£700	£2250	£7500
as	£130	£350	£1000
Vespasian			
aureus..	£425	£1150	£2800
denarius	£20	£65	£200
sestertius	£100	£285	£875
as dupondius	£40	£110	£350
Titus			
aureus..	£450	£1250	£3000
denarius	£40	£120	£330
sestertius	£130	£375	£1150
dupondius or as	£50	£140	£450
Domitian			
aureus..	£450	£1200	£3000
denarius	£20	£55	£175
*sestertius	£90	£275	£900
dupondius or as	£35	£325	£295
ae semis	£30	£80	£250

Galba

Domitian

Sabina

	F	VF	EF
Nerva			
aureus	£800	£2600	£7200
denarius	£40	£110	£375
sestertius	£140	£425	£1750
as	£55	£170	£575
Trajan			
aureus	£400	£1000	£2900
denarius	£17	£50	£150
sestertius	£65	£200	£650
dupondius or as	£25	£85	£300
Hadrian			
aureus	£500	£1150	£3200
denarius (provinces)	£30	£90	£250
denarius other types	£20	£55	£170
sestertius	£70	£220	£695
sestertius (Britannia std)	£2250	£7500	—
dupondius or as	£30	£100	£350
Sabina			
denarius	£25	£70	£225
*sestertius	£110	£300	£1000
as or dupondius	£50	£165	£475
Aelius Ceasar			
denarius	£65	£200	£500
sestertius	£135	£400	£1200
as or dupondius	£55	£165	£550
Antoninus Pius			
aureus	£295	£750	£2400
denarius	£15	£45	£140
sestertius Britannia legends	£450	£1350	£5500
sestertius other types	£40	£130	£475
dupondius or As Britannia	£50	£65	£260
dupondius or As other types	£20	£65	£260
Faustina Senior			
denarius	£15	£45	£140
sestertius	£30	£125	£450
as or dupondius	£20	£60	£225
Marcus Aurelius			
aureus	£375	£850	£2500
*denarius	£15	£40	£120
sestertius	£40	£140	£475
as or dupondius	£22	£65	£230
Faustina Junior			
*denarius	£15	£45	£135
sestertius	£36	£130	£400
as or dupondius	£18	£55	£200
Lucius Verus			
denarius	£20	£60	£200
sestertius	£55	£175	£650
as or dupondius	£25	£75	£300
Lucilla			
denarius	£20	£55	£175
sestertius	£45	£160	£550
Commodus			
denarius	£15	£45	£125
*sestertius	£40	£120	£450
sestertius (Vict. Brit)	£90	£275	£850
as or dupondius	£20	£60	£220
Crispina			
denarius	£20	£60	£190
as or dupondius	£30	£85	£265
Pertinax			
*denarius	£190	£550	£1350

Marcus Aurelius

Faustina Junior

Commodus

Pertinax

Caracalla

	F	VF	EF
Didius Julianus			
denarius	£375	£850	£1850
sestertius	£250	£650	£2100
Pescennius Niger			
denarius	£180	£650	£1800
Clodius Albinus			
denarius	£40	£100	£295
sestertius	£130	£500	£2000
as	£70	£225	£775
Septimius Severus			
aureus	£495	£1250	£3800
aureus (VICT BRIT)	£1000	£3000	£7000
denarius	£12	£35	£95
denarius (VICT BRIT)	£25	£75	£195
sestertius (VICT BRIT REV)	£290	£800	£2800
sestertius other types	£60	£200	£650
dupondius or as	£45	£125	£375
Julia Domna			
denarius	£12	£35	£95
sestertius	£65	£200	£600
as or dupondius	£45	£130	£390
Caracalla			
*denarius	£12	£35	£95
denarius (VICT BRIT)	£25	£80	£210
sestertius	£75	£225	£775
sestertius (VICT BRIT)	£220	£650	£2250
supondius or as	£40	£120	£375
dupondius or as (VICT BRIT)	£85	£250	£775
antoninianus	£25	£70	£175
Plautilla			
denarius	£22	£55	£150
Geta			
denarius	£12	£35	£95
denarius (VICT BRIT)	£30	£85	£225
sestertius	£100	£300	£875
sestertius (VICT BRIT)	£220	£650	£2250
dupondius or as	£65	£185	£575
dupondius (VICT BRIT)	£95	£275	£850
Macrinus			
antoninianus	£75	£225	£500
denarius	£30	£85	£225
*sestertius	£195	£550	£2200
Diadumenian			
*denarius	£65	£175	£450
dupondius or As	£120	£350	£1100
Elagabalus			
aureus	£600	£1800	£5000
denarius	£12	£35	£95
dupondius or As	£50	£140	£475
antoninianus	£18	£55	£150
Julia Paula			
denarius	£30	£85	£250
Aquilla Severa			
denarius	£50	£135	£375
Julia Soaemias			
denarius	£22	£55	£140
Julia Maesa			
denarius	£15	£40	£115
Severus Alexander			
aureus	£350	£900	£2700
*denarius	£12	£30	£90
sestertius	£28	£85	£275
dupondius or As	£24	£70	£225

Macrinus

Diadumenian

Severus Alexander

Maximinus

	F	VF	EF
Orbiana			
denarius	£55	£145	£375
Julia Mamaea			
denarius	£13	£35	£100
Maximinus I			
denarius	£15	£45	£100
*sestertius	£30	£90	£300
as	£27	£75	£250
Maximus			
denarius	£50	£140	£400
sestertius	£55	£150	£430
Balbinus & Pupienus			
antoninanus	£60	£175	£450
denarius	£50	£160	£420
Gordian III			
antoninianus	£8	£22	£60
denarius	£10	£33	£85
sestertius	£22	£70	£180
Philip I			
antoninianus "Animal Den"			
lion, stag, antelope, wolf & twins	£20	£50	£125
antoninianus	£8	£22	£60
*sestertius	£25	£75	£200
Otacilla Severa			
antoniniaus	£10	£25	£70
sestertius	£25	£80	£275
Philip II			
antoninianus	£10	£25	£70
Trajan Decius			
antoninianus	£8	£22	£60
Herennius Etruscilla			
antoninianus	£10	£25	£70
Herennius Etruscus			
antoninianus	£15	£50	£130
Hostilian			
antoninianus	£30	£90	£265
Trebonianus Gallus			
antoninianus	£12	£27	£70
Volusian			
antoninianus	£12	£30	£75
Aemilian			
*antoninianus	£45	£135	£325
Valerian I			
antoninianus	£8	£20	£55
Diva Mariniana			
antoninianus	£40	£110	£300
Gallienus			
*silver antoninianus	£8	£20	£55
ae antoninianus	£5	£15	£40
ae denarius	£45	£125	£375
Salonina			
ae antoninianus	£7	£18	£45
Valerian II			
billon antoninianus	£12	£35	£95
Saloninus			
antoninianus	£12	£35	£95
Macrianus			
billon antoninianus	£40	£100	£265
Quietus			
billon antoninianus	£40	£100	£265
Postumus			
silver antoninianus	£8	£22	£60
*ae antoninianus	£5	£15	£40
sestertius	£45	£145	£450

Philip I

Aemillian

Gallienus

Postumus

123

	F	VF	EF
Laelianus			
antoninianus	£115	£285	£700
Marius			
antoninianus	£35	£90	£235
Victorinus			
ae antoninianus.................................	£5	£15	£40
Claudius II Gothicus			
ae antoninianus.................................	£4	£14	£38
Tetricus I			
ae antoninianus.................................	£5	£15	£40
Tetricus II			
ae antoninianus.................................	£7	£17	£45
Quintillus			
*ae antoninianus	£13	£35	£85
Aurelian			
ae antoninianus.................................	£6	£17	£50
Vabalathus & Aurelian			
ae antoninianus	£25	£60	£175
Severina			
*ae antoninianus	£12	£35	£95
Tacitus			
ae antoninianus.................................	£10	£27	£75
Florian			
ae antoninianus.................................	£25	£75	£200
Probus			
ae antoninianus.................................	£5	£16	£45
antoninianus (military or imp. busts).	£10	£25	£65
Carus			
ae antoninianus.................................	£12	£35	£95
Numerian			
ae antoninianus.................................	£12	£35	£95
Carinus			
ae antoninianus.................................	£11	£30	£80
Magna Urbica			
ae antoninianus	£60	£160	£400
Diocletian			
ae argenteus	£80	£250	£600
ae antoninianus.................................	£7	£22	£65
ae follis (London Mint).......................	£12	£35	£95
Ae follis (other mints)	£10	£25	£70
Maximianus			
ae follis (London mint).......................	£12	£35	£95
*ae follis (other mints)	£10	£25	£70
Carausius			
aureus	£5250	£15,000	—
denarius	£275	£800	£2250
antoninianus	£25	£55	£250
with full silvering............................	£30	£90	£395
legionary antoninianus......................	£70	£190	£725
Expectate Veni antoninianus.............	£85	£260	—
in the name of Diocletian or Maximian	£30	£90	£400
Allectus			
aureus	£6500	£20,000	—
antoninianus	£25	£65	£300
with full silvering............................	£35	£100	£450
quinarius	£25	£65	£250
Constantius I			
ae follis (London mint).......................	£14	£35	£110
ae follis (other mints)........................	£10	£25	£70
Galerius			
ae follis (London mint).......................	£12	£30	£90
ae follis (other mints)........................	£8	£22	£60
Galeria Valeria			
follis..	£30	£75	£200

Quintillus

Severina

Maximianus

Severus II

	F	VF	EF
Severus II			
ae follis (London mint)......................	£38	£95	£255
*ae follis (other mints)	£30	£75	£200
Maximinus II			
ae follis (London mint)......................	£14	£35	£110
*ae follis (other mints)	£7	£18	£50
Maxentius			
follis...	£8	£22	£60
Romulus			
ae follis	£35	£90	£275
Licinius I			
follis (London mint)	£8	£22	£65
follis (other mints)..............................	£7	£18	£55
ae 3..	£6	£16	£45
Licinius II			
ae 3..	£9	£22	£60
Constantine I			
follis (London mint)	£8	£20	£55
as above—helmeted bust...............	£15	£45	£125
follis (other mints)..............................	£6	£15	£45
ae 3..	£5	£13	£40
ae 3 (London mint)............................	£8	£20	£55
Urbs Roma ae 3/4...........................	£4	£12	£40
Faustina			
ae 3 (London mint)............................	£60	£150	£375
ae 3 (other mints)..............................	£16	£40	£120
Helena			
*ae 3 (London mint)...........................	£60	£150	£375
ae 3 (other mints)..............................	£16	£40	£120
Theodora			
ae 4..	£8	£22	£60
Crispus			
ae 3 (London mint).............................	£10	£25	£75
*ae 3...	£7	£18	£55
Delmatius			
ae 3/4	£14	£35	£90
Hanniballianus Rex			
ae 4..	£90	£250	£650
Constantine II			
ae 3 (London Mint)	£10	£25	£75
ae 3..	£7	£18	£50
ae 4..	£3	£8	£30
Constans			
*ae 2 (centenionalis).........................	£10	£25	£70
ae 3 (half centenionalis)	£6	£20	£50
ae 4..	£3	£8	£30
Constantius II			
*siliqua	£22	£65	£160
ae 2 (centenionalis)	£6	£20	£50
ae 3 (half centenionalis)	£6	£17	£45
ae 4..	£2	£7	£28
Magnentius			
double centenionalis.........................	£50	£150	£475
centenionalis.....................................	£12	£35	£95
Decentius			
double centenionalis.........................	£65	£195	£600
centenionalis.....................................	£15	£45	£130
Vetranio			
ae 2 (centenionalis)	£45	£135	£400
ae 3 (half centenionalis)	£38	£110	£325
Constantius Gallus			
centenionalis.....................................	£12	£35	£90
Julian II			
*siliqua	£24	£65	£170
ae 1..	£40	£125	£360
ae 3 (helmeted bust)	£10	£25	£75

Maximinus II

Helena

Crispus

Julian II

	F	VF	EF
Jovian			
ae 1	£75	£225	£575
ae 3	£13	£35	£95
Valentinian I			
gold solidus	£110	£275	£600
siliqua	£26	£65	£145
ae 3	£5	£15	£50
Valens			
gold solidus	£110	£275	£600
*siliqua	£22	£60	£145
ae 3	£5	£15	£50
Procopius			
ae 3	£50	£150	£450
Gratian			
silver milliarense	£165	£500	£1200
*siliqua	£24	£60	£150
ae 3	£5	£15	£50
Valentinian II			
siliqua	£25	£65	£150
ae 2	£12	£28	£80
ae 4	£5	£12	£35
Theodosius I			
siliqua	£28	£75	£180
ae 2	£12	£30	£85
Aelia Flaccilla			
ae 2	£25	£70	£220
Magnus Maximus			
solidus	£700	£1800	£4500
siliqua	£50	£80	£195
*ae 2	£28	£70	£175
Flavius Victor			
silver sliqua	£100	£275	£680
Eugenius			
silver siliqua	£120	£300	£750
Arcadius			
gold solidus	£100	£250	£550
silver siliqua	£25	£65	£160
ae 2	£11	£28	£75
Eudoxia			
ae 3	£22	£60	£180
Honorius			
gold solidus	£100	£250	£550
silver siliqua	£30	£75	£190
ae 4	£6	£15	£45
Constantine III			
silver siliqua	£120	£300	£750

Valens

Gratian

Magnus Maximus

ae = bronze; ae 1, 2, 3, 4 = bronze coins in descending order of size.

Illustrations by courtesy of Classical Numismatic Group/Seaby Coins.

A SIMPLIFIED PRICE GUIDE
TO

ENGLISH HAMMERED COINS

PART I

959–1485

INTRODUCTION

We have taken our starting point for hammered coin prices back to the Anglo-Saxon reign of Edgar; who could reasonably claim to be the first king of All England. Also it is from this time onwards that we start to get regular "portraits" as well as moneyers and mints on most issues. This gives a total of eight rulers to the list of kings prior to the Norman Conquest and most of these have coin issues that can be purchased quite reasonably. It is also worth pointing out here that of course coins had previously been struck in England for approximately 1000 years prior to our listings by Celtic, Roman and earlier Saxon rulers, details of which can be found in more specific publications.

PRICING

The prices given in the following pages are intended to be used as a "Pocket book guide" to the values of the *most common* coins within any denomination of any one reign. The price quoted is what a collector may expect to pay for such a piece in the condition indicated. For more detailed information we recommend the reader to one of the many specialist publications.

GRADING

The prices quoted are for three different grades of condition: Fine (F), Very Fine (VF) and Extremely Fine (EF). A "Fine" coin is assumed to be a fairly worn, circulated, piece but with all or most of the main features and lettering still clear. "Very Fine" is a middle grade with a small amount of wear and most details fairly clear. For this edition we have included the prices for coins in Extremely Fine condition where appropriate, although very few hammered coins actually turn up in this grade (i.e. nearly mint state with hardly any wear). In some instances the prices quoted are theoretically based and are only included to provide a guide. It is important to note that on all hammered coins the very nature of striking, i.e. individually, by hand, means hammered coinage is rarely a straight grade and when listed by a dealer the overall condition will often be qualified by terms such as: *weak in parts, struck off-centre, cracked or chipped flan, double struck,* etc. When applicable the price should be adjusted accordingly.

HISTORY

Below the heading for each monarch we have given a few historical notes as and when they apply to significant changes in the coinage.

EDGAR
(959–957

	F	VF	EF
Edgar Penny, non portrait (2 line inscription)............................	£150	£325	—

EDWARD THE MARTYR
(975–978)

	F	VF	EF
Edward, Penny, Portrait........................	£700	£1650	—

AETHELRED II
(978–1016)

	F	VF	EF
Aethelred II, Penny, First hand type	£90	£225	—

CNUT
(1016–1035)

	F	VF	EF
Cnut, Penny (Helmet type)	£65	£115	£200

HAROLD I
(1035–40)

	F	VF	EF
Harold I, Penny	£190	£460	—

HARTHACANUTE
(1035–42)

	F	VF	EF
Harthacanute, Penny, English Mint (in his own name)	£700	£1600	—
Harthacanute, Penny, Danish type	£160	£440	—

Danish type

EDWARD THE CONFESSOR
(1042–66)

	F	VF	EF
Edward the Confessor, Penny	£80	£160	—

HAROLD II
(1066)

	F	VF	EF
Harold II, Penny	£450	£950	—

WILLIAM I
(1066–87)

The Norman Conquest had very little immediate effect on the coinage of England. The Anglo-Saxon standard of minting silver pennies was very high and the practice of the moneyer putting his name and mint town on the reverse continued as before, except with William's portrait of course. It is worth noting here that non-realistic, stylised portraits were used until the reign of Henry VII.

There are eight major types of pennies of which the last, the PAXS type, is by far the commonest.

	F	VF	EF
William I, Penny	£160	£325	£600

WILLIAM II
(1087–1100)

Very little change from his father's reign except that five new types were issued, most of which were much more crudely designed than previous, all are scarce.

	F	VF	EF
William II, Penny	£425	£900	—

HENRY I
(1100–35)

There are fifteen different types of penny for this reign of which the last two are the most common. Most issues are of a very poor standard both in workmanship and metal, the prices reflect a poor quality of issue.

	F	VF	EF
Henry I, Penny	£145	£350	—

STEPHEN
(1135–54)

This is historically a very complicated time for the coinage, mainly due to civil war and a consequential lack of central control in the country which resulted in very poor quality and deliberately damaged pieces. Coins were struck not only in the name of Stephen and his main rival claimant Matilda but also by their supporters. The commonest issue is the "Watford" type; so named, as are many issues, after the area in which a hoard was found.

	F	VF	EF
Stephen, Penny	£200	£550	—

HENRY II
(1154–89)

There were two distinct issues struck during this reign. The first, Cross and Crosslets or "Tealby" coinage (named after Tealby in Lincolnshire), continued to be very poorly made and lasted 20 years. However, in 1180 the new and superior "Short Cross" issue commenced, being issued from only twelve major

	F	VF	EF
Henry II, Penny, Tealby	£75	£200	—
Henry II, Penny, Short Cross	£40	£115	—

RICHARD I
(1189–1199)

There were no major changes during this reign, in fact pennies continued to be struck with his father Henry's name throughout the reign. The coins struck under Richard tend to be rather crude in style.

	F	VF	EF
Richard I, Penny	£55	£140	—

JOHN
(1199–1216)

As with his brother before him, there were no major changes during the reign of King John, and pennies with his father's name were struck throughout the reign, although they tended to be somewhat neater in style than those struck during the reign of Richard I.

	F	VF	EF
John, Penny.....................................	£40	£90	£175

HENRY III
(1216–72)

The coinage during Henry III's reign continued as before with the short cross issue. However, in 1247 a new long cross design was introduced to prevent clipping. This design was to last in one form or another for many centuries.

	F	VF	EF
Henry III, Penny, Short Cross	£25	£55	£125
Henry III, Penny, Long Cross...................	£20	£40	£100

EDWARD I
(1272–1307)

After a few years of issuing similar pieces to his father, in 1279 Edward I ordered a major re-coinage. This consisted of well-made pennies, halfpennies and farthings in relatively large quantities, and for a brief period a groat (four pence) was produced. The pennies are amongst the most common of all hammered coins.

	F	VF	EF
Edward I (and Edward II)			
Groat (often damaged)....................	£1600	£5500	—
Penny......................................	£18	£40	£100
Halfpenny.................................	£20	£50	£150
Farthing..................................	£15	£45	£140

Edward I halfpenny

EDWARD II
(1307–1327)

The coinage of Edward II differs in only a very few minor details from that of Edward I and are of similar value.

EDWARD III
(1327–77)

This was a long reign which saw major changes in the coinage, the most significant being the introduction of a gold coinage (based on the Noble, valued at 6s 8d, and its fractions) and a regular issue of a large silver groat (and half groat). The mints were limited to a few episcopal cities but coins of English type were also struck in the newly-acquired Calais.

	F	VF	EF
Gold			
Noble	£500	£1100	£2350
Half Noble	£320	£750	£1600
Quarter Noble	£180	£400	£725
Silver			
Groat	£50	£135	£400
Half Groat	£30	£85	£250
Penny	£20	£50	£135
Half Penny	£15	£40	£120
Farthing	£30	£70	£150

Gold Noble

RICHARD II
(1377–1399)

The denominations continued during this reign much as before. However, coins are quite rare mainly due to the lack of bullion gold and silver going into the mints, mainly because of an inbalance with European weights and fineness.

	F	VF	EF
Gold			
Noble	£675	£1400	£3000
Half Noble	£625	£1650	—
Quarter Noble	£325	£750	£1250
Silver			
Groat	£300	£825	—
Half Groat	£200	£480	—
Penny	£50	£175	—
Half Penny	£30	£90	—
Farthing	£100	£240	—

Groat

HENRY IV
(1399–1413)

Because of the continuing problems with the scarcity of gold and silver the coinage was reduced in weight in 1412, towards the end of the reign. All coins of this reign are quite scarce.

	F	VF
Gold		
Noble	£1200	£3000
Half Noble	£2150	£5000
Quarter Noble	£450	£1000
Silver		
Groat	£1600	£5000
Half Groat	£425	£950
Penny	£200	£600
Half Penny	£165	£425
Farthing	£600	£1350

Noble

HENRY V
(1413–22)

Monetary reform introduced towards the end of his father's reign in 1412 improved the supply of bullion and hence coins of Henry V are far more common. All of the main denominations continued as before.

	F	VF	EF
Gold			
Noble	£600	£1200	£2500
Half Noble	£500	£100	—
Quarter Noble	£250	£600	£1000
Silver			
Groat	£120	£350	—
Half Groat	£90	£260	—
Penny	£30	£100	—
Half Penny	£20	£75	—
Farthing	£130	£400	—

Half Groat

HENRY VI
(1422–61 and again 1470–71)

Although there were no new denominations during these reigns (see Edward IV below), Henry's first reign saw eleven different issues, each for a few years and distinguished by privy marks, i.e. crosses, pellets, annulets, etc.

HENRY VI *continued*

Gold	F	VF	EF
First reign—			
Noble	£450	£1100	£2000
Half Noble	£300	£800	£1450
Quarter Noble	£180	£400	£700
2nd reign—			
Angel	£1100	£2700	—
Half Angel	£1600	£4200	—

Silver	F	VF	EF
Groat	£40	£100	£200
Half Groat	£30	£75	£165
Penny	£25	£70	£150
Half Penny	£15	£45	£115
Farthing	£90	£225	

Groat

EDWARD IV
(1461–70 and again 1471–83)

The significant changes during these reigns were the replacement of the noble by the rose ryal (and revalued at 10 shillings) and the introduction of the angel at the old noble value. We also start to see mint-marks or initial marks appearing, usually at the top of the coin, they were used to denote the period of issue for dating purposes and often lasted for two to three years.

Gold	F	VF	EF
Ryal	£525	£1150	£1800
Half Ryal	£400	£900	£1500
Quarter Ryal	£275	£600	£1000
Angel	£425	£950	£1800
Half Angel	£350	£725	£1500

Silver	F	VF	EF
Groat	£40	£110	£265
Half Groat	£35	£90	£225
Penny	£35	£75	£175
Half Penny	£20	£70	—
Farthing	£230	£500	—

Gold Ryal

RICHARD III
(1483–85)

The close of the Yorkist Plantagenet and the beginning of the Medieval period come together at this time. There are no new significant numismatic changes but most coins of Richard whilst not really rare, continue to be very popular and priced quite high.

Gold	F	VF	EF
Angel	£1450	£3500	—
Half Angel	£2800	£7750	—

Silver	F	VF	EF
Groat	£380	£900	—
Half Groat	£450	£1200	—
Penny	£180	£475	—
Half Penny	£140	£365	—
Farthing	£725	£1850	—

Groat

PART II: 1485–1663

Among the more significant features of the post-Renaissance period as it affected coinage is the introduction of realistic portraiture during the reign of Henry VII. We also have a much wider and varied number of new and revised denominations, for example eleven different gold denominations of Henry VIII and the same number of silver for Elizabeth I. Here we only mention the introduction or changes in the main denominations, giving a value for all of them, once again listing the commonest type.

HENRY VII
(1485–1509)

The gold sovereign of 20 shillings makes its first appearance in 1489 as does the testoon (later shilling) in about 1500. The silver penny was re-designed to a rather crude likeness of the sovereign.

	F	VF	EF
Gold			
Sovereign	£7500	£19,000	—
Ryal	£7750	£23,500	—
Angel	£380	£850	£1600
Half Angel	£340	£750	£1400
Silver			
Testoon 1/-	£5500	£12,000	—
Groat	£55	£145	£400
Half Groat	£30	£80	£200
Penny	£30	£80	£175
Half Penny	£20	£60	—
Farthing	£140	£450	—

Profile Groat

Sovereign-style penny

HENRY VIII
(1509–47)

After a long initial period of very little change in the coinage, in 1526 there were many, with an attempt to bring the gold/silver ratio in line with the continental currencies. Some gold coins only lasted a short time and are very rare. The crown (in gold) makes its first appearance. Towards the end of the reign we see large issues of debased silver coins (with a high copper content) bearing the well-known facing portrait of the ageing King. These tend to turn up in poor condition.

Gold			
Sovereign	£2400	£6750	—
Half Sovereign	£425	£1100	—
Angel	£385	£850	£1700
Half Angel	£300	£750	£1400
Quarter Angel	£350	£825	—
George Noble	£3500	£9500	—
Half George Noble	Rare	Rare	—
Crown of the rose	Rare	Rare	—
Crown of the double rose	£350	£850	£1500
Half Crown of the double rose	£300	£750	—
Silver			
Testoon 1/-	£575	£1875	—
Groat	£80	£250	£450
Half Groat	£45	£120	£250
Penny	£30	£110	£200
Half Penny	£25	£75	—
Farthing	£220	£600	—

Facing Groat

Crown of the double rose

EDWARD VI
(1547–53)

Some of the coins struck in the first few years of this short reign could really be called Henry VIII posthumous issues as there is continuity in both name and style from his father's last issue. However, overlapping this period are portrait issues of the boy King, particularly shillings (usually poor quality coins). This period also sees the first dated English coin (shown in Roman numerals). In 1551 however, a new coinage was introduced with a restored silver quality from the Crown (dated 1551) down to the new sixpence and threepence.

	F	VF	EF
Gold			
Sovereign (30s)	£2875	£7500	—
Half Sovereign	£800	£2300	—
Crown	£900	£2400	—
Half Crown	£875	£2250	—
Angel	£4000	£12,000	—
Half Angel	—	—	—
Sovereign (20s)	£1875	£4750	—
Silver			
Crown	£575	£1500	—
Half Crown	£450	£1100	—
Shilling	£85	£350	£850
Sixpence	£90	£380	—
Groat	£625	£1700	—
Threepence	£170	£575	—
Half Groat	£250	£650	—
Penny	£50	£200	—
Half Penny	£150	£500	—
Farthing	£750	£2350	—

Base Shilling, obverse

Fine Shilling

MARY
(1553–54)

The early coins of Mary's sole reign are limited and continue to use the same denominations as Edward, except that the gold ryal was reintroduced.

	F	VF
Gold		
Sovereign (30s)	£2800	£7000
Ryal	£8250	—
Angel	£950	£2500
Half Angel	£2000	£5250
Silver		
Groat	£100	£375
Half Groat	£675	£1800
Penny	£450	£1450

Groat

PHILIP & MARY
(1554–58)

After a very short reign alone, Mary married Philip of Spain and they technically ruled jointly (although not for very long in practise) until her death. After her marriage we see both her and Philip on the shillings and sixpences.

	F	VF
Gold		
Angel	£2000	£5350
Half Angel	£4500	—
Silver		
Shilling	£275	£925
Sixpence	£250	£900
Groat	£100	£375
Half Groat	£325	£850
Penny	£75	£225

Shilling

ELIZABETH I
(1558–1603)

As might be expected with a long reign there are a number of significant changes in the coinage which include several new denominations—so many in silver that every value from the shilling downwards was marked and dated to distinguish them. Early on we have old base Edward VI shillings countermarked to a new reduced value (not priced here). Also due to a lack of small change and the expense of making a miniscule farthing we have a new threehalfpence and threefarthings. Finally we see the beginnings of a milled (machine produced) coinage for a brief period from 1561–71.

	F	VF	EF
Gold			
Sovereign (30s)	£2400	£6000	—
Ryal (15s)	£4500	£12,000	—
Angel	£500	£1200	—
Half Angel	£475	£1100	—
Quarter Angel	£400	£925	—
Pound (20s)	£1300	£3250	—
Half Pound	£700	£1750	—
Crown	£650	£1500	—
Half Crown	£600	£1500	—
Silver			
Crown	£900	£2400	—
Half Crown	£625	£1700	—
Shilling	£75	£275	£750
Sixpence	£45	£150	£400
Groat	£50	£165	£300
Threepence	£35	£120	£250
Half Groat	£25	£65	—
Threehalfpence	£30	£100	—
Penny	£25	£70	£135
Threefarthings	£55	£170	—
Half Penny	£25	£70	£100

Shilling

Milled Sixpence

JAMES I
(1603–25)

Although the size of the gold coinage remains much the same as Elizabeth's reign, the name and weight or value of the denominations have several changes, i.e. Pound = Sovereign = Unite = Laurel. A new four shilling gold coin (thistle crown) was introduced. A number of the silver coins now have their value in Roman numerals on the coin. Relatively few angels were made from this period onwards and they are usually found pierced.

	F	VF	EF		F	VF	EF
Gold				Sixpence	£45	£160	—
Sovereign (20s)	£1000	£2400	—	Half Groat	£18	£45	£85
Unite	£370	£800	£1750	Penny	£18	£35	£70
Double crown/half unite	£300	£650	£1350	Half Penny	£15	£30	£50
Crown	£175	£400	£850				
Thistle Crown	£200	£500	£850				
Half Crown	£165	£350	—				
Rose Ryal (30s)	£1325	£3200	—				
Spur Ryal (15s)	£2300	£6750	—				
Angel (pierced)	£400	£825	—				
Half Angel (Unpierced)	£1400	£4250	—				
Laurel	£370	£775	—				
Half Laurel	£325	£725	—				
Quarter Laurel	£190	£425	£850				
Silver							
Crown	£500	£1300	—				
Half Crown	£210	£650	—				
Shilling	£55	£210	—				

CHARLES I
(1625–49)

This reign is probably the most difficult to simplify as there are so many different issues and whole books have been produced on this period alone. From the beginning of the King's reign and throughout the Civil War, a number of mints operated for varying lengths of time, producing both regular and irregular issues. The Tower mint was taken over by Parliament in 1642 but before this a small quantity of milled coinage was produced alongside the regular hammered issues. The Court then moved to Oxford from where, for the next three years, large quantities of gold and silver were struck (including rare triple unites and large silver pounds). The most prolific of the provincial mints were those situated at Aberystwyth, York, Oxford, Shrewsbury, Bristol, Exeter, Truro, Chester and Worcester as well as some smaller mints mainly situated in the West Country. Among the more interesting coins of the period are the pieces struck on unusually-shaped flans at Newark and Pontefract whilst those towns were under siege. As many of the coins struck during the Civil War were crudely struck on hastily gathered bullion and plate, they provide a fascinating area of study. The prices indicated below are the minimum for the commonest examples of each denomination irrespective of town of origin.

	F	VF	EF
Gold			
Triple Unite (£3)	£3400	£8500	—
Unite	£400	£925	—
Double crown/Half unite	£325	£700	—
Crown	£175	£410	—
Angel (pierced)	£500	£1200	—
Silver			
Pound (20 shillings)	£1500	£3250	—
Half Pound	£650	£1450	—
Crown	£280	£750	—
Half Crown	£60	£175	—
Shilling	£40	£150	£425
Sixpence	£45	£165	£400
Groat	£50	£135	£275
Threepence	£45	£125	£250
Half Groat	£20	£50	£100
Penny	£15	£35	£90
Half Penny	£15	£35	£55

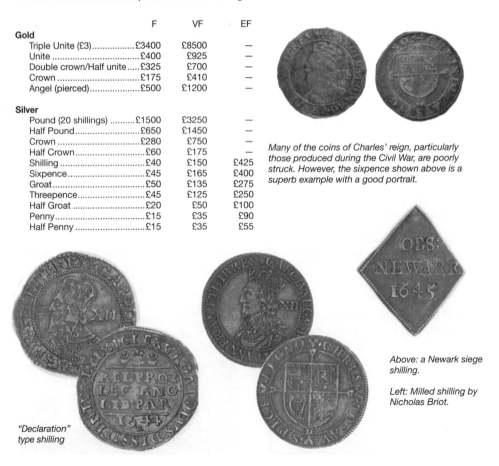

Many of the coins of Charles' reign, particularly those produced during the Civil War, are poorly struck. However, the sixpence shown above is a superb example with a good portrait.

Above: a Newark siege shilling.

Left: Milled shilling by Nicholas Briot.

"Declaration" type shilling

THE COMMONWEALTH
(1649–60)

After the execution of Charles I, Parliament changed the design of the coinage. They are simple non-portrait pieces with an English legend.

	F	VF	EF
Gold			
Unite	£700	£1300	—
Double crown/Half unite	£500	£1150	—
Crown	£450	£1000	—
Silver			
Crown	£565	£1150	£2500
Half Crown	£175	£460	£1500
Shilling	£125	£265	£650
Sixpence	£100	£270	£600
Half Groat	£30	£85	£185
Penny	£30	£80	£165
Half Penny	£25	£75	£125

Unite

CHARLES II
(1660–85)

Although milled coins had been produced for Oliver Cromwell in 1656–58, after the Restoration of the monarchy hammered coins continued to be produced until 1663, when the machinery was ready to manufacture large quantities of good milled pieces.

	F	VF	EF
Gold			
Unite	£825	£2000	—
Double crown/Half unite	£700	£1900	—
Crown	£675	£1800	—
Silver			
Half Crown	£140	£500	—
Shilling	£120	£325	—
Sixpence	£100	£300	—
Fourpence	£30	£75	£140
Threepence	£30	£75	£130
Twopence	£20	£45	£85
Penny	£25	£55	£110

Halfcrown

A COMPREHENSIVE PRICE GUIDE
TO THE COINS OF

THE
UNITED KINGDOM
1656–2004

including

ENGLAND
SCOTLAND
ISLE OF MAN
GUERNSEY, JERSEY, ALDERNEY

also

IRELAND

When referring to this price guide one must bear a number of important points in mind. The points listed here have been taken into consideration during the preparation of this guide and we hope that the prices given will provide a true reflection of the market at the time of going to press. Nevertheless, the publishers can accept no liability for the accuracy of the prices quoted.

1. "As struck" examples with flaws will be worth less than the indicated price.
2. Any coin which is particularly outstanding, with an attractive natural toning or in superb state will command a much *higher* price than that shown.
3. These prices refer strictly to the British market, and do not reflect outside opinions.
4. Some prices given for coins not seen in recent years are estimates based on a knowledge of the market.
5. In the case of coins of high rarity, prices are not generally given.
6. In the listing, "—" indicates, where applicable, one of the following:
    a. Metal or bullion value only
    b. Not usually found in this grade
    c. Not collected in this condition
7. Proof coins are listed in FDC under the UNC column.
8. All prices are quoted in £ sterling, exclusive of VAT (where applicable).

FIVE GUINEAS

CHARLES II (1660–85)

	F	VF	EF
1668 First bust	£1200	£3000	£7000
1668 — Elephant	£1200	£3000	£7500
1669 —	£1400	£3250	—
1669 — Elephant	£1500	£3500	—
*1670 —	£1500	£3500	£8250
1671 —	£1500	£3500	£8500
1672 —	£1500	£3500	£7500
1673 —	£1500	£3500	£7500
1674 —	£1500	£3500	£8250
1675 —	£1500	£3500	£7500
1675 — Elephant	£1500	£3250	—
1675 — Elephant & Castle		Extremely rare	
1676 —	£1500	£3500	£8000
1676 — Elephant & Castle	£1250	£3000	£7000
1677 —	£1300	£3000	£7000
1677/5 —Elephant		Extremely rare	
1677 — Elephant & Castle	£1400	£3500	£8000
1678 —	£1500	£3500	£8000
1678 — Elephant & Castle	£1500	£3750	£8500
1678/7—Second Bust	£1500	£3200	—
1679 —	£1200	£3000	£7000
1680 —	£1200	£3000	£7000
1680 — Elephant & Castle		Extremely rare	
1681 —	£1200	£3000	£7000
1681 — Elephant & Castle	£1500	£3500	£8000
1682 —	£1250	£3000	£7000
1682 — Elephant & Castle	£1250	£3000	£7000
1683 —	£1500	£3000	£7000
1683 — Elephant & Castle	£1500	£3600	£8000
1684 —	£1200	£2500	£7000
1684 — Elephant & Castle	£1200	£3000	£7000

JAMES II (1685–88)

	F	VF	EF
1686	£1500	£4000	£9000
1687	£1200	£3000	£8500
1687 Elephant & Castle	£1500	£3000	£9000
1688	£1500	£4000	£10000
1688 Elephant & Castle	£1500	£4000	£10000

WILLIAM AND MARY (1688–94)

	F	VF	EF
*1691	£1200	£3000	£7500
1691 Elephant & Castle	£1400	£3000	£8000
1692	£1200	£3000	£7500
1692 Elephant & Castle	£1400	£3000	£8000
1693	£1200	£3000	£7500
1693 Elephant & Castle	£1600	£3250	£9000
1694	£1400	£3500	£9000
1694 Elephant & Castle	£1500	£3500	£9500

WILLIAM III (1694–1702)

	F	VF	EF
1699 First bust	£1200	£3500	£7250
1699 — Elephant & Castle	£1500	£4000	£9000
1700 —	£1300	£3500	£8000
1701 Second bust "fine work"	£1200	£3500	£8000

ANNE (1702–14)

Pre-Union with Scotland

	F	VF	EF
1703 VIGO below bust	—	—	£4500

	F	VF	EF
*1705	£1500	£3000	£8000
1706	£1250	£3000	£9000
Post-Union (different shields)			
1706	£1700	£3250	£8000
1709 Narrow shields	£1500	£3250	£8000
1711 Broader shields	£1500	£3250	£8000
1713 —	£1500	£3250	£8000
1714 —	£1500	£3250	£8000
1714/3	£1600	£3500	£8500

GEORGE I (1714–27)

	F	VF	EF
1716	£1600	£3750	£9000
1717	£1700	£4000	£9500
1720	£1700	£4000	£9500
1726	£1600	£3500	£9000

GEORGE II (1727–60)

	F	VF	EF
1729 Young head	£1200	£3000	£7500
1729 — E.I.C. below head	£1200	£3000	£7500
1731 —	£1200	£3000	£7000
1735 —	£1200	£3000	£7000
1738 —	£1200	£3000	£7000
1741 —	£1200	£3000	£7000
1746 Old head, LIMA	£1250	£3200	£7000
1748 —	£1000	£2500	£7000
1753 —	£1000	£2500	£7000

GEORGE III (1760–1820)

	F	VF	EF
1770 Patterns	—	—	£45000
1773	—	—	£45000
1777	—	—	£45000

TWO GUINEAS

	F	VF	EF

CHARLES II (1660–85)

	F	VF	EF
1664 First bust	£800	£2500	—
*1664 — Elephant	£800	£2000	£4500
1665 —		Extremely rare	
1669 —		Extremely rare	
1671 —	£800	£3000	£4250
1675 Second bust	£850	£2500	£4250
1676 —	£700	£2250	—
1676 — Elephant & Castle	£700	£2250	—
1677 —	£700	£2250	£4500
1677 — Elephant & Castle		Extremely rare	
1678/7 —	£700	£2200	—
1678 — Elephant		Extremely rare	
1678 — Elephant & Castle	£700	£2200	—
1679 —	£700	£2200	—
1680 —	£800	£2500	—
1681 —	£700	£2200	£4500
1682 — Elephant & Castle	£700	£2200	£5000
1683 —	£700	£2200	£4500
1683 — Elephant & Castle	£900	£3000	—
1684 —	£800	£2500	—
1684 — Elephant & Castle	£900	£2500	£6000

JAMES II (1685–88)

	F	VF	EF
1687	£900	£2500	£5000
*1688/7	£1000	£2750	£9000

WILLIAM AND MARY (1688–94)

	F	VF	EF
1691 Elephant & Castle		Extremely rare	
1693	£800	£2200	£5000
1693 Elephant & Castle	£900	£2500	£5000
1694	£750	£2200	£4500
1694 Elephant & Castle	£850	£2500	£5000

WILLIAM III (1694–1702)

	F	VF	EF
1701 "fine work"	£120	£3000	£4700

ANNE (1702–14)

	F	VF	EF
1709	£600	£1400	£3750
1711	£600	£1400	£3750
1713	£600	£1400	£3750
1714	£650	£1500	£4000

GEORGE I (1714–27)

	F	VF	EF
1717	£600	£1700	£4000
1720	£600	£1700	£4500
*1726	£500	£1500	£3750

	F	VF	EF

GEORGE II (1727–60)

	F	VF	EF
1734 Young head 4 over 3	£1400	£3000	–
1735 —	£450	£1200	£2700
*1738 —	£375	£700	£1700
1739 —	£375	£700	£1750
1739 Intermediate head	£400	£800	£2000
1740 —	£400	£800	£2000
1748 Old head	£400	£1100	£3000
1753 —	£500	£1400	£3500

GEORGE III (1760–1820)

	F	VF	EF
1768 Patterns only	–	–	£20000
1773 Patterns only	–	–	£20000
1777 Patterns only	–	–	£20000

GUINEAS

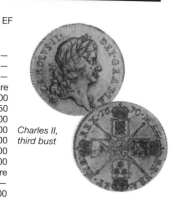

Charles II, third bust

CHARLES II (1660–85)

	F	VF	EF
1663 First bust	£700	£2200	–
1663 — Elephant below	£575	£2000	–
1664 Second bust	£500	£1750	–
1664 — Elephant		Extremely rare	
1664 Third bust	£475	£1500	£4000
1664 — Elephant	£600	£1800	£4250
1665 —	£450	£1500	£3500
1665 — Elephant	£500	£1600	£4500
1666 —	£450	£1600	£4500
1667 —	£450	£1600	£4000
1668 —	£450	£1600	£4000
1668 — Elephant		Extremely rare	
1669 —	£500	£1750	–
*1670 —	£450	£1600	£4000
1671 —	£450	£1600	£4000
1672 —	£450	£1600	£4500
1672 Fourth bust	£400	£1400	£3500
1673 Third bust	£600	£2000	£4500
1673 Fourth bust	£400	£1200	£3000
1674 —	£450	£1500	–
1674 — Elephant & Castle		Extremely rare	
1675 —	£400	£1500	£4000
1675 — CRAOLVS Error		Extremely rare	
*1675 — Elephant & Castle	£500	£1600	£4000
1676 —	£350	£1200	£3000
1676 — Elephant & Castle	£400	£1500	£3500
1677 —	£350	£1200	£3000
1677/5 — Elephant 7 over 5		Extremely rare	
1677 — Elephant & Castle	£400	£1600	£4000
1678 —	£350	£1200	£3000
1678 — Elephant		Extremely rare	
1678 — Elephant & Castle	£500	£1800	–

Charles II, fourth bust, elephant & castle below

	F	VF	EF
1679 —	£350	£1200	£3000
1679 — Elephant & Castle	£500	£1750	—
1680 —	£350	£1200	£3000
1680 — Elephant & Castle	£600	£2000	—
1681 —	£400	£1500	£4000
1681 — Elephant & Castle	£500	£1600	—
1682 —	£400	£1500	£3500
1682 — Elephant & Castle	£425	£1600	£4000
1683 —	£350	£1200	£3000
1683 — Elephant & Castle	£600	£2000	£4000
1684 —	£375	£1400	£4000
1684 — Elephant & Castle	£425	£1500	£4000

James II, first bust, elephant & castle below

JAMES II (1685–1688)

	F	VF	EF
1685 First bust	£350	£1200	£4000
*1685 — Elephant & Castle	£500	£1800	£4000
1686 —	£400	£1500	£3500
1686 — Elephant & Castle		Extremely rare	
1686 Second bust	£300	£1200	£3000
1686 — Elephant & Castle	£500	£2000	£4500
1687 —	£300	£1200	£3000
1687 —Elephant & Castle	£350	£1500	£4000
*1688 —	£300	£1200	£5000
1688 — Elephant & Castle	£350	£1500	£4000

James II, second bust

WILLIAM AND MARY (1688–94)

	F	VF	EF
1689	£350	£1600	£4000
*1689 Elephant & Castle	£350	£1600	£4000
1690	£350	£1600	£4000
1690 Elephant & Castle	£500	£1750	£4250
1691	£350	£1600	£4000
1691 Elephant & Castle	£350	£1600	£4000
1692	£350	£1600	£4000
1692 Elephant	£500	£2000	£4750
1692 Elephant & Castle	£400	£2000	£4000
1693	£350	£1750	£4000
1693 Elephant		Extremely rare	
1693 Elephant & Castle		Extremely rare	
1694	£300	£1750	£4000
1694 Elephant & Castle	£400	£2000	£4000

WILLIAM III (1694–1702)

	F	VF	EF
1695 First bust	£250	£1000	£3000
1695 — Elephant & Castle	£350	£1250	£4000
1696 —	£300	£1500	£3750
1696 — Elephant & Castle		Extremely rare	
1697 —	£300	£1500	£3700
1697 Second bust	£270	£1500	£3700
1697 — Elephant & Castle	£800	£3000	—
1698 —	£225	£1200	£3000
1698 — Elephant & Castle	£350	£1500	£4000
1699 —	£300	£1500	£4000
1699 — Elephant & Castle		Extremely rare	
1700 —	£225	£1200	£3000
1700 — Elephant & Castle	£800	£3000	—
1701 —	£225	£1200	£3000
1701 — Elephant & Castle		Extremely rare	
1701 Third bust "fine work"	£450	£1800	£4250

ANNE (1702–1714)

	F	VF	EF
1702 (Pre-Union) First bust	£400	£1250	£3500
1703 — VIGO below	£4000	£10000	£20000
1705 —	£450	£1500	£4000
1706 —	£450	£1500	£4000
1707 —	£500	£1800	£4250
1707 — (Post-Union)	£300	£1800	£2750
1707 — Elephant & Castle	£550	£1750	—
1707 Second bust		Extremely rare	
1708 First bust		Extremely rare	
1708 Second bust	£300	£1000	£3500
1708 — Elephant & Castle	£700	£1700	£3500
1709 —	£325	£1100	£3000
1709 — Elephant & Castle	£550	£1500	£3500
1710 Third bust	£300	£800	£2000
1711 —	£300	£800	£2000
1712 —	£300	£800	£2000
*1713 —	£300	£800	£2000
1714 —	£300	£800	£2000
1714 GRΛTIΛ	£600	£1200	£3000

GEORGE I (1714–27)

	F	VF	EF
*1714 First bust (Prince Elector)	£1000	£2500	£4000
1715 Second bust	£350	£1200	£3000
1715 Third bust	£300	£1200	£3000
1716 —	£300	£1200	£3000
1716 Fourth bust	£250	£1000	£2200
1717 —	£250	£100	£2500
1718 —		Extremely rare	
1719 —	£250	£1200	£2500
1720 —	£275	£1200	£2700
1721 —	£275	£1200	£2700
1721 — Elephant & Castle		Extremely rare	
1722 —	£275	£1200	£2750
1722 — Elephant & Castle		Extremely rare	
1723 —	£275	£1250	£2800
1723 Fifth bust	£260	£1000	£2500
1724 —	£260	£1000	£2500
1725 —	£260	£1000	£2500
1726 —	£260	£1000	£2500
1726 — Elephant & Castle	£1000	£3000	£7500
1727 —	£275	£1200	£3000

GEORGE II (1727–60)

	F	VF	EF
1727 First young head, early large shield	£700	£2000	£4000
1727 — Larger lettering, early small shield	£375	£1200	£3000
1728 — —	£375	£1200	£3000
1729 2nd young head E.I.C. below	£500	£1500	£3500
1730 —	£350	£1200	£3000
1731 —	£300	£1000	£3000
1731 — E.I.C. below	£450	£1200	£3000
1732 —	£350	£1200	£2700
1732 — E.I.C. below	£425	£1200	£3200
1732 — Larger lettering obverse	£325	£1200	£2500
1732 — — E.I.C. below	£400	£1500	£3200
1733 — —	£270	£1100	£2250
1734 — —	£270	£1100	£2250
1735 — —	£270	£1100	£2250
1736 — —	£275	£1100	£2250
*1737 — —	£270	£1100	£2250

	F	VF	EF
1738 — —	£270	£1100	£2250
1739 Intermediate head	£275	£800	£2000
1739 — E.I.C. below........................	£275	£800	£2500
1740 —	£300	£900	£2750
1741/39 —		Extremely rare	
1743 —		Extremely rare	
1745 — Larger lettering obv. Older bust	£325	£1000	£3250
1745 — LIMA below..........................	£800	£2250	£5000
1746 — (GEORGIVS) Larger lettering obv.	£300	£800	£2700
1747 Old head, large lettering	£225	£500	£1250
1748 —	£225	£500	£1250
1749 —	£225	£500	£1250
1750 —	£225	£500	£1250
1751 — small lettering.......................	£225	£500	£1250
1753 —	£225	£500	£1250
1755 —	£225	£500	£1500
1756 —	£225	£500	£1250
1758 —	£225	£500	£1250
1759 —	£225	£500	£1250
1760 —	£225	£500	£1250

GEORGE III (1760–1820)

	F	VF	EF
1761 First head................................	£900	£2500	£4250
1763 Second head	£800	£1200	£4000
1764 —	£700	£1500	£3000
1765 Third head	£200	£425	£900
1766 —	£200	£425	£800
1767 —	£200	£425	£950
1768 —	£200	£425	£800
1769 —	£200	£425	£800
1770 —	£200	£425	£900
*1771 —	£200	£450	£800
1772 —	£200	£425	£800
1773 —	£200	£425	£800
1774 Fourth head	£120	£300	£500
1775 —	£120	£300	£500
1776 —	£120	£300	£500
1777 —	£120	£300	£500
1778 —	£125	£350	£600
1779 —	£120	£325	£500
1781 —	£120	£270	£500
1782 —	£120	£270	£500
1783 —	£120	£270	£500
1784 —	£120	£270	£500
1785 —	£120	£270	£500
1786 —	£120	£270	£500
1787 Fifth head, "Spade" reverse	£115	£270	£500
1788 —	£115	£270	£500
1789 —	£115	£270	£500
1790 —	£115	£270	£500
1791 —	£115	£270	£500
1792 —	£115	£270	£500
1793 —	£115	£270	£500
1794 —	£115	£270	£500
1795 —	£110	£220	£500
1796 —	£140	£250	£550
1797 —	£120	£275	£500
*1798 —	£110	£200	£400
1799 —	£160	£300	£600
*1813 Sixth head, "Military" reverse	£350	£900	£1650

(Beware of counterfeits of this series—many dangerous copies exist)

HALF GUINEAS

	F	VF	EF

CHARLES II (1660–85)

	F	VF	EF
1669 First bust	£325	£850	£3000
*1670 —	£275	£800	£2500
1671 —	£350	£1000	£3500
1672 —	£350	£1000	£3500
1672 Second bust	£300	£800	£2500
1673 —	£450	£1200	£3200
1674 —	£450	£1400	—
1675 —		Extremely rare	
1676 —	£300	£800	£2200
1676 — Elephant & Castle	£500	£2000	—
1677 —	£300	£800	£2500
1677 — Elephant & Castle	£400	£1300	—
1678 —	£375	£1000	£3000
1678 — Elephant & Castle	£350	£1000	£3500
1679 —	£300	£750	£2250
1680 —	£400	£1200	—
1680 — Elephant & Castle		Extremely rare	
1681 —	£400	£1200	—
1682 —	£400	£1200	£3000
1682 — Elephant & Castle	£450	£1350	—
1683 —	£270	£675	£2200
1683 — Elephant & Castle		Extremely rare	
1684 —	£300	£750	£2200
1684 — Elephant & Castle	£350	£900	£3000

JAMES II (1685–88)

	F	VF	EF
1686	£300	£800	£2700
1686 Elephant & Castle	£700	£3000	£5000
1687	£400	£1000	£3200
1688	£325	£1000	£3000

WILLIAM AND MARY (1688–94)

	F	VF	EF
1689 First busts	£400	£1500	£3500
1690 Second busts	£400	£1500	£3500
1691 —	£425	£1500	£3500
1691 — Elephant & Castle	£325	£1500	£3500
1692 —	£350	£900	£2500
*1692 — Elephant		Extremely rare	
1692 — Elephant & Castle	£325	£1500	£3750
1693 —		Extremely rare	
1694 —	£300	£1500	£3250

WILLIAM III (1694–1702)

	F	VF	EF
1695	£200	£600	£2500
1695 Elephant & Castle	£425	£1100	£3000
1696 —	£250	£800	£2500
1697 Larger Harp rev.	£275	£800	£2500
1698	£175	£550	£2000
1698 Elephant & Castle	£350	£800	£2500
*1699		Extremely rare	
1700	£200	£500	£2000
1701	£200	£500	£2000

	F	VF	EF

ANNE (1702–14)

	F	VF	EF
1702 (Pre-Union)	£300	£1200	£3000
1703 VIGO below bust	£3500	£9000	£15000
1705	£450	£1100	£4000
1707 (Post-Union)	£250	£800	£2000
1708	£325	£800	£2250
1709	£275	£750	£1800
1710	£275	£750	£1800
*1711	£275	£750	£1800
1712	£275	£750	£1800
1713	£275	£750	£1800
1714	£275	£750	£1800

GEORGE I (1714–27)

	F	VF	EF
1715 First bust	£225	£500	£1200
1717 —	£225	£500	£1200
*1718 —	£225	£500	£1200
1719 —	£225	£500	£1200
1720 —	£275	£650	£1400
1721 —		Extremely rare	
1721 — Elephant & Castle		Extremely rare	
1722 —	£225	£450	£1850
1723 —		Extremely rare	
1724 —	£275	£550	£1850
1725 Second bust	£200	£400	£1050
1726 —	£200	£400	£1050
1727 —	£220	£425	£1250

GEORGE II (1727–60)

	F	VF	EF
1728 Young head	£250	£700	£2000
1729 —	£300	£700	£2000
1729 — E.I.C.	£325	£1000	£2750
1730 —	£550	£1750	—
1730 — E.I.C.	£600	£1500	—
1731 —	£300	£100	£2750
1731 — E.I.C.		Extremely rare	
1732 —	£300	£700	£2200
1732 — E.I.C.		Extremely rare	
1733 —		Unknown	
1734 —	£200	£600	£1700
1735 —		Extremely rare	
1736 —	£225	£700	£2000
*1737 —		Extremely rare	
1738 —	£200	£600	£1700
1739 —	£200	£600	£1700
1739 — E.I.C.		Extremely rare	
1740 Intermediate head	£325	£9000	£2200
1743 —		Extremely rare	
1745 —	£300	£900	£2750
1745 — LIMA	£700	£2500	—
1746 —	£225	£600	£1600
1747 Old head	£300	£700	£2000
1748 —	£170	£600	£1200
1749 —		Extremely rare	
*1750 —	£200	£500	£1250
1751 —	£200	£500	£1250
1752 —	£200	£500	£1250
1753 —	£200	£500	£1250
1755 —	£200	£500	£1250

George II, young head

George II, old head

	F	VF	EF
1756 —	£200	£500	£1250
1758 —	£200	£500	£1250
1759 —	£200	£500	£1250
1760 —	£200	£500	£1250

George III, second head

GEORGE III (1760–1820)

	F	VF	EF
1762 First head	£400	£1000	£2250
1763 —	£400	£1200	£3000
1764 Second head	£125	£350	£700
1765 —	£400	£800	£2000
1766 —	£175	£400	£850
1768 —	£175	£400	£850
*1769 —	£170	£425	£900
1772 —		Extremely rare	
1773 —	£175	£400	£800
1774 —	£250	£550	£1500
1774 Third head		Extremely rare	
1775 —	£600	£1500	£3000
1775 Fourth head	£80	£200	£400
1775 — Proof		Extremely rare	
1776 —	£80	£200	£400
1777 —	£80	£200	£400
1778 —	£100	£225	£500
1779 —	£120	£225	£550
1781 —	£100	£225	£500
1783 —	£350	£1000	—
1784 —	£90	£200	£400
1785 —	£90	£200	£400
1786 —	£90	£200	£400

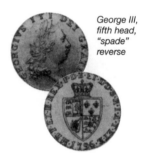

George III, fifth head, "spade" reverse

	F	VF	EF
1787 Fifth head, "Spade" rev.	£80	£170	£350
1788 —	£80	£170	£350
1789 —	£80	£200	£425
1790 —	£80	£170	£350
1791 —	£80	£170	£350
1792 —	£500	£1600	—
1793 —	£80	£170	£325
1794 —	£80	£170	£325
1795 —	£120	£200	£500
*1796 —	£85	£200	£350
1797 —	£85	£200	£350
1798 —	£85	£200	£350
1800 —	£175	£500	£1000
*1801 Sixth head, Shield in Garter rev.	£70	£125	£270
1802 —	£70	£125	£270
1803 —	£70	£125	£270
1804 Seventh head	£70	£125	£270
1805		Extremely Rare	

George III, sixth head

	F	VF	EF
1806 —	£70	£110	£250
1808 —	£70	£110	£250
1899 —	£70	£110	£250
1810 —	£70	£110	£250
1811 —	£100	£250	£500
1813 —	£100	£225	£450

THIRD GUINEAS

DATE	F	VF	EF

GEORGE III (1760–1820)

	F	VF	EF
*1797 First head, date in legend	£60	£100	£200
1798 — —	£60	£100	£200
1799 — —	£70	£110	£225
1800 — —	£55	£100	£200
1801 Date under crown	£55	£100	£200
1802 —	£55	£100	£200
1803 —	£55	£100	£200
1804 Second head	£60	£100	£200
1806 —	£60	£100	£200
1808 —	£60	£100	£200
1809 —	£60	£100	£200
*1810 —	£60	£100	£200
1811 —	£175	£400	£850
1813 —	£125	£200	£450

George III, date in legend

George III, date under crown

QUARTER GUINEAS

GEORGE I (1714–27)

	F	VF	EF
1718	£90	£175	£325

GEORGE III (1760–1820)

	F	VF	EF
*1762	£65	£150	£275

FIVE POUNDS

DATE	Mintage	F	VF	EF	UNC

GEORGE III (1760–1820)

	Mintage	F	VF	EF	UNC
1820 (pattern only)	—			Extremely rare	

GEORGE IV (1820–30)

	Mintage	F	VF	EF	UNC
*1826 proof only	—	—	—	£6,000	£10,000

VICTORIA (1837–1901)

	Mintage	F	VF	EF	UNC
1839 Proof Only	—	—	—	£16,000	£25,000
1887	53,844	£350	£525	£675	£875
1887 Proof	797	—	—	—	£2,250
1887 S on ground on rev. (Sydney Mint)				Excessively rare	
1893	20,405	£400	£650	£900	£1500
1893 Proof	773	—	—	—	£2750

EDWARD VII (1902–10)

	Mintage	F	VF	EF	UNC
1902	34,910	—	£400	£550	£775
1902 Matt proof	8,066	—	—	—	£750

DATE	MINTAGE	F	VF	EF	UNC

GEORGE V (1911–36)

| 1911 Proof only .... | 2,812 | — | — | — | £1,500 |

GEORGE VI (1937–52)

| *1937 Proof only................ | 5,501 | — | — | — | £675 |

Later issues are listed in the Decimal section.

TWO POUNDS

GEORGE III (1760–1820)

| 1820 (pattern only) .... | — | — | — | Extremely rare |

GEORGE IV (1820–30)

| 1823 St George reverse .... | — | £225 | £450 | £950 | £1700 |
| 1826 Proof only, shield reverse | — | — | — | £2750 | £4000 |

WILLIAM IV (1830–37)

| 1831 Proof only .... | 225 | — | — | £3000 | £5000 |

VICTORIA (1837–1901)

1887...................................	91,345	£170	£240	£375	£475
1887 Proof........................	797	—	—	—	£850
1887 S on ground of rev. (Sydney Mint)			Excessively rare		
1893...................................	52,212	£240	£350	£500	£675
1893 Proof........................	773	—	—	—	£1000

EDWARD VII (1902–10)

| 1902................................... | 45,807 | £150 | £200 | £300 | £380 |
| 1902 Matt proof................ | 8,066 | — | — | — | £350 |

GEORGE V (1911–36)

| 1911 Proof only .... | 2,812 | — | — | — | £650 |

GEORGE VI (1937–52)

| *1937 Proof only................ | 5,501 | — | — | — | £360 |

Later issues are listed in the Decimal section.

155

SOVEREIGNS

DATE	MINTAGE	F	VF	EF	UNC

GEORGE III (1760–1820)

DATE	MINTAGE	F	VF	EF	UNC
1817	3,235,239	£125	£240	£600	£1000
1818	2,347,230	£140	£240	£600	£1000
1819	3,574			Exceedingly rare	
1820	931,994	£140	£240	£600	£1100

GEORGE IV (1820–30)

DATE	MINTAGE	F	VF	EF	UNC
1821 First bust, St George reverse	9,405,114	£125	£225	£600	£1100
1821 — Proof	incl. above	—	—	—	£2750
1822 —	5,356,787	£95	£175	£450	£850
1823 —	616,770	£250	£700	£3000	—
1824 —	3,767,904	£125	£275	£700	£1200
1825 —	4,200,343	£225	£600	£2000	—
1825 Second bust, shield reverse	incl. above	£125	£250	£600	£1000
1826 —	5,724,046	£125	£250	£600	£1000
*1826 — Proof	—	—	—	—	£2500
1827 —	2,266,629	£150	£300	£600	£1000
1828 —	386,182	£800	£2000	£5500	—
1829 —	2,444,652	£160	£300	£600	£1100
1830 —	2,387,881	£160	£300	£600	£1100

WILLIAM IV (1830–37)

DATE	MINTAGE	F	VF	EF	UNC
1831	598,547	£200	£325	£700	£1200
*1831 Proof	—	—	—	—	£5000
1832	3,737,065	£200	£300	£750	£1250
1833	1,225,269	£200	£300	£750	£1250
1835	723,441	£200	£300	£750	£1250
1836	1,714,349	£200	£300	£750	£1250
1837	1,172,984	£200	£300	£750	£1250

VICTORIA (1837–1901)

Many of the gold coins struck at the colonial mints found their way into circulation in Britain, for the sake of completeness these coins are listed here. These can easily be identified by a tiny initial letter for the appropriate mint which can be found below the base of the reverse shield or, in the case of the St George reverse, below the bust on the obverse of the Young Head issues, or on the "ground" below the horse's hoof on the later issues.

YOUNG HEAD ISSUES

Shield reverse
(Note—Shield back sovereigns in Fine/VF condition, common dates, are normally traded as bullion + a percentage)

DATE	MINTAGE	F	VF	EF	UNC
1838	2,718,694	£80	£200	£500	£1200
1839	503,695	£125	£400	£1000	£2200
*1839 Proof	—	—	—	—	£2750
1841	124,054	£700	£1200	£3520	—
1842	4,865,375	—	£85	£175	£300
1843	5,981,968	—	£85	£175	£300
1843 "Narrow shield" variety	incl. above				Rare
1844	3,000,445	£65	£85	£175	£300
1845	3,800,845	£65	£85	£175	£300
1846	3,802,947	£65	£85	£175	£320
1847	4,667,126	£65	£80	£175	£300

DATE	MINTAGE	F	VF	EF	UNC
1848	2,246,701	£65	£80	£175	£350
1849	1,755,399	£65	£80	£175	£350
1850	1,402,039	£65	£80	£175	£375
1851	4,013,624	£65	£80	£175	£375
1852	8,053,435	£65	£80	£175	£375
1853	10,597,993	£60	£75	£140	£375
1853 Proof	—	—	—	—	£5500
1854	3,589,611	£90	£200	£475	£1000
1855	8,448,482	£80	£125	£200	£350
1856	4,806,160	£65	£80	£155	£300
1857	4,495,748	£65	£80	£155	£300
1858	803,234	£65	£80	£175	£375
1859	1,547,603	£65	£80	£155	£350
1859 "Ansell" (additional line on lower part of hair ribbon)	—	£170	£400	£2000	—
1860	2,555,958	£60	£75	£200	£300
1861	7,624,736	£60	£75	£140	£250
1862	7,836,413	—	£75	£140	£250
1863	5,921,669	—	£75	£140	£250
1863 Die No 827 on Truncation...			Extremely Rare		
1863 with Die number below shield	incl. above	£60	£75	£125	£275
1864 —	8,656,352	£60	£75	£125	£275
1865 —	1,450,238	£60	£75	£125	£275
1866 —	4,047,288	£60	£75	£125	£275
1868 —	1,653,384	£60	£75	£125	£275
1869 —	6,441,322	£60	£75	£125	£275
1870 —	2,189,960	£60	£75	£125	£275
1871 —	8,767,250	£60	£75	£125	£275
1872 —	8,767,250	£60	£75	£140	£275
1872 no Die number	incl. above	£60	£75	£140	£275
1873 with Die number	2,368,215	£55	£70	£130	£275
1874	520,713	£800	—	—	—

M below (Melbourne Mint)

1872	748,180	£60	£75	£175	£400
1873	—		Extremely rare		
1874	1,373,298	£60	£75	£150	£400
1879			Extremely rare		
1880	3,053,454	£200	£500	£1750	—
1881	2,325,303	£70	£100	£200	£400
1882	2,465,781	£80	£75	£175	£375
1883	2,050,450	£100	£200	£600	—
1884	2,942,630	£60	£75	£150	£400
1885	2,967,143	£60	£75	£150	£400
1886	2,902,131	£400	£1500	£3000	—
1887	1,916,424	£300	£700	£2000	£3750

"S" below the shield indicates that the coin was struck at the Sydney Mint

S below (Sydney Mint)

1871	2,814,000	£60	£65	£140	£400
1872	1,815,000	£60	£65	£140	£400
1873	1,478,000	£60	£65	£140	£400
1875	2,122,000	£60	£65	£140	£400
1877	1,590,000	£60	£65	£140	£400
1878	1,259,000	£60	£65	£150	£400
1879	1,366,000	£60	£65	£140	£400
1880	1,459,000	£60	£65	£140	£400
1881	1,360,000	£60	£75	£170	£400
1882	1,298,000	£60	£65	£140	£400
1883	1,108,000	£60	£75	£170	£400
1884	1,595,000	£60	£65	£140	£400
1885	1,486,000	£60	£65	£140	£400
1886	1,667,000	£60	£65	£140	£400
1887	1,000,000	£60	£75	£170	£375

"M" below the horse's hoof above the date indicates that the coin was struck at the Melbourne Mint

DATE	MINTAGE	F	VF	EF	UNC
St George & Dragon reverse					
1871	incl. above	—	£60	£85	£175
1872	incl. above	—	£60	£85	£175
1873	incl. above	—	£60	£85	£175
1874	incl. above	—	£60	£85	£175
1876	3,318,866	—	£60	£85	£175
1878	1,091,275	—	£60	£85	£175
1879	20,013	£100	£300	£750	—
1880	3,650,080	—	£60	£85	£175
1884	1,769,635	—	£60	£85	£175
1885	717,723	—	£60	£85	£175
M below (Melbourne Mint)					
1872	incl. above	—	£60	£100	£175
1873	752,199	—	£60	£100	£175
1874	incl. above	—	£60	£100	£175
1875	incl. above	—	£60	£100	£175
1876	2,124,445	—	£60	£100	£175
1877	1,487,316	—	£60	£100	£175
1878	2,171,457	—	£60	£100	£175
1879	2,740,594	—	£60	£100	£175
1880	incl. above	—	£60	£100	£175
1881	incl. above	—	£60	£100	£175
1882	incl. above	—	£60	£100	£175
1883	incl. above	—	£60	£100	£175
1884	incl. above	—	£60	£100	£175
1885	incl. above	—	£60	£100	£175
1886	incl. above	—	£60	£100	£175
1887	incl. above	—	£60	£100	£175
S below (Sydney Mint)					
1871	2,814,000	—	£60	£110	£225
1872	incl. above	—	£60	£110	£225
1873	incl. above	—	£60	£110	£225
1874	1,899,000	—	£60	£100	£325
1875	inc above	—	£60	£100	£200
1876	1,613,000	—	£60	£100	£225
1877	—			Extremely rare	
1879	incl. above	—	£60	£100	£225
1880	incl. above	—	£60	£100	£225
1881	incl. above	—	£60	£100	£225
1882	incl. above	—	£60	£100	£225
1883	incl. above	—	£60	£100	£225
1884	incl. above	—	£60	£100	£225
1885	incl. above	—	£60	£100	£225
1886	incl. above	—	£60	£100	£225
1887	incl. above	—	£60	£100	£225
JUBILEE HEAD ISSUES					
*1887	1,111,280	—	—	£70	£100
1887 Proof	797	—	—	—	£700
1888	2,717,424	—	—	£60	£100
1889	7,257,455	—	—	£60	£100
1890	6,529.887	—	—	£60	£100
1891	6,329,476	—	—	£60	£100
1892	7,104,720	—	—	£60	£100
M below (Melbourne Mint)					
1887	940,000	£60	£85	£125	—
1888	2,830,612	£55	£70	£110	£120
1889	2,732,590	£55	£70	£110	£120
1890	2,473,537	£55	£70	£110	£120
1891	2,749,592	£55	£70	£110	£120
1892	3,488,750	£55	£70	£110	£120
1893	1,649,352	£55	£70	£110	£120

DATE	MINTAGE	F	VF	EF	UNC
S below (Sydney Mint)					
1887	1,002,000	£55	£150	£225	£500
1888	2,187,000	—	£75	£100	£135
1889	3,262,000	—	£75	£100	£135
1890	2,808,000	—	£75	£100	£135
1891	2,596,000	—	£75	£100	£135
1892	2,837,000	—	£75	£100	£135
1893	1,498,000	—	£75	£100	£135
OLD HEAD ISSUES					
*1893	6,898,260	—	—	£65	£85
1893 Proof	773	—	—	—	£650
1894	3,782,611	—	—	£65	£85
1895	2,285,317	—	—	£65	£85
1896	3,334,065	—	—	£65	£85
1898	4,361,347	—	—	£65	£85
1899	7,515,978	—	—	£65	£85
1900	10,846,741	—	—	£65	£85
1901	1,578,948	—	—	£65	£85
M below (Melbourne Mint)					
1893	1,914,000	—	—	£90	£120
1894	4,166,874	—	—	£90	£100
1895	4,165,869	—	—	£90	£100
1896	4,456,932	—	—	£90	£100
1897	5,130,565	—	—	£90	£100
1898	5,509,138	—	—	£90	£100
1899	5,579,157	—	—	£90	£100
1900	4,305,904	—	—	£90	£100
1901	3,987,701	—	—	£90	£100
P below (Perth Mint)					
1899	690,992	£60	£100	£275	£1000
1900	1,886,089	—	—	£90	£150
1901	2,889,333	—	—	£90	£150
S below (Sydney Mint)					
1893	1,346,000	—	—	£75	£100
1894	3,067,000	—	—	£75	£100
1895	2,758,000	—	—	£75	£100
1896	2,544,000	—	—	£100	£140
1897	2,532,000	—	—	£75	£100
1898	2,548,000	—	—	£75	£100
1899	3,259,000	—	—	£75	£100
1900	3,586,000	—	—	£75	£100
1901	3,012,000	—	—	£75	£100

EDWARD VII (1902–10)

	MINTAGE	F	VF	EF	UNC
*1902	4,737,796	—	—	£60	£75
1902 Matt proof	15,123	—	—	—	£140
1903	8,888,627	—	—	£60	£75
1904	10,041,369	—	—	£60	£75
1905	5,910,403	—	—	£60	£75
1906	10,466,981	—	—	£60	£75
1907	18,458,663	—	—	£60	£75
1908	11,729,006	—	—	£60	£75
1909	12,157,099	—	—	£60	£75
1910	22,379,624	—	—	£60	£75
C below (Ottawa Mint)					
1908 Satin finish Proof only	633		Extremely rare		
1909	16,300	—	£80	£220	—
1910	28,020	—	£80	£220	—

DATE	MINTAGE	F	VF	EF	UNC
M below (Melbourne Mint)					
1902	4,267,157	—	—	£75	£110
1903	3,521,780	—	—	£75	£110
1904	3,743,897	—	—	£75	£110
1905	3,633,838	—	—	£75	£110
1906	3,657,853	—	—	£75	£110
1907	3,332,691	—	—	£75	£110
1908	3,080,148	—	—	£75	£110
1909	3,029,538	—	—	£75	£110
1910	3,054,547	—	—	£75	£110
P below (Perth Mint)					
1902	3,289,122	—	—	£75	£110
1903	4,674,783	—	—	£75	£110
1904	4,506,756	—	—	£75	£110
1905	4,876,193	—	—	£75	£110
1906	4,829,817	—	—	£75	£110
1907	4,972,289	—	—	£75	£110
1908	4,875,617	—	—	£75	£110
1909	4,524,241	—	—	£75	£110
1910	4,690,625	—	—	£75	£110
S below (Sydney Mint)					
1902	2,813,000	—	—	£75	£110
1902 Proof	incl. above		Extremely rare		
1903	2,806,000	—	—	£75	£110
1904	2,986,000	—	—	£75	£110
1905	2,778,000	—	—	£75	£110
1906	2,792,000	—	—	£75	£110
1907	2,539,000	—	—	£75	£110
1908	2,017,000	—	—	£75	£110
1909	2,057,000	—	—	£75	£110
1910	2,135,000	—	—	£75	£110

GEORGE V (1911–36)

(Extra care should be exercised when purchasing as good quality forgeries exist of virtually all dates and mintmarks)

DATE	MINTAGE	F	VF	EF	UNC
1911	30,044,105	—	—	£60	£85
1911 Proof	3,764	—	—	—	£300
1912	30,317,921	—	—	£60	£85
1913	24,539,672	—	—	£60	£85
1914	11,501,117	—	—	£60	£85
1915	20,295,280	—	—	£60	£85
1916	1,554,120	—	—	£60	£90
1917	1,014,714	£1250	£2000	£4000	—
1925	4,406,431	—	—	£60	£90
C below (Ottawa Mint)					
1911	256,946	—	£70	£90	£125
1913	3,715	£100	£120	£400	—
1914	14,891	£100	£180	£300	—
1916	6,111		Extremely rare		
1917	58,845	—	£70	£110	£125
1918	106,516	—	£70	£110	£125
1919	135,889	—	£70	£110	£125
I below (Bombay Mint)					
1918	1,295,372	—	—	£75	—
M below (Melbourne Mint)					
1911	2,851,451	—	—	£75	£100
1912	2,469,257	—	—	£75	£100
1913	2,323,180	—	—	£75	£100
1914	2,012,029	—	—	£75	£100
1915	1,637,839	—	—	£75	£100

DATE	MINTAGE	F	VF	EF	UNC
1916	1,273,643	—	—	£75	£100
1917	934,469	—	—	£75	£100
1918	4,969,493	—	—	£75	£100
1919	514,257	—	—	£90	£125
1920	530,266	—	£1250	£2250	—
1921	240,121	—	—	£5000	—
1922	608,306	—	£1750	£4500	—
1923	510,870	—	—	£75	£110
1924	278,140	—	—	£80	£125
1925	3,311,622	—	—	£75	£100
1926	211,107	—	—	£75	£100
1928	413,208	—	£550	£1250	£2000
1929	436,719	—	£500	£1500	£2000
1930	77,547	—	£75	£150	£200
1931	57,779	—	£140	£300	£350

P below (Perth Mint)

DATE	MINTAGE	F	VF	EF	UNC
1911	4,373,165	—	—	£75	£100
1912	4,278,144	—	—	£75	£100
1913	4,635,287	—	—	£75	£100
1914	4,815,996	—	—	£75	£100
1915	4,373,596	—	—	£75	£100
1916	4,096,771	—	—	£75	£100
1917	4,110,286	—	—	£75	£100
1918	3,812,884	—	—	£75	£100
1919	2,995,216	—	—	£75	£100
1920	2,421,196	—	—	£75	£100
1921	2,134,360	—	—	£75	£100
1922	2,298,884	—	—	£75	£100
1923	2,124,154	—	—	£75	£100
1924	1,464,416	—	—	£80	£140
1925	1,837,901	—	—	£90	£225
1926	1,313,578	—	£100	£1000	£1800
1927	1,383,544	—	—	£110	£450
1928	1,333,417	—	—	£100	£160
1929	1,606,625	—	—	£75	£100
1930	1,915,352	—	—	£75	£100
1931	1,173,568	—	—	£75	£100

S below (Sydney Mint)

DATE	MINTAGE	F	VF	EF	UNC
1911	2,519,000	—	—	£70	£90
1912	2,227,000	—	—	£70	£90
1913	2,249,000	—	—	£70	£90
1914	1,774,000	—	—	£70	£90
1915	1,346,000	—	—	£70	£90
1916	1,242,000	—	—	£70	£90
1917	1,666,000	—	—	£70	£90
1918	3,716,000	—	—	£70	£90
1919	1,835,000	—	—	£70	£90
1920	—		Excessively rare		
1921	839,000	—	£600	£1500	—
1922	578,000		Extremely rare		
1923	416,000		Extremely rare		
1924	394,000	—	£400	£800	£1250
1925	5,632,000	—	—	£75	£100
1926	1,031,050		Extremely rare		

SA below (Pretoria Mint)

DATE	MINTAGE	F	VF	EF	UNC
1923	719		Extremely rare		
1923 Proof	655		Extremely rare		
1924	3,184		Extremely rare		
1925	6,086,264	—	£60	£80	£95
1926	11,107,611	—	£60	£80	£95
1927	16,379,704	—	£60	£80	£95
1928	18,235,057	—	£60	£80	£95

DATE	MINTAGE	F	VF	EF	UNC
1929	12,024,107	—	—	£80	£95
1930	10,027,756	—	—	£80	£95
1931	8,511,792	—	—	£80	£95
1932	1,066,680	—	—	£90	£110

GEORGE VI (1937–52)

	MINTAGE	F	VF	EF	UNC
*1937 Proof only	5,501	—	—	£350	£700

ELIZABETH II (1952–   )

Pre Decimal Issues

	MINTAGE	F	VF	EF	UNC
1957	2,072,000	—	—	—	£65
1958	8,700,140	—	—	—	£60
1959	1,358,228	—	—	—	£70
1962	3,000,000	—	—	—	£60
1963	7,400,000	—	—	—	£60
1964	3,000,000	—	—	—	£60
1965	3,800,000	—	—	—	£60
1966	7,050,000	—	—	—	£60
1967	5,000,000	—	—	—	£60
1968	4,203,000	—	—	—	£60

Later issues are included in the Decimal section.

HALF SOVEREIGNS

GEORGE III (1760–1820)

	MINTAGE	F	VF	EF	UNC
1817	2,080,197	£55	£90	£200	£325
1818	1,030,286	£55	£90	£200	£350
1820	35,043	£55	£90	£200	£350

GEORGE IV (1820–30)

	MINTAGE	F	VF	EF	UNC
1821 First bust, ornate shield reverse	231,288	£200	£600	£1500	£2650
1821 — Proof	unrecorded	—	—	£2000	£3000
1823 First bust, Plain shield rev.	224,280	£70	£150	£400	£675
1824 —	591,538	£70	£150	£425	£675
1825 —	761,150	£70	£150	£425	£675
1826 bare head, shield with full legend reverse	344,830	£70	£130	£400	£600
1826 — Proof	unrecorded	—	—	£750	£1000
1827 —	492,014	£75	£150	£400	£650
1828 —	1,224,754	£70	£135	£400	£675

WILLIAM IV (1830–37)

	MINTAGE	F	VF	EF	UNC
1831 Proof only	unrecorded	—	—	£750	£1400
1834	133,899	£100	£200	£500	£800
1835	772,554	£100	£300	£425	£775
1836	146,865	£90	£200	£500	£850
1836 obverse from 6d die	incl. above	£600	£1200	£2270	—
1837	160,207	£100	£200	£475	£750

VICTORIA (1837–1901)

YOUNG HEAD ISSUES
Shield reverse

DATE	MINTAGE	F	VF	EF	UNC
1838	273,341	£60	£90	£225	£450
1839 Proof only	1,230	—	—	—	£1200
1841	508,835	£65	£90	£260	£500
1842	2,223,352	—	£65	£200	£300
1843	1,251,762	£65	£90	£260	£500
1844	1,127,007	£60	£70	£240	£350
1845	887,526	£100	£300	£700	£1000
1846	1,063,928	£60	£80	£220	£375
1847	982,636	£60	£80	£220	£375
1848	410,595	£60	£80	£220	£375
1849	845,112	—	£75	£180	£325
1850	179,595	£100	£200	£500	£800
1851	773,573	—	£75	£200	£350
1852	1,377,671	—	£80	£200	£350
1853	2,708,796	—	£70	£180	£300
1853 Proof	unrecorded	—	—	—	£2800
1854	1,125,144		Extremely rare		
1855	1,120,362	—	£75	£180	£325
1856	2,391,909	—	£75	£180	£325
1857	728,223	—	£80	£190	£350
1858	855,578	—	£80	£190	£350
1859	2,203,813	—	£70	£180	£325
1860	1,131,500	—	£70	£180	£325
1861	1,130,867	—	£70	£180	£325
1862	unrecorded	£275	£800	£2500	—
1863	1,571,574	—	£70	£180	£325
1863 with Die number	incl. above	—	£65	£180	£325
1864 —	1,758,490	—	£70	£180	£325
1865 —	1,834,750	—	£70	£180	£325
1866 —	2,058,776	—	£70	£180	£325
1867 —	992,795	—	£70	£180	£325
1869 —	1,861,764	—	£65	£180	£325
1870 —	1,159,544	—	£65	£175	£275
1871 —	2,062,970	—	£60	£150	£275
1872 —	3,248,627	—	£65	£150	£275
1873 —	1,927,050	—	£60	£150	£275
1874 —	1,884,432	—	£60	£150	£275
1875 —	516,240	—	£60	£150	£275
1876 —	2,785,187	—	£60	£150	£250
1877 —	2,197,482	—	£60	£130	£275
1878 —	2,081,941	—	£60	£130	£275
1879 —	35,201	—	£60	£140	£275
1880 —	1,009,049	—	£60	£140	£275
1880 no Die number	incl. above	—	£60	£140	£275
1883 —	2,870,457	—	£60	£135	£225
1884 —	1,113,756	—	£60	£125	£225
1885 —	4,468,871	—	£60	£125	£225
M below (Melbourne Mint)					
1873	165,034	£50	£110	£350	—
1877	80,016	£50	£110	£350	—
1881	42,009	£60	£175	£450	—
1882	107,522	£60	£100	£400	—
1884	48,009	£60	£100	£350	—
1885	11,003	£70	£200	£800	—
1886	38,008	£60	£110	£450	—
1887	64,013	£75	£225	£800	£1750
S below (Sydney Mint)					
1871	180,000 (?)	£60	£95	£400	—
1872	356,000	£65	£110	£400	—
1875	unrecorded	£55	£90	£450	—

Date	Mintage	F	VF	EF	UNC
1879............................	94,000	£55	£90	£450	—
1880............................	80,000	£55	£900	£400	—
1881............................	62,000	£55	£100	£400	—
1882............................	52,000	£100	£400	£1500	—
1883............................	220,000	£55	£80	£450	—
1886............................	82,000	£55	£80	£375	—
1887............................	134,000	£55	£80	£1500	—

JUBILEE HEAD ISSUES

Date	Mintage	F	VF	EF	UNC
1887............................	871,770	—	£45	£65	£80
1887 Proof....................	797	—	—	—	£350
1890............................	2.266,023	—	£50	£70	£125
1891............................	1,079,286	—	£50	£70	£125
1892............................	13,680,486	—	—	£60	£120
1893............................	4,426,625	—	—	£65	£120

M below (Melbourne Mint)

1887	incl. above	£50	£100	£275	£450
1893............................	110,024	£60	£125	£375	—

S below (Sydney Mint)

1887	incl. above	£50	£90	£250	£400
1889............................	64,000	£60	£100	£250	—
1891............................	154,000	£60	£120	£275	—

OLD HEAD ISSUES

Date	Mintage	F	VF	EF	UNC
1893............................	incl. above	—	£40	£55	£90
1893 Proof....................	773	—	—	—	£500
1894............................	3,794,591	—	£40	£60	£90
1895............................	2,869,183	—	£40	£60	£90
1896............................	2,946,605	—	£40	£60	£90
1897............................	3,568,156	—	£40	£60	£90
1898............................	2,868,527	—	£40	£60	£90
1899............................	3,361,881	—	£40	£60	£90
1900............................	4,307,372	—	£40	£60	£90
1901............................	2,037,664	—	£40	£60	£90

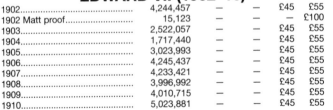

M below (Melbourne Mint)

1893	unrecorded		Extremely rare		
1896............................	218,946	£50	£100	£300	—
1899............................	97,221	£50	£100	£300	—
1900............................	112,920	£50	£100	£300	—

P below (Perth Mint)

1899............................			Proof Unique		
1900	119,376	£125	£300	£500	—

S below (Sydney Mint)

1893	250,000	£60	£100	£275	—
1897............................	unrecorded	£50	£90	£275	—
1900............................	260,00	£50	£80	£275	—

EDWARD VII (1902–10)

Date	Mintage	F	VF	EF	UNC
1902............................	4,244,457	—	—	£45	£55
1902 Matt proof..........	15,123	—	—	—	£100
1903............................	2,522,057	—	—	£45	£55
1904............................	1,717,440	—	—	£45	£55
1905............................	3,023,993	—	—	£45	£55
1906............................	4,245,437	—	—	£45	£55
1907............................	4,233,421	—	—	£45	£55
1908............................	3,996,992	—	—	£45	£55
1909............................	4,010,715	—	—	£45	£55
1910............................	5,023,881	—	—	£45	£55

DATE		F	VF	EF	UNC
M below (Melbourne Mint)					
1906	82,042	—	£40	£80	£150
1907	405,034	—	£40	£80	£150
1908	incl. above	—	£40	£80	£200
1909	186,094	—	£40	£80	£150
P below (Perth Mint)					
1904	60,030	£100	£150	£550	—
1908	24,668	£100	£150	£550	—
1909	44,022	£70	£130	£350	—
S below (Sydney Mint)					
1902	84,000	—	£45	£100	£200
1902 Proof				Extremely rare	
1903	231,000	—	£45	£100	£150
1906	308,00	—	£45	£100	£175
1908	538,000	—	£45	£100	£175
1910	474,000	—	£45	£100	£175

GEORGE V (1911–36)

		F	VF	EF	UNC
1911	6,104,106	—	£35	£50	£75
1911 Proof	3,764	—	—	—	£175
1912	6,224,316	—	£35	£50	£75
1913	6,094,290	—	£35	£50	£75
1914	7,251,124	—	£35	£50	£75
1915	2,042,747	—	£35	£50	£75
M below (Melbourne Mint)					
1915	125,664	—	—	£70	£125
P below (Perth Mint)					
1911	130,373	—	—	£70	£100
1915	136,219	—	—	£70	£100
1918	unrecorded	£120	£275	£600	—
S below (Sydney Mint)					
1911	252,000	—	—	£70	£110
1912	278,000	—	—	£70	£110
1914	322,000	—	—	£70	£110
1915	892,000	—	—	£70	£110
1916	448,000	—	—	£70	£110
SA below (Pretoria Mint)					
1923 Proof only	655	—	—	—	£350
1925	946,615	—	—	£40	£75
1926	806,540	—	—	£40	£75

GEORGE VI (1937–52)

		F	VF	EF	UNC
1937 Proof only	5,501	—	—	—	£165

Later issues are included in the Decimal section.

CROWNS

DATE	F	VF	EF	UNC

OLIVER CROMWELL

	F	VF	EF	UNC
1658 8 over 7 (always).................................	£1800	£3200	£4250	—
1658 Dutch Copy		Extremely rare		
1658 Patterns. In Various Metals................		Extremely rare		

CHARLES II (1660–85)

	F	VF	EF	UNC
1662 First bust, rose (2 varieties)	£120	£700	£3250	—
1662 — no rose (2 varieties)......................	£120	£700	£3250	—
1663 —	£125	£700	£3300	—
1664 Second bust	£100	£600	£3250	—
1665 —	£750	—	—	—
*1666 —	£115	£700	£3300	—
1666 — error RE.X for REX		Extremely rare		
1666 — Elephant below bust	£280	£1000	£4000	—
1667 —	£100	£500	£2500	—
1668/7 — 8 over 7	£100	£500	—	—
1668 —	£90	£500	£2750	—
1669/8 — 9 over 8	£350	£800	—	—
1669 —	£275	£800	£3500	—
1670/69 — 70 over 69	£140	£700	—	—
1670 —	£120	£600	£3250	—
1671...	£100	£600	£500	—
1671 Third bust	£90	£450	£2750	—
1672 —	£90	£450	£2750	—
1673 —	£90	£450	£2750	—
1674 —		Extremely rare		
1675 —	£1000	—	—	—
1675/3 —	£625	£2000	—	—
1676 —	£90	£500	£3000	—
1677 —	£100	£500	£3000	—
1677/6 — 7 over 6	£120	£800	—	—
1678/7 —	£120	£800	—	—
1678/7 — 8 over 7	£125	—	—	—
1679 —	£100	£600	£3000	—
1679 Fourth bust	£90	£600	£3000	—
1680 Third bust	£120	£600	£3000	—
1680/79 — 80 over 79	£120	£600	—	—
1680 Fourth bust	£100	£550	£3000	—
1680/79 — 80 over 79	£125	£800	—	—
1681 —	£100	£500	£3000	—
1681 — Elephant & Castle below bust.......	£2500	£5000	—	—
1682/1 —	£95	£550	£3000	—
1682 — edge error QVRRTO for QVARTO .	£350	—	—	—
1683 —	£400	£1000	£4000	—
1684 —	£325	£1100	—	—

JAMES II (1685–88)

	F	VF	EF	UNC
1686 First bust	£175	£800	£3500	—
1686 — No stops on obv	£325	£1000	—	—
1687 Second bust...................................	£150	£600	£2500	—
1688/7 — 8 over 7...................................	£170	£700	—	—
*1688 —	£160	£700	£2750	—

WILLIAM AND MARY (1688–94)

	F	VF	EF	UNC
1691	£300	£800	£3500	—
1692	£300	£800	£3500	—
1692 2 over upside down 2	£300	£800	£3500	—

DATE	F	VF	EF	UNC

WILLIAM III (1694–1702)

DATE	F	VF	EF	UNC
1695 First bust	£70	£240	£1050	—
1696 —	£60	£240	£1000	—
1696 — no stops on obv.	£225	—	—	—
1996 — no stops obv./rev.	£250	—	—	—
1696 — GEI for DEI	£300	£850	—	—
1696 Second bust				Unique
1696 Third bust	£70	£250	£1050	—
1697 —	£600	£2000	£1500	—
1700 Third bust variety edge year DUODECIMO	£80	£300	£1000	—
1700 — edge year DUODECIMO TERTIO..	£80	£300	£1000	—

ANNE (1702–14)

DATE	F	VF	EF	UNC
1703 First bust, VIGO	£260	£900	£3300	—
1705 — Plumes in angles on rev.	£425	£1500	£4500	—
1706 — Roses & Plumes in angles on rev...	£140	£500	£1750	—
1707 — —	£140	£500	£1800	—
1707 Second bust, E below	£110	£450	£950	—
1707 — Plain	£110	£450	£1000	—
1708 — E below	£110	£450	£1000	—
1708/7 — 8 over 7	£110	£600	—	—
1708 — Plain	£100	£500	£1000	—
1708 — — error BR for BRI		Extremely rare		
1708 — Plumes in angles on rev.	£150	£550	£1350	—
*1713 Third bust, Roses & Plumes in angles on rev.	£150	£500	£1150	—

GEORGE I (1714–27)

DATE	F	VF	EF	UNC
1716	£250	£650	£2750	—
1718 8 over 6	£250	£650	£2750	—
1720 20 over 18	£250	£650	£2750	—
1723 SSC in angles on rev. (South Sea Co.) £280	£700	£2750	—	
1726	£300	£800	£3500	—

GEORGE II (1727–60)

DATE	F	VF	EF	UNC
1732 Young head, Plain, Proof	—	£600	£4500	
1732 — Roses & Plumes in angles on rev ..	£150	£600	£1500	—
1734 — —	£150	£600	£1500	—
1735 — —	£150	£600	£1500	—
1736 — —	£170	£600	£1600	—
1739 — Roses in angles on rev	£150	£550	£1500	—
1741 — —	£150	£550	£1500	—
1743 Old head, Roses in angles on rev	£130	£550	£1200	—
*1746 — — LIMA below bust	£135	£550	£1200	—
1746 — Plain, Proof	—	—	£3500	—
1750 — —	£200	£600	£1500	—
1751 — —	£250	£700	£1800	—

GEORGE III (1760–1820)

DATE	F	VF	EF	UNC
Dollar with oval counterstamp	£125	£400	£750	—
Dollar with octagonal counterstamp	£175	£500	£800	—
1804 Bank of England Dollar, Britannia rev.	£100	£225	£450	—
1818 LVIII	£25	£70	£240	£550
1818 LIX	£25	£70	£240	£550
1819 LIX	£25	£70	£240	£550
1819 LIX 9 over 8	£30	£125	£400	—
1819 no stops on edge	£50	£120	£300	£600
1820 LX	£25	£70	£250	£550
1820 LX 20 over 19	£40	£125	£375	—

DATE	MINTAGE	F	VF	EF	UNC

GEORGE IV (1820–30)

1821 First bust, St George rev.

SECUNDO on edge 437,976		£30	£140	£420	£900
1821 – – Proof..........................Incl. above		–	–	–	£4000
1821 – – Proof TERTIO (error edge)Incl above		–	–	–	£4000
1822 – – SECUNDO................... 124,929		£30	£140	£420	£1000
1822 – – TERTIO......................Incl above		£30	£140	£420	£1000
1823 – – Proof only				Extremely rare	
1826 Second bust, shield rev, SEPTIMO					
Proof only...		–	–	£1750	£2500

WILLIAM IV (1830–37)

				UNC
1831 Proof only W.W. on truncation............	–	–		£8000
1831 Proof only W. WYON on truncation....	–	–		£9500
1834 Proof only	–	–	–	–

VICTORIA (1837–1901)

YOUNG HEAD ISSUES

1839 Proof only	–	–	–	–	£3500
1844 Star stops on edge.................	94,248	£32	£150	£700	£2000
1844 Cinquefoil stops on edge ...	incl. above	£30	£150	£700	£2000
*1845 Star stops on edge............	159,192	£32	£150	£700	£2000
1845 Cinquefoil stops on edge ...	incl. above	£30	£150	£700	£2000
1847...	140,976	£40	£160	£750	£2200

GOTHIC HEAD ISSUES (Proof only)

1847 mdcccxlvii UNDECIMO on edge	8,000	£400	£700	£1200	£2200
1847 – Plain edge......................	–	–	–	–	£3000
1853 mdcccliii SEPTIMO on edge	460	–	–	–	£5000
1853 – Plain edge....................	–	–	–	–	£7000

JUBILEE HEAD ISSUES

*1887	173,581	£10	£22	£50	£100
1887 Proof..............................	1,084	–	–	–	£375
1888 Narrow date......................	131,899	£12	£25	£70	£150
1888 Wide date	incl above	£25	£60	£300	–
1889...	1,807,224	£10	£20	£45	£100
1890...	997,862	£12	£25	£60	£170
1891...	556,394	£12	£25	£60	£170
1892...	451,334	£12	£25	£70	£200

Victoria, young head

OLD HEAD ISSUES (Regnal date on edge in Roman numerals)

1893 LVI......................................	497,845	£12	£30	£120	£300
1893 LVII.....................................	incl. above	£14	£35	£175	£400
1893 Proof..................................	1,312	–	–	–	£425
1894 LVII.....................................	144,906	£14	£45	£150	£375
1894 LVIII....................................	incl. above	£14	£45	£150	£375
1895 LVIII	252,862	£12	£35	£130	£375
1895 LIX	incl. above	£12	£35	£130	£375
1896 LIX	317,599	£14	£35	£130	£400
1896 LX	incl. above	£12	£35	£130	£350
1897 LX	262,118	£12	£35	£130	£350
1897 LXI	incl. above	£12	£35	£130	£400
1898 LXI	166,150	£14	£40	£130	£400
1898 LXII	incl. above	£12	£35	£130	£350
1899 LXII	166,300	£12	£35	£130	£350
1899 LXIII	incl. above	£12	£35	£130	£350
1900 LXIII	353,356	£12	£35	£130	£350
1900 LXIV	incl. above	£12	£52	£130	£350

Victoria, Jubilee head

169

DATE	MINTAGE	F	VF	EF	UNC

EDWARD VII (1901–10)

DATE	MINTAGE	F	VF	EF	UNC
1902	256,020	£25	£50	£100	£150
1902 "Matt Proof"	15,123	—	—	—	£150

GEORGE V (1910–36)

DATE	MINTAGE	F	VF	EF	UNC
1927 Proof only	15,030	—	£55	£90	£170
1928	9,034	£55	£90	£170	£300
1929	4,994	£55	£90	£170	£300
1930	4,847	£55	£90	£170	£320
1931	4,056	£55	£90	£170	£300
1932	2,395	£80	£175	£300	£500
1933	7,132	£55	£75	£160	£300
*1934	932	£400	£700	£1400	£2000
1935 Jubilee issue. Incuse edge inscription	714,769	£8	£12	£16	£25
1935 — — error edge inscription	incl. above	—	—	—	£1500
1935 — Specimen in box	incl. above	—	—	—	£45
1935 — Proof	incl. above	—	—	—	£150
1935 — Proof. Raised edge inscription	2,500	—	—	£175	£300
1935 — — fine lettering	incl. above	—	—	—	£1000
1935 — — error edge inscription	incl. above	—	—	—	£1500
1935 — Gold proof	30	—	—	—	£12,000
1936	2,473	£80	£190	£250	£475

GEORGE VI (1936–52)

DATE	MINTAGE	F	VF	EF	UNC
1937 Coronation	418,699	£9	£14	£20	£30
1937 Proof	26,402	—	—	—	£35
1951 Festival of Britain, Proof-like	1,983,540	—	—	£3	£6

ELIZABETH II (1952–)

Pre-Decimal issues (Five Shillings)

DATE	MINTAGE	F	VF	EF	UNC
*1953	5,962,621	—	—	£3	£6
1953 Proof	40,000	—	—	—	£20
1960	1,024,038	—	—	£3	£6
1960 Polished dies	70,000	—	—	—	£8
1965 Churchill	19,640,000	—	—	—	£1

Later issues are listed in the Decimal section.

DOUBLE FLORINS

VICTORIA (1837–1901)

DATE	MINTAGE	F	VF	EF	UNC
1887 Roman I	483,347	£10	£18	£40	£70
1887 Roman I Proof	incl. above	—	—	—	£275
1887 Arabic 1	incl. above	£10	£18	£40	£70
1887 Arabic 1 Proof	incl. above	—	—	—	£275
1888	243,340	£12	£30	£75	£100
1888 Second I in VICTORIA an inverted 1	incl. above	£20	£35	£75	£250
1889	1,185,111	£15	£23	£40	£90
1889 inverted 1	incl. above	£20	£35	£75	£300
1890	782,146	£12	£33	£55	£105

Patterns were also produced in 1911, 1914 and 1950 and are all extremely rare.

HALFCROWNS

DATE	MINTAGE	F	VF	EF	UNC

OLIVER CROMWELL

1656				Extremely rare	
1658	£850	£1500	£2750	—	
1658 Proof in Gold				Extremely rare	

CHARLES II (1660–1685)

1663 First bust	£85	£400	£2000	—	
1663 — no stops on obv.	£120	£600	—	—	
1664 Second bust	£120	£500	£2200	—	
1666 Third bust	£800	—	—	—	
1666 — Elephant	£700	£1500	—	—	
1667/4 — 7 over 4				Extremely rare	
1668/4 — 8 over 4	£175	—	—	—	
1669 —	£350	£1200	—	—	
1669/4 — 9 over 4	£175	£750	—	—	
1670 —	£75	£400	£2000	—	
1670 — MRG for MAG	£300	£1000	—	—	
1671 —	£75	£300	£2200	—	
1671/0 — 1 over 0	£90	£500	£2400	—	
1672 —	£80	£500	£2200	—	
1672 Fourth bust	£95	£500	£2200	—	
1673 —	£80	£250	£2000	—	
1673 — Plumes both sides				Extremely rare	
1673 — Plume below bust	£1500	—	—	—	
1674 —	£80	£400	—	—	
1675 —	£90	£300	£1500	—	
1676 —	£90	£300	£1250	—	
1676 — inverted 1 in date	£100	£350	£1500	—	
1677 —	£80	£350	£1200	—	
1678 —	£200	£700	—	—	
1679 — GRATTA error				Extremely rare	
1679 —	£80	£300	£1500	—	
1680 —	£140	£600	—	—	
1681/0 — 1 over 0	£150	—	—	—	
1681 —	£100	£325	£1750	—	
1681 — Elephant & Castle	£1700	—	—	—	
1682 —	£100	£350	£2500	—	
1683 —	£100	£350	£2200	—	
1683 — Plume below bust				Extremely rare	
1684/3 — 4 over 3	£175	£700	£3000	—	

JAMES II (1685–1688)

1685 First bust	£125	£550	£2000	—	
1686 —	£125	£550	£2000	—	
1686/5 — 6 over 5	£140	£600	—	—	
1686 — V over S	£220	£600	—	—	
1687 —	£130	£550	£1400	—	
1687/6 — 7 over 6	£140	£600	—	—	
1687 Second bust	£140	£450	£1600	—	
1688 —	£140	£450	£1600	—	

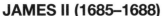

WILLIAM AND MARY (1688–1694)

1689 First busts; first shield	£70	£300	£1200	—	
1689 — — no pearls in crown	£70	£300	£1200	—	
1689 — — FRA for FR	£120	£300	£1200	—	
1689 — — No stop on obv	£70	£300	£1200	—	
1689 — Second shield	£70	£300	£1200	—	
1689 — — no pearls in crown	£70	£325	£1200	—	

171

DATE	MINTAGE	F	VF	EF	UNC
1690 — —		£100	£500	£1600	—
1690 — — error GRETIA for GRATIA		£200	£700	£2500	—
1691 Second busts		£100	£325	£1400	—
1692 —		£100	£400	£1500	—
1693 —		£100	£400	£1500	—
1693 — 3 over inverted 3		£110	£450	£1500	—

WILLIAM III (1694–1702)

1696 First bust, large shields, early harp		£50	£200	£700	—
1696 — — — B (Bristol) below bust		£60	£200	£900	—
1696 — — — C (Chester)		£70	£300	£900	—
1696 — — — E (Exeter)		£100	£400	£1150	—
1696 — — — N (Norwich)		£80	£300	£1000	—
1696 — — — y (York)		£80	£350	£1000	—
1696 — — — — Scottish arms at date				Extremely rare	
1696 — — ordinary harp		£65	£250	—	—
1696 — — — C		£70	£300	—	—
1696 — — — E		£70	£300	—	—
1696 — — — N		£125	£550	£1600	—
1696 — Small shields, ordinary harp		£50	£200	£600	—
1696 — — — B		£60	£250	£800	—
1696 — — — C		£60	£250	£900	—
1696 — — — E		£80	£300	—	—
1696 — — — N		£70	£300	£1100	—
1696 — — — y		£70	£300	£1100	—
1696 Second bust				Only one known	
1697 First bust, large shields, ordinary harp		£60	£250	£700	—
1697 — — — GRR for GRA				Extremely rare	
1697 — — — B		£55	£250	£850	—
1697 — — — C		£55	£300	£900	—
1697 — — — E		£70	£300	£900	—
1697 — — — N		£70	£300	£900	—
1697 — — — y		£70	£300	£900	—
1698 — —		£60	£250	£800	—
1698/7 — — 8 over 7				Extremely rare	
1699 — —		£80	£275	£1000	—
1699 — — Scottish arms at date				Extremely rare	
1700 — —		£60	£250	£700	—
1701 — —		£75	£275	£700	—
1701 — — No stops on rev		£80	£275	—	—
1701 — — Elephant & Castle below				Fair £1150	
1701 — — Plumes in angles on rev.		£150	£500	£1200	—

ANNE (1702–1714)

1703 Plain (pre-Union)		£500	£2000	—	—
1703 VIGO below bust		£100	£300	£900	—
1704 Plumes in angles on rev.		£140	£500	£1500	—
1705 —		£100	£450	£1200	—
1706 Roses & Plumes in angles on rev.		£75	£300	£900	—
*1707 —		£75	£300	£900	—
1707 Plain (post-Union)		£65	£200	£550	—
1707 E below bust		£65	£200	£550	—
1707 — SEPTIMO edge				Extremely rare	
1708 Plain		£65	£250	£800	—
1708 E below bust		£65	£250	£800	—
1708 Plumes in angles on rev.		£65	£250	£800	—
1709 Plain		£60	£225	£600	—
1709 E below bust		£200	£750	—	—
1710 Roses & Plumes in angles on rev.		£65	£250	£800	—
1712 —		£65	£250	£800	—
1713 Plain		£65	£250	£800	—
1713 Roses & Plumes in angles on rev.		£65	£250	£800	—
1714 —		£65	£250	£800	—
1714/3 4 over 3		£100	£350	—	—

DATE	MINTAGE	F	VF	EF	UNC

GEORGE I (1714–1727)

DATE	MINTAGE	F	VF	EF	UNC
1715 Roses & Plumes in angles on rev.		£160	£475	£1800	—
1715 Plain edge...				Extremely rare	
1717 —		£160	£500	£1700	—
*1720 —		£160	£500	£1700	—
1720/17 20 over 17		£160	£500	—	—
1723 SSC in angles on rev.		£160	£550	£1600	—
1726 Small Roses & Plumes in angles on rev...	£2000	£10000	—	—	

GEORGE II (1727–1760)

DATE	MINTAGE	F	VF	EF	UNC
1731 Young head, Plain, proof only	—	—	£4000	—	
1731 — Roses & Plumes in angles on rev.........	£75	£325	£900	—	
1732 — —	£75	£325	£900	—	
1734 — —	£75	£325	£900	—	
1735 — —	£75	£325	£900	—	
1736 — —	£75	£325	£900	—	
1739 — Roses in angles on rev.	£70	£275	£800	—	
1741/39 — — 41 over 30	£125	£400	—	—	
1741 — —	£70	£275	£800	—	
1743 Old head, Roses in angles on rev.	£60	£150	£600	—	
1745 — —	£60	£150	£600	—	
1745 — LIMA below bust..................................	£60	£150	£600	—	
1746 — —	£60	£150	£600	—	
1746/5 — — 6 over 5	£65	£170	£650	—	
1746 — Plain, Proof	—	—	£1400	—	
1750 — —	£85	£350	£950	—	
1751 — —	£100	£400	£1100	—	

GEORGE III (1760–1820)

DATE	MINTAGE	F	VF	EF	UNC
1816 "Bull head"	—	£15	£60	£175	£350
1817 —..	8,092,656	£15	£60	£175	£350
1817 "Small head".....................	incl. above	£15	£60	£175	£350
1818 —..	2,905,056	£15	£60	£175	£350
1819/8 — 9 over 8.........................	incl. above			Extremely rare	
1819 —..	4,790,016	£15	£60	£175	£350
1820 —..	2,396,592	£25	£80	£250	£600

GEORGE IV (1820–30)

DATE	MINTAGE	F	VF	EF	UNC
1820 First bust, first reverse........	incl. above	£20	£50	£200	£400
1821 — —	1,435,104	£20	£50	£200	£400
1821 — — Proof..........................	incl. above	—	—	—	£1000
1823 — —	2,003,760	£600	£1500	£5000	—
1823 — Second reverse.............	incl. above	£20	£50	£180	£400
1824 — —	465,696	£25	£65	£200	£500
1824 Second bust, third reverse .	incl. above			Extremely rare	
*1825 — —	2,258,784	£20	£50	£140	£325
1826 — —	2,189,088	£15	£50	£140	£325
1826 — — Proof..........................	incl. above	—	—	—	£1200
1828 — —	49,890	£40	£90	£275	£600
1829 — —	508,464	£45	£90	£275	£500

WILLIAM IV (1830–37)

DATE	MINTAGE	F	VF	EF	UNC
1831...	—			Extremely rare	
1831 Proof (W.W. in script & block)	—	—	—	—	£750
1834 W.W. in block.......................	993,168	£20	£60	£175	£425
1834 W.W. in script.......................	incl. above	£20	£60	£175	£425
1835...	281,952	£25	£70	£220	£450
*1836...	1,588,752	£20	£50	£200	£450
1836/5 6 over 5	incl. above	£40	£100	£400	—
1837...	150,526	£30	£100	£350	£750

DATE	MINTAGE	F	VF	EF	UNC

VICTORIA (1837–1901)

YOUNG HEAD ISSUES

DATE	MINTAGE	F	VF	EF	UNC
1839 (two varieties)	—	£400	£1200	£3500	—
1839 Proof	—	—	—	—	£2250
1840	386,496	£30	£170	£400	£700
1841	42,768	£300	£600	£1500	£2500
1842	486,288	£30	£80	£400	£700
1843	454,608	£70	£175	£700	£1100
*1844	1,999,008	£20	£50	£300	£650
1845	2,231,856	£20	£50	£300	£650
1846	1,539,668	£25	£60	£300	£700
1848 Plain 8	367,488	£60	£175	£600	£1600
1848/6	incl. above	£50	£150	£500	£1600
1849	261,360	£40	£80	£400	£800
1849 Small date	incl. above	£60	£150	£600	£1000
1850	484,613	£30	£75	£400	£900
1853 Proof only	—	—	—	—	£1800
1874	2,188,599	£15	£35	£150	£300
1875	1,113,483	£15	£35	£150	£300
1876	633,221	£15	£35	£150	£300
1876/5 6 over 5	incl. above	£20	£50	£200	£500
1877	447,059	£15	£35	£150	£300
1878	1,466,323	£15	£35	£150	£300
1879	901,356	£20	£40	£175	£300
1880	1,346,350	£15	£40	£125	£300
1881	2,301,495	£15	£40	£125	£275
1882	808,227	£15	£40	£125	£275
1883	2,982,779	£15	£40	£125	£275
1884	1,569,175	£15	£40	£125	£275
1885	1,628,438	£15	£40	£125	£275
1886	891,767	£15	£40	£125	£275
1887	1,438,046	£15	£40	£125	£275

JUBILEE HEAD ISSUES

DATE	MINTAGE	F	VF	EF	UNC
1887	incl. above	£5	£8	£16	£40
1887 Proof	1,084	—	—	—	£125
1888	1,428,787	£8	£15	£35	£70
1889	4,811,954	£8	£14	£35	£70
1890	3,228,111	£8	£14	£45	£100
1891	2,284,632	£8	£15	£45	£100
1892	1,710,946	£8	£14	£50	£110

OLD HEAD ISSUES

DATE	MINTAGE	F	VF	EF	UNC
1893	1,792,600	£7	£15	£40	£85
1893 Proof	1,312	—	—	—	£135
1894	1,524,960	£10	£25	£60	£140
1895	1,772,662	£8	£18	£50	£120
1896	2,148,505	£7	£15	£45	£110
1897	1,678,643	£7	£15	£40	£110
1898	1,870,055	£7	£15	£40	£110
1899	2,865,872	£7	£15	£40	£110
1900	4,479,128	£7	£15	£40	£110
1901	1,516,570	£7	£15	£40	£110

EDWARD VII (1901–10)

DATE	MINTAGE	F	VF	EF	UNC
1902	1,316,008	£8	£20	£55	£90
1902 "Matt Proof"	15,123	—	—	—	£110
*1903	274,840	£65	£225	£700	£1500
1904	709,652	£50	£175	£400	£900
1905	166,008	£175	£450	£900	£2250
1906	2,886,206	£10	£35	£150	£450
1907	3,693,930	£10	£35	£150	£450
1908	1,758,889	£15	£50	£220	£700
1909	3,051,592	£10	£50	£175	£600
1910	2,557,685	£8	£28	£80	£320

GEORGE V (1910–36)

First issue

DATE	MINTAGE	F	VF	EF	UNC
1911	2,914,573	£7	£20	£50	£100
1911 Proof	6,007	—	—	—	£80
1912	4,700,789	£6	£14	£40	£90

George V first type reverse

DATE	MINTAGE	F	VF	EF	UNC
1913	4,090,169	£6	£12	£45	£100
1914	18,333,003	£3	£8	£30	£60
1915	32,433,066	£3	£8	£25	£55
1916	29,530,020	£3	£8	£25	£50
1917	11,172,052	£3	£8	£25	£65
1918	29,079,592	£3	£8	£20	£50
1919	10,266,737	£4	£10	£25	£70
Second issue—debased silver					
1920	17,982,077	£2	£7	£18	£50
1921	23,677,889	£2	£7	£16	£50
1922	16,396,724	£2	£7	£16	£50
1923	26,308,526	£6	£7	£15	£35
1924	5,866,294	£7	£14	£40	£110
1925	1,413,461	£12	£40	£160	£450
1926	4,473,516	£4	£15	£40	£100
Third issue—Modified effigy					
1926	incl. above	£4	£10	£30	£75
1927	6,837,872	£3	£8	£24	£45
Fourth issue—New shield reverse					
1927 Proof	15,000	—	—	—	£45
1928	18,762,727	£2	£5	£12	£25
1929	17,632,636	£2	£5	£12	£25
1930	809,051	£7	£35	£120	£350
1931	11,264,468	£2	£5	£15	£30
1932	4,793,643	£2	£5	£20	£70
1933	10,311,494	£2	£5	£15	£40
1934	2,422,399	£3	£8	£40	£100
1935	7,022,216	£2	£5	£12	£20
*1936	7,039,423	£2	£5	£10	£18

George V, fourth issue, new shield reverse

GEORGE VI (1936–52)

	MINTAGE	F	VF	EF	UNC
1937	9,106,440	—	£2	£4	£10
1937 Proof	26,402	—	—	—	£12
1938	6,426,478	£1	£3	£10	£17
1939	15,478,635	—	£1	£3	£8
1940	17,948,439	—	£1	£3	£6
1941	15,773,984	—	£1	£3	£6
1942	31,220,090	—	£1	£3	£6
1943	15,462,875	—	£1	£3	£6
*1944	15,255,165	—	£1	£3	£6
1945	19,849,242	—	£1	£3	£6
1946	22,724,873	—	£1	£3	£6
Cupro-nickel					
1947	21,911,484	—	£1	£2	£4
1948	71,164,703	—	£1	£2	£4
1949	28,272,512	—	£1	£2	£6
1950	28,335,500	—	£1	£2	£6
1950 Proof	17,513	—	£1	£2	£9
1951	9,003,520	—	£1	£2	£6
1951 Proof	20,000	—	—	—	£9
1952			Only one known		

ELIZABETH II (1952–   )

	MINTAGE	F	VF	EF	UNC
1953	4,333,214	—	—	£1	£3
1953 Proof	40,000	—	—	—	£5
1954	11,614,953	—	£1	£3	£15
1955	23,628,726	—	—	£1	£4
1956	33,934,909	—	—	£1	£4
1957	34,200,563	—	—	£1	£4
1958	15,745,668	—	£1	£3	£16
1959	9,028,844	—	£1	£5	£18
1960	19,929,191	—	—	£1	£2
1961	25,887,897	—	—	—	£1
1961 Polished dies	incl. above	—	—	£1	£2
1962	24,013,312	—	—	—	£1
1963	17,625,200	—	—	—	£1
1964	5,973,600	—	—	—	£1
1965	9,778,440	—	—	—	£1
1966	13,375,200	—	—	—	£1
1967	33,058,400	—	—	—	—

FLORINS

DATE	MINTAGE	F	VF	EF	UNC

VICTORIA (1837–1901)

YOUNG (CROWNED) HEAD ISSUES

"Godless" type (without D.G.—"Dei Gratia")

DATE	MINTAGE	F	VF	EF	UNC
1848 "Godless" Pattern only plain edge	—			Very rare	
1848 "Godless" Pattern only milled edge	—			Extremely rare	
*1849	413,820	£15	£40	£100	£250

"Gothic" type i.e. date in Roman numerals in obverse legend

"brit." in legend. No die no.

DATE	MINTAGE	F	VF	EF	UNC
1851 mdcccli Proof	1,540			Extremely rare	
1852 mdccclii	1,014,552	£16	£40	£140	£300
1853 mdcccliii	3,919,950	£16	£40	£140	£300
1853 — Proof	incl. above	—	—	—	£1500
1854 mdcccliv	550,413	£500	—	—	—
1855 mdccclv	831,017	£16	£40	£140	£300
1856 mdccclvi	2,201,760	£16	£40	£140	£350
1857 mdccclvii	1,671,120	£16	£40	£140	£350
1858 mdccclviii.........................	2,239,380	£16	£40	£140	£350
1859 mdccclix	2,568,060	£16	£40	£140	£350
1860 mdccclx............................	1,475,100	£18	£50	£170	£340
1862 mdccclxii	594,000	£70	£200	£600	£1500
1863 mdccclxiii	938,520	£200	£400	£1500	£2000

"brit" in legend. Die no. below bust

DATE	MINTAGE	F	VF	EF	UNC
1864 mdccclxiv	1,861,200	£16	£40	£140	£300
1864 Gothic Piedfort flan	incl. above			Extremely rare	
1865 mdccclxv	1,580,044	£15	£40	£140	£350
1866 mdccclxvi	914,760	£15	£40	£140	£350
*1867 mdccclxvii	423,720	£25	£75	£250	£550
1867—only 42 arcs in border	incl. above			Extremely rare	

"britt" in legend. Die no. below bust

DATE	MINTAGE	F	VF	EF	UNC
1868 mdccclxviii........................	896,940	£15	£40	£140	£300
1869 mdccclxix	297,000	£20	£45	£175	£400
1870 mdccclxx	1,080,648	£15	£40	£125	£275
1871 mdccclxxi	3,425,605	£15	£40	£125	£275
1872 mdccclxxii	7,199,690	£14	£40	£125	£275
1873 mdccclxxiii........................	5,921,839	£14	£40	£125	£275
1874 mdccclxxiv	1,642,630	£14	£40	£125	£275
1874 — iv over iii in date	incl. above	£25	£60	£150	£275
1875 mdccclxxv	1,117,030	£14	£40	£140	£275
1876 mdccclxxvi	580,034	£20	£50	£150	£300
1877 mdccclxxvii........................	682,292	£14	£40	£125	£300
1877 — 48 arcs in border no W.W.	incl. above	£15	£45	£140	£325
1877 — 42 arcs	incl. above	£15	£45	£140	£325
1877 — — no die number	incl. above			Extremely rare	
1878 mdccclxxviii with die number	1,786,680	£15	£40	£150	£325
1879 mdccclxxix no die no	1,512,247			Extremely rare	
1879 — 48 arcs in border...........	incl. above	£14	£40	£150	£300
1879 — no die number..............	incl. above			Extremely rare	
1879 — 38 arcs, no W.W..	incl. above	£14	£50	£150	£300
1880 mdccclxxx Younger portrait	—			Extremely rare	
1880 — 34 arcs, Older portrait....	2,167,170	£12	£40	£125	£275
1881 mdccclxxxi — —	2,570,337	£12	£40	£125	£275
1881 — xxɪ̄i broken puncheon ...	incl. above	£20	£60	£150	£300
1883 mdccclxxxiii — —	3,555,667	£12	£40	£125	£275
1884 mdccclxxxiv —	1,447,379	£12	£40	£125	£275
1885 mdccclxxxv — —	1,758,210	£12	£40	£125	£275
1886 mdccclxxxvi — —	591,773	£12	£40	£125	£275
1887 mdccclxxxvii — —..............	1,776,903	£22	£70	£220	£450
1887 — 46 arcs	incl. above	£22	£75	£240	£475

"Godless" florin

"Gothic" florin

DATE	MINTAGE	F	VF	EF	UNC
JUBILEE HEAD ISSUES					
1887	incl. above	£4	£8	£18	£40
1887 Proof..............................	1,084	—	—	—	£100
1888...	1,547,540	£5	£10	£35	£90
1889...	2,973,561	£5	£12	£35	£90
1890...	1,684,737	£8	£22	£70	£200
1891...	836,438	£15	£50	£140	£325
1892...	283,401	£22	£60	£180	£475
VICTORIA – OLD HEAD ISSUES					
1893...	1,666,103	£5	£14	£32	£75
1893 Proof..............................	1,312	—	—	—	£110
1894...	1,952,842	£8	£22	£55	£130
1895	2,182,968	£7	£20	£55	£110
1896...	2,944,416	£6	£16	£40	£85
1897...	1,699,921	£6	£16	£40	£85
1898...	3,061,343	£6	£16	£40	£85
1899...	3,966,953	£6	£16	£40	£85
*1900	5,528,630	£6	£16	£40	£80
1901...	2,648,870	£6	£16	£40	£80

EDWARD VII (1901–10)

*1902	2,189,575	£7	£14	£40	£80
1902 "Matt Proof"	15,123	—	—	—	£70
1903...	1,995,298	£10	£30	£85	£300
1904...	2,769,932	£10	£30	£80	£300
1905...	1,187,596	£45	£120	£400	£900
1906...	6,910,128	£10	£30	£90	£300
1907...	5,947,895	£11	£30	£90	£300
1908...	3,280,010	£12	£45	£175	£550
1909...	3,482,829	£10	£40	£175	£500
1910...	5,650,713	£8	£25	£70	£200

GEORGE V (1910–36)

First issue					
1911...	5,951,284	£4	£8	£30	£75
1911 Proof..............................	6,007	—	—	—	£70
1912...	8,571,731	£3	£11	£30	£85
1913...	4,545,278	£5	£16	£35	£100
1914...	21,252,701	£3	£14	£22	£45
1915...	12,367,939	£3	£14	£22	£45
1916...	21,064,337	£3	£14	£22	£45
1917...	11,181,617	£3	£14	£25	£60
1918...	29,211,792	£3	£14	£22	£45
1919...	9,469,292	£3	£15	£30	£70
Second issue *– debased silver*					
1920...	15,387,833	£2	£12	£32	£70
1921...	34,863,895	£2	£12	£30	£50
1922...	23,861,044	£2	£12	£30	£50
1923...	21,546,533	£2	£10	£25	£55
1924...	4,582,372	£5	£15	£55	£120
1925...	1,404,136	£12	£35	£150	£325
1926...	5,125,410	£5	£15	£40	£80
Fourth issue *– new reverse*					
1927 Proof only	101,497	—	—	—	£40
1928...	11,087,186	£2	£4	£12	£25
1929...	16,397,279	£2	£4	£12	£25
1930...	5,753,568	£2	£5	£15	£40
1931...	6,556,331	£2	£5	£12	£30
1932...	717,041	£8	£20	£120	£300
1933...	8,685,303	£2	£5	£15	£35
1935...	7,540,546	£2	£5	£10	£20
*1936	9,897,448	£2	£4	£9	£20

DATE	MINTAGE	F	VF	EF	UNC

GEORGE VI (1936–52)

DATE	MINTAGE	F	VF	EF	UNC
1937	13,006,781	–	£1	£3	£6
1937 Proof	26,402	–	–	–	£8
1938	7,909,388	£1	£2	£8	£16
1939	20,850,607	£1	£2	£3	£5
1940	18,700,338	£1	£2	£3	£5
1941	24,451,079	£1	£2	£3	£5
1942	39,895,243	£1	£2	£3	£5
1943	26,711,987	£1	£2	£3	£5
*1944	27,560,005	£1	£2	£3	£5
1945	25,858,049	£1	£2	£3	£5
1946	22,300,254	£1	£2	£3	£5

Cupro-nickel

DATE	MINTAGE	F	VF	EF	UNC
1947	22,910,085	–	–	£1	£3
1948	67,553,636	–	–	£1	£3
1949	28,614,939	–	–	£1	£5
1950	24,357,490	–	–	£2	£7
1950 Proof	17,513	–	–	£1	£8
1951	27,411,747	–	–	£2	£8
1951 Proof	20,000	–	–	–	£8

ELIZABETH II (1952–   )

DATE	MINTAGE	F	VF	EF	UNC
1953	11,958,710	–	–	–	£2
1953 Proof	40,000	–	–	–	£5
1954	13,085,422	–	–	£5	£25
1955	25,887,253	–	–	£1	£3
1956	47,824,500	–	–	£1	£3
1957	33,071,282	–	–	£4	£25
1958	9,564,580	–	–	£3	£15
1959	14,080,319	–	–	£4	£25
1960	13,831,782	–	–	£1	£3
1961	37,735,315	–	–	£1	£2
1962	35,147,903	–	–	£1	£2
1963	26,471,000	–	–	£1	£2
1964	16,539,000	–	–	£1	£2
1965	48,163,000	–	–	–	£1.50
1966	83,999,000	–	–	–	£1.50
1967	39,718,000	–	–	–	£1.50

SHILLINGS

OLIVER CROMWELL

1658	£500	£850	£1500	–
1658 Dutch Copy			Extremely rare	

CHARLES II (1660–85)

*1663 First bust	£65	£180	£700	–
1663 — GARTIA error			Extremely rare	
1663 — Irish & Scottish shields transposed	£125	£450	–	–
1666 — Elephant below bust	£325	£850	£2500	–
1666 "Guinea" head, elephant	£1500	£3500	–	–
1666 Second bust			Extremely rare	
1668 —	£60	£200	£700	–
1668/7 — 8 over 7	£60	£225	–	–
1668 Second bust	£60	£200	£700	–
1669/6 First bust variety			Extremely rare	
1669			Extremely rare	
1669 Second bust			Extremely rare	
1670 —	£80	£325	£1000	–
1671 —	£100	£350	£1100	–
1671 — Plume below, plume in centre rev.	£250	£600	£2000	–
1672 —	£75	£225	£900	–
1673 —	£90	£350	£900	–

DATE	F	VF	EF	UNC
1673 — Plume below, plume in centre rev.	£225	£600	£2000	—
1673/2 — 3 over 2..................................	£120	£500	—	—
1674/3 — 4 over 3..................................	£120	£500	—	—
1674 —..	£90	£300	£900	—
1674 — Plume below bust, plume in centre rev.	£250	£600	£2000	—
1674 — Plume rev. only...........................	£300	£600	£2000	—
1674 Third bust	£250	£750	—	—
1675 Second bust..................................	£110	£350	—	—
1675/4 — 5 over 4..................................	£150	£550	—	—
1675 — Plume below bust, plume in centre rev.	£250	£650	£2000	—
1675 Third bust	£225	£600	—	—
1675/3 — 5 over 3..................................	£225	£600	—	—
1676 Second bust	£75	£220	£750	—
1676/5 — 6 over 5..................................	£85	£350	—	—
1676 — Plume below bust, plume in centre rev.	£250	£700	£2200	—
1677 —..	£70	£250	£900	—
1677 — Plume below bust	£250	£550	£1800	—
1678 —..	£80	£300	£900	—
1678/7 — 8 over 7..................................	£90	£400	—	—
1679 —..	£80	£250	£800	—
1679 — Plume below bust, plume in centre rev.	£300	£700	£2200	—
1679 — Plume below bust	£300	£650	£2200	—
1679 — 9 over 7....................................	£90	£400	—	—
1680 —..		Extremely rare		
1680 — Plume below bust, plume in centre rev.	£350	£800	£2800	—
1680/79 — — 80 over 79	£325	£1000	—	—
1681 —..	£140	£400	£1200	—
1681 — 1 over 0....................................	£140	£400	£1200	—
1681/0 Elephant & Castle below bust	£2000	—	—	—
1682/1 — 2 over 1	£500	—	—	—
1683 —..		Extremely rare		
1683 Fourth (Larger) bust	£175	£500	£1800	—
1684 —..	£125	£450	£1500	—

William III First bust

JAMES II (1685–88)

	F	VF	EF	UNC
1685..	£100	£350	£1000	—
1685 Plume in centre rev. rev		Extremely rare		
1685 No stops on rev.	£150	£600	—	—
1686..	£110	£325	£1100	—
1686/5 6 over 5	£110	£325	£1100	—
1687..	£125	£400	£1200	—
1687/6 7 over 6	£110	£400	£1200	—
1688..	£110	£400	£1200	—
1688/7 last 8 over 7	£120	£400	£1200	—

William III Second bust

WILLIAM & MARY (1688–94)

	F	VF	EF	UNC
1692	£110	£350	£1250	—
1692 inverted 1....................................	£150	£350	£1400	—
1693..	£110	£350	£1250	—

William III Third bust

WILLIAM III (1694–1702)

Provincially produced shillings carry privy marks or initials below the bust:
B: Bristol. C: Chester. E: Exeter. N: Norwich. Y or y: York.

	F	VF	EF	UNC
1695 First bust	£35	£100	£450	—
1696 —..	£30	£75	£350	—
1696 — no stops on rev.	£50	£120	£600	—
1696 — MAB for MAG		Extremely rare		
1696 — 1669 error		Extremely rare		
1696 — 1669 various GVLELMVS errors		Extremely rare		
1696 — B below bust	£40	£120	£500	—
1696 — C...	£40	£120	£500	—
1696 — E...	£45	£120	£600	—
1696 — N	£40	£110	£500	—

William III Fourth bust

William III Fifth bust

179

DATE	F	VF	EF	UNC
1696 — y	£35	£110	£500	—
1696 — Y..	£35	£110	£500	—
1696 Second bust			Only one known	
1696 Third bust C below	£150	£350	£900	—
1696 — Y..			Extremely rare	
1697 First bust	£35	£90	£300	—
1697 — GRI for GRA error			Extremely rare	
1697 — Scottish & Irish shields transposed			Extremely rare	
1697 — Irish arms at date................................			Extremely rare	
1697 — no stops on rev	£45	£150	£600	—
1697 — GVLELMVS error..............................			Extremely rare	
1697 — B	£40	£110	£500	—
1697 — C	£40	£110	£500	—
1697 — E	£40	£110	£500	—
1697 — N	£40	£110	£500	—
1697 — — no stops on obv..............................			Extremely rare	
1697 — y	£40	£110	£450	—
1697 — — arms of France & Ireland transposed			Extremely rare	
1697 — Y..	£40	£110	£450	—
1697 Third bust	£35	£110	£450	—
1697 — B	£40	£110	£450	—
1697 — C	£40	£110	£450	—
1697 — — Fr.a error	£70	£220	—	—
1697 — — no stops on obv..............................	£65	£200	—	—
1697 — — arms of Scotland at date.................			Extremely rare	
1697 — E..	£40	£110	£500	—
1697 — N	£40	£110	£500	—
1697 — y	£50	£120	£425	—
1697 Third bust variety..................................	£40	£85	£300	—
1697 — B	£40	£120	£450	—
1697 — C	£75	£350	—	—
1698 —	£60	£200	£600	—
1698 — Plumes in angles of rev.	£200	£450	£1100	—
1698 Fourth bust "Flaming hair"	£125	£400	£1250	—
1699 —	£90	£275	£1000	—
1699 Fifth bust	£80	£170	£550	—
1699 — Plumes in angles on rev.	£95	£275	£800	—
1699 — Roses in angles on rev.	£95	£275	£800	—
1700 —	£45	£100	£350	—
1700 — Small round oo in date....................	£45	£100	£350	—
1700 — no stop after DEI			Extremely rare	
1700 — Plume below bust	£1150	£2500	—	—
1701 —	£75	£200	£475	—
1701 — Plumes in angles on rev.	£95	£275	£800	—

Anne, VIGO below bust

ANNE (1702–14)

	F	VF	EF	UNC
1702 First bust (pre-Union with Scotland).........	£60	£300	£600	—
1702 — Plumes in angles on rev.	£70	£275	£600	—
*1702 — VIGO below bust	£70	£220	£600	—
1702 — — colon before ANNA			Extremely rare	
1703 Second bust, VIGO below	£50	£170	£450	—
1704 — Plain	£450	£1200	—	—
1704 — Plumes in angles on rev.	£60	£150	£600	—
1705 — Plain	£60	£175	£550	—
1705 — Plumes in angles on rev.	£55	£175	£550	—
1705 — Roses & Plumes in angles on rev.........	£55	£175	£500	—
1707 — —	£50	£170	£500	—
1707 Second bust (post-Union) E below bust ..	£40	£90	£400	—
1707 — E* below bust....................................	£70	£200	£600	—
1707 Third bust, Plain	£30	£75	£300	—
1707 — Plumes in angles on rev.	£40	£150	£600	—
1707 — E below bust	£35	£80	£350	—
1707 "Edinburgh" bust, E* below			Extremely rare	
1708 Second bust, E below	£40	£80	£400	—
1708 — E below bust	£45	£150	£600	—
1708/7 — — 8 over 7			Extremely rare	
1708 — Roses & Plumes in angles on rev.........	£80	£250	£600	—

Anne, E below bust

DATE	MINTAGE	F	VF	EF	UNC
1708 Third bust, Plain		£35	£85	£300	—
1708 — Plumes in angles on rev.		£45	£120	£400	—
1708 Third bust, E below bust		£45	£160	£450	—
1708/7 — — 8 over 7		£80	£225	—	—
1708 — Roses & Plumes in angles on rev.		£50	£150	£475	—
1708 "Edinburgh" bust, E* below		£50	£150	£475	—
1709 Third bust, Plain		£35	£90	£400	—
1709 "Edinburgh" bust, E* below		£45	£150	£500	—
1709 — E no star (filled in die?)		£70	£160	£450	—
1710 Third bust, Roses & Plumes in angles		£50	£120	£500	—
1710 Fourth bust, Roses & Plumes in angles		£50	£140	£500	—
1711 Third bust, Plain		£60	£120	£375	—
1711 Fourth bust, Plain		£22	£50	£150	—
1712 — Roses & Plumes in angles on rev.		£50	£100	£350	—
1713 — —		£50	£90	£300	—
1713/2 — 3 over 2		£45	£150	—	—
1714 — —		£55	£85	£300	—
1714/3 —				Extremely rare	

GEORGE I (1714–27)

DATE	MINTAGE	F	VF	EF	UNC
*1715 First bust, Roses & Plumes in angles on rev.		£45	£150	£525	—
1716 — —		£80	£300	£800	—
1717 — —		£55	£170	£600	—
1718 — —		£45	£110	£500	—
1719 — —		£110	£270	£800	—
1720 — —		£40	£110	£350	—
1720/18 — —		£100	£300	£1000	—
1720 — Plain		£35	£100	£375	—
1721 — Roses & Plumes in angles on rev.		£50	£160	£600	—
1721/0 — — 1 over 0		£50	£160	£600	—
1721 — Plain		£100	£300	£900	—
1721/19 — — 21 over 19		£125	£250	—	—
1722 — Roses & Plumes in angles on rev.		£70	£175	£600	—
1723 — —		£70	£175	£600	—
1723 — SSC in angles of rev.		£20	£50	£175	—
1723 — SSC rev., Arms of France at date		£70	£150	£700	—
1723 Second bust, SSC in angles on rev.		£40	£90	£400	—
1723 — Roses & Plumes in angles		£50	£120	£650	—
1723 — WCC (Welsh Copper Co) below bust		£300	£750	£2750	—
1724 — Roses & Plumes in angles on rev.		£50	£125	£450	—
1724 — WCC below bust		£300	£800	£2750	—
1725 — Roses & Plumes in angles on rev.		£50	£140	£600	—
1725 — — no stops on obv.		£70	£200	£600	—
1725 — WCC below bust		£325	£900	£2950	—
1726 — .		£325	£900	£3000	—
1726 — Roses & Plumes in angles on rev.		£300	£1200	—	—
1727 — —				Extremely rare	
1727 — — no stops on obv.				Extremely rare	

GEORGE II (1727–60)

DATE	MINTAGE	F	VF	EF	UNC
1727 Young head, Plumes in angles on rev.		£55	£250	£475	—
1727 — Roses & Plumes in angles on rev.		£55	£150	£475	—
1728 — —		£55	£150	£475	—
1728 — Plain		£60	£200	£600	—
1729 — Roses & Plumes in angles on rev.		£50	£150	£475	—
1731 — —		£60	£150	£475	—
1731 — Plumes in angles on rev.		£60	£300	£700	—
1732 — Roses & Plumes in angles on rev.		£50	£150	£475	—
1734 — —		£50	£150	£475	—
1735 — —		£50	£150	£475	—
1736 — —		£50	£150	£475	—
1736/5 — — 6 over 5		£60	£200	£600	—
1737 — —		£50	£150	£4750	—
*1739 — Roses in angles on rev.		£30	£100	£300	—
1739/7 — — 9 over 7				Extremely rare	
1741 — —		£30	£100	£300	—
1741/39 — — 41 over 39				Extremely rare	
1743 Old head, Roses in angles on rev.		£25	£70	£300	—
1745 — —		£25	£70	£300	—
1745 — — LIMA beow bust		£20	£70	£275	—

George II Young head

DATE	MINTAGE	F	VF	EF	UNC
1745/3 — — — 5 over 3		£50	£150	£400	—
1746 — — —		£50	£150	£600	—
1746/5 — — — 6 over 5		£100	£275	—	—
1746 — Plain, Proof	—	—	£1000	—
*1747 — Roses in angles on rev.		£30	£80	£300	—
1750 — Plain		£35	£120	£350	—
1750/6 — — 0 over 6		£50	£140	£475	—
1751 — —		£100	£250	£625	—
1758 — —		£15	£40	£105	—

GEORGE III (1760–1820)

*1763 "Northumberland" bust		£275	£450	£825	—
1787 rev. no semée of hearts in 4th shield		£15	£30	£80	—
1787 — No stop over head		£15	£30	£80	
1787 — No stop at date		£15	£30	£80	
1787 — No stops on obv		£18	£35	£85	—
1787 rev. with semée of hearts in shield		£15	£30	£80	—
1798 "Dorrien Magens" bust		—	—	£6000	—

NEW COINAGE—shield in garter reverse

1816	—	£8	£18	£50	£100
1817	3,031,360	£8	£18	£50	£100
1817 GEOE for GEOR	incl. above	£100	£200	£400	—
1818	1,342,440	£8	£20	£70	£140
1819	7,595,280	£8	£18	£50	£100
1819/8 9 over 8	incl. above	£10	£30	£70	—
1820	7,975,440	£8	£18	£45	£100

George II Old head

GEORGE IV (1820–30)

1821 First bust, first reverse	2,463,120	£10	£40	£120	£300
1821 — — Proof	incl. above	—	—	—	£650
1823 — Second reverse	693,000	£20	£55	£190	£325
1824 — —	4,158,000	£10	£40	£125	£325
1825 — —	2,459,160	£20	£40	£125	£400
1825/3 — — 5 over 3	incl. above		Extremely rare		
1825 Second bust, third reverse	incl. above	£4	£14	£50	£110
1825 — — Roman I	incl. above		Extremely rare		
1826 — —	6,351,840	£4	£14	£45	£110
1826 — — Proof	incl. above	—	—	—	£400
1827 — —	574,200	£20	£50	£140	£350
1829 — —	879,120	£15	£50	£140	£325

WILLIAM IV (1830–37)

1831 Proof only	—	—	—	—	£400
1834	3,223,440	£10	£30	£100	£300
1835	1,449,360	£10	£30	£100	£300
1836	3,567,960	£10	£30	£100	£300
1837	478,160	£12	£40	£125	£425

George III "Northumberland" shilling

VICTORIA (1837–1901)

YOUNG HEAD ISSUES
First head

1838 WW on truncation	1,956,240	£10	£30	£125	£250
1839 —	5,666,760	£10	£30	£125	£250
Second head					
1839 WW on truncation, Proof only	incl. above	—	—	—	£425
1839 no WW	incl. above	£10	£30	£110	£250
1840	1,639,440	£10	£30	£110	£275
1841	875,160	£10	£30	£110	£275
1842	2,094,840	£10	£30	£110	£275
1843	1,465,200	£10	£35	£12	£280
1844	4,466,880	£8	£30	£100	£250
1845	4,082,760	£8	£30	£100	£250
1846	4,031,280	£8	£30	£100	£250
1848 last 8 of date over 6	1,041,480	£40	£75	£400	£600
1849	845,480	£12	£40	£125	£350

DATE	MINTAGE	F	VF	EF	UNC
1850	685,080	£300	£650	£1400	£3000
1851	470,071	£25	£100	£250	£500
1851/49 51 over 49	incl. above	£125	£600	—	—
1852	1,306,574	£10	£30	£100	£250
1853	4,256,188	£10	£30	£100	£250
1853 Proof	incl. above	—	—	—	£400
1854	552,414	£70	£150	£500	£1000
1854/1 4 over 1	incl. above	£140	£500	—	—
1855	1,368,400	£8	£30	£100	£200
1856	3,168,000	£8	£30	£100	£200
1857	2,562,120	£8	£30	£100	£200
1857 error F:G with inverted G	incl. above	£100	£300	—	—
1858	3,108,600	£8	£30	£110	£200
1859	4,561,920	£8	£30	£110	£200
1860	1,671,120	£8	£30	£110	£220
1861	1,382,040	£9	£35	£125	£300
1862	954,320	£40	£100	£250	£600
1863	859,320	£80	£200	£400	£800
1863/1 3 over 1			Extremely rare		

Victoria Small Jubilee head

Die no. added above date up to 1879

DATE	MINTAGE	F	VF	EF	UNC
1864	4,518,360	£8	£25	£80	£175
1865	5,619,240	£8	£25	£80	£175
1866	4,984,600	£8	£25	£80	£175
1866 error BBITANNIAR	incl. above	£70	£150	—	—
1867	2,166,120	£8	£30	£90	£175

Victoria Large Jubilee head

Third head—with die no

DATE	MINTAGE	F	VF	EF	UNC
1867	incl. above	£50	£100	—	—
1868	3,330,360	£8	£30	£75	£175
1869	736,560	£8	£30	£75	£175
1870	1,467,471	£8	£30	£75	£175
1871	4,910,010	£8	£30	£75	£175
1872	8,897,781	£8	£30	£75	£175
1873	6,489,598	£8	£30	£75	£175
1874	5,503,747	£8	£30	£75	£175
1875	4,353,983	£8	£30	£75	£175
1876	1,057,487	£8	£30	£75	£175
1877	2,989,703	£8	£30	£75	£175
1878	3,127,131	£8	£30	£75	£175
1879	3,611,507	£20	£55	£200	£400

Fourth head—no die no

DATE	MINTAGE	F	VF	EF	UNC
1879 no Die no.	incl. above	£7	£22	£65	£150
1880	4,842,786	£7	£22	£65	£150
1881	5,255,332	£7	£22	£65	£150
1882	1,611,786	£12	£40	£150	£300
1883	7,281,450	£6	£22	£55	£110
1884	3,923,993	£6	£22	£55	£110
1885	3,336,526	£6	£22	£55	£110
1886	2,086,819	£6	£22	£55	£110
1887	4,034,133	£7	£24	£55	£110

JUBILEE HEAD ISSUES

DATE	MINTAGE	F	VF	EF	UNC
1887	incl. above	£2	£5	£9	£22
1887 Proof	1,084	—	—	—	£60
1888	4,526,856	£4	£9	£20	£45
1889	7,039,628	£25	£80	£275	—
1889 Large bust (until 1892)	incl. above	£5	£10	£40	£70
1890	8,794,042	£5	£10	£40	£70
*1891	5,665,348	£5	£10	£40	£70
1892	4,591,622	£5	£10	£40	£70

OLD HEAD ISSUES

DATE	MINTAGE	F	VF	EF	UNC
1893	7,039,074	£4	£8	£22	£50
1893 small lettering	incl. above	£3	£8	£22	£50
1893 Proof	1,312	—	—	—	£75
1894	5,953,152	£7	£20	£50	£100
1895	8,880,651	£6	£18	£40	£80
1896	9,264,551	£6	£15	£40	£70
1897	6,270,364	£5	£10	£40	£70
*1898	9,768,703	£5	£10	£40	£60
1899	10,965,382	£5	£10	£40	£60
1900	10,937,590	£5	£10	£40	£70
1901	3,426,294	£5	£10	£40	£60

Victoria Old or Veiled head

DATE	MINTAGE	F	VF	EF	UNC

EDWARD VII (1901–10)

DATE	MINTAGE	F	VF	EF	UNC
1902	7,809,481	£3	£12	£45	£65
1902 Proof matt	13,123	—	—	—	£65
1903	2,061,823	£6	£30	£80	£300
1904	2,040,161	£6	£30	£80	£300
1905	488,390	£50	£150	£500	£1150
1906	10,791,025	£3	£10	£40	£100
1907	14,083,418	£3	£10	£40	£100
1908	3,806,969	£8	£20	£90	£275
1909	5,664,982	£8	£20	£80	£260
*1910	26,547,236	£2	£8	£40	£85

GEORGE V (1910–36)

First issue

DATE	MINTAGE	F	VF	EF	UNC
1911	20,065,901	£2	£6	£16	£40
1911 Proof	6,007	—	—	—	£50
*1912	15,594,009	£2	£7	£22	£60
1913	9,011,509	£4	£15	£40	£80
1914	23,415,843	£1	£5	£20	£35
1915	39,279,024	£1	£5	£20	£35
1916	35,862,015	£1	£5	£20	£35
1917	22,202,608	£1	£5	£20	£35
1918	34,915,934	£1	£5	£20	£35
1919	10,823,824	£1	£6	£24	£40

Second issue — debased silver

DATE	MINTAGE	F	VF	EF	UNC
1920	22,825,142	—	£2	£15	£35
1921	22,648,763	—	£2	£15	£35
1922	27,215,738	—	£2	£15	£35
1923	14,575,243	—	£2	£15	£30
1924	9,250,095	£3	£6	£35	£80
1925	5,418,764	£2	£5	£30	£80
1926	22,516,453	—	£4	£18	£80

Third issue — Modified bust

DATE	MINTAGE	F	VF	EF	UNC
1926	incl. above	—	£3	£20	£35
1927 —	9,247,344	£1	£3	£20	£35

Fourth issue — large lion and crown on rev., date in legend

DATE	MINTAGE	F	VF	EF	UNC
1927	incl. above	£1	£2	£15	£35
1927 Proof	15,000	—	—	—	£30
1928	18,136,778	—	£2	£10	£30
1929	19,343,006	—	£2	£12	£30
1930	3,172,092	—	£2	£15	£40
1931	6,993,926	—	£2	£10	£30
1932	12,168,101	—	£2	£10	£30
1933	11,511,624	—	£2	£10	£30
*1934	6,138,463	—	£2	£12	£35
1935	9,183,462	—	£2	£6	£16
1936	11,910,613	—	£2	£4	£12

George V First obverse

GEORGE VI (1936–52)

E = England rev. (lion standing on large crown). S = Scotland rev. (lion seated on small crown holding sword and mace)

DATE	MINTAGE	F	VF	EF	UNC
1937 E	8,359,122	—	£1	£2	£6
1937 E Proof	26,402	—	—	—	£12
1937 S	6,748,875	—	£1	£2	£5
1937 S Proof	26,402	—	—	—	£12
1938 E	4,833,436	—	£1	£7	£14
1938 S	4,797,852	—	£1	£7	£14
1939 E	11,052,677	—	£1	£2	£6
1939 S	10,263,892	—	£1	£2	£6
1940 E	11,099,126	—	—	£2	£6
1940 S	9,913,089	—	—	£2	£6

George V Second obverse

DATE	MINTAGE	F	VF	EF	UNC
1941 E	11,391,883	—	—	£2	£6
1941 S	8,086,030	—	—	£2	£4
1942 E	17,453,643	—	—	£2	£4
1942 S	13,676,759	—	—	£2	£4
1943 E	11,404,213	—	—	£2	£4
1943 S	9,824,214	—	—	£2	£4
*1944 E	11,586,751	—	—	£2	£4
*1944 S	10,990,167	—	—	£2	£4
1945 E	15,143,404	—	—	£2	£5
1945 S	15,106,270	—	—	£2	£5
1946 E	16,663,797	—	—	£2	£5
1946 S	16,381,501	—	—	£2	£5
Cupro-nickel					
1947 E	12,120,611	—	—	—	£2
1947 S	12,283,223	—	—	—	£2
1948 E	45,576,923	—	—	—	£2
1948 S	45,351,937	—	—	—	£2
1949 E	19,328,405	—	—	—	£5
1949 S	21,243,074	—	—	—	£5
1950 E	19,243,872	—	—	—	£5
1950 E Proof	17,513	—	—	—	£15
1950 S	14,299,601	—	—	—	£5
1950 S Proof	17,513	—	—	—	£15
1951 E	9,956,930	—	—	—	£5
1951 E Proof	20,000	—	—	—	£15
1951 S	10,961,174	—	—	—	£5
1951 S Proof	20,000	—	—	—	£15

English reverse

Scottish reverse

ELIZABETH II (1952–   )

E = England rev. (shield with three lions). S = Scotland rev. (shield with one lion).

DATE	MINTAGE	F	VF	EF	UNC
1953 E	41,942,894	—	—	—	£1
1953 E Proof	40,000	—	—	—	£3
1953 S	20,663,528	—	—	—	£1
1953 S Proof	40,000	—	—	—	£3
*1954 E	30,262,032	—	—	—	£2
*1954 S	26,771,735	—	—	—	£2
1955 E	45,259,908	—	—	—	£2
1955 S	27,950,906	—	—	—	£2
1956 E	44,907,008	—	—	—	£8
1956 S	42,853,639	—	—	—	£8
1957 E	42,774,217	—	—	—	£1
1957 S	17,959,988	—	—	—	£9
1958 E	14,392,305	—	—	—	£9
1958 S	40,822,557	—	—	—	£1
1959 E	19,442,778	—	—	—	£1
1959 S	1,012,988	£1	£2	£4	£15
1960 E	27,027,914	—	—	—	£1
1960 S	14,376,932	—	—	—	£1
1961 E	39,816,907	—	—	—	£1
1961 S	2,762,558	—	—	—	£3
1962 E	36,704,379	—	—	—	£1
1962 S	17,475,310	—	—	—	£1
1963 E	49,433,607	—	—	—	£1
1963 S	32,300,000	—	—	—	£1
1964 E	8,590,900	—	—	—	£1
1964 S	5,239,100	—	—	—	£1
1965 E	9,216,000	—	—	—	£1
1965 S	2,774,000	—	—	—	£2
1966 E	15,002,000	—	—	—	£1

English reverse

Scottish reverse

SIXPENCES

DATE	F	VF	EF	UNC

OLIVER CROMWELL

1658 Patterns by Thos. Simon & Tanner

	F	VF	EF	UNC
Four varieties		Extremely rare		

CHARLES II (1660–85)

	F	VF	EF	UNC
1674..	£60	£200	£600	—
1675..	£60	£200	£600	—
1675/4 5 over 4	£70	£220	£675	—
1676..	£60	£200	£600	—
1676/5 6 over 5	£75	£200	£600	—
*1677	£60	£200	£600	—
1678/7	£60	£200	£600	—
1679..	£55	£200	£600	—
1680..	£70	£225	£650	—
1681..	£60	£200	£625	—
1682/1	£60	£200	£625	—
1682..	£60	£200	£625	—
1683..	£60	£200	£625	—
1684..	£60	£200	£625	—

JAMES II (1685–88)

	F	VF	EF	UNC
1686 Early shields	£90	£325	£750	—
1687/6 — 7 over 6..	£90	£325	£750	—
1687 Late shields	£90	£325	£725	—
1687/6 — 7 over 6	£85	£320	£725	—
1688 —	£85	£320	£750	—

WILLIAM & MARY (1688–94)

	F	VF	EF	UNC
*1693	£100	£300	£850	—
1693 error inverted 3	£110	£350	£900	—
1694..	£110	£375	£925	—

WILLIAM III (1694–1702)

Provincially produced sixpences carry privy marks or initials below the bust:
B: Bristol. C: Chester. E: Exeter. N: Norwich. Y or y: York.

	F	VF	EF	UNC
1695 First bust, early harp in 4th shield on rev.	£30	£90	£300	—
1696 — —	£30	£90	£300	—
1696 — — French arms at date		Extremely rare		
1696 — — Scottish arms at date		Extremely rare		
1696 — — DFI for DEI.....................................		Extremely rare		
1696 — — No stops on obv.	£25	£80	£300	—
1696 — — B	£35	£90	£350	—
1696 — — — B over E		Extremely rare		
1696 — — C..	£35	£90	£400	—
1696 — — E..	£35	£90	£400	—
1696 — — N..	£35	£90	£400	—
1696 — — y..	£35	£90	£400	—
1696 — — Y..	£35	£90	£400	—
1696 — Later harp	£35	£175	£400	—
1696 — — B	£40	£175	£400	—
1696 — — — no stops on obv.........................	£40	£175	£400	—
1696 — — C..	£60	£300	£800	—
1696 — — N..	£50	£275	—	—
1696 Second bust..	£200	£500	—	—
1697 First bust, later harp	£30	£70	£275	—
1697 — — Arms of France & Ireland transposed		Extremely rare		

DATE	MINTAGE	F	VF	EF	UNC
1697 — — B..		£40	£100	£400	—
1697 — — C..		£40	£100	£400	—
1697 — — — Irish shield at date				Extremely rare	
1697 — — E..		£40	£100	£400	—
1697 — — N..		£40	£100	£400	—
1697 — — error GVLIEMVS				Extremely rare	
1697 — — y..		£35	£90	£375	—
1697 — — — Irish shield at date				Extremely rare	
1697 Second bust		£95	£250	£900	—
1697 Third bust		£25	£60	£180	—
1697 — error GVLIEIMVS..............................				Extremely rare	
1697 — B		£30	£100	£400	—
1697 — IRA for FRA				Extremely rare	
1697 — C...		£35	£140	£400	—
1697 — E...		£35	£140	£400	—
1697 — Y...		£35	£140	£400	—
1698 —		£40	£150	£425	—
1698 — Plumes in angles on rev.		£50	£175	£525	—
1699 —		£55	£220	£600	—
1699 — Plumes in angles on rev.		£55	£220	£550	—
1699 — Roses in angles on rev.		£70	£225	£600	—
1699 — — error GᵛLIELMVS				Extremely rare	
1700 —		£40	£85	£325	—
1700 — Plume below bust		£1500	—	—	—
1701 —		£45	£100	£375	—

ANNE (1702–14)

1703 VIGO below bust Before Union with Scotland	£35	£100	£375	—
1705 Plain..		£40	£140	£400	—
*1705 Plumes in angles on rev.		£45	£140	£400	—
1705 Roses & Plumes in angles on rev.		£40	£95	£375	—
1707 Roses & Plumes in angles on rev.		£40	£95	£350	—
1707 (Post-Union), Plain...............................		£30	£70	£275	—
1707 E (Edinburgh) below bust		£25	£65	£250	—
1707 Plumes in angles on rev...........................		£30	£80	£300	—
1708 Plain..		£30	£80	£250	—
1708 E below bust.......................................		£25	£70	£250	—
1708 E* below bust		£35	£85	£300	—
1708 "Edinburgh" bust E* below		£35	£90	£325	—
1708 Plumes in angles on rev.........................		£35	£90	£300	—
1710 Roses & Plumes in angles on rev.		£35	£90	£325	—
1711 Plain..		£20	£40	£135	—

GEORGE I (1714–27)

*1717 Roses & Plumes in angles on rev.		£70	£200	£500	—
1717 Plain edge..				Extremely rare	
1720 —		£70	£175	£475	—
1723 SSC in angles on rev.		£18	£45	£175	—
1723 Larger lettering		£18	£45	£175	—
1726 Small Roses & Plumes in angles on rev. ..		£80	£225	£650	—

GEORGE II (1727–60)

1728 Young head, Plain.................................		£70	£200	£450	—
1728 — Proof		—	—	£2500	—
1728 — Plumes in angles on rev.		£40	£110	£325	—
1728 — Roses & Plumes in angles on rev.........		£35	£125	£300	—
1731 — —		£35	£125	£300	—
*1732 — —		£35	£125	£300	—
1734 — —		£35	£125	£300	—
1735 — —		£35	£125	£300	—
1735/4 5 over 4		£35	£125	£300	—
1736 — —		£35	£125	£300	—
1739 — Roses in angles on rev.		£25	£60	£175	—
1741 —		£28	£60	£175	—

187

DATE	MINTAGE	F	VF	EF	UNC
1743 Old head, Roses in angles on rev............		£20	£50	£150	—
1745 — —		£20	£50	£150	—
1745 — — 5 over 3		£20	£55	£160	—
1745 — Plain, LIMA below bust......................		£20	£50	£160	—
1746 — — —		£20	£50	£160	—
1746 — — Proof..		—	—	£700	—
1750 — —		£30	£100	£300	—
1751 — —		£28	£80	£275	—
1757 — —		£12	£25	£60	—
1758 — —		£12	£25	£60	—

GEORGE III (1760–1820)

1787 rev. no semée of hearts on 4th shield		£10	£22	£45	—
1787 rev. with semée of hearts		£10	£22	£45	—

NEW COINAGE

1816	—	£5	£14	£40	£95
1817	10,921,680	£5	£14	£40	£95
1818..	4,284,720	£6	£18	£60	£125
1819..	4,712,400	£5	£14	£40	£95
1819 very small 8 in date	incl. above	£5	£14	£40	£95
1820..	1,488,960	£5	£14	£40	£95

GEORGE IV (1820–30)

*1821 First bust, first reverse	863,280	£12	£25	£75	£200
1821 error BBRITANNIAR............		£50	£200	£650	—
1821 — — Proof.........................	incl. above	—	—	—	£475
1824 — Second (garter) reverse .	633,600	£12	£25	£75	£180
1825 —	483,120	£12	£25	£75	£180
1826 — —	689,040	£18	£50	£125	£300
1826 Second bust, third (lion on crown) reverse	incl. above	£10	£25	£65	£125
1826 — — Proof.........................	incl. above	—	—	—	£200
1827 — —	166,320	£18	£50	£150	£275
1828 — —	15,840	£16	£40	£125	£250
1829 — —	403,290	£12	£40	£110	£230

WILLIAM IV (1830–37)

1831..	1,340,195	£11	£25	£85	£200
1831 Proof....................................	incl. above	—	—	—	£275
*1834	5,892,480	£11	£25	£85	£200
1835..	1,552,320	£11	£25	£85	£200
1836..	1,987,920	£11	£30	£110	£225
1837..	506,880	£14	£35	£140	£300

VICTORIA (1837–1901)

YOUNG HEAD ISSUES
First head

1838..	1,607,760	£7	£22	£60	£150
1839..	3,310,560	£7	£22	£60	£150
1839 Proof..................................	incl. above	—	—	—	£300
1840..	2,098,800	£7	£22	£60	£150
1841..	1,386,000	£7	£24	£70	£160
1842..	601,920	£7	£22	£70	£150
1843..	3,160,080	£7	£24	£50	£150
1844..	3,975,840	£7	£20	£45	£150
1844 Large 44 in date................	incl. above	£10	£30	£85	£225
1845..	3,714,480	£7	£22	£50	£160
1846..	4,226,880	£7	£22	£50	£160
1848..	586,080	£20	£70	£200	£400
1848/6 final 8 over 6..................	incl. above	£35	£75	£200	—
1850..	498,960	£7	£25	£60	£160
1850/3 0 over 3	incl. above	£15	£25	£80	£220

DATE	MINTAGE	F	VF	EF	UNC
1851	2,288,107	£7	£24	£50	£170
1852	904,586	£7	£24	£50	£180
1853	3,837,930	£7	£24	£50	£160
1853 Proof	incl above	—	—	—	£325
1854	840,116	£50	£150	£400	£850
1855	1,129,684	£7	£20	£50	£140
1855/3 last 5 over 3	incl. above	£10	£30	£60	£170
1856	2,779,920	£7	£20	£50	£150
1857	2,233,440	£7	£20	£50	£150
1858	1,932,480	£7	£20	£50	£150
1859	4,688,640	£7	£20	£50	£150
1859/8 9 over 8	incl. above	£10	£30	£60	£190
1860	1,100,880	£8	£22	£60	£190
1862	990,000	£30	£75	£200	£550
1863	491,040	£30	£75	£200	£600

Die no. added above date from 1864 to 1879

1864	4,253,040	£7	£22	£60	£140
1865	1,631,520	£7	£22	£60	£135
1866	4,140,080	£7	£22	£60	£135
1866 no Die no.	incl. above	£15	£60	£150	£240

Second head

1867	1,362,240	£7	£20	£60	£140
1868	1,069,200	£7	£20	£55	£130
1869	388,080	£7	£20	£55	£130
1870	479,613	£7	£20	£55	£130
1871	3,662,684	£6	£20	£50	£100
1871 no Die no.	incl. above	£6	£20	£50	£100
1872	3,382,048	£6	£20	£50	£100
1873	4,594,733	£6	£20	£50	£100
1874	4,225,726	£6	£20	£50	£100
1875	3,256,545	£6	£20	£50	£100
1876	841,435	£6	£20	£55	£100
1877	4,066,486	£6	£20	£55	£100
1877 no Die no	incl. above	£6	£20	£55	£100
1878	2,624,525	£6	£20	£55	£100
1878 Dritanniar Error	incl. above	£60	£200	—	—
1879	3,326,313	£6	£18	£50	£100
1879 no Die no	incl. above	£5	£18	£50	£100
1880 no Die no	3,892,501	£5	£18	£50	£100

Third head

1880	incl above	£6	£18	£40	£80
1881	6,239,447	£6	£18	£40	£80
1882	759,809	£7	£25	£80	£220
1883	4,986,558	£6	£16	£35	£80
1884	3,422,565	£6	£16	£35	£80
1885	4,652,771	£6	£16	£35	£80
1886	2,728,249	£6	£16	£35	£70
1887	3,675,607	£6	£16	£35	£70

JUBILEE HEAD ISSUES

*1887 Shield reverse	incl. above	£3	£5	£10	£25
1887 — Proof	incl. above	—	—	—	£50
1887 Six Pence in wreath reverse	incl. above	£3	£5	£10	£25
1888 —	4,197,698	£4	£7	£20	£40
*1889 —	8,738,928	£4	£7	£25	£50
1890 —	9,386,955	£4	£7	£25	£50
1891 —	7,022,734	£4	£7	£25	£50
1892 —	6,245,746	£4	£8	£28	£60
1893 —	7,350,619	£250	£500	£1250	£2000

OLD HEAD ISSUES

1893	incl. above	£4	£8	£18	£40
1893 Proof	1,312	—	—	—	£60
1894	3,467,704	£7	£14	£40	£75
1895	7,024,631	£6	£14	£35	£60
1896	6,651,699	£4	£9	£30	£50
1897	5,031,498	£4	£9	£30	£50
1898	5,914,100	£4	£9	£30	£45
1899	7,996,80	£4	£9	£30	£45
1900	8,984,354	£4	£9	£30	£45
1901	5,108,757	£4	£9	£28	£45

Jubilee head, shield reverse

Jubilee head, wreath reverse

DATE	MINTAGE	F	VF	EF	UNC

EDWARD VII (1901–10)

1902	6,367,378	£2	£6	£25	£45
1902 "Matt Proof"	15,123	—	—	—	£45
1903	5,410,096	£5	£15	£45	£120
1904	4,487,098	£7	£25	£75	£200
1905	4,235,556	£6	£20	£60	£140
1906	7,641,146	£4	£10	£35	£90
1907	8,733,673	£4	£10	£40	£80
*1908	6,739,491	£7	£25	£55	£200
1909	6,584,017	£5	£15	£45	£125
1910	12,490,724	£2	£5	£20	£40

Edward VII

GEORGE V (1910–36)

First issue

1911	9,155,310	£1	£3	£10	£35
1911 Proof	6,007	—	—	—	£30
1912	10,984,129	£1	£3	£20	£40
1913	7,499,833	£1	£6	£22	£50
1914	22,714,602	£1	£2	£10	£25
*1915	15,694,597	£1	£3	£12	£35
1916	22,207,178	£1	£2	£8	£25
1917	7,725,475	£4	£12	£30	£70
1918	27,553,743	£1	£2	£12	£25
1919	13,375,447	£1	£3	£12	£30
1920	14,136,287	£1	£3	£10	£25

George V, first reverse above and second reverse below

Second issue—debased silver

1920	incl. above	£1	£3	£10	£28
1921	30,339,741	£1	£3	£10	£28
1922	16,878,890	£1	£2	£10	£28
1923	6,382,793	£3	£8	£40	£85
1924	17,444,218	£1	£5	£10	£25
1925	12,720,558	£1	£2	£10	£25
1925 Broad rim	incl. above	£1	£2	£10	£25
1926 —	21,809,621	£1	£2	£10	£25

Third issue—Modified bust

1926	incl. above	£1	£2	£10	£30
1927	8,924,873	—	£1	£10	£30

Fourth issue—New design (oakleaves)

1927 Proof only	15,000	—	—	—	£20
1928	23,123,384	—	£1	£7	£20
1929	28,319,326	—	£1	£7	£20
1930	16,990,289	—	£1	£8	£24
1931	16,873,268	—	£1	£7	£20
1932	9,406,117	—	£1	£7	£25
1933	22,185,083	—	£1	£7	£20
1934	9,304,009	£1	£2	£9	£22
1935	13,995,621	—	£1	£5	£10
*1936	24,380,171	—	£1	£5	£10

GEORGE VI (1936–52)

First type

1937	22,302,524	—	—	£1	£4
1937 Proof	26,402	—	—	—	£5
1938	13,402,701	—	£1	£3	£12
1939	28,670,304	—	—	£1	£5
1940	20,875,196	—	—	£1	£5
1941	23,086,616	—	—	£1	£5
1942	44,942,785	—	—	£1	£4
1943	46,927,111	—	—	£1	£4
1944	36,952,600	—	—	£1	£4
1945	39,939,259	—	—	£1	£3
1946	43,466,407	—	—	£1	£3

George VI first reverse

Cupro-nickel

1947	29,993,263	—	—	£1	£3
1948	88,323,540	—	—	£1	£3

Second type—new cypher on rev.

1949	41,335,515	—	—	£1	£3

George VI second reverse

DATE	MINTAGE	F	VF	EF	UNC
1950..	32,741,955	–	–	£1	£3
1950 Proof	17,513	–	–	–	£5
1951..	40,399,491	–	–	£1	£3
1951 Proof...............................	20,000	–	–	–	£5
1952..	1,013,477	£3	£8	£20	£50

ELIZABETH II (1952–   )

1953..	70,323,876	–	–	–	£2
1953 Proof...............................	40,000	–	–	–	£4
1954..	105,241,150	–	–	–	£3
1955..	109,929,554	–	–	–	£1
1956..	109,841,555	–	–	–	£1
1957..	105,654,290	–	–	–	£1
1958..	123,518,527	–	–	–	£3
1959..	93,089,441	–	–	–	£1
1960..	103,283,346	–	–	–	£3
1961..	115,052,017	–	–	–	£3
1962..	166,483,637	–	–	–	25p
1963..	120,056,000	–	–	–	25p
1964..	152,336,000	–	–	–	25p
1965..	129,644,000	–	–	–	25p
1966..	175,676,000	–	–	–	25p
1967..	240,788,000	–	–	–	25p

GROATS OR FOURPENCES

DATE	MINTAGE	F	VF	EF	UNC

The earlier fourpences are included in the Maundy oddments section as they are generally considered to have been issued for the Maundy ceremony.

WILLIAM IV (1831–37)

*1836	–	£7	£15	£40	£70
1837..	962,280	£7	£15	£40	£70

VICTORIA (1838–1901)

1837..	Extremely Rare Proofs or Patterns only				
1837 Last 8 over 8 on its side		£10	£18	£50	£95
1838..	2,150,280	£7	£12	£30	£70
1839..	1,461,240	£7	£14	£32	£70
1839 Proof...............................	incl. above				Rare
1840..	1,496,880	£7	£12	£30	£70
1840 Small 0 in date..................	incl. above	£7	£12	£30	£70
1841..	344,520	£7	£14	£35	£70
1842/1 2 over 1	incl. above	£7	£14	£35	£70
1842..	724,680	£7	£14	£35	£70
1843..	1,817640	£7	£14	£35	£80
1843 4 over 5.............................	incl. above	£7	£14	£35	£70
1844..	855,360	£7	£14	£35	£80
1845..	914,760	£7	£14	£35	£80
1846..	1,366,200	£7	£14	£35	£75
1847 7 over 6.............................	225,720	£12	£25	£100	–
1848..	712,800	£7	£14	£30	£70
1848/6 8 over 6	incl. above	£25	£100	–	–
1848/7 8 over 7	incl. above	£8	£20	£50	£90
1849..	380,160	£7	£14	£35	£70
1849/8 9 over 8	incl. above	£8	£20	£50	£100
*1851..	594,000	£18	£50	£160	£300
1852..	31,300	£40	£100	£300	–
1853..	11,880	£40	£100	£375	–
1853 Proof Milled Rim	incl. above	–	–	–	£450
1853 Plain edge Proof................		Extremely rare			
1854..	1,096,613	£7	£14	£35	£60
1855..	646,041	£7	£14	£35	£65
1888 Jubilee Head	–	£7	£14	£35	£65

THREEPENCES

DATE	MINTAGE	F	VF	EF	UNC

The earlier threepences are included in the Maundy oddments section.

WILLIAM IV (1830–37)

(issued for use in the West Indies)

DATE	MINTAGE	F	VF	EF	UNC
1834		£6	£12	£45	£90
1835		£6	£12	£45	£90
1836		£6	£12	£45	£90
1837		£6	£12	£50	£100

VICTORIA (1837–1901)

YOUNG HEAD ISSUES

Victoria first type

DATE	MINTAGE	F	VF	EF	UNC
1838 BRITANNIAB error				Extremely rare	
1838	—	£6	£18	£50	£100
1839	—	£6	£18	£50	£100
1940	—	£6	£18	£50	£100
1841	—	£6	£18	£50	£110
1842	—	£6	£18	£50	£110
1843	—	£6	£18	£40	£90
1844	—	£6	£18	£60	£125
*1845	1,319,208	£7	£18	£40	£125
1846	52,008	£7	£22	£70	£140
1847	4,488			Extremely rare	
1848	incl. above				
1849	131,208	£7	£20	£55	£125
1850	954,888	£7	£18	£40	£90
1851	479,065	£6	£18	£50	£90
1851 5 over 8	incl. above	£10	£20	£80	—
1852	4,488			Extremely rare	
1853	36,168	£20	£50	£100	£220
1854	1,467,246	£6	£18	£45	£90
1855	383,350	£6	£18	£45	£90
1856	1,013,760	£6	£18	£50	£90
1857	1,758,240	£6	£18	£50	£90
1858	1,441,440	£6	£18	£50	£85
1858 BRITANNIAB error	incl. above			Extremely rare	
1858/6 final 8 over 6	incl. above	£8	£25	£80	—
1858/5 final 8 over 5	incl. above	£8	£25	£80	—
1859	3,579,840	£6	£18	£45	£80
1860	3,405,600	£6	£18	£45	£80
1861	3,294,720	£6	£18	£45	£80
1862	1,156,320	£6	£18	£45	£80
1863	950,400	£10	£25	£70	£125
1864	1,330,560	£6	£18	£45	£95
1865	1,742,400	£6	£18	£45	£100
1866	1,900,800	£6	£18	£45	£95
1867	712,800	£6	£18	£45	£95
1868	1,457,280	£6	£18	£45	£85
1868 RRITANNIAR error	incl. above	£50	£100	£225	—
1869	—	£30	£60	£175	£300
1870	1,283,218	£5	£16	£45	£70
1871	999,633	£5	£16	£40	£70
1872	1,293,271	£5	£16	£40	£70
1873	4,055,550	£5	£16	£40	£70
1874	4,427,031	£5	£16	£40	£70
1875	3,306,500	£5	£16	£40	£70
1876	1,834,389	£5	£16	£40	£70
1877	2,622,393	£5	£16	£40	£70
1878	2,419,975	£5	£16	£40	£70
1879	3,140,265	£5	£16	£40	£70
1880	1,610,069	£5	£16	£40	£70
1881	3,248,265	£5	£16	£40	£70
1882	472,965	£6	£20	£60	£125
1883	4,369,971	£5	£10	£30	£50
1884	3,322,424	£5	£10	£30	£50

DATE	MINTAGE	F	VF	EF	UNC
1885	5,183,653	£5	£10	£30	£50
1886	6,152,669	£5	£10	£30	£50
1887	2,780,761	£5	£10	£30	£50
JUBILEE HEAD ISSUES					
1887	incl. above	£1	£3	£9	£18
1887 Proof	incl. above	—	—	—	£40
1888	518,199	£2	£5	£18	£35
*1889	4,587,010	£2	£5	£18	£35
1890	4,465,834	£2	£5	£18	£35
1891	6,323,027	£2	£5	£18	£35
1892	2,578,226	£2	£5	£18	£40
1893	3,067,243	£8	£25	£100	£200
OLD HEAD ISSUES					
1893	incl. above	£1	£3	£15	£30
1893 Proof	incl. above	—	—	—	£40
1894	1,608,603	£2	£6	£24	£50
1895	4,788,609	£1	£5	£22	£50
1896	4,598,442	£1	£5	£18	£35
1897	4,541,294	£1	£5	£18	£35
1898	4,567,177	£1	£5	£18	£35
*1899	6,246,281	£1	£5	£18	£35
1900	10,644,480	£1	£5	£18	£35
1901	6,098,400	£1	£5	£14	£30

Victoria
Jubilee head

Victoria
Old or Veiled
head

EDWARD VII (1901–10)

	MINTAGE	F	VF	EF	UNC
1902	8,268,480	£1	£2	£7	£15
1902 "Matt Proof"	incl. above	—	—	—	£15
1903	5,227,200	£1	£4	£20	£40
1904	3,627,360	£2	£7	£35	£75
1905	3,548,160	£1	£4	£25	£60
1906	3,152,160	£1	£4	£20	£50
1907	4,831,200	£1	£4	£20	£50
1908	8,157,600	£1	£3	£20	£50
1909	4,055,040	£1	£4	£20	£45
*1910	4,563,380	£1	£3	£18	£35

GEORGE V (1910–36)

First issue	MINTAGE	F	VF	EF	UNC
1911	5,841,084	—	—	£3	£10
1911 Proof	incl. above	—	—	—	£20
1912	8,932,825	—	—	£3	£10
1913	7,143,242	—	—	£3	£10
1914	6,733,584	—	—	£3	£10
1915	5,450,617	—	—	£3	£10
1916	18,555,201	—	—	£3	£8
1917	21,662,490	—	—	£3	£8
7918	20,630,909	—	—	£3	£8
1919	16,845,687	—	—	£3	£8
1920	16,703,597	—	—	£3	£8
Second issue—debased silver					
1920	incl. above	—	—	£3	£10
1921	8,749,301	—	—	£3	£10
1922	7,979,998	—	—	£3	£10
1925	3,731,859	—	—	£5	£25
1926	4,107,910	—	—	£7	£25
Third issue—Modified bust					
1926	incl. above	—	—	£7	£20
Fourth issue—new design (oakleaves)					
1927 Proof only	15,022	—	—	—	£40
1928	1,302,106	£2	£6	£20	£50
1930	1,319,412	£1	£3	£8	£25
1931	6,251,936	—	—	£2	£6
*1932	5,887,325	—	—	£2	£6
1933	5,578,541	—	—	£2	£6
1934	7,405,954	—	—	£2	£6
1935	7,027,654	—	—	£2	£6
1936	3,328,670	—	—	£2	£6

George V,
fourth issue oak
leaves
design reverse

GEORGE VI (1936–52)

Silver

DATE	MINTAGE	F	VF	EF	UNC
*1937	8,148,156	—	—	£1	£3
1937 Proof	26,402	—	—	—	£5
1938	6,402,473	—	—	£1	£3
1939	1,355,860	—	—	£4	£12
1940	7,914,401	—	—	£1	£3
1941	7,979,411	—	—	£1	£3
1942	4,144,051	£2	£5	£12	£32
1943	1,397,220	£2	£5	£12	£35
1944	2,005,553	£5	£12	£35	£75
1945	Only one known				

Brass—lareger size, 12 sided, "Thrift" design

DATE	MINTAGE	F	VF	EF	UNC
1937	45,707,957	—	—	£1	£3
1937 Proof	26,402	—	—	—	£4
1938	14,532,332	—	—	£1	£12
1939	5,603,021	—	—	£2	£25
1940	12,636,018	—	—	£1	£8
1941	60,239,489	—	—	£1	£4
1942	103,214,400	—	—	£1	£5
1943	101,702,400	—	—	£1	£5
1944	69,760,000	—	—	£1	£6
1945	33,942,466	—	—	£1	£10
1946	620,734	£3	£20	£100	£300
1948	4,230,400	—	—	—	£30
1949	464,000	£4	£20	£110	£350
1950	1,600,000	—	£2	£20	£100
1950 Proof	17,513	—	—	—	£10
1951	1,184,000	—	£2	£20	£100
1951 Proof	20,000	—	—	—	£10
1952	25,494,400	—	—	—	£7

George VI "Thrift" design of the brass 3d

ELIZABETH II (1952–   )

DATE	MINTAGE	F	VF	EF	UNC
1953	30,618,000	—	—	—	£1
1953 Proof	40,000	—	—	—	£5
1954	41,720,000	—	—	—	£5
1955	41,075,200	—	—	—	£4
1956	36,801,600	—	—	—	£4
1957	24,294,500	—	—	—	£3
1958	20,504,000	—	—	—	£7
1959	28,499,200	—	—	—	£4
1960	83,078,400	—	—	—	£2
1961	41,102,400	—	—	—	£1
1962	51,545,600	—	—	—	£1
1963	39,482,866	—	—	—	£1
1964	44,867,200	—	—	—	—
1965	27,160,000	—	—	—	—
1966	53,160,000	—	—	—	—
1967	151,780,800	—	—	—	—

TWO PENCES

It is generally accepted that earlier issues of the small silver twopences were only produced for inclusion with the Maundy sets, q.v., except for those listed below.

		F	VF	EF	UNC
1797 "Cartwheel"		£18	£40	£220	£625
1797 Copper Proofs	Many varieties from £500+				

VICTORIA (1837–1901)

For use in the Colonies

		F	VF	EF	UNC
1838		£4	£10	£18	£30
1848		£4	£12	£20	£35

"Cartwheel" twopence

THREE-HALFPENCES

DATE	F	VF	EF	UNC

WILLIAM IV (1830–37)

For use in the Colonies

	F	VF	EF	UNC
1834	£6	£16	£32	£70
1835 over 4	£6	£16	£32	£70
1836	£8	£18	£35	£75
1837	£12	£35	£100	£175

VICTORIA (1837–1901)

For use in the Colonies

	F	VF	EF	UNC
1838	£6	£15	£32	£60
1839	£6	£15	£32	£60
1840	£7	£18	£40	£75
1841	£6	£15	£30	£60
1842	£6	£18	£35	£70
1843	£6	£15	£30	£60
1860	£9	£20	£60	£110
1862	£9	£20	£60	£110

PENNIES

DATE	MINTAGE	F	VF	EF	UNC

The earlier small silver pennies are included in the Maundy oddments section.

GEORGE III (1760–1820)

	MINTAGE	F	VF	EF	UNC
*1797 "Cartwheel", 10 laurel leaves	8,601,600	£15	£32	£140	£400
1797 — 11 laurel leaves	incl. above	£15	£32	£140	£400
1806 Third type	—	£5	£12	£55	£120
1807	—	£5	£12	£55	£125
1808					Unique

GEORGE IV (1820–30)

	MINTAGE	F	VF	EF	UNC
1825	1,075,200	£9	£32	£90	£250
*1826 (varieties)	5,913,600	£9	£32	£90	£250
1826 Proof	—	—	—	£90	£150
1827	1,451,520	£90	£300	£1000	—

WILLIAM IV (1830–37)

	MINTAGE	F	VF	EF	UNC
1831 (varieties)	806,400	£14	£40	£175	£350
1831 Proof	—	—	—	£175	£350
1834	322,560	£14	£40	£175	£350
1837	174,720	£14	£40	£175	£350

"Cartwheel" penny

VICTORIA (1837–1901)

YOUNG HEAD ISSUES

Copper

	MINTAGE	F	VF	EF	UNC
1839 Proof	unrecorded	—	—	—	£700
*1841	913,920	£7	£14	£60	£175
1841 No colon after REG	incl. above	£7	£14	£60	£175
1843	483,840	£30	£100	£500	£1000
1844	215,040	£8	£20	£70	£200
1845	322,560	£8	£22	£80	£220

DATE	MINTAGE	F	VF	EF	UNC
1846	483,840	£10	£25	£90	£220
1846 FID: DEF colon spaced	incl. above	£10	£20	£90	£200
1846 FID:DEF colon close	incl. above	£10	£20	£90	£200
1847	430,080	£8	£20	£80	£200
1848	161,280	£8	£20	£70	£200
1848/7 final 8 over 7	incl. above	£7	£20	£70	£200
1848/6 final 8 over 6	incl. above	£12	£30	£100	—
1849	268,800	£45	£140	£600	—
1851	268,800	£10	£30	£100	£300
1853	1,021,440	£4	£10	£40	£80
1853 Proof	—	—	—	—	£375
1854	6,720,000	£5	£12	£50	£80
1854/3 4 over 3	incl. above	£8	£20	£80	—
1855	5,273,856	£5	£12	£50	£100
1856	1,212,288	£20	£60	£200	£400
1857 Plain trident	752,640	£5	£16	£50	£100
1857 Ornamental trident	incl. above	£5	£16	£50	£100
1858/7 final 8 over 7	incl. above	£4	£14	£40	£85
1858/3 final 8 over 3	incl. above	£20	£60	£200	—
1858	1,599,040	£5	£15	£50	£120
1859	1,075,200	£7	£24	£60	£200
1860/59	32,256	£300	£500	£1750	—

Bronze

DATE	MINTAGE	F	VF	EF	UNC
1860 Beaded border	5,053,440	£5	£15	£50	£130
1860 Toothed border	incl. above	£5	£15	£50	£140
1860 — Piedfort flan	—		Extremely rare		
1861	36,449,280	£4	£10	£40	£120
1862	50,534,400	£4	£10	£40	£120
1862 8 over 6	incl. above		Extremely rare		
1863	28,062,720	£4	£8	£40	£120
1863 Die no below date	incl. above		Extremely rare		
1864 Plain 4	3,440,640	£15	£75	£400	£800
1864 Crosslet 4	incl. above	£15	£75	£400	£1000
1865	8,601,600	£6	£15	£45	£200
1865/3 5 over 3	incl. above	£15	£60	£200	—
1866	9,999,360	£5	£15	£40	£200
1867	5,483,520	£5	£15	£40	£200
*1868	1,182,720	£9	£40	£125	£275
1869	2,580,480	£60	£175	£500	£1600
1870	5,695,022	£7	£25	£100	£275
1871	1,290,318	£30	£100	£300	£1000
1872	8,494,572	£6	£20	£45	£120
1873	8,494,200	£6	£20	£45	£120
1874	5,621,865	£6	£20	£45	£120
1874 H	6,666,240	£6	£20	£45	£120
1874 Later (older) bust	incl. above	£10	£25	£60	£200
1875	10,691,040	£6	£20	£60	£150
1875 H	752,640	£35	£90	£500	£1200
1876 H	11,074,560	£5	£12	£45	£140
1877	9,624,747	£5	£14	£50	£140
1878	2,764,470	£5	£14	£50	£140
1879	7,666,476	£4	£12	£50	£125
1880	3,000,831	£4	£12	£50	£125
1881	2,302,362	£5	£12	£50	£125
1881 H	3,763,200	£5	£12	£50	£125
1882 H	7,526,400	£5	£12	£50	£125
1882 no H	—		Extremely Rare		
1883	6,237,438	£5	£14	£50	£110
1884	11,702,802	£5	£14	£50	£110
1885	7,145,862	£4	£14	£50	£110
1886	6,087,759	£4	£14	£50	£110
1887	5,315,085	£4	£14	£50	£110

Victoria copper penny

Victoria bronze penny

DATE	MINTAGE	F	VF	EF	UNC
1888..............................	5,125,020	£4	£14	£50	£110
1889..............................	12,559,737	£4	£14	£50	£110
1890..............................	15,330,840	£4	£14	£50	£110
1891..............................	17,885,961	£4	£12	£45	£110
1892..............................	10,501,671	£4	£12	£45	£110
1893..............................	8,161,737	£4	£12	£45	£110
1894..............................	3,883,452	£7	£25	£75	£175

OLD HEAD ISSUES

DATE	MINTAGE	F	VF	EF	UNC
1895 Trident 2mm from P(ENNY)	5,395,830	£4	£18	£70	£200
1895 Trident 1mm from P............	incl. above	—	£2	£15	£45
1896..............................	24,147,156	—	£2	£15	£40
*1897	20,756,620	—	£2	£15	£40
1898..............................	14,296,836	—	£2	£16	£40
1899..............................	26,441,069	—	£2	£14	£40
1900..............................	31,778,109	—	£2	£13	£35
1901..............................	22,205,568	—	£2	£7	£20

EDWARD VII (1901–10)

DATE	MINTAGE	F	VF	EF	UNC
1902..............................	26,976,768	—	£1	£8	£22
1902 "Low tide" to sea line	incl. above	—	£5	£20	£50
1903..............................	21,415,296	—	£3	£14	£50
1904..............................	12,913,152	—	£4	£20	£80
1905..............................	17,783,808	—	£3	£14	£45
1906..............................	37,989,504	—	£3	£14	£40
1907..............................	47,322,240	—	£3	£14	£40
*1908	31,506,048	—	£3	£14	£45
1909..............................	19,617,024	—	£3	£20	£70
1910..............................	29,549,184	—	£3	£14	£40

GEORGE V (1910–36)

DATE	MINTAGE	F	VF	EF	UNC
1911..............................	23,079,168	—	£3	£12	£32
1912..............................	48,306,048	—	£3	£12	£32
*1912 H..............................	16,800,000	—	£3	£25	£90
1913..............................	65,497,812	—	£3	£12	£40
1914..............................	50,820,997	—	£3	£12	£40
1915..............................	47,310,807	—	£3	£12	£40
1916..............................	86,411,165	—	£3	£12	£40
1917..............................	107,905,436	—	£3	£12	£40
1918..............................	84,227,372	—	£3	£12	£40
1918 H..............................	3,660,800	£1	£8	£80	£240
1918 KN..............................	incl. above	£7	£60	£300	£1000
1919..............................	113,761,090	—	£2	£12	£40
1919 H..............................	5,209,600	£1	£10	£70	£250
1919 KN..............................	incl. above	£8	£70	£350	£1200
1920..............................	124,693,485	—	£2	£12	£25
1921..............................	129,717,693	—	£2	£12	£25
1922..............................	16,346,711	—	£2	£12	£40
1926..............................	4,498,519	—	£6	£20	£75
1926 Modified effigy..................	incl above	£7	£25	£300	£500
1927..............................	60,989,561	—	£2	£8	£30
1928..............................	50,178,00	—	£2	£8	£30
1929..............................	49,132,800	—	£2	£8	£30
1930..............................	29,097,600	—	£2	£15	£45
1931..............................	19,843,200	—	£2	£8	£35
1932..............................	8,277,600	—	£2	£10	£35
1933..............................			Only 7 examples known		
1934..............................	13,965,600	—	£2	£8	£32
1935..............................	56,070,000	—	—	£2	£9
1936..............................	154,296,000	—	—	£2	£8

DATE	MINTAGE	F	VF	EF	UNC

GEORGE VI (1936–52)

DATE	MINTAGE	F	VF	EF	UNC
1937	88,896,000	—	—	—	£3
1937 Proof	26,402	—	—	—	£5
1938	121,560,00	—	—	—	£3
1939	55,560,000	—	—	—	£4
1940	42,284,400	—	—	—	£6
1944	42,600,000	—	—	—	£6
1945	79,531,200	—	—	—	£5
1946	66,855,600	—	—	—	£3
1947	52,220,400	—	—	—	£3
1948	63,961,200	—	—	—	£3
1949	14,324,400	—	—	—	£3
1950	240,000	£3	£7	£14	£22
1950 Proof	17,513	—	—	—	£14
1951	120,000	£5	£9	£18	£35
1951 Proof	20,000	—	—	—	—

ELIZABETH II (1952–)

DATE	MINTAGE	F	VF	EF	UNC
*1953	1,308,400	—	—	£1	£4
1953 Proof	40,000	—	—	—	£6
1954	Only one known				
1961	48,313,400	—	—	—	£1
1962	143,308,600	—	—	—	50p
1963	125,235,600	—	—	—	50p
1964	153,294,000	—	—	—	50p
1965	121,310,400	—	—	—	50p
1966	165,739,200	—	—	—	50p
1967	654,564,000	—	—	—	—

Later issues are included in the Decimal section.

HALFPENNIES

DATE		F	VF	EF	UNC

CHARLES II (1660–85)

DATE	F	VF	EF	UNC
1672	£50	£175	£750	—
1672 CRAOLVS error		Extremely rare		
1673	£50	£175	£750	—
1673 CRAOLVS error		Extremely rare		
1673 No rev. stop	£70	£250	—	—
1673 No stops on obv.		Extremely rare		
1675	£50	£175	£700	—
1675 No stops on obv.	£50	£200	—	—

JAMES II (1685–88)

DATE	F	VF	EF	UNC
1685 (tin)	£100	£500	£2250	—
1686 (tin)	£110	£500	£2250	—
1687 (tin)	£100	£50	£2250	—

WILLIAM & MARY (1688–94)

Tin

DATE	F	VF	EF	UNC
1689 Small draped busts, edge dated	£300	—	—	—
1690 Large cuirassed busts, edge dated	£110	£350	£2000	—
1691 — date on edge and in exergue	£110	£350	£2000	—
1692 — —	£110	£350	£2000	—

DATE	F	VF	EF	UNC

Copper
*1694 Large cuirassed busts, date in exergue .	£35	£125	£850	—
1694 — — GVLIEMVS error	Extremely rare			
1694 — — MΛRIΛ error	Extremely rare			
1694 — — No stops on rev.	Extremely rare			

WILLIAM III (1694–1702)

1695 First issue (date in exergue)	£30	£80	£500	—
1695 — No stop after GVLIEMVS on obv.	£50	£100	—	—
1695 — No stop after BRITANNIA on rev.	£50	£100	—	—
1696 —	£30	£100	£525	—
1696 — TERTVS error	Extremely rare			
1697 —	£30	£90	£500	—
1697 — No stop after TERTIVS on obv.	£50	£100	—	—
1698 —	£30	£90	£600	—
1698 Second issue (date in legend)	£30	£120	—	—
1698 — No stop after date	£45	£100	—	—
1699 —	£30	£90	£500	—
1699 — No stop after date	£45	£120	—	—
1699 Third issue (date in exergue) (Britannia with right hand on knee)	£35	£90	£500	—
1699 — No stop after date	Extremely rare			
1699 — BRITΛNNIΛ error	£80	£175	—	—
1699 — TERTVS error	Extremely rare			
1699 — No stop on rev.	Extremely rare			
1699 — No stops on obv.	£80	£175	—	—
1700 —	£30	£90	£500	—
1700 — No stops on obv.	£75	£175	—	—
1700 — No stops after GVLIELMUS	£75	£175	—	—
1700 — BRITVANNIA error	Extremely rare			
1700 — GVIELMS error	£75	£175	—	—
1700 — GVLIEEMVS error	£50	£160	—	—
*1701 —	£35	£90	£500	—
1701 — BRITΛNNIΛ error	£50	£160	—	—
1701 — No stops on obv.	Extremely rare			
1701 — inverted As for Vs	£60	£175	—	—

GEORGE I (1714–27)

*1717 "Dump" issue	£40	£110	£500	
1718 —	£28	£100	£400	—
1719 Second issue	£25	£100	£400	—
1720 —	£25	£100	£400	—
1721 —	£25	£85	£400	—
1721 — Stop after date	£35	£100	—	—
1722 —	£25	£85	£400	—
1722 — inverted A for V on obv.	£40	£125	—	—
1723 —	£25	£85	£400	—
1723 — No stop on rev.	£30	£90	—	—
1724 —	£25	£85	£400	—

GEORGE II (1727–60)

1729 Young head	£22	£50	£225	—
1729 — No stop on rev.	£25	£60	£200	—
1730 — .	£15	£45	£200	—
1730 — GEOGIVS error	£30	£80	£400	—
1730 — Stop after date	£25	£70	£250	—
1730 — No stop after REX on obv.	£30	£80	£270	—
1731 —	£20	£50	£225	—
1731 — No rev. stop	£25	£70	£240	—
1732 —	£20	£50	£200	—
1732 — No rev. stop	£25	£70	£250	—
1733 —	£20	£50	£200	—

DATE	MINTAGE	F	VF	EF	UNC
1734/3 — 4 over 3..........................		£30	£125	—	—
1734 — No stop on obv.		£30	£125	—	—
1735 —..		£20	£40	£200	—
1736 —..		£20	£40	£175	—
1737 —..		£20	£40	£175	—
1738 —..		£20	£40	£175	—
1739 —..		£18	£40	£175	—
1740 Old head.............................		£15	£40	£160	—
1742 —..		£15	£40	£160	—
1742/0 — 2 over 0........................		£20	£75	£240	—
1743 —..		£15	£40	£175	—
1744 —..		£15	£40	£175	—
1745 —..		£15	£40	£175	—
1746 —..		£15	£40	£175	—
1747 —..		£15	£40	£175	—
1748 —..		£15	£40	£175	—
1749 —..		£15	£40	£175	—
1750 —..		£15	£40	£175	—
*1751 —...		£15	£40	£175	—
1752 —..		£15	£40	£175	—
1753 —..		£15	£40	£175	—
1754 —..		£15	£40	£175	—

George II old head

GEORGE III (1760–1820)

First type—Royal Mint

	MINTAGE	F	VF	EF	UNC
1770..		£10	£35	£175	—
1770 No stop on rev.		£20	£55	£180	—
1771..		£10	£35	£200	—
1771 No stop on rev.		£20	£60	£200	—
1772 Error GEORIVS		£40	£100	£500	
1772..		£9	£28	£150	—
1772 No stop on rev		£20	£60	£175	—
1773..		£9	£28	£150	—
1773 No stop after REX................		£25	£60	—	—
1773 No stop on rev.		£20	£40	£145	—
1774..		£9	£28	£145	—
*1775		£10	£28	£130	—

Second type—Soho Mint

	MINTAGE	F	VF	EF	UNC
*1799		£2	£6	£30	£65

Third type

	MINTAGE	F	VF	EF	UNC
1806..		£2	£6	£30	£65
1807..		£2	£6	£30	£65

George III first type

GEORGE IV (1820–30)

	MINTAGE	F	VF	EF	UNC
1825..............................	215,040	£8	£28	£70	£140
1826 (varieties)	9,031,630	£7	£25	£50	£125
1826 Proof....................	—	—	—	£80	£140
1827..............................	5,376,000	£8	£25	£70	£120

WILLIAM IV (1830–37)

	MINTAGE	F	VF	EF	UNC
1831..............................	806,400	£7	£22	£70	£175
1831 Proof.................................	—	—	—	—	£225
1834..............................	537,600	£7	£22	£70	£175
1837..............................	349,440	£7	£22	£70	£175

George III second type

VICTORIA (1837–1901)

YOUNG HEAD ISSUES

Copper

	MINTAGE	F	VF	EF	UNC
1838..............................	456,960	£4	£15	£40	£100
1839 Proof.................................	268,800	—	—	—	£250

DATE	MINTAGE	F	VF	EF	UNC
1841	1,0745,200	£4	£15	£40	£100
1843	967,680	£15	£40	£100	£220
1844	1,075,200	£4	£15	£40	£100
1845	1,075,200	£40	£100	£350	£800
1846	860,160	£6	£15	£40	£125
1847	725,640	£6	£15	£40	£125
1848	322,560	£6	£15	£40	£125
1848/7 final 8 OVER 7	incl. above	£7	£15	£50	£130
1851	215,040	£5	£14	£40	£120
1852	637,056	£5	£12	£40	£120
1853	1,559,040	£4	£7	£20	£60
1853/2 3 over 2	incl. above	£10	£20	£40	£125
1853 Proof	—	—	—	—	£200
1854	12,354,048	£4	£8	£30	£60
1855	1,455,837	£4	£8	£30	£60
1856	1,942,080	£6	£14	£45	£110
1857	1,820,720	£5	£12	£30	£70
1858	2,472,960	£4	£10	£30	£70
1858/7 final 8 over 7	incl. above	£4	£10	£30	£70
1858/6 final 8 over 6	incl. above	£4	£10	£30	£70
1859	1,290,240	£5	£15	£35	£100
1859/8 9 over 8	incl. above	£4	£10	£30	£65
1860	unrecorded		£600	£1750	£5000

Victoria copper halfpenny

Bronze

1860 Beaded border	6,630,400	£3	£9	£30	£120
1860 Toothed border		£4	£12	£40	£125
1861	54,118,400	£3	£9	£30	£100
1862 Die letter A, B or C to left of lighthouse				Extremely rare	
1862	61,107,200	£3	£9	£30	£75
1863	15,948,800	£3	£9	£30	£75
1864	537,600	£3	£10	£40	£100
1865	8,064,000	£4	£15	£50	£100
1865/3 5 over 3	incl. above	£15	£40	£200	—
1866	2,508,800	£5	£15	£50	£100
1867	2,508,800	£5	£15	£45	£100
1868	3,046,400	£4	£10	£40	£125
1869	3,225,600	£7	£30	£60	£225
1870	4,350,739	£5	£15	£50	£130
1871	1,075,280	£30	£80	£200	£500
1872	4,659,410	£4	£10	£35	£90
1873	3,404,880	£4	£10	£35	£90
1874	1,347,655	£5	£20	£60	£140
1874 H	5,017,600	£3	£10	£30	£125
1875	5,430,815	£3	£8	£30	£100
1875 H	1,254,400	£4	£10	£35	£85
1876 H	5,809,600	£4	£10	£30	£90
1877	5,209,505	£3	£10	£30	£90
1878	1,425,535	£5	£20	£60	£125
1879	3,582,545	£3	£10	£30	£80
1880	2,423,465	£4	£12	£40	£100
1881	2,007,515	£4	£12	£35	£90
1881 H	1,792,000	£3	£10	£30	£75
1882 H	4,480,000	£3	£10	£30	£90
1883	3,000,725	£3	£10	£30	£70
1884	6,989,580	£3	£10	£30	£70
1885	8,600,574	£3	£10	£30	£70
1886	8,586,155	£3	£10	£25	£70
1887	10,701,305	£3	£10	£25	£70
1888	6,814,670	£3	£10	£25	£70
1889	7,748,234	£3	£10	£25	£70
1889/8 9 over 8	incl. above	£10	£30	£75	—
1890	11,254,235	£3	£10	£25	£70

Victoria bronze halfpenny

DATE	MINTAGE	F	VF	EF	UNC
1891	13,192,260	£3	£10	£25	£70
1892	2,478,335	£3	£10	£25	£75
1893	7,229,344	£3	£10	£25	£70
1894	1,767,635	£5	£12	£35	£100

OLD HEAD ISSUES

1895	3,032,154	£1	£4	£15	£40
1896	9,142,500	£1	£4	£10	£35
1897	8,690,315	£1	£4	£10	£35
1898	8,595,180	£1	£4	£10	£35
1899	12,108,001	£1	£4	£10	£35
1900	13,805,190	£1	£4	£10	£30
1901	11,127,360	£1	£2	£6	£15

EDWARD VII (1901–10)

1902	13,672,960	£2	£4	£8	£22
1902 "Low tide"	incl. above	£6	£15	£50	£125
*1903	11,450,880	£2	£5	£18	£40
1904	8,131,200	£2	£5	£18	£40
1905	10,124,800	£2	£5	£18	£40
1906	16,849,280	£2	£5	£18	£40
1907	16,849,280	£2	£5	£18	£40
1908	16,620,800	£2	£5	£18	£40
1909	8,279,040	£2	£5	£18	£40
1910	10,769,920	£2	£5	£18	£40

GEORGE V (1910–36)

1911	12,570,880	—	£3	£12	£30
1912	21,185,920	—	£2	£12	£30
1913	17,476,480	—	£2	£14	£35
1914	20,289,111	—	£2	£12	£35
1915	21,563,040	£1	£3	£14	£35
1916	39,386,143	—	£2	£12	£35
1917	38,245,436	—	£2	£12	£30
1918	22,321,072	—	£2	£12	£30
1919	28,104,001	—	£2	£12	£30
1920	35,146,793	—	£2	£12	£30
1921	28,027,293	—	£2	£12	£30
*1922	10,734,964	—	£2	£15	£40
1923	12,266,282	—	£2	£12	£30
1924	13,971,038	—	£2	£10	£30
1925	12,216,123	—	£2	£10	£30
1925 Modified effigy	incl. above	£2	£5	£20	£50
1926	6,172,306	—	£2	£10	£32
1927	15,589,622	—	£2	£10	£30
1928	20,935,200	—	£2	£8	£25
1929	25,680,000	—	£2	£8	£25
1930	12,532,800	—	£2	£8	£25
1931	16,137,600	—	£2	£8	£25
1932	14,448,000	—	£2	£8	£25
1933	10,560,000	—	£2	£8	£25
1934	7,704,000	—	£2	£12	£30
1935	12,180,000	—	£1	£6	£15
1936	23,008,800	—	£1	£5	£8

GEORGE VI (1936–52)

1937	24,504,000	—	—	£1	£2
1937 Proof	26,402	—	—	£1	£5
1938	40,320,000	—	—	£1	£4
1939	28,924,800	—	—	£1	£4

DATE	MINTAGE	F	VF	EF	UNC
1940	32,162,400	—	—	£1	£5
1941	45,120,000	—	—	£1	£5
1942	71,908,800	—	—	£1	£3
1943	76,200,000	—	—	£1	£3
1944	81,840,000	—	—	£1	£3
1945	57,000,000	—	—	£1	£3
1946	22,725,600	—	—	£1	£5
1947	21,266,400	—	—	£1	£3
1948	26,947,200	—	—	£1	£2
*1949	24,744,000	—	—	£1	£2
1950	24,153,600	—	—	£1	£4
1950 Proof	17,513	—	—	£1	£5
1951	14,868,000	—	—	£1	£5
1951 Proof	20,000	—	—	£1	£5
1952	33,78,400	—	—	£1	£2

ELIZABETH II (1952–)

DATE	MINTAGE	F	VF	EF	UNC
1953	8,926,366	—	—	—	£1
1953 Proof	40,000	—	—	—	£3
*1954	19,375,000	—	—	—	£3
1955	18,799,200	—	—	—	£3
1956	21,799,200	—	—	—	£3
1957	43,684,800	—	—	—	£1
1958	62,318,400	—	—	—	£1
1959	79,176,000	—	—	—	£1
1960	41,340,000	—	—	—	£1
1962	41,779,200	—	—	—	£1
1963	45,036,000	—	—	—	20p
1964	78,583,200	—	—	—	20p
1965	98,083,200	—	—	—	20p
1966	95,289,600	—	—	—	20p
1967	146,491,200	—	—	—	10p

Later issues are included in the Decimal section.

FARTHINGS

DATE	F	VF	EF	UNC

OLIVER CROMWELL

Undated (copper) Draped bust, shield rev. Variations   Extremely rare

CHARLES II (1660–85)

Copper

	F	VF	EF	UNC
1672	£40	£200	£700	—
*1673	£40	£200	£500	—
1673 CAROLA for CAROLO error	£70	£300	—	—
1673 No stops on obv.			Extremely rare	
1673 No stop on rev.			Extremely rare	
1674	£40	£175	£500	—
1675	£40	£175	£500	—
1675 No stop after CAROLVS			Extremely rare	
1679	£45	£200	£550	—
1679 No stop on rev.	£60	£225	—	—
Tin				
1684 with date on edge	£150	£375	—	—
1685 —			Extremely rare	

DATE	F	VF	EF	UNC

JAMES II (1685–88)

	F	VF	EF	UNC
1684 (tin) Cuirassed bust			Extremely rare	
1685 (tin) —	£125	£400	£1250	—
1686 (tin) —	£125	£400	£1250	—
1687 (tin) —			Extremely rare	
1687 (tin) Draped bust	£160	£600	—	—

WILLIAM & MARY (1688–94)

	F	VF	EF	UNC
1689 (tin) Small draped busts	£500	—	—	—
1689 (tin) — with edge date 1690			Extremely rare	
1690 (tin) Large cuirassed busts	£120	£400	£1500	—
1690 (tin) — with edge date 1689			Extremely rare	
1691 (tin) —	£125	£400	—	—
1692 (tin) —	£120	£500	£1500	—
1694 (copper) —	£50	£175	£650	—
1694 No stop after MARIΛ			Extremely rare	
1694 No stop on obv.			Extremely rare	
1694 No stop on rev.			Extremely rare	
1694 Unbarred As in BRITANNIA			Extremely rare	

WILLIAM III (1694–1702)

	F	VF	EF	UNC
1695 First issue (date in exergue)	£35	£125	£500	—
1695 — GVLIELMV error			Extremely rare	
1696 —	£35	£125	£500	—
1697 —	£35	£125	£450	—
1697 — GVLIELMS error			Extremely rare	
1698 —	£125	£400	—	—
1698 Second issue (date in legend)	£40	£150	£600	—
1699 First issue	£40	£150	£550	—
1699 Second issue	£40	£150	£575	—
1699 — No stop after date	£40	£140	—	—
1700 First issue	£28	£90	£450	—
1700 — error RRITANNIA			Extremely rare	

ANNE (1702–14)

	F	VF	EF	UNC
*1714	£240	£400	£700	—

GEORGE I (1714–27)

	F	VF	EF	UNC
*1717 First small "Dump" issue	£100	£300	£700	—
1719 Second issue	£25	£100	£325	—
1719 — No stop on rev.	£60	£300	—	—
1719 — No stops on obv.	£60	£300	—	—
1720 —	£25	£75	£350	—
*1721 —	£25	£75	£350	—
1721/0 — Last 1 over 0	£40	£130	—	—
1722 —	£25	£75	£250	—
1723 —	£30	£100	£350	—
1723 — R over sideways R in REX			Extremely rare	
1724 —	£30	£100	£350	—

George I, first type

GEORGE II (1727–60)

	F	VF	EF	UNC
1730 Young head	£14	£50	£200	—
1731 —	£14	£50	£200	—
1732 —	£14	£60	£225	—
1733 —	£14	£60	£200	—
1734 —	£14	£60	£200	—
1734 — No stop on obv.	£30	£100	£300	—

George I second type

DATE	MINTAGE	F	VF	EF	UNC
1735 —		£12	£50	£175	—
1735 — 3 over 5		£20	£70	£250	—
1736 —		£12	£50	£175	—
1737 —		£12	£50	£175	—
1739 —		£12	£50	£175	—
1741 Old Head		£12	£50	£175	—
1744 —		£11	£45	£160	—
1746 —		£11	£45	£160	—
1746 — V over LL in GEORGIVS				Extremely rare	
1749 —		£15	£40	£175	—
1750 —		£12	£35	£160	—
1754 —		£9	£25	£150	—
1754 — 4 over 0		£18	£40	£175	—

George III, third (Soho Mint) issue

GEORGE III (1760–1820)

	MINTAGE	F	VF	EF	UNC
1771 First (London) issue		£18	£50	£200	—
1773 —		£11	£40	£125	—
1773 — No stop on rev.		£18	£40	£125	—
1773 — No stop after REX		£25	£70	£160	—
1774 —		£10	£30	£140	—
1775 —		£10	£30	£140	—
1797 Second (Soho Mint) issue				Patterns only	
*1799 Third (Soho Mint) issue		£2	£8	£32	£70
*1806 Fourth (Soho Mint) issue		£2	£8	£32	£70
1807 —		£2	£8	£32	£70

George III, fourth (Soho Mint) issue

GEORGE IV (1820–30)

	MINTAGE	F	VF	EF	UNC
1821 First bust (laureate, draped), first reverse (date in exergue)...	2,688,000	£2	£9	£40	£80
*1822 —	5,924,350	£2	£9	£40	£80
1823 —	2,365,440	£2.50	£10	£40	£80
1823 I for 1 in date	incl. above	£15	£60	£175	—
1825 —	4,300.800	£2.50	£10	£40	£80
1826 —	6,666,240	£2.50	£8	£40	£80
1826 Second bust (couped, date below), second reverse (ornament in exergue)	incl. above	£2.50	£10	£40	£75
1826 — Proof	—	—	—	—	£175
1827 —	2,365,440	£2.50	£9	£35	£100
1828 —	2,365,440	£2.50	£9	£35	£100
1829 —	1,505,280	£2.50	£10	£40	£100
1830 —	2,365,440	£2.50	£8	£35	£100

WILLIAM IV (1830–37)

	MINTAGE	F	VF	EF	UNC
1831	2,688,000	£5	£12	£35	£100
1831 Proof	—	—	—	—	£200
1834	1,935,360	£5	£12	£35	£100
1835	1.720,320	£5	£12	£30	£100
1836	1,290.240	£5	£12	£40	£100
1837	3.010,560	£5	£12	£35	£110

VICTORIA (1837–1901)

FIRST YOUNG HEAD (COPPER) ISSUES

	MINTAGE	F	VF	EF	UNC
1838	591,360	£4	£12	£35	£80
1839	4,300,800	£4	£12	£35	£75
1839 Proof	—	—	—	—	£150
1840	3,010,560	£4	£12	£35	£70
1841	1,720,320	£4	£12	£35	£80
1842	1,290,240	£8	£25	£70	£160
1843	4,085,760	£5	£10	£35	£70

DATE	MINTAGE	F	VF	EF	UNC
1843 I for 1 in date		£45	£150	£275	—
1844...............................	430,080	£45	£100	£400	£800
1845...............................	3,225,600	£5	£10	£35	£70
1846...............................	2,580,480	£6	£18	£45	£90
*1847	3,879,720	£5	£10	£35	£75
1848...............................	1,290,240	£5	£10	£35	£75
1849...............................	645,120	£20	£50	£140	£300
1850...............................	430,080	£5	£10	£35	£70
1851...............................	1,935,360	£6	£20	£55	£140
1851 D over sideways D in DEI ...	incl. above	£25	£50	£150	—
1852...............................	822,528	£7	£20	£50	£120
1853...............................	1,028,628	£4	£7	£30	£50
1853 Proof.........................	—	—	—	—	£325
1854...............................	6,504,960	£4	£10	£35	£50
1855...............................	3,440,640	£4	£10	£35	£50
1856...............................	1,771,392	£8	£15	£50	£120
1856 R over E in VICTORIA........	incl. above	£20	£50	£120	—
1857...............................	1,075,200	£4	£10	£35	£55
1858...............................	1,720,320	£3	£8	£35	£50
1859...............................	1,290,240	£9	£25	£60	£150
1860...............................	unrecorded	£750	£1800	£4000	—

Victoria Young Head first (copper) issue

SECOND YOUNG OR "BUN" HEAD (BRONZE) ISSUES

1860 Toothed border	2,867,200	£2	£5	£26	£80
1860 Beaded border	incl. above	£3	£7	£30	£85
1860 Toothed/Beaded border mule	incl. above		Extremely rare		
1861...............................	8,601,600	£2	£5	£25	£80
1862...............................	14,336,000	£1	£5	£25	£70
1862 Large 8 in date..................	incl. above		Extremely rare		
1863...............................	1,433,600	£20	£50	£150	£325
1864...............................	2,508,800	£1	£5	£25	£60
1865...............................	4,659,200	£1	£5	£25	£56
1865 5 over 2.......................	incl. above	£8	£15	£35	—
1866...............................	3,584,000	£1	£5	£20	£60
1867...............................	5,017,600	£1	£5	£25	£60
1868...............................	4,851,210	£1	£5	£25	£60
1869...............................	3,225,600	£1	£8	£30	£70
1872...............................	2,150,400	£1	£5	£25	£60
1873...............................	3,225,620	£1	£5	£25	£60
1874 H	3,584,000	£1	£5	£25	£70
1874 H both Gs over sideways G	incl. above	£100	£200	£500	—
1875...............................	712,760	£3	£10	£35	£80
1875 H	6,092,800	£1	£5	£20	£60
1876 H	1,175,200	£2	£10	£35	£80
*1878	4,008,540	£1	£4	£18	£50
1879...............................	3,977,180	£1	£4	£18	£50
1880...............................	1,842,710	£1	£4	£18	£50
1881...............................	3,494,670	£1	£4	£18	£50
1881 H	1,792,000	£1	£4	£18	£50
1882 H	1,792,000	£1	£5	£18	£50
1883...............................	1,128,680	£4	£15	£45	£80
1884...............................	5,782,000	£1	£4	£16	£35
1885...............................	5,442,308	£1	£4	£16	£35
1886...............................	7,707,790	£1	£4	£16	£35
1887...............................	1,340,800	£1	£4	£16	£35
1888...............................	1,887,250	£1	£4	£16	£35
1890...............................	2,133,070	£1	£4	£16	£35
1891...............................	4,959,690	£1	£4	£16	£35
1892...............................	887,240	£2	£7	£30	£35
1893...............................	3,904,320	£1	£4	£16	£35
1894...............................	2,396,770	£1	£4	£16	£35
1895...............................	2,852,852	£10	£25	£60	£140

Victoria Young Head second (bronze) issue

DATE	MINTAGE	F	VF	EF	UNC
OLD HEAD ISSUES					
1895 Bright finish	incl. above	£1	£2	£14	£22
1896 —	3,668,610	£1	£2	£14	£20
1897 —	4,579,800	£1	£2	£14	£20
1897 Dark finish	incl. above	£1	£2	£14	£20
1898 —	4,010,080	£1	£2	£14	£20
1899 —	3,864,616	£1	£2	£14	£20
1900 —	5,969,317	£1	£2	£14	£20
*1901 —	8,016,460	£1	£2	£6	£14

EDWARD VII (1901–10)

DATE	MINTAGE	F	VF	EF	UNC
1902..................................	5,125,120	50p	£1	£7	£12
1903..................................	5,331,200	50p	£1	£8	£15
1904..................................	3,628,800	£1	£2	£12	£25
1905..................................	4,076,800	50p	£1	£8	£20
1906..................................	5,340,160	50p	£1	£8	£15
*1907	4,399,360	50p	£1	£7	£15
1908..................................	4,264,960	50p	£1	£7	£14
1909..................................	8,852,480	50p	£1	£7	£14
1910..................................	2,298,400	£1	£6	£15	£45

GEORGE V (1910–36)

DATE	MINTAGE	F	VF	EF	UNC
1911..................................	5,196,800	25p	50p	£5	£10
1912..................................	7,669,760	25p	50p	£4	£10
1913..................................	4,184,320	25p	50p	£5	£10
1914..................................	6,126,988	25p	50p	£4	£10
1915..................................	7,129,255	25p	50p	£4	£12
1916..................................	10,993,325	25p	50p	£4	£10
*1917	21,434,844	25p	50p	£4	£10
1918..................................	19,362,818	25p	50p	£4	£10
1919..................................	15,089,425	25p	50p	£4	£10
1920..................................	11,480,536	25p	50p	£4	£8
1921..................................	9,469,097	25p	50p	£4	£8
1922..................................	9,956,983	25p	50p	£4	£8
1923..................................	8,034,457	25p	50p	£4	£8
1924..................................	8,733,414	25p	50p	£4	£8
1925..................................	12,634,697	25p	50p	£4	£8
1926 Modified effigy..................	9,792,397	25p	50p	£4	£8
1927	7,868,355	25p	50p	£4	£8
1928	11,625,600	25p	50p	£4	£8
1929	8,419,200	25p	50p	£4	£8
1930	4,195,200	25p	50p	£4	£8
1931	6,595,200	25p	50p	£4	£8
1932	9,292,800	25p	50p	£4	£8
1933	4,560,000	25p	50p	£4	£8
1934	3,052,800	25p	50p	£4	£8
1935	2.227,200	£1	£2	£8	£20
1936	9,734,400	25p	50p	£3	£6

GEORGE VI (1936–52)

DATE	MINTAGE	F	VF	EF	UNC
1937..................................	8,131,200	—	—	50p	£1
1937 Proof...............................	26,402	—	—	£1	£4
1938..................................	7,449,600	—	—	£1	£5
1939..................................	31,440,000	—	—	50p	£1
1940..................................	18,360,000	—	—	50p	£1
1941..................................	27,312,000	—	—	50p	£1
1942..................................	28,857,600	—	—	50p	£1
1943..................................	33,345,600	—	—	50p	£1
1944..................................	25,137,600	—	—	50p	£1
1945..................................	23,736,000	—	—	50p	£1

DATE	MINTAGE	F	VF	EF	UNC
1946	24,364,800	—	—	50p	£1
1947	14,745,600	—	—	50p	£1
1948	16,622,400	—	—	50p	£1
*1949	8,424,000	—	—	50p	£1
1950	10,324,800	—	—	50p	£1
1950 Proof	17,513	—	—	50p	£3
1951	14,016,000	—	—	50p	£1
1951 Proof	20,000	—	—	50p	£3
1952	5,251,200	—	—	50p	£1

ELIZABETH II (1952–   )

	MINTAGE	F	VF	EF	UNC
1953	6,131,037	—	—	—	£1
1953 Proof	40,000	—	—	—	£2
*1954	6,566,400	—	—	—	£1
1955	5,779,200	—	—	—	£1
1956	1,996,800	—	50p	£1	£2

HALF FARTHINGS

DATE	MINTAGE	F	VF	EF	UNC

GEORGE IV (1820–30)

	MINTAGE	F	VF	EF	UNC
1828 (two different obverses) (issued for Ceylon)	7,680,000	£9	£20	£45	£90
1830 (large or small date) (issued for Ceylon)	8,766,320	£9	£20	£45	£85

WILLIAM IV (1830–37)

	MINTAGE	F	VF	EF	UNC
1837 (issued for Ceylon)	1,935,360	£20	£55	£140	£220

VICTORIA (1837–1901)

	MINTAGE	F	VF	EF	UNC
1839	2,042,880	£5	£10	£30	£65
1842	unrecorded	£4	£8	£25	£65
1843	3,440,640	£3	£6	£20	£40
1844	6,451,200	£3	£6	£15	£40
1844 E over N in REGINA	incl. above	£10	£45	£100	—
1847	3,010,560	£6	£12	£30	£60
1851	unrecorded	£5	£12	£35	£60
1851 5 over 0	unrecorded	£8	£20	£60	£125
1852	989,184	£5	£12	£40	£65
1853	955,224	£5	£15	£45	£85
1853 Proof	incl. above	—	—	—	£175
1854	677,376	£8	£25	£70	£125
1856	913,920	£8	£25	£70	£125
1868	unrecorded	—	—	—	Rare
1868	unrecorded	—	—	—	Rare

THIRD FARTHINGS

DATE	MINTAGE	F	VF	EF	UNC

GEORGE IV (1820–30)

| 1827 (issued for Malta)............... | unrecorded | £5 | £15 | £35 | £90 |

WILLIAM IV (1830–37)

| 1835 (issued for Malta)............... | unrecorded | £7 | £16 | £40 | £95 |

VICTORIA (1837–1901)

1844 (issued for Malta)...............	1,301,040	£10	£24	£70	£140
1844 RE for REG	incl. above	£30	£60	£250	—
1866..	576,000	£6	£14	£30	£55
1868..	144,000	£6	£14	£30	£55
1876..	162,000	£6	£14	£30	£55
1878..	288,000	£6	£14	£30	£55
1881..	144,000	£6	£14	£30	£55
1884..	144,000	£6	£14	£30	£55
1885..	288,000	£6	£14	£30	£55

EDWARD VII (1902–10)

| 1902 (issued for Malta)............... | 288,000 | £3 | £7 | £20 | £30 |

GEORGE V (1911–36)

| 1913 (issued for Malta)............... | 288,000 | £3 | £7 | £20 | £30 |

QUARTER FARTHINGS

DATE	MINTAGE	F	VF	EF	UNC

VICTORIA (1837–1901)

1839 (issued for Ceylon).............	3,840,000	£10	£25	£50	£100
1851 (issued for Ceylon).............	2,215,680	£10	£25	£50	£100
1852 (issued for Ceylon).............	incl. above	£10	£25	£50	£100
1853 (issued for Ceylon).............	incl. above	£10	£25	£50	£100
1853 Proof...................................	—	—	—	—	£400

EMERGENCY ISSUES

DATE   F   VF   EF   UNC

GEORGE III (1760–1820)

To alleviate the shortage of circulating coinage during the Napoleonic Wars the Bank of England firstly authorised the countermarking of other countries' coins, enabling them to pass as English currency. The coins, countermarked with punches depicting the head of George III, were mostly Spanish American 8 reales of Charles III. Although this had limited success it was later decided to completely overstrike the coins with a new English design on both sides—specimens that still show traces of the original host coin's date are avidly sought after by collectors. This overstriking continued for a number of years although all the known coins are dated 1804. Finally, in 1811 the Bank of England issued silver tokens which continued up to 1816 when a completely new regal coinage was introduced.

DOLLAR
Oval countermark of George III

	F	VF	EF	UNC
On "Pillar" type 8 reales	£165	£650	£1000	—
*On "Portrait" type.............	£200	£350	£750	—

Octagonal countermark of George III

	F	VF	EF	UNC
On "Portrait" type..............	£200	£600	£850	—

HALF DOLLAR
Oval countermark of George III

	F	VF	EF	UNC
On "Portrait" type 4 reales	£200	£400	£850	—

FIVE SHILLINGS OR ONE DOLLAR
These coins were overstruck on Spanish-American coins

	F	VF	EF	UNC
*1804	£100	£250	£450	—

— With details of original coin still visible add from 10%.

BANK OF ENGLAND TOKENS

THREE SHILLINGS

	F	VF	EF	UNC
1811 Draped bust..............	£35	£45	£100	—
1812 —	£35	£50	£125	—
1812 Laureate bust	£35	£45	£100	—
1813 —	£35	£45	£100	—
1814 —	£35	£45	£100	—
1815 —	£35	£45	£100	—
1816 —	£125	£250	£850	—

ONE SHILLING AND SIXPENCE

	F	VF	EF	UNC
1811 Draped bust..............	£20	£45	£75	£145
1812 —	£20	£45	£75	£145
*1812 Laureate bust	£20	£45	£75	£145
1812 Proof in platinum				Unique
1813 —	£20	£35	£65	£125
1813 Proof in platinum				Unique
1814 —	£20	£35	£65	£125
1815 —	£20	£35	£65	£125
1816 —	£20	£35	£65	£125

NINEPENCE

	F	VF	EF	UNC
1812 Pattern only	—	—		Very Rare

MAUNDY SETS

CHARLES II (1660–85)

DATE	F	VF	EF	UNC
Undated	£135	£190	£450	—
1670	£120	£170	£415	—
1671	£110	£165	£390	—
1672	£110	£160	£390	—
1673	£110	£160	£390	—
1674	£115	£165	£395	—
1675	£110	£165	£390	—
1676	£120	£170	£395	—
1677	£110	£160	£385	—
1678	£160	£230	£475	—
1679	£115	£175	£400	—
1680	£110	£165	£400	—
1681	£130	£185	£415	—
1682	£120	£165	£400	—
1683	£120	£170	£400	—
1684	£190	£250	£500	—

JAMES II (1685–88)

DATE	F	VF	EF	UNC
1686	£140	£200	£400	—
1687	£140	£200	£415	—
1688	£170	£220	£450	—

WILLIAM & MARY (1688–94)

DATE	F	VF	EF	UNC
1689	£425	£625	£900	—
1691	£260	£330	£575	—
1692	£265	£360	£600	—
1693	£230	£300	£535	—
1694	£210	£270	£495	—

WILLIAM III (1694–1702)

DATE	F	VF	EF	UNC
1698	£150	£220	£475	—
1699	£230	£320	£600	—
1700	£160	£230	£485	—
1701	£150	£215	£460	—

ANNE (1702–14)

DATE	F	VF	EF	UNC
1703	£135	£230	£450	—
1705	£125	£210	£445	—
1706	£130	£205	£435	—
1708	£230	£315	£550	—
1709	£145	£230	£450	—
1710	£155	£235	£470	—
1713	£135	£225	£450	—

GEORGE I (1714–27)

DATE	F	VF	EF	UNC
1723	£130	£215	£440	—
1727	£125	£205	£425	—

GEORGE II (1727–60)

DATE	F	VF	EF	UNC
1729	£110	£165	£360	—
1731	£110	£165	£360	—
1732	£100	£155	£330	—
1735	£100	£155	£330	—
1737	£100	£155	£335	—
1739	£100	£155	£335	—
1740	£100	£155	£335	—
1743	£135	£190	£360	—
1746	£95	£150	£315	—
1760	£105	£160	£325	—

GEORGE III (1760–1820)

DATE	MINTAGE	F	VF	EF	UNC
1763		£90	£135	£260	—
1766		£90	£135	£275	—
1772		£95	£140	£280	—
1780		£90	£135	£260	—
1784		£90	£140	£270	—
1786		£90	£140	£270	—
1792 Wire		£125	£180	£280	£425
1795		£60	£85	£130	£190
1800		£55	£80	£125	£180
New Coinage					
1817		£85	£110	£155	£250
1818		£80	£100	£150	£235
1820		£80	£100	£150	£240

GEORGE IV (1820–30)

DATE	F	VF	EF	UNC
1822	—	£85	£150	£230
1823	—	£85	£150	£230
1824	—	£85	£150	£230
1825	—	£80	£145	£220
1826	—	£80	£145	£220
1827	—	£80	£145	£230
1828	—	£80	£145	£220
1829	—	£80	£145	£220
1830	—	£80	£145	£220

WILLIAM IV (1830–37)

DATE	F	VF	EF	UNC
1831	—	£90	£155	£245
1831 Proof	—	—	—	£450
1832	—	£90	£155	£255
1833	—	£90	£155	£255
1834	—	£90	£155	£255
1835	—	£90	£155	£250
1836	—	£90	£155	£255
1837	—	£95	£160	£260

VICTORIA (1837–1901)
YOUNG HEAD ISSUES

DATE	MINTAGE	F	VF	EF	UNC
1838	4,158	—	—	£110	£185
1839	4,125	—	—	£120	£200
1839 Proof	unrecorded	—	—	£225	£425
1840	4,125	—	—	£145	£210
1841	2,574	—	—	£145	£220
1842	4,125	—	—	£145	£225
1843	4,158	—	—	£115	£195
1844	4,158	—	—	£150	£225
1845	4,158	—	—	£105	£180
1846	4,158	—	—	£150	£250
1847	4,158	—	—	£225	£325
1848	4,158	—	—	£225	£325
1849	4,158	—	—	£165	£230
1850	4,158	—	—	£120	£190
1851	4,158	—	—	£125	£200
1852	4,158	—	—	£240	£360
1853	4,158	—	—	£250	£375

DATE	MINTAGE	EF	UNC
1853 Proof	unrecorded	–	£500
1854	4,158	£120	£195
1855	4,158	£130	£200
1856	4,158	£110	£180
1857	4,158	£120	£195
1858	4,158	£110	£180
1859	4,158	£105	£170
1860	4,158	£120	£185
1861	4,158	£120	£200
1862	4,158	£125	£195
1863	4,158	£125	£195
1864	4,158	£120	£185
1865	4,158	£125	£195
1866	4,158	£125	£185
1867	4,158	£120	£195
1868	4,158	£105	£180
1869	4,158	£130	£205
1870	4,458	£105	£170
1871	4,488	£100	£160
1872	4,328	£100	£160
1873	4,162	£90	£150
1874	4,488	£90	£150
1875	4,154	£90	£150
1876	4,488	£90	£145
1877	4,488	£85	£120
1878	4,488	£85	£140
1879	4,488	£85	£140
1880	4,488	£85	£140
1881	4,488	£85	£140
1882	4,146	£85	£150
1883	4,488	£75	£120
1884	4,488	£75	£120
1885	4,488	£75	£120
1886	4,488	£75	£120
1887	4,488	£90	£145

JUBILEE HEAD ISSUES

DATE	MINTAGE	EF	UNC
1888	4,488	£80	£110
1889	4,488	£75	£105
1890	4,488	£80	£110
1891	4,488	£75	£105
1892	4,488	£75	£110

OLD HEAD ISSUES

DATE	MINTAGE	EF	UNC
1893	8,976	£65	£85
1894	8,976	£70	£90
1895	8,976	£65	£85
1896	8,976	£65	£85
1897	8,976	£65	£85
1898	8,976	£65	£85
1899	8,976	£65	£85
1900	8,976	£65	£80
1901	8,976	£65	£80

EDWARD VII (1902–110)

DATE	MINTAGE	EF	UNC
1902	8,976	£50	£70
1902 Matt proof	15,123	–	£80
1903	8,976	£50	£70
1904	8,976	£60	£85
1905	8,976	£60	£90
1906	8,800	£55	£75
1907	8,760	£50	£75
1908	8,769	£50	£75
1909	1,983	£75	£125
1910	1,440	£85	£140

GEORGE V (1911–136)

DATE	MINTAGE	EF	UNC
1911	1,786	£65	£110
1911 Proof	6,007	–	£115
1912	1,246	£70	£110
1913	1,228	£70	£110

DATE	MINTAGE	EF	UNC
1914	982	£75	£125
1915	1,293	£70	£110
1916	1,128	£65	£105
1917	1,237	£65	£110
1918	1,375	£65	£105
1919	1,258	£65	£105
1920	1,399	£65	£110
1921	1,386	£70	£115
1922	1,373	£65	£110
1923	1,430	£70	£115
1924	1,515	£70	£115
1925	1,438	£65	£105
1926	1,504	£65	£105
1927	1,647	£70	£110
1928	1,642	£70	£110
1929	1,761	£70	£110
1930	1,724	£65	£105
1931	1,759	£65	£105
1932	1,835	£65	£105
1933	1,872	£65	£100
1934	1,887	£65	£100
1935	1,928	£70	£115
1936	1,323	£80	£125

GEORGE VI (1936–52)

DATE	MINTAGE	EF	UNC
1937	1,325	£60	£90
1937 Proof	20,900	£60	£90
1938	1,275	£65	£105
1939	1,234	£65	£105
1940	1,277	£65	£105
1941	1,253	£70	£110
1942	1,231	£65	£105
1943	1,239	£65	£105
1944	1,259	£65	£105
1945	1,355	£65	£105
1946	1,365	£65	£105
1947	1,375	£70	£110
1948	1,385	£70	£110
1949	1,395	£70	£110
1950	1,405	£70	£110
1951	1,468	£70	£110
1952	1,012	£80	£130

ELIZABETH II (1952–)

DATE	MINTAGE	EF	UNC
1953	1,025	–	£450
1954	1,020	–	£95
1955	1,036	–	£95
1956	1,088	–	£95
1957	1,094	–	£95
1958	1,100	–	£95
1959	1,106	–	£95
1960	1,112	–	£95
1961	1,118	–	£95
1962	1,125	–	£95
1963	1,131	–	£95
1964	1,137	–	£95
1965	1,143	–	£95
1966	1,206	–	£95
1967	986	–	£100
1968	964	–	£100
1969	1,002	–	£95
1970	980	–	£95

Later issues are listed in the Decimal section.
Sets in contemporary dated boxes are usually worth a higher premium. For example approximately £10 can be added to sets from Victoria to George VI in contemporary undated boxes and above £15 for dated boxes.

MAUNDY ODDMENTS
SINGLE COINS

DATE	F	VF	EF

It is nowadays considered that the early small denomination silver coins 4d–1d were originally struck for the Maundy ceremony although undoubtedly many subsequently circulated as small change—therefore they are listed here under "Maundy

CHARLES II (1660–85)

DATE	F	VF	EF
Undated	£33	£50	£100
1670	£40	£60	£110
1671	£28	£45	£90
1672	£28	£45	£90
1673	£28	£45	£90
1674	£29	£48	£90
1675	£28	£45	£90
1676	£28	£45	£90
*1677	£25	£40	£90
1678	£28	£45	£90
1679	£25	£40	£80
1680	£29	£42	£85
1681	£30	£45	£90
1682	£28	£45	£95
1683	£29	£45	£95
1684	£28	£45	£95

JAMES II (1685–88)

DATE	F	VF	EF
1686	£33	£48	£95
1687	£33	£45	£105
1688	£33	£50	£95

WILLIAM & MARY (1688–94)

DATE	F	VF	EF
*1689	£28	£45	£95
1690	£38	£55	£120
1691	£40	£60	£120
1692	£50	£65	£130
1693	£48	£70	£135
1694	£45	£65	£130

WILLIAM III (1694–1702)

DATE	F	VF	EF
1698	£45	£55	£115
1699	£40	£55	£115
1700	£45	£60	£115
1701	£45	£60	£120
1702	£37	£50	£100

ANNE (1702–14)

DATE	F	VF	EF
1703	£40	£60	£115
1704	£30	£55	£100
1705	£40	£60	£110
1706	£35	£55	£105
1708	£35	£55	£105
1709	£37	£60	£110
1710	£30	£45	£85
*1713	£35	£55	£105

GEORGE I (1714–27)

DATE	F	VF	EF
1717	£33	£55	£95
1721	£30	£55	£90
1723	£40	£60	£110
1727	£38	£55	£105

DATE	F	VF	EF	UNC
GEORGE II (1727–60)				
1729......................................	£33	£50	£80	—
1731......................................	£33	£50	£80	—
1732......................................	£31	£47	£75	—
1735......................................	£33	£52	£83	—
1737......................................	£32	£47	£80	—
1739......................................	£33	£47	£80	—
1740......................................	£30	£45	£80	—
1743......................................	£55	£80	£120	—
*1746	£30	£43	£75	—
1760......................................	£33	£47	£80	—
GEORGE III (1760–1820)				
1763 Young head	£25	£43	£65	—
1765......................................	£295	£550	£795	—
1766......................................	£30	£48	£80	—
1770......................................	£75	£110	£160	—
1772......................................	£45	£65	£110	—
1780......................................	£30	£45	£75	—
1784......................................	£30	£45	£75	—
1786......................................	£30	£45	£80	—
1792 Older head, Thin 4	—	£60	£80	£130
1795......................................	—	£22	£40	£65
1800......................................	—	£20	£37	£55
*1817 New coinage	—	£25	£40	£60
1818......................................	—	£30	£40	£60
1820......................................	—	£27	£45	£65
GEORGE IV (1820–30)				
1822......................................	—	—	£33	£55
1823......................................	—	—	£33	£50
1824......................................	—	—	£35	£58
1826......................................	—	—	£33	£55
1827......................................	—	—	£33	£55
1828......................................	—	—	£33	£55
1829......................................	—	—	£33	£55
1830......................................	—	—	£32	£50
WILLIAM IV (1830–37)				
1831–37	—	—	£35	£55
VICTORIA (1837–1901)				
1838–87 (Young Head)	—	—	£13	£20
1841 & 1857	—	—	£20	£30
1888–92 (Jubilee Head)..........	—	—	£12	£19
1893–1909 (Old Head.............	—	—	£9	£16
EDWARD VII (1901–10)				
1902–08.................................	—	—	£10	£15
1909 & 1910	—	—	£13	£20
GEORGE V (1910–36)				
1911–36.................................	—	—	£13	£19
GEORGE VI (1936–52)				
1937–52.................................	—	—	£13	£21
ELIZABETH II (1952–)				
1953......................................	—	—	£60	£90
1954–85.................................	—	—	£16	£21
1986–2002.............................	—	—	£19	£25

DATE	F	VF	EF	UNC

THREEPENCE

CHARLES II (1660–85)

DATE	F	VF	EF	UNC
Undated	£33	£45	£100	—
1670	£28	£40	£85	—
1671	£28	£40	£85	—
1672	£27	£40	£85	—
1673	£27	£40	£80	—
1674	£28	£38	£85	—
1675	£30	£40	£90	—
1676	£31	£42	£90	—
1677	£30	£40	£85	—
1678	£25	£41	£90	—
1679	£23	£33	£80	—
1680	£25	£40	£90	—
1681	£28	£42	£90	—
1682	£30	£42	£90	—
1683	£30	£41	£90	—
1684	£31	£43	£95	—

JAMES II (1685–88)

DATE	F	VF	EF	UNC
1685	£30	£45	£95	—
1686	£30	£45	£95	—
1687	£25	£40	£90	—
1688	£40	£70	£130	—

WILLIAM & MARY (1688–94)

DATE	F	VF	EF	UNC
1689	£30	£42	£95	—
1690	£42	£60	£115	—
1691	£140	£200	£275	—
1692	£50	£70	£125	—
1693	£90	£145	£210	—
1694	£48	£70	£125	—

WILLIAM III (1694–1702)

DATE	F	VF	EF	UNC
1698	£40	£60	£110	—
1699	£36	£55	£95	—
1700	£45	£70	£120	—
1701	£38	£50	£95	—

ANNE (1702–14)

DATE	F	VF	EF	UNC
1703	£38	£50	£100	—
1704	£30	£42	£80	—
1705	£35	£50	£95	—
1706	£30	£45	£90	—
1707	£30	£42	£85	—
1708	£30	£45	£85	—
1709	£30	£45	£90	—
1710	£25	£45	£80	—
1713	£30	£50	£95	—

GEORGE I (1714–27)

DATE	F	VF	EF	UNC
1717	£33	£45	£85	—
1721	£33	£45	£85	—
1723	£40	£50	£95	—
1727	£40	£55	£100	—

GEORGE II (1727–60)

DATE	F	VF	EF	UNC
1729	£35	£45	£80	—
1731	£35	£45	£80	—
1732	£35	£45	£80	—

DATE	F	VF	EF	UNC
1735	£35	£48	£85	—
1737	£35	£45	£80	—
1739	£33	£45	£80	—
1740	£30	£40	£75	—
1743	£30	£40	£70	—
1746	£28	£40	£70	—
1760	£33	£45	£80	—

GEORGE III (1760–1820)

1762	£14	£25	£40	—
1763	£14	£25	£40	—
1765	£215	£325	£550	—
1766	£27	£40	£70	—
1770	£32	£45	£70	—
1772	£25	£40	£65	—
1780	£28	£40	£65	—
1784	£28	£42	£70	—
1786	£28	£40	£65	—
1792	—	£45	£75	£130
1795	—	£22	£35	£55
1800	—	£25	£40	£60
1817	—	£25	£35	£85
1818	—	£20	£33	£80
1820	—	£25	£35	£85

GEORGE IV (1820–30)

1822	—	—	£43	£85
1823	—	—	£40	£80
1824	—	—	£43	£85
1825–30	—	—	£40	£80

WILLIAM IV (1830–37)

1831–1836	—	—	£50	£90
1837	—	—	£60	£110

VICTORIA (1837–1901)

1838	—	—	£60	£115
1839	—	—	£70	£140
1840	—	—	£75	£150
1841	—	—	£85	£165
1842	—	—	£90	£175
1843	—	—	£65	£115
1844	—	—	£75	£150
1845	—	—	£50	£100
1846	—	—	£110	£190
1847	—	—	£185	£325
1848	—	—	£185	£325
1849	—	—	£85	£160
1850	—	—	£65	£110
1851	—	—	£65	£120
1852	—	—	£200	£350
1853	—	—	£225	£375
1854	—	—	£70	£130
1855	—	—	£70	£130
1856	—	—	£60	£110
1957	—	—	£80	£150
1858	—	—	£65	£130
1859	—	—	£55	£110
1860	—	—	£75	£140
1861	—	—	£70	£135
1862	—	—	£75	£140
1863	—	—	£77	£150
1864	—	—	£70	£130
1865	—	—	£75	£140

DATE	F	VF	EF	UNC
1866	—	—	£70	£130
1867	—	—	£80	£140
1868	—	—	£60	£120
1869	—	—	£80	£150
1870	—	—	£60	£115
1871	—	—	£60	£120
1872	—	—	£55	£105
1873	—	—	£50	£95
1874	—	—	£45	£85
1875	—	—	£45	£85
1876	—	—	£45	£85
1877	—	—	£45	£85
1878	—	—	£45	£85
1879	—	—	£48	£90
1880	—	—	£45	£85
1881	—	—	£45	£85
1882	—	—	£65	£130
1883	—	—	£45	£85
1884	—	—	£40	£80
1885	—	—	£40	£80
1886	—	—	£40	£80
1887	—	—	£50	£100
1888–1892 (Jubilee Head)	—	—	£30	£50
1893–1901 (Old Head)	—	—	£20	£40

EDWARD VII (1901–10)

	F	VF	EF	UNC
1902	—	—	£20	£40
1903	—	—	£25	£50
1904	—	—	£30	£60
1905	—	—	£40	£70
1906	—	—	£30	£60
1907	—	—	£30	£60
1908	—	—	£25	£50
1909	—	—	£30	£65
1910	—	—	£40	£80

GEORGE V (1910–36)

	F	VF	EF	UNC
1911–34	—	—	£20	£35
1935	—	—	£30	£50
1936	—	—	£35	£60

GEORGE VI (1936–52)

	F	VF	EF	UNC
1937–52	—	—	£30	£50

ELIZABETH II (1952–)

	F	VF	EF	UNC
1953	—	—	£65	£110
1954–85	—	—	£25	£40
1986–2003	—	—	£30	£45

TWOPENCE

CHARLES II (1660–85)

	F	VF	EF	UNC
Undated	£33	£45	£95	—
1668	£38	£48	£110	—
1670	£28	£45	£90	—
1671	£27	£45	£90	—
1672	£27	£42	£90	—
1673	£30	£45	£95	—
1671	£28	£45	£95	—
1675	£28	£42	£95	—
1676	£28	£42	£90	—
1677	£25	£42	£90	—

DATE	F	VF	EF	UNC
1678...............................	£28	£40	£90	—
1679...............................	£22	£35	£75	—
1680...............................	£24	£39	£85	—
1681...............................	£25	£40	£90	—
1682...............................	£27	£40	£92	—
1683...............................	£27	£40	£95	—
1684...............................	£30	£45	£95	—

JAMES II (1685–88)

*1686	£30	£40	£90	—
1687...............................	£35	£47	£95	—
1688...............................	£28	£40	£85	—

WILLIAM & MARY (1688–94)

1689...............................	£22	£37	£80	—
1691...............................	£27	£40	£90	—
1692...............................	£50	£85	£125	—
1693...............................	£36	£50	£100	—
1694...............................	£29	£42	£90	—

WILLIAM III (1694–1702)

1698...............................	£40	£60	£110	—
1699...............................	£30	£50	£90	—
1700...............................	£33	£55	£100	—
1701...............................	£38	£60	£105	—

ANNE (1702–14)

1703...............................	£33	£50	£100	—
1704...............................	£26	£38	£75	—
1705...............................	£30	£50	£90	—
1706...............................	£30	£50	£90	—
1707...............................	£25	£42	£80	—
1708...............................	£27	£43	£85	—
1709...............................	£35	£55	£105	—
1710...............................	£23	£38	£75	—
1713...............................	£40	£65	£115	—

GEORGE I (1714–27)

1717...............................	£25	£40	£70	—
1721...............................	£22	£35	£65	—
1723...............................	£25	£50	£80	—
1726...............................	£22	£40	£70	—
1727...............................	£27	£47	£80	—

GEORGE II (1727–60)

1729...............................	£22	£35	£60	—
1731...............................	£22	£35	£60	—
1732...............................	£24	£36	£65	—
1735...............................	£22	£35	£60	—
1737...............................	£22	£35	£60	—
1739...............................	£24	£37	£62	—
1740...............................	£22	£35	£65	—
1743...............................	£22	£35	£60	—
1746...............................	£23	£39	£62	—
1756...............................	£20	£30	£55	—
1759...............................	£20	£30	£55	—
1760...............................	£25	£40	£65	—

GEORGE III (1760–1820)

1763...............................	£19	£35	£50	—
1765...............................	£225	£375	£650	—

DATE	F	VF	EF	UNC
1766	£20	£28	£44	—
1772	£18	£26	£42	—
1780	£18	£27	£42	—
1784	£20	£30	£45	—
1786	£20	£28	£45	—
1792	—	£33	£45	£75
1795	—	£16	£25	£35
1800	—	£14	£22	£33
1817	—	£18	£33	£45
1818	—	£14	£24	£35
1820	—	£14	£25	£35

GEORGE IV (1820–30)

	F	VF	EF	UNC
1822–30	—	—	£20	£33

WILLIAM IV (1830–37)

	F	VF	EF	UNC
1831–37	—	—	£22	£35

VICTORIA (1837–1901)

	F	VF	EF	UNC
1838–87 (Young Head)	—	—	£13	£20
1888–92 (Jubilee Head)	—	—	£11	£18
1893–1901 (Old Head	—	—	£9	£16

EDWARD VII (1901–10)

	F	VF	EF	UNC
1902–08	—	—	£9	£16
1909	—	—	£11	£22
1910	—	—	£12	£25

GEORGE V (1910–36)

	F	VF	EF	UNC
1911–34	—	—	£12	£22
1935	—	—	£15	£25
1936	—	—	£17	£30

GEORGE VI (1936–52)

	F	VF	EF	UNC
1937–47	—	—	£13	£22
1948–52	—	—	£15	£25

ELIZABETH II (1952–)

	F	VF	EF	UNC
1953	—	—	£48	£75
1954–85	—	—	£17	£23
1986–2003	—	—	£17	£25

PENNY

CHARLES II (1660–85)

DATE	F	VF	EF	UNC
Undated	£35	£50	£100	—
1670	£27	£50	£90	—
1671	£27	£50	£90	—
1672	£30	£50	£90	—
1673	£30	£50	£90	—
*1674	£30	£50	£90	—
1675	£30	£50	£90	—
1676	£35	£55	£100	—
1677	£27	£50	£90	—
1678	£100	£170	£225	—
1679	£45	£70	£120	—
1680	£30	£50	£95	—
1681	£55	£85	£140	—
1682	£32	£60	£105	—
1683	£32	£60	£105	—
1684	£140	£180	£250	—

Charles II

DATE	F	VF	EF	UNC

JAMES II (1685–88)

	F	VF	EF	UNC
*1685	£35	£50	£90	—
1686	£35	£47	£90	—
1687	£42	£55	£110	—
1688	£40	£47	£90	—

James II

WILLIAM & MARY (1688–94)

	F	VF	EF	UNC
1689	£325	£450	£600	—
1690	£50	£75	£110	—
1691	£47	£75	£120	—
1692	£90	£150	£250	—
1693	£55	£75	£115	—
1694	£47	£70	£105	—

WILLIAM III (1694–1702)

	F	VF	EF	UNC
1698	£50	£70	£110	—
1699	£170	£250	£350	—
1700	£52	£70	£115	—
1701	£50	£70	£100	—

ANNE (1702–14)

	F	VF	EF	UNC
1703	£40	£55	£110	—
1705	£40	£55	£100	—
1706	£40	£52	£90	—
1708	£150	£200	£300	—
1709	£35	£47	£85	—
1710	£85	£140	£200	—
1713	£42	£60	£95	—

GEORGE I (1714–27)

	F	VF	EF	UNC
1716	£27	£40	£60	—
1718	£25	£37	£60	—
1720	£30	£40	£60	—
1723	£37	£50	£90	—
1725	£30	£42	£60	—
1726	£30	£42	£60	—
1727	£37	£50	£90	—

GEORGE II (1727–60)

	F	VF	EF	UNC
1729	£32	£50	£75	—
1731	£32	£42	£60	—
1732	£24	£35	£55	—
1735	£24	£35	£48	—
1737	£25	£35	£48	—
1739	£25	£35	£48	—
1740	£28	£37	£48	—
1743	£24	£38	£50	—
1746	£30	£45	£60	—
1750	£20	£30	£42	—
1752	£20	£30	£42	—
1753	£20	£30	£42	—
1754	£20	£30	£42	—
1755	£24	£35	£48	—
1756	£20	£30	£42	—
1757	£20	£30	£42	—
1758	£20	£32	£50	—
1759	£20	£30	£42	—
1760	£28	£38	£55	—

George II

DATE	F	VF	EF	UNC
GEORGE III (1760–1820)				
1763	£22	£35	£45	—
1766	£20	£28	£40	—
1772	£22	£30	£40	—
1780	£20	£28	£40	—
1781	£18	£27	£37	—
1784	£16	£27	£37	—
1786	£17	£28	£38	—
1792	—	£35	£45	£60
1795	—	£18	£25	£35
1800	—	£17	£24	£33
*1817	—	£16	£20	£30
1818	—	£16	£20	£30
1820	—	£16	£21	£32
GEORGE IV (1820–30)				
1822–30	—	—	£16	£28
WILLIAM IV (1830–37)				
1831–37	—	—	£17	£30
VICTORIA (1837–1901)				
1838–87 (Young Head)	—	—	£10	£18
1888–92 (Jubilee Head)	—	—	£9	£17
1893–1901 (Old Head)	—	—	£8	£15
EDWARD VII (1901–10)				
1902–08	—	—	£8	£14
1909	—	—	£12	£20
1910	—	—	£15	£30
GEORGE V (1910–36)				
1911–14	—	—	£12	£20
1915	—	—	£13	£24
1916–19	—	—	£12	£20
1920	—	—	£13	£25
1921–28	—	—	£12	£20
1929	—	—	£15	£26
1930–34	—	—	£12	£20
1935	—	—	£15	£26
1936	—	—	£17	£30
GEORGE VI (1936–52)				
1937–40	—	—	£14	£25
1941	—	—	£15	£28
1942–47	—	—	£14	£27
1948–52	—	—	£16	£30
ELIZABETH II (1952–)				
1953	—	—	£90	£180
1965–85	—	—	£17	£28
1986–2003	—	—	£20	£32

DECIMAL COINAGE

Since the introduction of the Decimal system in the UK, many coins have been issued for circulation purposes in vast quantities. In addition, from 1982 sets of coins to non-proof standard, and including examples of each denomination found in circulation, have been issued each year. For 1982 and 1983 they were to "circulation" standard and described as "Uncirculated". Individual coins from these sets are annotated "Unc" on the lists that follow. From 1984 to the present day they were described as "Brilliant Uncirculated" (BU on the lists), and from around 1986 these coins are generally distinguishable from coins intended for circulation. They were from then produced by the Proof Coin Division of the Royal Mint (rather than by the Coin Production Room which produces circulation-standard coins). For completeness however, we have included the annotations Unc and BU back to 1982, the start year for these sets.

It is emphasised that the abbreviations Unc and BU in the left-hand columns adjacent to the date refer to an advertising description or to an engineering production standard, not the preservation condition or grade of the coin concerned. Where no such annotation appears adjacent to the date, the coin is circulation-standard for issue as such.

We have included the "mintage" figures for circulation coins down to Twenty-five pence. Strictly speaking, these figures are for coins issued by the Royal Mint up to December 31, 2003. The figure given for the 1997 Two Pounds, for example, is considerably less than the actual quantity struck, because many were scrapped before issue due to failing an electrical conductivity test. Figures are not available for commemorative £5, £2 and 50p coins dated 2000 or since, their totals are included in the definitive version of the coins concerned. We have included the figures for non-circulation-standard coins where known. Where a coin is available in uncirculated grade at, or just above, face value no price has been quoted.

Base metal Proof issues of circulation coinage (£2 or £1 to one or H penny) of the decimal series were only issued, as with Unc or BU, as part of Year Sets, but many of these sets have been broken down into individual coins, hence the appearance of the latter on the market.

The lists do not attempt to give details of die varieties, except where there was an obvious intention to change the appearance of a coin, e.g. 1992 20p.

FIVE POUNDS (Sovereign series)

This series is all minted in gold, and, except where stated, have the St George reverse. BU coins bear a U in a circle.

DATE	Mintage	UNC
1980 Proof	10,000	£450
1981 Proof	5,400	£450
1982 Proof	2,500	£480
1984 BU	15,104	£400
1984 Proof	8,000	£475
1985 New portrait BU	13,626	£400
1985 — Proof	6,130	£480
1986 BU	7,723	£400
1987 Uncouped portrait BU	5,694	£400
*1988 BU	3,315	£400
1989 500th Anniversary of the Sovereign. Enthroned portrayal obverse and Crowned shield reverse BU	2,937	£550
1989 — Proof	5000	£650
1990 BU	1,226	£400
1990 Proof	1,721	£500
1991 BU	976	£400
1991 Proof	1,336	£550
1992 BU	797	£400
1992 Proof	1,165	£550
1993 BU	906	£400
1993 Proof	1,078	£550
1994 BU	1,000	£400
1994 Proof	918	£550
1995 BU	1,000	£400
1995 Proof	1,250	£550
1996 BU	901	£400
1996 Proof	742	£550
1997 BU	802	£400
1997 Proof	860	£600
1998 New portrait BU	825	£425
1998 Proof	789	£650
1999 BU	991	£425
1999 Proof	1,000	£650
2000 ("Bullion")	10,000	£350
2000 BU	994	£450
2000 Proof	3,000	£650
2001 BU	1,000	£450
2001 Proof	3,500	£650
2002 Shield rev. ("Bullion")	—	£350
2002 BU	—	£450
2002 Proof	3,000	£650
2003 BU	—	£425
2003 Proof	—	—
2004 Proof	—	—

The obverse of the 1989 gold coins portray HM the Queen enthroned

FIVE POUNDS (Crown series)

This series commenced in 1990 when the "Crown" was declared legal tender at £5, instead of 25p as all previous issues continued to be. Mintage is in cupro-nickel unless otherwise stated. BU includes those in individual presentation folders, and those in sets sold with stamp covers and/or banknotes.

	Mintage	
1990 Queen Mother's 90th Birthday.	2,761,431	£8
1990 — BU	48,477	£10
1990 — Silver Proof	56,800	£32
1990 — Gold Proof	2,500	£525

DATE	Mintage	UNC
1993 Coronation 40th Anniversary	1,834,655	£8
1993 — BU	—	£10
1993 — Proof	—	£15
1993 — Silver Proof	100,000	£32
1993 — Gold Proof	2,500	£525
1996 HM the Queen's 70th Birthday	2,396,100	£8
1996 — BU	—	£10
1996 — Proof	—	£15
1996 — Silver Proof	70,000	£32
1996 — Gold Proof	2,127	£650
*1997 Royal Golden Wedding	1,733,000	£8
1997 — BU	—	£10
1997 — — with £5 note	5,000	£55
1997 — Proof	—	£20
1997 — Silver Proof	75,000	£32
1997 — Gold Proof	2,750	£650
1998 Prince of Wales 50th birthday	1,407,300	£7
1998 — BU	—	£12
1998 — Proof	—	£20
1998 — Silver Proof	—	£40
1998 — Gold Proof	—	£650
1999 Princess of Wales Memorial.	1,600,000	£9
1999 — BU	—	£12
1999 — Proof	—	£20
1999 — Silver Proof	350,000	£40
1999 — Gold Proof	7,500	£650
1999 Millennium	3,796,300	£8
1999 — BU	—	£15
1999 — Proof	—	£22
1999 — Silver Proof	100,000	£40
1999 — Gold Proof	2,500	£600
*2000 —	3,147,092*	£8
2000 — BU	—	£15
2000 — — with special Millennium Dome mintmark	—	£12
2000 — Proof	—	£22
2000 — Silver Proof with gold highlight	50,000	£40
2000 — Gold Proof	2,500	£575
2000 Queen Mother's 100th Birthday	incl. above*	£7
2000 — BU	—	£12
2000 — Silver Proof	100,000	£40
2000 — — Piedfort	14,850	£175
2000 — Gold Proof	3,000	£550
*2001 Victorian Era.	851,491	£7
2001 — BU	—	£12
2001 — Proof	—	£20
2001 — Silver Proof	100,000	£40
2001 — Gold Proof	3,000	£550
2001 — — with frosted relief	750	£850
*2002 Golden Jubilee	3,687,882*	£7
2002 — BU	—	£12
2002 — Proof	—	£20
2002 — Silver Proof	75,000	£40
2002 — Gold Proof	5,502	£550
2002 Queen Mother Memorial	incl. above*	£7
2002 — BU	—	£12
2002 — Silver Proof	25,000	£40
2002 — Gold Proof	3,000	£550
2003 Coronation Jubilee	1,307,010	—
2003 — BU	—	—
2003 — Proof	—	—
2003 — Silver Proof	—	—
2003 — Gold Proof	—	—
2004 Entente Cordiale Centenary	—	—
2004 — Proof Reverse Frosting	—	—
2004 — Silver Proof	—	—
2004 — Gold Proof	—	—
2004 — Platinum Proof Piedfort	501	—

DOUBLE SOVEREIGN

As with the Sovereign series Five Pound coins, those listed under this heading bear the St George reverse, except where otherwise stated, and are minted in gold. They are, and always have been, legal tender at £2, and have a diameter indentical to that of the base metal Two Pound coins listed further below under a different heading. The denomination does not appear on Double Sovereigns.

DATE	Mintage	UNC
1980 Proof	10,000	£200
1982 Proof	2,500	£200
1983 Proof	12,500	£180
1985 New Portrait Proof	5,849	£200
1987 Proof	14,301	£200
1988 Proof	12,743	£200
1989 500th Anniversary of the Sovereign. Enthroned portrayal obverse and Crowned shield reverse Proof	14,936	£240
1990 Proof	4,374	£200
1991 Proof	3,108	£220
1992 Proof	2,608	£220
1993 Proof	2,155	£220
1996 Proof	3,167	£220
1998 New Portrait Proof	4,500	£225
2000 Proof	2,250	£275
2002 Shield reverse Proof	8,000	£300
2003 Proof	2,250	—
2004 Proof	—	—

TWO POUNDS

This series commenced in 1986 with nickel-brass commemorative coins, with their associated base metal and precious metal BU and proof coins. From 1997 (actually issued in 1998) a thinner bi-metal version commenced with a reverse theme of the advance of technology, and from this date the coin was specifically intended to circulate. This is true also for the parallel issues of anniversary and commemorative Two Pound issues in 1999 and onwards. All have their BU and proof versions, as listed below.

DATE		UNC
*1986 Commonwealth Games	8,212,184	£6
1986 — BU		£7
1986 — Proof		£10
1986 — Silver BU		£15
1986 — — Proof		£18
1986 — Gold Proof		£250
1989 Tercentenary of Bill of Rights.	4,392,825	£7
1989 — BU (issued in folder with Claim of Right)		£20
1989 — Proof (issued as pair with Claim of Right)		£28
1989 — Silver Proof (Pair as above)		£40
1989 — — — Piedfort (Pair as above)		£60
*1989 Tercentenary of Claim of Right (issued in Scotland)	381,400	£12
1989 — BU (see above)		£20
1989 — Proof (see above)		£28
1989 — Silver Proof (see above)		£40
1989 — — — Piedfort (see above)		£60
*1994 Tercentenary of the Bank of England	1,443,116	£5
1994 — BU		£7
1994 — Proof		£10
1994 — Silver Proof		£28
1994 — — — Piedfort		£65
1994 — Gold Proof		£400
1994 — — — with Double Sovereign obverse (no denomination)		£575
1995 50th Anniversary of End of WWII.	4,394,566	£5

DATE		UNC
1995 — BU		£6
1995 — Proof		£10
1995 — Silver Proof		£35
1995 — — — Piedfort		£55
1995 — Gold Proof		£450
1995 50th Anniversary of The United Nations	1,668,575	£5
1995 — BU		£6
1995 — Proof		£10
1995 — Silver Proof		£35
1995 — Silver Proof Piedfort		£60
1995 — Gold Proof		£450
*1996 European Football Championships	5,195,350	£5
1996 — BU		£6
1996 — Proof		£8
1996 — Silver Proof		£32
1996 — — — Piedfort		£55
1996 — Gold Proof		£450
*1997	13,734,625	£4
1997 BU		£8
1997 Proof		£12
1997 Silver Proof		£25
1997 — — Piedfort		£45
1997 Gold Proof (red (outer) and yellow (inner) 22ct)		£355
1998 New Portrait		£3
1998 — BU	91,110,375	£7
1998 Proof		£10
1998 Silver Proof		£32
1999	33,719,000	£3
*1999 Rugby World Cup	4,933,000	£3
1999 — BU		£4
1999 — Silver Proof (gold plated ring)		£32
1999 — — — Piedfort (Hologram)		£85
1999 — Gold Proof		£355
2000	25,770,000	£3
2000 BU		£4
2000 Proof		£10
2000 Silver Proof		£32
2000 Gold Proof		£355
2001	37,843,500*	—
2001 BU		£3
2001 Proof		£10
2001 Marconi	*Incl. in above**	£3
2001 — BU		£4
2001 — Proof		£10
2001 — Silver Proof (gold plated ring)		£30
2001 — — — Piedfort		£85
2001 — Gold Proof		£355
2002	15,521,000*	—
2002 BU		£3
2002 Proof		£10
2002 Commonwealth Games (4 versions)	*Incl in above**	£3
2002 — — BU (issued in set of 4)		£4
2002 — — Proof (issued in set of 4)		£10
2002 — Silver Proof (issued in set of 4)		£32
2002 — — — Piedfort (painted) (issued in set of 4)		£85
2002 — Gold (issued in set of 4)		£300
2003	15,922,250*	—
2003 BU		—
2003 Proof		£10
2003 DNA Double Helix	*Incl in above**	—
2003 — BU		—
2003 — Proof		£10
2003 — Silver Proof (Gold-plated ring)		£30
2003 — — Piedfort		—
2003 — Gold Proof		£300
2004 BU		—
2004 Proof		—

DATE		UNC
2004 Trevithick Steam Locomotive	....	—
2004 — BU	....	—
2004 — Proof	....	—
2004 — Silver BU	....	—
2004 — — Proof (Gold-plated ring)	....	—
2004 — — — Piedfort	....	—
2004 — Gold Proof	....	—

SOVEREIGN

All are minted in gold, bear the St George reverse except where stated, and are legal tender at one pound.

DATE	MINTAGE	UNC
1974	5,002,566	£55
1976	4,150,000	£55
1978	6,550,000	£55
1979	9,100,000	£55
1979 Proof	50,000	£75
1980	5,100,000	£55
1980 Proof	91,200	£75
1981	5,000,000	£55
1981 Proof	32,960	£75
1982	2,950,000	£55
1982 Proof	22,500	£75
1983 Proof	21,250	£75
1984 Proof	19,975	£85
1985 New portrait Proof	17,242	£85
1986 Proof	17,579	£85
1987 Proof	22,479	£85
1988 Proof	18,862	£90
1989 500th Anniversary of the Sovereign—details as Five Pounds (Sov. Series). Proof	23,471	£200
1990 Proof	8,425	£130
1991 Proof	7,201	£130
1992 Proof	6,854	£150
1993 Proof	6,090	£150
1994 Proof	7,165	£150
1995 Proof	9,500	£150
1996 Proof	9,110	£150
1997 Proof	9,177	£165
1998 New Portrait Proof	11,349	£165
1999 Proof	11,903	£175
2000 (first Unc issue since 1982)	129,069	£55
2000 Proof	12,159	£135
2001	49,458	£55
2001 Proof	10,000	£135
2002 Shield Rev. ("bullion")	71,815	£60
2002 Proof	20,500	£135
2003 ("bullion")	40,447	£60
2003 Proof	—	£140
2004 ("bullion")	—	£60
2004 Proof	—	£150

HALF SOVEREIGN

Legal Tender at 50 pence, otherwise the notes for the Sovereign apply.

DATE	MINTAGE	UNC
1980 Proof only	86,700	£40
1982	2,500,000	£40
1982 Proof	21,590	£45
1983 Proof	19,710	£50
1984 Proof	19,505	£50
1985 New portrait Proof	15,800	£45
1986 Proof	17,075	£45
1987 Proof	20,687	£45
1988 Proof	18,266	£50
1989 500th Anniversary of the Sovereign (details as Five Pounds (Sov. Series) Proof	21,824	£100
1990 Proof	7,889	£55
1991 Proof	6,076	£55
1992 Proof	5,915	£65
1993 Proof	4,651	£65
1994 Proof	7,167	£70
1995 Proof	7,500	£70
1996 New Portrait Proof	7,340	£70
1997 Proof	9,177	£70
1998 Proof	7,496	£70
1999 Proof	9,403	£70
2000	146,542	£40
2000 Proof	9,708	£70
2001	94,736	£40
2001 Proof	7,500	£70
2002 Shield reverse ("bullion")	59,568	£70
2002 Proof	—	£40
2003 ("bullion")	42,083	£40
2003 Proof	—	£70
2004 ("bullion")	—	£40
2004 Proof	—	£70

ONE POUND

Introduced into circulation in 1983 to replace the £1 note, all are minted in nickel-brass unless otherwise stated. The reverse changes yearly, the Royal coat of arms being the "definitive" version. Unc or BU may come either in a presentation folder or from a set.

DATE		UNC
1983 Royal coat of arms	443,053,510	£5
1983 — Unc	1,134,000	£7
1983 — Proof	107,800	£10
1983 — Silver Proof	50,000	£30
1983 — — — Piedfort	10,000	£120
1984 Scottish Thistle	146,256,501	£4
1984 — BU	199,430	£6
1984 — Proof	106,520	£7
1984 — Silver Proof	44,855	£32
1984 — — — Piedfort	15,000	£60
1985 New portrait. Welsh Leek	228,430,749	£3
1985 — BU	213,679	£6
1985 — Proof	102,015	£7
1985 — Silver Proof	50,000	£30
1985 — — — Piedfort	15,000	£50
1986 Northern Ireland Flax	10,409,501	£3
1986 — BU		£6

1983, 1993, 1998, 2003

1984, 1989

DATE		UNC
1986 — Proof		£8
1986 — Silver Proof		£35
1986 — — — Piedfort		£55
1987 English Oak	39,298,502	£3
1987 — BU		£6
1987 — Proof		£10
1987 — Silver Proof		£30
1987 — — — Piedfort		£50
1988 Crowned Royal Arms	7,118,825	£2
1988 — BU		£6
1988 — Proof		£10
1988 — Silver Proof		£32
1988 — — — Piedfort		£55
1989 Scottish Thistle	70,580,501	£2
1989 — BU		£6
1989 — Proof		£8
1989 — Silver Proof		£28
1989 — — — Piedfort		£50
1990 Welsh Leek		£2
1990 — BU	97,269,302	£5
1990 — Proof		£8
1990 — Silver Proof		£28
1991 Northern Ireland Flax	38,443,575	£2
1991 — BU		£6
1991 — Proof		£8
1991 — Silver Proof		£32
1992 English Oak	36,320,487	£2
1992 — BU		£5
1992 — Proof		£8
1992 — Silver Proof		£32
1993 Royal Coat of Arms	114,744,500	£2
1993 — BU		£5
1993 — Proof		£10
1993 — Silver Proof		£34
1993 — — — Piedfort		£65
1994 Scottish Lion	29,752,525	£2
1994 — BU		£6
1994 — Proof		£8
1994 — Silver Proof		£32
1994 — — — Piedfort		£65
1995 Welsh Dragon	34,503,501	£2
1995 — BU		£6
1995 — — (Welsh)		£8
1995 — Proof		£10
1995 — Silver Proof		£34
1995 — — — Piedfort		£65
1996 Northern Ireland Celtic-style Cross	89,886,000	£3
1996 — BU		£6
1996 — Proof		£8
1996 — Silver Proof		£33
1996 — — — Piedfort		£65
1997 English Lions	57,117,450	£3
1997 — BU		£6
1997 — Proof		£8
1997 — Silver Proof		£35
1997 — — — Piedfort		£70
1998 New portrait. Royal Coat of Arms. BU		£7
1998 — Proof		£8
1998 — Silver Proof		£30
1998 — — — Piedfort		£45
1999 Scottish Lion. BU		£6
1999 — Proof		£8
1999 — Silver Proof		£35
1999 — — — Reverse Frosting		£45
1999 — — — Piedfort		£75
2000 Welsh Dragon	109,496,500	£2
2000 — BU		£6

1985, 1990

1986, 1991

1987, 1992

1988

1994, 1999

1995, 2000

1996, 2001

DATE		UNC
2000 — Proof	....	£8
2000 — Silver Proof	....	£35
2000 — — — Reverse Frosting	....	£40
2000 — — — Piedfort	....	£45
2001 Northern Ireland Celtic-style Cross.	....	£2
2001 — BU	58,093,731	£6
2001 — Proof	....	£8
2001 — Silver Proof	....	£35
2001 — — — Piedfort	....	£45
2002 English Lions	77,818,000	£2
2002 — BU	....	£6
2002 — Proof	....	£8
2002 — Silver Proof	....	£32
2002 — — — Piedfort	....	£50
2002 — Gold Proof	....	£160
2003 Royal Coat of Arms	40,648,500	—
2003 — BU	....	—
2003 — Proof	....	—
2003 — Silver Proof	....	—
2003 — — Piedfort	....	—
2004 Forth Railway Bridge	....	—
2004 — BU	....	—
2004 — Proof	....	—
2004 — Silver Proof	....	—
2004 — — — Piedfort	....	—
2004 — Gold Proof	....	—

1997, 2002

2004

FIFTY PENCE

Introduced as legal tender for 10 shillings to replace the banknote of that value prior to decimalisation, coins of the original size are no longer legal tender. Unless otherwise stated, i.e. for commemoratives, the reverse design is of Britannia. The reverse legend of NEW PENCE became FIFTY PENCE from 1982.

DATE		UNC
*1969	188,400,000	£3
1970	19,461,500	£4
1971 Proof	....	£8
1972 Proof	....	£8
*1973 Accession to EEC	89,775,000	£3
1973 — Proof	....	£5
1973 — Silver Proof Piedfort	....	£750
1974 Proof	....	£5
1975 Proof	....	£5
1976	43,746,500	£3
1976 Proof	....	£5
1977	49,536,000	£3
1977 Proof	....	£5
1978	72,005,000	£3
1978 Proof	....	£5
1979	58,680,000	£3
1979 Proof	....	£5
1980	89,086,000	£3
1980 Proof	....	£5
1981	74,002,000	£2
1981 Proof	....	£5
*1982	51,312,000	£1
1982 Unc	....	£2
1982 Proof	....	£5
1983	62,824,000	£1
1983 Unc	....	£3
1983 Proof	....	£5
1984 BU	....	£3
1984 Proof	....	£5
1985 New portrait	estimated approx 3,400,000	£1
1985 BU	....	£3
1985 Proof	....	£5

DATE	UNC
1986 BU	£4
1986 Proof	£5
1987 BU	£4
1987 Proof	£5
1988 BU	£4
1988 Proof	£5
1989 BU	£4
1989 Proof	£5
1990 BU	£4
1990 Proof	£5
1991 BU	£5
1991 Proof	£6
1992 BU	£9
1992 — Proof	£15

*1992 Presidency of EC Council and EC accession 20th anniversary (includes 1993 date) 109,000	£8
1992 — BU	—
1992 — Proof	—
1992 — Silver Proof	£30
1992 — — — Piedfort	£50
1992 — Gold Proof	£400
1993 BU	£5
1993 Proof 6,705,520	—
*1994 50th Anniversary of the Normandy Landings	£5
1994 — BU (also in presentation folder)	£6
1994 — Proof	£8
1994 — Silver Proof	£30
1994 — — — Piedfort	£60
1994 — Gold Proof	£425

1995 BU	£5
1995 Proof	£8
1996 BU	£5
1996 Proof	£7
1996 Silver Proof	£22
1997 BU	£8
1997 Proof	£10
1997 Silver Proof	£28
1997 new reduced size 456,364,100	£4
1997 BU	—
1997 Proof	£6
1997 Silver Proof	£28
1997 — — Piedfort	£40
1998 New portrait 64,306,500	£2

1998 BU	—
1998 Proof	£5
*1998 Presidency and 25th anniversary of EU entry 5,043,000	£2
1998 — BU	£4
1998 — Proof	£7
1998 — Silver Proof	£25
1998 — — — Piedfort	£65
1998 — Gold Proof	£275
*1998 50th Anniversary of the National Health Service 5,001,000	£2
1998 — BU	£4
1998 — Silver Proof (believed not issued as Cu-Ni proof)	£25
1998 — — — Piedfort	£75
1998 — Gold Proof	£275

1999 24,905,000	£2
1999 BU	£4
1999 Proof	£5
2000 .... 39,172,000*	£1
2000 BU	£2
2000 Proof	£5
*2000 150th Anniversary of Public Libraries ....*Incl in above*	£1
2000 — BU	£3
2000 — Proof	£8
2000 — Silver Proof	£30
2000 — — — Piedfort	£45
2000 — Gold proof	£250

DATE		UNC
2001	84,999,500	£1
2001 BU		£2
2001 Proof		£5
2002	23,757,500	—
2002 BU		£1
2002 Proof		£5
2002 Gold Proof	17,551,780*	£125
2003		—
2003 BU		£5
2003 Proof		—
2003 Suffragette	*Incl. in above**	—
2003 — BU		—
2003 — Proof		—
2003 — Silver Proof		—
2003 — — Piedfort		—
2003 — Gold Proof		—
2004		—
2004 BU		—
2004 Proof		—
2004 Roger Bannister		—
2004 — BU		—
2004 — Proof		—
2004 — Silver Proof		—
2004 — — Piedfort		—
2004 — Gold Proof		—

TWENTY-FIVE PENCE (CROWN)

This series is a continuation of the pre-decimal series, there having been four crowns to the pound. The coins below have a legal tender face value of 25p to this day, and are minted in cupro-nickel except where stated otherwise.

DATE	MINTAGE	UNC
1972 Royal Silver Wedding	7,452,100	£2
1972 — Proof	150,000	£6
1972 — Silver Proof	100,000	£20
1977 Silver Jubilee	37,061,160	£2
1977 — in Presentation folder	Incl. above	£3
1977 — Proof	193,000	£5
1977 — Silver Proof	377,000	£15
1980 Queen Mother 80th Birthday	9,306,000	£1.50
1980 — in Presentation folder	Incl. above	£3
1980 — Silver Proof	83,670	£28
*1981 Royal Wedding	26,773,600	£2
1981 — in Presentation folder	Incl. above	£3
1981 — Silver Proof	218,140	£25

TWENTY PENCE

DATE		UNC
1982		£1
1982 Unc		£2
1982 Proof		£5
1982 Silver Proof Piedfort		£40
1983		£1
1983 Unc		£2
1983 Proof		£5
1984		£1
1984 BU		£2
1984 Proof		£5
1985 New portrait		£1

DATE	UNC
1985 BU	£2
1985 Proof	£6
1986 BU	£4
1986 Proof	£5
1987	£1
1987 BU	£2
1987 Proof	£4
1988	£1
1988 BU	£2
1988 Proof	£4
1989	£1
1989 BU	£2
1989 Proof	£4
1990	£1
1990 BU	£1
1990 Proof	£4
1991	£1
1991 BU	£2
1991 Proof	£5
1992	£4
1992 Enhanced effigy	£2
1992 — BU	£2
1992 — Proof	£4
1993	£1
1993 BU	£2
1993 Proof	£4
1994	£1
1994 BU	£2
1994 Proof	£4
1995	£1
1995 BU	£2
1995 Proof	£4
1996	£1
1996 BU	£2
1996 Proof	£4
1996 Silver Proof	£15
1997	£1
1997 BU	£2
1997 Proof	£4
1998 New portrait	£1
1998 BU	£2
1998 Proof	£4
1999	£1
1999 BU	£2
1999 Proof	£4
2000	£1
2000 BU	£2
2000 Proof	£4
2000 Silver Proof	£25
2001	£1
2001 BU	£2
2001 Proof	£4
2002	£1
2002 BU	£2
2002 Proof	£4
2002 Gold Proof	£125
2003	—
2003 BU	£1
2003 Proof	£5
2004	—
2004 BU	—
2004 Proof	—

TEN PENCE

The series commenced before decimalisation with the legend NEW
PENCE, this changed to TEN PENCE from 1982. These "florin-sized"
coins up to 1992 are no longer legal tender.

DATE	UNC	DATE	UNC
1968	£1	1992 BU	£5
1969	£2	1992 Proof	£6
1970	£2	1992 Silver Proof	£17
1971	£2	1992 Size reduced (24.5mm diam)	£1
1971 Proof	£2	1992 — BU	£2
1972 Proof	£3	1992 — Proof	£4
1973	£2	1992 — Silver Proof	£17
1973 Proof	£4	1992 — — — piedfort	£40
1974	£2	1993 BU	£2
1974 Proof	£4	1993 Proof	£3
1975	£2	1994 BU	£2
1975 Proof	£4	1994 Proof	£3
1976	£2	1995	£1
1976 Proof	£4	1995 BU	£2
1977	£2	1995 Proof	£3
1977 Proof	£4	1996	£1
1978 Proof	£5	1996 BU	£2
1979	£2	1996 Proof	£3
1979 Proof	£4	1996 Silver Proof	£22
1980	£2	1997	£1
1980 Proof	£3	1997 BU	£2
1981	£2	1997 Proof	£3
1981 Proof	£3	1998 New portrait BU	£4
1982 Unc	£4	1998 Proof	£3
1982 Proof	£5	1999 BU	£3
1983 Unc	£3	1999 Proof	£3
1983 Proof	£2	2000	£1
1984 BU	£2	2000 BU	£2
1984 Proof	£3	2000 Proof	£3
1985 New portrait BU	£4	2000 Silver Proof	£24
1985 Proof	£3	2001	£1
1986 BU	£4	2001 BU	£2
1986 Proof	£3	2001 Proof	£3
1987 BU	£4	2002	£1
1987 Proof	£5	2002 BU	£2
1988 BU	£4	2002 Proof	£3
1988 Proof	£5	2002 Gold Proof	£150
1989 BU	£6	2003	—
1989 Proof	£5	2003 BU	£1
1990 BU	£6	2003 Proof	£3
1990 Proof	£5	2004	—
1991 BU	£6	2004 BU	—
1991 Proof	£5	2004 Proof	—

FIVE PENCE

This series commenced simultaneously with the Ten Pence (qv). They were the same size and weight as their predecessor, the shilling, and such coins up to 1990 are no longer legal tender.

DATE	UNC	DATE	UNC
1968	50p	1990 — — Piedfort	£30
1969	50p	1991	—
1970	55p	1991 BU	£1
1971	50p	1991 Proof	£3
1971 Proof	£4	1992	—
1972 Proof	£5	1992 BU	£1
1973 Proof	£5	1992 Proof	£3
1974 Proof	£5	1993 BU	50p
1975	50p	1993 Proof	£4
1975 Proof	£3	1994	—
1976 Proof	£5	1994 BU	£1
1977	50p	1994 Proof	£3
1977 Proof	£4	1995	—
1978	£1	1995 BU	£1
1978 Proof	£3	1995 Proof	£3
1979	£1	1996	—
1979 Proof	£3	1996 BU	£1
1980	£1	1996 Proof	£3
1980 Proof	£2	1996 Silver proof	£15
1981 Proof	£3	1997	—
1982 Unc	£3	1997 BU	£1
1982 Proof	£3	1997 Proof	£3
1983 Unc	£4	1998 New portrait	—
1983 Proof	£3	1998 BU	£1
1984 BU	£3	1998 Proof	£3
1984 Proof	£4	1999	—
1985 New Portrait. BU	£2	1999 BU	£1
1985 Proof	£4	1999 Proof	£3
1986 BU	£2	2000	—
1986 Proof	£4	2000 BU	£1
1987	—	2000 Proof	£3
1987 BU	£1	2000 Silver Proof	£20
1987 Proof	£3	2001	—
1988	—	2001 BU	—
1988 BU	£1	2001 Proof	£3
1988 Proof	£2	2002	—
1989	—	2002 BU	—
1989 BU	£1	2002 Proof	£3
1989 Proof	£4	2002 Gold Proof	£85
1990 BU	£2	2003	—
1990 Proof	£5	2003 BU	—
1990 Silver Proof	£15	2003 Proof	—
1990 Size reduced to 18mm	—	2004	—
1990 — BU	£1	2004 BU	—
1990 Proof	£2	2004 Proof	—
1990 Silver Proof	£15		

TWO PENCE

Dated from 1971, and legal tender from Decimal Day that year, early examples are found in the blue Specimen decimal set wallets of 1968. They were minted in bronze up to 1991, and mainly in copper-plated steel from 1992. However details of where this rule does not totally apply (1992, 1996, 1998–2000 and 2002) are given below. As with other denominations, "NEW" was replaced by the quantity of pence in word from 1982.

DATE	UNC	DATE	UNC
1971	50p	1991 BU	50p
1971 Proof	£2	1991 Proof	£1
1972 Proof	£3	1992 Copper plated steel	£1
1973 Proof	£3	1992 Bronze BU	£3
1974 Proof	£2	1992 — Proof	£1
1975	£1	1993	50p
1975 Proof	£2	1993 BU	£1
1976	50p	1993 Proof	£2
1976 Proof	£2	1994	25p
1977	50p	1994 BU	50p
1977 Proof	£2	1994 Proof	£2
1978	50p	1995	—
1978 Proof	£2	1995 BU	50p
1979	50p	1995 Proof	£2
1979 Proof	£2	1996	—
1980	50p	1996 BU	50p
1980 Proof	£2	1996 Proof	£2
1981	50p	1996 Silver Proof	£18
1981 Proof	£2	1997	—
1982 Unc	£2	1997 BU	50p
1982 Proof	£2	1997 Proof	£2
1983 Unc	£2	1998 New portrait	—
1983 — Error NEW instead of TWO	£250	1998 BU	50p
1983 Proof	£3	1998 Proof	£4
1984 BU	£1	1998 Bronze	£1
1984 Proof	£1	1999	£1
1985 New portrait	50p	1999 Bronze BU	£4
1985 BU	—	1999 — Proof	£5
1985 Proof	£1	2000	—
1986	25p	2000 BU	50p
1986 BU	50p	2000 Proof	£4
1986 Proof	£1	2000 Silver Proof	£15
1987	25p	2001	—
1987 BU	50p	2001 BU	50p
1987 Proof	£1	2001 Proof	£4
1988	25p	2002	—
1988 BU	50p	2002 BU	—
1988 Proof	£1	2002 Proof	£4
1989	25p	2002 Gold Proof	£85
1989 BU	50p	2003	—
1989 Proof	£1	2003 BU	—
1990	25p	2003 Proof	—
1990 BU	50p	2004	—
1990 Proof	£1	2004 BU	—
1991	25p	2004 Proof	,

ONE PENNY

The history of this coin is very similar to that of the Two Pence coin (qv) except that all 1998 examples were of copper-plated steel.

DATE	UNC	DATE	UNC
1971	25p	1990 Proof	£2
1971 Proof	£1	1991	25p
1972 Proof	£2	1991 BU	50p
1973	£1	1991 Proof	£2
1973 Proof	£2	1992 Copper-plated steel	£1
1974	£1	1992 Bronze BU	£2
1974 Proof	£2	1992 — Proof	£2
1975	£1	1993	25p
1975 Proof	£2	1993 BU	50p
1976	£1	1993 Proof	£1
1976 Proof	£2	1994	25p
1977	50p	1994 BU	50p
1977 Proof	£1	1994 Proof	£1
1978	£1	1995	25p
1978 Proof	£2	1995 BU	50p
1979	£1	1995 Proof	£1
1979 Proof	£2	1996	—
1980	£1	1996 BU	50p
1980 Proof	£2	1996 Proof	£1
1981	£1	1996 Silver Proof	£16
1981 Proof	£2	1997	—
1982 Legend changed to ONE PENNY	50p	1997 BU	50p
1982 Unc	£1	1997 Proof	£1
1982 Proof	£2	1998 New portrait	25p
1983	50p	1998 — BU	50p
1983 Unc	£1	1998 Proof	£2
1983 Proof	£1	1999	£2
1984	50p	1999 Bronze BU	£3
1984 BU	£1	1999 Bronze Proof	£1
1984 Proof	£1	2000	—
1985 New portrait	25p	2000 BU	50p
1985 BU	50p	2000 Proof	£2
1985 Proof	£1	2000 Silver Proof	£20
1986	25p	2001	—
1986 BU	50p	2001 BU	—
1986 Proof	£1	2001 Proof	£2
1987	25p	2002	—
1987 BU	50p	2002 BU	—
1987 Proof	£1	2002 Proof	£3
1988	25p	2002 Gold Proof	£65
1988 BU	50p	2003	—
1988 Proof	£3	2003 BU	£1
1989	25p	2003 Proof	£3
1989 BU	50p	2004	—
1989 Proof	£2	2004 BU	—
1990	25p	2004 Proof	—
1990 BU	50p		

HALF PENNY

No longer legal tender, its history tracks that of the Two Pence and One Penny.

DATE	UNC
1971	25p
1971 Proof	£1
1972 Proof	£5
1973	50p
1973 Proof	£3
1974	50p
1974 Proof	£2
1975	50p
1975 Proof	£2
1976	50p
1976 Proof	£2
1977	50p
1977 Proof	£2
1978	75p
1978 Proof	£2
1979	£1
1979 Proof	£2

DATE	UNC
1980	50p
1980 Proof	£1
1981	£1
1981 Proof	£2
1982 Legend changed to HALF PENNY	50p
1982 Unc	£1
1982 Proof	£3
1983	25p
1983 Unc	£1
1983 Proof	£4
1984	£4
1984 BU	£5
1984 Proof	£5

MAUNDY SETS

DATE AND PLACE OF ISSUE	MINTAGE	UNC
1971 Tewkesbury Abbey	1,018	£95
1972 York Minster	1,026	£100
1973 Westminster Abbey	1,004	£95
1974 Salisbury Cathedral	1,042	£95
1975 Peterborough Cathedral	1,050	£95
1976 Hereford Cathedral	1,158	£95
1977 Westminster Abbey	1,138	£105
1978 Carlisle Cathedral	1,178	£95
1979 Winchester Cathedral	1,188	£95
1980 Worcester Cathedral	1,198	£95
1981 Westminster Abbey	1,178	£95
1982 St David's Cathedral	1,218	£95
1983 Exeter Cathedral	1,228	£95
1984 Southwell Minster	1,238	£95
1985 Ripon Cathedral	1,248	£95
1986 Chichester Cathedral	1,378	£95
1987 Ely Cathedral	1,390	£100
1988 Lichfield Cathedral	1,402	£100
1989 Birmingham Cathedral	1,353	£100
1990 Newcastle Cathedral	1,523	£105
1991 Westminster Abbey	1,384	£105
1992 Chester Cathedral	1,424	£105
1993 Wells Cathedral	1,440	£105
1994 Truro Cathedral	1,433	£105
1995 Coventry Cathedral	1,466	£105
1996 Norwich Cathedral	1,629	£110
1997 Birmingham Cathedral	1,786	£110
1998 Portsmouth Cathedral	1,654	£110
1999 Bristol Cathedral	1,676	£110
2000 Lincoln Cathedral	1,686	£125

DATE AND PLACE OF ISSUE	MINTAGE	UNC
2000 Proof	13,180	£135
2001 Westminster Abbey	1,132	£130
2002 Canterbury Cathedral	1,681	£130
2002 Gold Proof	2,002	£550
2003 Gloucester Cathedral	1,601	£130
2004 Liverpool Cathedral	—	£135

In keeping with ancient tradition the Royal Maundy sets are made up of four silver coins of 4p, 3p, 2p and 1p. The designs for the reverse of the coins are a crowned numeral in a wreath of oak leaves—basically the same design that has been used for Maundy coins since Charles II.

PROOF AND SPECIMEN SETS

The following listings are an attempt to include all officially marketed products from the Royal Mint of two coins or more, but excluding those which included non-UK coins. It is appreciated that not all have been advertised as new to the public, but it is assumed that at some time they have been, or will be, available. In a few cases, therefore, the prices may be conjectural but are, nevertheless, attempts at listing realistic value, in some instances based on an original retail price. In the case of Elizabeth II sets, if no metal is stated in the listing, the coins in the sets are of the same metal as the circulation coin equivalent.

DATE	FDC
GEORGE IV	
1826 £5–farthing (11 coins)	£18,000
WILLIAM IV	
1831 Coronation £2–farthing (14 coins)	£16,500
VICTORIA	
1839 "Una and the Lion" £5–farthing (15 coins)	£35,000
1853 Sovereign–quarter farthing, including "Gothic"crown (16 coins)	£27,500
1887 Golden Jubilee £5–3d (11 coins)	£7500
1887 Golden Jubilee Crown–3d (7 coins)	£1250
1893 £5–3d (10 coins)	£8500
1893 Crown–3d (6 coins)	£1500
EDWARD VII	
1902 Coronation £5–Maundy penny, matt proofs (13 coins)	£2000
1902 Coronation Sovereign–Maundy penny, matt proofs (11 coins)	£850
GEORGE V	
1911 Coronation £5–Maundy penny (12 coins)	£2550
1911 Sovereign–Maundy penny (10 coins)	£850
1911 Coronation Halfcrown–Maundy penny (8 coins)	£450
1927 New types Crown–3d (6 coins)	£350

DATE	FDC

GEORGE VI
1937 Coronation £5–half sovereign (4 coins) £1550
1937 Coronation Crown–farthing including Maundy money (15 coins) £175
1950 Mid-century Halfcrown–farthing (9 coins) £65
1951 Festival of Britain, Crown–farthing (10 coins)... £85

ELIZABETH II
1953 Proof Coronation Crown–farthing (10 coins) £55
1953 Currency (plastic) set halfcrown–farthing (9 coins)... £12
1968 Specimen decimal set 10p, 5p and 1971-dated bronze in blue wallet (5 coins) £2.50
1970 Proof Last £sd coins (issued from 1972) Halfcrown–halfpenny (8 coins)................. £18
1971 Proof (issued 1973) 50p–Hp (6 coins) £12
1972 Proof (issued 1976) 50p–Hp (7 coins including Silver Wedding crown)..................... £15
1973 Proof (issued 1976) 50p–Hp (6 coins) £14
1974 Proof (issued 1976) 50p–Hp (6 coins) £16
1975 Proof (issued 1976) 50p–Hp (6 coins) £16
1976 Proof 50p–Hp (6 coins) £16
1977 Proof 50p–Hp (7 coins including Silver Jubilee crown)... £15
1978 Proof 50p–Hp (6 coins) £15
1979 Proof 50p–Hp (6 coins) £16
1980 Proof gold sovereign series (4 coins) £750
1980 — 50p–Hp (6 coins) £15
1981 Proof £5, sovereign, Royal Wedding Silver crown, 50p–Hp (9 coins)...................... £650
1981 — 50p–Hp (6 coins) £17
1982 Proof gold sovereign series (4 coins) £750
1982 — 50p–Hp (7 coins) £16
1982 Uncirculated 50p–Hp (7 coins).. £11
1983 Proof gold double-sovereign to half sovereign (3 coins)... £350
1983 — £1–Hp (8 coins)... £20
1983 Uncirculated £1–Hp (8 coins) (includes Benson & Hedges and Martini sets).......... £25
1983 — 50p –Hp (7 coins) (H. J. Heinz sets) £12
1984 Proof gold five pounds, sovereign and half-sovereigns (3 coins)............................. £650
1984 — £1 (Scottish rev.)–Hp (8 coins) £16
1984 BU £1 (Scottish rev.)–Hp (8 coins) £15
1985 New portrait proof gold sovereign series (4 coins).. £750
1985 Proof £1–1p in de luxe case (7 coins) £25
1985 — in standard case £18
1985 BU £1–1p in folder (7 coins) £15
1986 Proof gold Commonwealth Games £2, sovereign and half sovereign (3 coins)........ £450
1986 — Commonwealth Games £2–1p, de luxe case (8 coins) £25
1986 — — in standard case (8 coins) £23
1986 BU £2–1p in folder (8 coins) £15
1987 Proof gold Britannia set (4 coins) £800
1987 — — £25 and £10 (2 coins) £150
1987 — — double- to half sovereign (3 coins).. £325
1987 — £1–1p in de luxe case (7 coins) £28
1987 — £1–1p in standard case (7 coins) £20
1987 BU £1–1p in folder (7 coins) £12
1988 Proof gold Britannia set (4 coins) £750
1988 — — £25 and £10 (2 coins) £150
1988 — — double- to half sovereign (3 coins).. £325
1988 — £1–1p in de luxe case (7 coins) £30
1988 — £1–1p in standard case (7 coins) £25
1988 BU £1–1p in folder (7 coins) (includes Bradford & Bingley sets)............................. £12
1989 Proof gold Britannia set (4 coins) £760
1989 — — £25 and £10 (2 coins) £150
1989 — — 500th anniversary of the sovereign series set (4 coins) £950
1989 — — double- to half sovereign (3 coins).. £600
1989 — Silver Bill of Rights £2, Claim of Right £2 (2 coins) £42
1989 — — Piedfort as above (2 coins)... £85
1989 BU £2 in folder (2 coins).. £15
1989 Proof £2 (both)–1p in de luxe case (9 coins) £35
1989 — in standard case (9 coins).. £30

DATE	FDC
1989 BU £1–1p in folder (7 coins)	£18
1990 Proof gold Britannia set (4 coins)...	£800
1990 — — sovereign series set (4 coins)	£875
1990 — — double- to half sovereign (3 coins)...................................	£400
1990 — silver 5p, 2 sizes (2 coins)	£20
1990 — £1–1p in de luxe case (8 coins)	£32
1990 — £1–1p standard case (8 coins)	£25
1990 BU £1–1p in folder (8 coins)	£16
1991 Proof gold Britannia set (4 coins)	£775
1991 — — sovereign series set (4 coins)	£1000
1991 — — double- to half sovereign (3 coins)...................................	£450
1991 — £1–1p in de luxe case (7 coins)	£30
1991 — £1–1p in standard case (7 coins)	£25
1991 BU £1–1p in folder (7 coins)	£16
1992 Proof gold Britannia set (4 coins)	£775
1992 — — sovereign series set (4 coins)	£900
1992 — — double- to half sovereign (3 coins)...................................	£450
1992 — £1–1p including two each 50p and 10p in de luxe case (9 coins)...............	£35
1992 — £1–1p as above in standard case (9 coins)	£30
1992 BU £1–1p as above in folder (9 coins)	£15
1992 Proof silver 10p, two sizes (2 coins)	£35
1993 Proof gold Britannia set 1 (4 coins)	£900
1993 — — sovereign series set (4 coins plus silver Pistrucci medal)	£1000
1993 — — double- to half sovereign (3 coins)...................................	£500
1993 — Coronation anniversary £5–1p in de luxe case (8 coins)	£38
1993 — — in standard case (8 coins)	£35
1993 BU £1–1p including 1992 EU 50p (8 coins)................................	£15
1994 Proof gold Britannia set (4 coins)	£825
1994 — — sovereign series set (4 coins)	£1000
1994 — — £2 to half sovereign (3 coins)	£550
1994 — Bank of England Tercentenary £2–1p in de luxe case (8 coins)	£35
1994 — — in standard case (8 coins)	£32
1994 BU £1–1p in folder (7 coins)	£16
1994 Proof gold 1992 and 1994 50p (2 coins)	£145
1994 — "Family silver" set £2–50p (3 coins)	£45
1995 Proof gold Britannia set (4 coins)	£810
1995 — — sovereign series (4 coins)	£1,250
1995 — — £2 to half sovereign (3 coins)	£525
1995 — 50th Anniversary of WWII £2–1p in de luxe case (8 coins)	£35
1995 — — as above in standard case (8 coins)	£32
1995 BU as above in folder (8 coins)	£15
1995 Proof "Family Silver" set £2 (two) and £1 (3 coins)	£50
1996 Proof gold Britannia set (4 coins)	£950
1996 — — sovereign series set (4 coins)	£1000
1996 — — double- to half sovereign (3 coins)...................................	£525
1996 — Royal 70th Birthday £5–1p in de luxe case (9 coins)...............	£45
1996 — — as above in standard case (9 coins)	£38
1996 BU Football £2–1p in folder (8 coins)	£15
1996 Proof gold Britannia £10 and half-sovereign (2 coins)	£450
1996 — — sovereign and silver £1 (2 coins)......................................	£165
1996 — — "Family silver" set £5–£1 (3 coins)	£45
1996 — silver 25th Anniversary of Decimal currency £1–1p (7 coins)	£130
1996 Circulation and BU 25th Anniversary of Decimalisation 2s 6d–Hd (misc.) and £1–1p in folder (14 coins)........................	£45
1997 Proof gold Britannia set (4 coins)	£1000
1997 — — sovereign series set (4 coins)...	£950
1997 — — — £2 to half sovereign (3 coins).......................................	£520
1997 — — Silver Britannia set (4 coins)	£100
1997 — Golden Wedding £5–1p in red leather case	£50
1997 — — as above in standard case (10 coins)................................	£38
1997 BU £2 to 1p in folder (9 coins)...	£20
1997 Proof silver 50p set, two sizes (2 coins)	£35
1997/1998 Proof silver £2 set, both dates (2 coins)...........................	£18
1998 Proof gold Britannia set (4 coins)	£1000
1998 — — sovereign series set (4 coins)	£1000

DATE	FDC
1998 — — — double- to half sovereign (3 coins)	£500
1998 Proof silver Britannia set (4 coins)	£95
1998 — Prince of Wales £5–1p (10 coins) in red leather case	£42
1998 — — as above in standard case (10 coins)	£36
1998 BU £2–1p in folder (9 coins)	£15
1998 Proof silver European/NHS 50p set (2 coins)	£50
1998 BU Britannia/EU 50p set (2 coins)	£5
1999 Proof gold Britannia set (4 coins)	£1000
1999 — — sovereign series set (4 coins)	£1000
1999 — — — £2 to half sovereign (3 coins)	£500
1999 — Princess Diana £5–1p in red leather case (9 coins)	£50
1999 — — as above in standard case (9 coins)	£38
1999 BU £2–1p (8 coins) in folder	£15
1999 Proof "Family Silver" set. Both £5, £2 and £1 (4 coins)	£45
1999 Britannia Millennium set. Bullion £2 and BU £5 (2 coins)	£25
1999/2000 Reverse frosted proof set, two x £1 (2 coins)	£65
2000 Proof gold Britannia set (4 coins)	£1000
2000 — — sovereign series set (4 coins)	£1000
2000 — — — double- to half sovereign (3 coins)	£500
2000 — Millennium £5–1p in red leather case (10 coins)	£50
2000 — — as above in de luxe case (10 coins)	£40
2000 — — as above in standard case (10 coins)	£35
2000 — Silver set Millennium £5 to 1p plus Maundy (13 coins)	£135
2000 BU £2–1p set in folder (9 coins)	£12
2000 Millennium "Time Capsule" BU £5 to 1p (9 coins)	£25
2001 Proof gold Britannia set (4 coins)	£825
2001 — — sovereign series set (4 coins)	£1000
2001 — — — £2–half sovereign (3 coins)	£500
2001 — silver Britannia set (4 coins)	£100
2001 — Victoria £5–1p in Executive case (10 coins)	£75
2001 — — as above in red leather case (10 coins)	£50
2001 — — as above in "Gift" case (10 coins)	£45
2001 — — as above in standard case (10 coins)	£35
2001 BU £2–1p in folder (9 coins)	£15
2002 Proof gold Britannia set (4 coins)	£825
2002 — — sovereign series set, all Shield rev. (4 coins)	£1000
2002 — — — double- to half sovereign (3 coins)	£450
2002 — — Golden Jubilee set £5–1p plus Maundy (13 coins)	£2500
2002 — Golden Jubilee £5–1p in Executive case (9 coins)	£65
2002 — — as above in red leather de luxe case (9 coins)	£45
2002 — — as above in "Gift" case (9 coins)	£40
2002 — — as above in standard case (9 coins)	£30
2002 BU £2–1p (8 coins) in folder	£15
2002 Proof Gold Commonwealth Games £2 set (4 coins)	£1200
2002 — Silver Piedfort Commonwealth Games £2 set (4 coins)	£200
2002 — — Commonwealth Games £2 set (4 coins)	£100
2002 — Commonwealth Games £2 set (4 coins)	£25
2002 BU Commonwealth Games £2 set (4 coins) in folder	£15
2003 Proof gold Britannia set (4 coins)	£950
2003 — — — £50–£10 (3 coins)	£400
2003 — — — type set, one of each £100 reverse (4 coins)	£1350
2003 — — sovereign series set (4 coins)	£1000
2003 — — — series £2–half sovereign (3 coins)	£425
2003 — silver Britannia set (4 coins)	£100
2003 — — — type set (one of each £2 reverse) (4 coins)	£75
2003 — £5 to 1p, two of each £2 and 50p in Executive case (11 coins)	£75
2003 — — as above in red leather case (11 coins)	£45
2003 — — as above in standard case (11 coins)	£40
2003 BU £2 (two)–1p in folder (10 coins)	£15
2003 Proof silver Piedfort set. DNA £2, £1 and Suffragette 50p (3 coins)	£150
2003 Proof "Family Silver" set £5, Britannia and DNA £2, £1 and Suffragette 50p (5 coins)	£140
2003 Circ & BU "God Save the Queen" coronation anniversary set 5s/0d to ¼d (1953) and £5 to 1p (2003) in folder (19 coins)	£70
2003 Circulation or bullion "Royal Sovereign" collection, example of each Elizabeth II date (21 coins)	£2500

DATE	FDC
2004 Proof gold Britannia set (4 coins)	£815
2004 — — £50 to £10 (3 coins)	£395
2004 — — Sovereign series set (4 coins)	£985
2004 — — — Series £2-half sovereign (3 coins)...	£439
2004 (Issue date) Royal Portrait gold sovereign set, all proof except the first: Gillick, Machin, Maklouf and Rank-Broadley sovereigns, and the 2nd, 3rd and 4th of above half-sovereigns, various dates (7 coins)...	£750
2004 Proof silver Britannia set (4 coins)	£95
2004 — "Family Silver" set £5, Britannia and Trevithick £2, £1 and Bannister 50p (5 coins)	£145
2004 — Silver Piedfort set, Trevithick £2, £1 and Bannister 50p (3 coins)	£145
2004 — £2 to 1p, two each of £2 and 50p in Executive case (10 coins)	£65
2004 — — as above in red leather case (10 coins)...	£40
2004 — — as above in standard case (10 coins)..	£30
2004 BU £2 to 1p in folder (10 coins)...	£14
2004 "New Coinage" set, Trevithick £2, £1 and Bannister 50p (3 coins)..	£9

In addition to the above the Royal Mint produce the BU sets detailed above in Wedding and in Baby gift packs each year. Also the following patterns have been made available:

1999 (dated 1994) Bi-metal £2, plus three unprocessed or part-processed elements....................	—
2003 (dated 2004–7) Proof gold £1 featuring future reverse Bridge designs, hall-marked on edge (4 coins)	—
2003 — — silver £1 as above (4 coins)..	—
2004 — "Heraldic Traditions" silver £1-sized hall-marked (4 coins)	£98

SCOTLAND

The coins illustrated are pennies representative of the reign, unless otherwise stated.

	F	VF
DAVID I (1124–53)		
Berwick, Carlisle, Edinburgh and Roxburgh Mints		
Penny	£600	£1500

David I

	F	VF
HENRY (1136–52)		
Bamborough, Carlisle and Corbridge Mints for the Earl of Huntingdon and Northumberland		
Penny	£1300	£4000

Henry

	F	VF
MALCOLM IV (1153–65)		
Berwick and Roxburgh Mints		
Penny (5 different types)...............................	£3500	£9500

	F	VF
WILLIAM THE LION (1165–1214)		
Berwick, Edinburgh, Dun (Dunbar?), Perth and Roxburgh Mints		
Penny	£100	£200

William the Lion

	F	VF
ALEXANDER II (1214–49)		
Berwick and Roxburgh Mints		
Penny	£750	£1600

Alexander II

ALEXANDER III (1249–86)

FIRST COINAGE (1250–80)
Pennies struck at the Mints at

	F	VF
Aberdeen..	£100	£300
Ayr	£100	£325
Berwick...	£85	£185
"Dun" (Dumfries?)..	£145	£375
Edinburgh...	£55	£165
Forfar...	£145	£425
Forres	£150	£400
Glasgow	£165	£435
Inverness	£165	£385
Kinghorn	£185	£450
Lanark..	£165	£385
Montrose	£275	£600
Perth...	£85	£185
Renfrew	£200	£600
Roxburgh..	£85	£200
St Andrews	£125	£300
Sterling	£180	£450

Alexander III

SECOND COINAGE (1280–86)

	F	VF
Penny	£50	£100
Halfpenny	£100	£225
Farthing	£175	£450

JOHN BALIOL (1292–1306)

FIRST COINAGE *(Rough Surface issue)*

	F	VF
Penny	£125	£275
Halfpenny	Extremely rare	

SECOND COINAGE *(Smooth Surface issue)*

	F	VF
Penny	£175	£350
Halfpenny	£235	£550
Farthing	£600	£1400

John Baliol

ROBERT BRUCE (1306–29)

	F	VF
Berwick Mint		
*Penny	£300	£850
Halfpenny	£450	£1100
Farthing	Extremely Rare	

Robert Bruce

DAVID II (1329–71)

	F	VF
Aberdeen and Edinburgh Mints		
Noble	Extremely Rare	
Groat	£85	£250
Halfgroat	£100	£250
Penny	£55	£125
Halfpenny	£200	£450
Farthing	£550	£1550

David II

ROBERT II (1371–90)

	F	VF
Dundee, Edinburgh and Perth Mints		
Groat	£100	£200
Halfgroat	£100	£250
Penny	£85	£250
Halfpenny	£150	£400

Robert II

ROBERT III (1390–1406)

	F	VF
Aberdeen, Dumbarton, Edinburgh, Perth Mints		
*Lion or crown	£500	£1100
Demy lion or halfcrown	£500	£1000
Groat	£65	£175
Halfgroat	£120	£325
Penny	£200	£450
Halfpenny	£300	£800

JAMES I (1406–37)

	F	VF
Aberdeen, Edinburgh, Inverness, Linlithgow, Perth, Stirling Mints		
Demy	£400	£900
Half demy	£500	£1000
Groat	£175	£350
Penny	£130	£325
Halfpenny	£350	£900

JAMES II (1437–60)

	F	VF
Aberdeen, Edinburgh, Linlithgow, Perth, Roxburgh, Stirling Mints		
Demy	£500	£1100
Lion	£650	£1700
Half lion	Extremely rare	
*Groat	£175	£550
Halfgroat	£500	£1100
Penny (billon)	£350	£700

Robert III Lion

JAMES III (1460–88)

	F	VF
Aberdeen, Berwick and Edinburgh Mints		
Rider	£850	£1850
Half rider	£1000	£2200
Quarter rider	£1100	£2600
Unicorn	£750	£1800
Groat	£200	£450
Halfgroat	£500	£900
Penny (silver)	£200	£500
Plack (billon)	£90	£300
Half plack	Extremely rare	
Penny (billon)	£100	£300
Farthing (copper)	£250	£325

James III Groat, Berwick Mint

JAMES IV (1488–1513)

James IV

	F	VF
Edinburgh Mint		
Unicorn	£675	£1500
Half unicorn	£550	£1100
Lion or crown	£800	£1750
Half lion	£1500	£3500
Groat	£400	£800
Halfgroat	£400	£800
Penny (silver)	£400	£1200
Plack	£60	£150
Half plack	£120	£250
*Penny (billon)	£60	£150

JAMES V (1513–42)

	F	VF
Edinburgh Mint		
Unicorn	£1000	£2500
Half Unicorn	£1450	£4000
Crown	£600	£1300
Ducat or Bonnet piece	£2000	£4500
Two-thirds ducat	£1850	£3200
One -third ducat	£2500	£4500
*Groat	£150	£400
One-third groat	£145	£375
Plack	£45	£145
Bawbee	£35	£115
Half bawbee	£75	£175
Quarter bawbee		Extremely rare

James V Edinburgh Groat

MARY (1542–67)

Edinburgh and Stirling Mints

FIRST PERIOD (1542–58)

	F	VF
Crown	£950	£2350
Twenty shillings	£1800	£3500
Lions (Forty-four shillings)	£900	£2500
Half lions (Twenty-two shillings)	£700	£1700
Ryals (Three pounds)	£2000	£5000
Half ryal	£2750	£6000
Portrait testoon	£1000	£4000
*Non-portrait testoon	£175	£485
Half testoon	£165	£455
Bawbee	£55	£115
Half bawbee	£85	£200
Penny (facing bust)	£175	£500
Penny (no bust)		Extremely rare
Lion	£35	£100
Plack	£35	£100

SECOND PERIOD (Francis and Mary, 1558–60)

	F	VF
Ducat (Sixty shillings)		Extremely rare
Non-portrait testoon	£165	£475
Half testoon	£185	£525
12 penny groat	£100	£250
Lion	£45	£100

Mary First Period Testoon

THIRD PERIOD (Widowhood, 1560–65)

	F	VF
Portrait testoon	£800	£2500
Half testoon	£950	£3000

FOURTH PERIOD (Henry and Mary, 1565–67)

	F	VF
Portrait ryal		Extremely rare
Non-portrait ryal	£200	£550
Two-third ryal	£350	£650

	F	VF
One-third ryal	£450	£1000
Testoon	£225	£850

FIFTH PERIOD (Second widowhood, 1567)

Non-portrait ryal	£250	£650
Two thirds ryal	£225	£600
One-third ryal	£275	£750

JAMES VI
(Before accession to the English throne)
(1567–1603)

FIRST COINAGE (1567–71)

Ryal	£185	£550
Two-thirds ryal	£180	£500
One-third ryal	£185	£500

SECOND COINAGE (1571–80)

Twenty pounds	Extremely rare	
Noble (or half merk)	£85	£350
Half noble (or quarter merk)	£80	£275
Two merks or Thistle dollar	£1200	£2000
Merk	£1200	—

THIRD COINAGE (1580–81)

Ducat	£2000	£5000
Sixteen shillings	£1100	£2500
Eight shillings	£850	£2200
Four shillings	£850	£2250
Two shillings	Extremely rare	

James VI Fourth coinage thirty shillings

FOURTH COINAGE (1582–88)

Lion noble	£2500	£6500
Two-third lion noble	£2500	£6500
One-third lion noble	£3000	£7750
Forty shillings	£2500	£7600
*Thirty shillings	£325	£850
Twenty shillings	£300	£700
Ten shillings	£200	£500

FIFTH COINAGE (1588)

Thistle noble	£1500	£3250

SIXTH COINAGE (1591–93)

"Hat" piece	£2500	£6000
"Balance" half merk	£175	£400
"Balance" quarter merk	£350	£800

SEVENTH COINAGE (1594–1601)

Rider	£500	£1000
Half rider	£400	£1000
Ten shillings	£100	£275
Five shillings	£110	£300
Thirty pence	£100	£275
Twelve pence	£80	£300

EIGHTH COINAGE (1601–04)

Sword and sceptre piece	£275	£500
Half sword and sceptre piece	£225	£400
Thistle-merk	£75	£200
Half thistle-merk	£50	£175
Quarter thistle-merk	£50	£175
Eighth thistle-merk	£50	£185

	F	VF
Billon and copper issues		
Eightpenny groat	£25	£60
Fourpenny groat	£150	—
Twopenny plack	£75	£200
Hardhead	£100	£250
Twopence	£70	£250
Penny plack	£80	£200
Penny	£130	£400

JAMES VI
(After accession to the English throne)
(1603–25)

	F	VF
Unit	£385	£750
Double crown	£500	£1400
British crown	£500	£1000
Halfcrown	£300	£700
Thistle crown	£300	£600
Sixty shillings	£285	£650
*Thirty shillings	£85	£275
Twelve shillings	£80	£225
Six shillings	£300	£700
Two shillings	£55	£250
One shilling	£85	£300
Copper twopence	£35	£100
Copper penny	£35	£100

James VI after accession thirty shillings

CHARLES I (1625–49)

FIRST COINAGE (1625–36)

	F	VF
Unit	£600	£850
Double crown	£1200	£2500
British crown	£1700	£5000
Sixty shillings	£300	£750
Thirty shillings	£85	£250
Twelve shillings	£85	£180
Six shillings	£200	£425
Two shillings	£75	£325
One shilling	£75	£325

SECOND COINAGE (1636)

	F	VF
Half merk	£55	£200
Forty penny piece	£60	£175
Twenty penny piece	£65	£300

THIRD COINAGE (1637–42)

	F	VF
Unit	£500	£1300
Half unit	£600	£1750
British crown	£500	£1700
British half crown	£355	£1000
Sixty shillings	£285	£950
*Thirty shillings	£80	£250
Twelve shillings	£70	£200
Six shillings	£65	£185
Half merk	£55	£165
Forty pence	£35	£100
Twenty pence	£30	£85
Three shillings	£50	£150
Two shillings	£50	£155
Twopence (copper)	£30	£85
Penny	Extremely rare	
Twopence (CR crowned)	£10	£35
Twopence (Stirling turner)	£10	£25

Charles I Third coinage thirty shillings

F   VF

CHARLES II (1660–85)

FIRST COINAGE

Four merks

	F	VF
1664 Thistle above bust	£500	£1000
1664 Thistle below bust	£600	£1000
1665	Extremely rare	
1670	£400	£800
1673	£400	£900
1674 F below bust	£450	£900
1675	£450	£900

Two merks

	F	VF
1664 Thistle above bust	£200	£600
1664 Thistle below bust	£225	£700
1670	£180	£600
1673	£180	£600
1673 F below bust	£285	£950
1674	£255	£950
1674 F below bust	£225	£850
1675	£165	£500

Merk

	F	VF
1664	£80	£200
1665	£80	£220
1666	£150	£420
1668	£80	£220
1669	£100	£250
1670	£85	£285
1671	£70	£185
1672	£70	£185
1673	£70	£220
1674	£70	£220
1674 F Below bust	£80	£225
*1675 F below bust	£100	£300
1675	£100	£320

Charles II two merks

Half merk

	F	VF
1664	£120	£300
1665	£100	£250
1666	£120	£350
1667	£100	£300
1668	£100	£300
1669	£110	£325
1670	£100	£350
1671	£75	£225
1672	£75	£220
1673	£80	£200
1675 F below bust	£120	£300
1675	£90	£225

SECOND COINAGE

Dollar

	F	VF
1676	£300	£750
1679	£300	£800
1680	£400	£1200
1681	£300	£800
1682	£275	£700

Half Dollar

	F	VF
1675	£250	£650
1676	£300	£800
1681	£190	£500

Quarter Dollar

	F	VF
1675	£100	£250
1676	£100	£255
1677	£175	£450

	F	VF
1679	£100	£350
1680	£120	£400
1681	£100	£350
1682	£130	£350
Eighth Dollar		
1676	£75	£175
1677	£75	£175
1678/7		Rare
1679	£225	£650
1680	£100	£225
1682	£200	£500
Sixteenth Dollar		
1677	£60	£150
1678/7	£75	£175
1679/7		Rare
1680	£200	£500
1681	£100	£225
Twopence CR crowned	£35	£125
Bawbees	£65	£175
Turners	£35	£125

James VII ten shillings

JAMES VII (1685–89)

	F	VF
Sixty shillings		
1688 proof only	—	£1250
Forty shillings		
1687	£115	£400
1688	£155	£450
Ten shillings		
*1687	£100	£275
1688	£125	£375

WILLIAM & MARY (1689–94)

	F	VF
Sixty shillings		
1691	£200	£750
1692	£250	£750
Forty shillings		
1689	£200	£400
1690	£100	£325
1691	£130	£400
1692	£120	£350
1693	£125	£425
1694	£130	£425
Twenty shillings		
1693	£200	£650
1694	£350	£1000
Ten shillings		
1689	Extremely rare	
1690	£200	£400
*1691	£150	£275
1692	£100	£250
1694	£175	£450
Five shillings		
1691	£125	£350
1694	£70	£220
Bawbee		
1691–94	£65	£130
Bodle		
1691–94	£40	£85

William & Mary ten shillings

	F	VF

WILLIAM II (1694–1702)

	F	VF
Pistole	£2300	£5000
Half pistole	£2700	£6000
Forty shillings		
1695	£130	£350
1696	£125	£300
1697	£190	£400
1698	£130	£300
1699	£200	£675
1700	Extremely rare	
Twenty shillings		
1695	£100	£300
1696	£100	£300
1697	£175	£550
1698	£125	£375
1699	£125	£350
Ten shillings		
*1695	£85	£265
1696	£85	£200
1697	£85	£200
1698	£100	£250
1699	£175	£400
Five shillings		
1695	£75	£300
1696	£55	£150
1697	£75	£200
1699	£60	£265
1700	£65	£255
1701	£80	£285
1702	£90	£325
Bawbee		
1695–97	£35	£150
Bodle		
1695–97	£45	£155

William II ten shillings

ANNE (1702–14)

PRE-UNION 1702–7

	F	VF
Ten shillings		
1705	£100	£275
1706	£125	£450
Five shillings		
1705	£35	£125
*1706	£45	£150

Anne five shillings

POST-UNION 1707–14
See listing in English section.

JAMES VIII (The Old Pretender) (1688–1766)

A number of Guineas and Crowns in various metals were struck in 1828 using original dies prepared by Norbert Roettiers, all bearing the date 1716. These coins are extremely rare and are keenly sought after.

ISLE OF MAN

DATE	F	VF	EF	UNC
PENNY				
*1709 Cast	£30	£75	£175	—
1709 Silver cast Proof	—	—	—	£1250
1709 Brass	£30	£82	£175	
*1733 "Quocunque"	£25	£40	£150	£250
1733 "Ouocunoue"	£25	£50	£185	£400
1733 Bath metal "Quocunque"	£15	£35	£150	—
1733 Silver Proof	—	—	—	£500
1733 Bronze Proof	—	—	—	£285
1733 Proof	—	—	—	£425
1733 Cap frosted	£15	£35	£150	£225
1733 Brass, cap frosted	£25	£45	£175	£335
1733 Silver Proof cap frosted	—	—	—	£350
1733 Bronze annulets instead of pellets	£35	£65	£225	£475
1758	£16	£30	£125	£250
1758 Proof	—	—	—	£400
1758 Silver Proof	—	—	—	£650
*1786 Engrailed edge	£18	£32	£140	£300
1786 Engrailed edge Proof	—	—	—	£350
1786 Plain edge Proof	—	—	—	£675
1786 Pellet below bust	£18	£45	£165	£350
*1798	£18	£45	£135	£275
1798 Proof	—	—	—	£245
1798 Bronze Proof	—	—	—	£245
1798 Copper-gilt Proof	—	—	—	£1150
1798 Silver Proof	—	—	—	£1650
1813	£20	£40	£100	£200
1813 Proof	—	—	—	£250
1813 Bronze Proof	—	—	—	£200
1813 Copper-gilt Proof	—	—	—	£1650
1839	£15	£30	£85	£165
1839 Proof	—	—	—	£275
HALF PENCE				
*1709 Cast	£35	£50	£155	—
1709 Brass	£40	£150	£330	—
1723 Silver	£525	£1000	£2000	—
1723 Copper	£230	£475	£1150	£1650
1733 Copper	£20	£40	£150	£250
1733 Bronze	£25	£40	£150	£250
1733 Silver Proof plain cap	—	—	—	£350
1733 Silver Proof frosted cap	—	—	—	—
1733 Bronze Proof	—	—	—	£275
1733 Bath metal plain cap	£25	£35	£140	—
1733 Bath metal frosted cap	£25	£35	£145	—
*1758	£25	£35	£150	£250
1758 Proof	—	—	—	£500
1786 Engrailed edge	£15	£30	£75	£200
1786 Proof engrailed edge	—	—	—	£250
1786 Plain edge	£25	£50	£165	£225
1786 Proof plain edge	—	—	—	£450
1786 Bronze Proof	—	—	—	£250
1798	£20	£30	£75	£200
1798 Proof	—	—	—	£250
1798 Bronze Proof	—	—	—	£225

DATE	F	VF	EF	UNC
1798 Copper-gilt Proof	—	—	—	£750
1798 Silver Proof	—	—	—	£1000
1813	£15	£30	£75	£155
1813 Proof	—	—	—	£225
1813 Bronze Proof	—	—	—	£200
1813 Copper-gilt Proof	—	—	—	£800
1839	£15	£30	£50	£100
1839 Bronze Proof	—	—	—	£250

FARTHING

	F	VF	EF	UNC
*1839 Copper	£15	£30	£55	£150
1839 Bronze Proof	—	—	—	£250
1839 Copper-gilt Proof	—	—	—	£1500

The last issue of coins made in the Isle of Man had been in 1839 but in 1970 Spink & Son Ltd was commissioned to produce a modern coinage for the Isle of Man Government which was struck at the Royal Mint. From 1973 onwards the Pobjoy Mint took over the contract and has been a very prolific producer of definitive and commemorative issues. It is not proposed to give a complete listing of all these coins but the Crown and 25p, which from the collector's point of view are the most interesting in the series, have been selected. Additionally a special 50p coin is issued to celebrate Christmas each year.

The listings that follow are of the ordinary uncirculated cupro-nickel crown-size coins. The Island has also issued most of the coins listed in other metals, including silver, gold and platinum in non proof and proof form and in 1984 some were also issued in silver clad cupro-nickel in proof form.

DATE	UNC
1970 Manx Cat	£6
1972 Royal Silver Wedding	£5
1974 Centenary of Churchill's birth	£4
1975 Manx Cat	£6
1976 Bi-Centenary of American Independence	£5
1976 Centenary of the Horse Drawn Tram	£4
1977 Silver Jubilee	£4
1977 Silver Jubilee Appeal	£4
1978 25th Anniversary of the Coronation	£4
1979 300th Anniversary of Manx Coinage	£4
1979 Millennium of Tynwald (5 coins)	£12
1980 Winter Olympics	£4
1980 Derby Bicentennial	£4
1980 22nd Olympics (3 coins)	£10
1980 80th Birthday of Queen Mother	£4
1981 Duke of Edinburgh Award Scheme (4 coins)	£10
1981 Year of Disabled (4 coins)	£10
1981 Prince of Wales' Wedding (2 coins)	£6
1982 12th World Cup—Spain (4 coins)	£12
1982 Maritime Heritage (4 coins)	£12
1983 Manned Flight (4 coins)	£12
1984 23rd Olympics (4 coins)	£12
1984 Quincentenary of College of Arms (4 coins)	£12
1984 Commonwealth Parliamentary Conference (4 coins)	£12
1985 Queen Mother (6 coins)	£12
1986 13th World Cup—Mexico (6 coins)	£12
1986 Prince Andrew Wedding (2 coins)	£8
1987 200th Anniversary of the United States Constitution	£5

DATE	UNC
1987 America's Cup Races (5 coins)	£12
1988 Bicentenary of Steam Navigation (6 coins)	£15
1988 Australia Bicentennial (6 coins)	£15
1988 Manx Cat	£5
1989 Royal Visit	£5
1989 Bicentenary of the Mutiny on the Bounty (4 coins)	£14
1989 Persian Cat	£6
1989 Bicentenary of Washington's Inauguration (4 coins)	£12
*1990 150th Anniversary of the Penny Black	£10
1990 World Cup—Italy (4 coins)	£12
1990 25th Anniversary of Churchill's Death (2 coins)	£8
1990 Alley Cat	£6
1990 Queen Mother's 90th Birthday	£6
1991 Norwegian Forest Cat	£6
1991 Centenary of the American Numismatic Association	£5
1991 1992 America's Cup	£6
1991 10th Anniversary of Prince of Wales' Wedding (2 coins)	£8
1992 Discovery of America (4 coins)	£15
1992 Siamese Cat	£7
1992 1992 America's Cup	£5
1993 Maine Coon Cat	£5
1993 Preserve Planet Earth—Dinosaurs (2 coins)	£9
1994 Preserve Planet Earth—Mammoth	£6
1994 Year of the Dog	£6
1994 World Football Cup (6 coins)	£24
1994 Japanese Bobtail Cat	£6
1994 Normandy Landings (8 coins)	£35
1994 Preserve Planet Earth—Endangered Animals (3 coins)	£17
1995 Man in Flight—Series i (8 coins)	£50
1995 Man in Flight—Series ii (8 coins)	£50
*1995 Queen Mother's 95th Birthday	£7
1995 Year of the Pig	£7
1995 Turkish Cat	£7
1995 Preserve Planet Earth—Egret and Otter	£9
1995 America's Cup	£7
*1995 Aircraft of World War II (19 coins)	£85
1995 Famous World Inventions—Series i (12 coins)	£55
1996 Year of the Rat	£7
1996 70th Birthday of HM the Queen	£10
1996 The Flower Fairies—Series i (4 coins)	£32
1996 Famous World Inventions—Series ii (6 coins)	£32
*1996 Olympic Games (6 coins)	£27
1996 Preserve Planet Earth—Killer Whale and Razorbill	£10
1996 Burmese Cat	£9
1996 Robert Burns (4 coins)	£20
1996 King Arthur & the Knights of the Round Table (5 coins)	£28
1996 European Football Championships (8 coins)	£45
1996 Football Championships Winner	£10
1996 Explorers (2 coins)	£17
1997 Year of the Ox	£10
*1997 The Flower Fairies—Series ii (4 coins)	£21
1997 Royal Golden Wedding (2 coins)	£12
1997 Explorers—Eriksson and Nansen (2 coins)	£12
1997 Long-haired Smoke Cat	£8
1997 10th Anniversary of the "Cats on Coins" series (silver only)	£31
1997 90th Anniversary of the TT Races (4 coins)	£25
1998 The Millennium (16 coins issued over 3 years)	—
1998 Year of the Tiger	£10
1998 FIFA World Cup (4 coins)	£25
1998 Birman Cat	£10
1998 The Flower Fairies—Series iii (4 coins)	£25
1998 18th Winter Olympics, Nagano (4 coins)	£25
1998 Explorers—Vasco da Gama and Marco Polo (2 coins)	£15

DATE	UNC
1998 125th Anniversary of Steam Railway (8 coins)	£50
1998 International Year of the Oceans (4 coins)	£28
1999 50th Birthday of HRH the Prince of Wales	£8
1999 Year of the Rabbit	£8
1999 27th Olympics in Sydney (5 coins)	£30
1999 Rugby World Cup (6 coins)	£35
1999 Wedding of HRH Prince Edward and Sophie Rhys-Jones	£9
1999 Queen Mother's 100th Birthday (4 coins)	£22
1999 The Millennium (4 coins)	£22
1999 Titanium Millennium crown	£7
*2000 Year of the Dragon	£7
2000 Scottish Fold cat	£7
2000 Millennium—own a piece of time	£7
2000 Explorers, Francisco Piarro and Wilem Brents (2 coins)	£12
2000 Life and times of the Queen Mother (4 coins)	£22
2000 Queen Mother's 100th Birthday	£7
2000 60th Anniversary of the Battle of Britain	£7
2000 BT Global Challenge	£7
2000 18th Birthday of HRH Prince William	£7
2001 Year of the Snake	£7
2001 The Somali cat	£7
2001 Life and times of the Queen Mother (2 coins)	£12
2001 Explorers, Martin Frobisher and Roald Amundsen (2 coins)	£12
2001 75th Birthday of HM the Queen	£7
2001 Joey Dunlop	£7
2001 Harry Potter (6 coins)	£55
2002 Year of the Horse	£8
2002 The XIX Winter Olympiad, Salt Lake City (2 coins)	£14
2002 World Cup 2002 in Japan/Korea (4 coins)	£30
2002 The Bengal Cat	£10
*2002 The Queen's Golden Jubilee—i (1 coin)	£12
*2002 Introduction of the Euro	£10
2002 The Queen's Golden Jubilee—ii (4 coins)	£40
2002 A Tribute to Diana Princess of Wales—5 years on	£15
2003 Year of the Goat	£8
*2003 The Balinese Cat	£10
2003 Anniversary of the "Star of India"	£12
2003 Lord of the Rings (5 coins)	£50
2004 Olympics (4 coins)	£40
2004 100 Years of Powered Flight (2 coins)	£20

GUERNSEY

DATE	F	VF	EF	UNC
TEN SHILLINGS				
*1966	—	£2	£3	£5
1966 Proof	—	—	—	£10
THREEPENCE				
1956	50p	£1	£2	£3
1956 Proof	—	—	—	£8
1959	50p	£1	£2	£3
1966 Proof	—	—	—	£8

EIGHT DOUBLES				
1834	£4	£8	£30	£100
*1858 5 berries	£3	£7	£30	£100
1858 4 berries	£3	£7	£30	£100
1864 1 stalk	£2	£3	£20	£48
1864 3 stalks	£2	£3	£18	£55
1868	£4	£7	£18	£45
1874	£3	£4	£8	£35
1885H	£3	£4	£7	£25
1889H	£2	£3	£5	£22
1893H small date	£2	£3	£5	£22
1893H large date	£2	£3	£5	£22
1902H	£2	£3	£5	£20
1903H	£2	£3	£5	£20
1910	£2	£3	£5	£22
1911H	£2	£3	£6	£28
1914H	50p	£2	£4	£18
1918H	50p	£2	£4	£15
1920H	50p	£2	£4	£15
1934H	60p	£2	£4	£20
1934H Proof	—	—	—	£85
1938H	60p	£2	£4	£15
1945H	50p	£1	£3	£8
1947H	40p	£1	£3	£8
1949H	40p	£1	£3	£8
1956	30p	50p	£2	£6
1956	30p	50p	£2	£6
1959	30p	50p	£2	£6
1966 Proof	—	—	—	£15

FOUR DOUBLES				
1830	£3	£8	£35	£70
1830 Mule with obv. St Helena Hd	—	£650	—	—
1858	£5	£10	£40	£70
1864 Single stalk	£1	£5	£10	£40
1864 3 stalks	31	£5	£12	£45
1868	£2	£6	£18	£55
1874	£1	£5	£15	£50
1885H	£1	£5	£12	£25
1889H	£1	£2	£9	£20
1893H	£1	£2	£9	£20
1902H	£1	£2	£6	£17
1903H	£1	£2	£9	£20
1906H	£1	£2	£6	£17
1908H	£1	£2	£6	£17
1910H	£1	£2	£6	£17
1911H	£1	£2	£5	£15
1914H	£1	£2	£9	£28
1918H	£1	£2	£8	£25
1920H	£1	£2	£6	£17
1945H	£1	£2	£6	£15
1949H	£1	£2	£8	£25
1956	50p	£1	£3	£8
1966 Proof	—	—	—	£10

DATE	F	VF	EF	UNC
TWO DOUBLES				
1858..	£5	£8	£35	£120
1868 Single stick	£5	£10	£40	£125
1868 3 stalks	£6	£12	£60	£130
1874..	£3	£8	£35	£80
1885H..	£2	£5	£8	£25
1889H..	£2	£3	£6	£18
1899H..	£2	£4	£12	£30
1902..	£2	£3	£10	£25
1902H..	£2	£3	£10	£25
1906H..	£2	£3	£10	£25
1908H..	£2	£4	£10	£25
1911H..	£2	£4	£13	£28
1914H..	£2	£4	£13	£28
1917H..	£6	£16	£51	£115
1918H..	£2	£3	£7	£18
*1920H..	£2	£3	£7	£17
1929H..	£1	£2	£5	£10
ONE DOUBLE				
*1830..	£2	£3	£15	£30
1868..	£3	£9	£25	£75
1868/30	£4	£6	£20	£65
1885H..	£1	£2	£4	£12
1889H..	50p	£1	£3	£12
1893H..	50p	£1	£3	£12
1899H..	50p	£1	£3	£12
1902..	50p	£1	£3	£12
1903H..	50p	£1	£3	£12
1911H..	50p	£1	£5	£12
1911 (new shield)	50p	£1	£3	£12
1914H..	50p	£1	£5	£12
1929H..	50p	£1	£3	£12
1933H..	50p	£1	£3	£12
1938H..	50p	£1	£3	£12

DECIMAL COINAGE

Ordinary circulating coinage from 1986 onwards is usually available in uncirculated condition at a small premium above face value thus it is not listed here. The coins listed are cupro-nickel unless otherwise stated.

	UNC
ONE HUNDRED POUNDS—Gold	
1994 50th Anniversary of Normandy Landings. Proof	£500
1995 Anniversary of the Liberation. Proof...	£500
FIFTY POUNDS—Gold	
1994 50th Anniversary of Normandy Landings. Proof	£250
1995 Anniversary of the Liberation. Proof...	£250
TWENTY-FIVE POUNDS—Gold	
1994 50th Anniversary of Normandy Landings	£175
1994 — Proof	£200
1995 Anniversary of the Liberation. Proof...	£175
1996 European Football Championships. Proof	£175
1997 Royal Golden Wedding. Proof..	£225
1998 Royal Air Force. Proof	£175
2000 Queen Mother 100th Birthday. Proof	£185
2001 Queen Victoria centennial	£200
2001 HM the Queen's 75th Birthday	£175
2002 Princess Diana memorial..	£200
2002 Duke of Wellington	£200
TEN POUNDS	
1994 50th Anniversary of Normandy Landings. Gold proof....................	£85
1995 Anniversary of the Liberation. Gold proof	£85
2000 Century of Monarchy. Silver proof...	£85
2001 19th Century Monarchy. Silver proof..	£85
2002 18th Century Monarchy. Silver proof..	£85

DATE   UNC

FIVE POUNDS

1995 Queen Mother's 95th birthday	£15
1995 — Silver proof	£40
1995 — Small size gold	£100
1996 HM the Queen's 70th birthday	£12
1996 — Silver proof	£35
1996 European Football Championships	£15
1996 — Silver proof	£40
1997 Royal Golden Wedding	£15
1997 — Silver proof	£40
1997 — Small size gold. BU	£52
1997 Castles of the British Isles—Castle Cornet, Guernsey	£12
1997 — Silver proof	£42
1997 Castles of the British Isles—Caernarfon Castle. Silver proof	£42
1997 Castles of the British Isles—Leeds Castle. Silver proof	£44
1998 Royal Air Force.	£6
1998 Royal Air Force. Silver proof	£44
1999 Millennium. Brass	£15
1999 — Silver proof	£34
1999 Wedding of HRH Prince Edward and Sophie Rhys-Jones	£15
1999 — Silver proof	£50
1999 Queen Mother	£15
1999 — Silver proof	£50
1999 Winston Churchill	£8
1999 — Gold	£650
2000 Queen Mother's 100th Birthday	£6
2000 — Silver proof	£40
2000 — Small size gold. Proof	£50
*2000 Centuries of the British Monarchy	£15
2000 — Silver proof	£45
2000 — Small size gold. Proof	£45
2001 The Reign of Queen Victoria	£6
2001 — Proof	£12
2001 — Silver proof	£35
2001 HM the Queen's 75th Birthday	£5
2001 — Silver proof	£35
2001 — Small size gold. Proof	£45
2001 19th Century Monarchy	£8
2001 — Silver proof	£35
2001 — Small size gold. Proof	£45
2002 Golden Jubilee (two types)	£5
2002 — Silver proof	£40
2002 Princess Diana memorial	£6
2002 — Proof	£30
2002 — Gold proof	£550
2002 Century of Monarchy	£6
2002 — Silver proof	£35
2002 — Small size gold. Proof	£45
2002 Queen Mother Memoriam	£8
2002 — Proof	£15
2002 — Silver proof	£35
2002 — Small size gold. Proof	£45
2003 Duke of Wellington	—
2003 — Silver proof	—
2003 — Gold proof	—

TWO POUNDS

1985 40th anniversary of Liberation	£8
1985 — Proof	£20
1985 — Silver proof	£30
*1986 Commonwealth Games, in plastic case	£10
1986 — in special folder	£10
1986 — .500 Silver	£19
1986 — .925 Silver proof	£30
1987 900th anniv. of death of William the Conqueror, in folder	£10
1987 — Silver proof	£30
1987 — Gold proof	£900

DATE	UNC

1988 William II, in presentation folder £9
1988 — Silver proof.. £30
1989 Henry I, in presentation folder £9
1989 — Silver proof.. £30
*1989 Royal Visit.. £9
1989 — Silver proof.. £30
1990 Queen Mother's 90th birthday.. £9
1990 — Silver proof.. £35
1991 Henry II, in presentation folder £9
1991 — Silver proof.. £35
1993 40th Anniversary of the Coronation.. £9
1993 — Silver proof.. £34
*1994 Anniversary of the Normandy Landings....................................... £
1994 — Silver proof.. £
1995 50th Anniversary of Liberation .... £
1995 — Silver proof.. £
1995 — Silver Piedfort proof £6
1997 Conserving Nature i.. £
1997 — Silver proof.. £
1998 Conserving Nature ii.. £

ONE POUND
1981.. £
1981 Gold proof £8
1981 Gold piedfort £25
1983 New specification, new reverse... £
1985 New design (in folder).. £
1995 Queen Mother's 95th Birthday. Silver proof .... £
1996 Queen's 70th Birthday. Silver proof... £28
1997 Royal Golden Wedding. Silver BU.. £12
1997 — Silver proof.. £28
1997 Castles of the British Isles—Tower of London. Silver proof only ... £22
1998 Royal Air Force. Silver proof.. £24
1999 Wedding of Prince Edward. Silver proof £28
1999 Queen Mother. Silver proof £28
1999 Winston Churchill. Silver proof... £25
2000 Millennium. Silver proof (gold plated)... £32
2000 Queen Mother's 100th Birthday. Silver proof £20
2001 HM the Queen's 75th Birthday. Silver proof £20

FIFTY PENCE
1969.. £2
1970.. £4
1971 Proof £6
1981.. £2
1982.. £2
1985 New design.. —
*2000 60th Anniversary of the Battle of Britain. £2
2000 — Silver proof.. £35
2000 — silver piedfort £50
2000 — Gold proof.. £250

TWENTY-FIVE PENCE
1972 Royal Silver Wedding £6
1972 — Silver proof.. £15
1977 Royal Silver Jubilee... £2
1977 — Silver proof.. £15
1978 Royal Visit £2
1978 — Silver proof.. £15
1980 Queen Mother's 80th birthday £3
1980 — Silver proof.. £15
1981 Royal Wedding £2
1981 — Silver proof.. £15

JERSEY

DATE	F	VF	EF	UNC

FIVE SHILLINGS
1966	—	£2	£4	£6
1966 Proof	—	£2	£6	£12

ONE QUARTER OF A SHILLING
1957	—	£1	£2	£5
1960 Proof	—	—	£2	£8
1964	—	—	£1	£4
1966	—	—	£1	£4

ONE TWELFTH OF A SHILLING

1877H	£1	£2	£12	£36
1877H Proof in nickel	—	—	—	£1000
1877 Proof only	—	—	—	£375
1877 Proof in nickel	—	—	—	£1000
1881	£2	£2	£10	£45
1888	£1	£2	£10	£35
1894	£1	£2	£10	£35
1909	£1	£2	£10	£25
1911	£1	£2	£4	£20
1913	£1	£2	£4	£20
1923 Spade shield	£1	£2	£4	£20
1923 Square shield	£1	£2	£4	£20
1926	£1	£2	£5	£30
1931	£1	£2	£4	£8
1933	£1	£2	£4	£8
1935	£1	£2	£4	£8
1937	£1	£2	£4	£8
1946	£1	£2	£4	£6
1947	25p	£2	£4	£7
"1945" GVI	10p	25p	50p	£4
"1945" QE2	10p	25p	50p	£4
1957	10p	35p	50p	£3
*1960 1660–1960 300th anniversary	10p	20p	40p	£3
1960 Mule	—	—	—	£100
1966 "1066–1966"	—	—	50p	£2

ONE THIRTEENTH OF A SHILLING
1841	£3	£7	£32	£150
1844	£3	£8	£32	£150
1851	£4	£12	£48	£155
1858	£3	£8	£36	£150
1861	£4	£12	£48	£150
1865 Proof only	—	—	—	£575
1866 with LCW	£1	£4	£30	£85
1866 without LCW Proof only	—	—	—	£300
1870	£3	£7	£32	£75
1871	£3	£7	£32	£75

ONE TWENTY-FOURTH OF A SHILLING
1877H	£2	£3	£7	£35
1877 Proof only	—	—	—	£225
1888	£2	£3	£7	£30
1894	£2	£3	£7	£30
1909	£2	£3	£7	£30
1911	£1	£2	£5	£25
1913	£1	£2	£5	£25

DATE	F	VF	EF	UNC
1923 Spade shield	£1	£2	£6	£25
1923 Square shield	£1	£2	£5	£25
1926	£1	£2	£5	£15
1931	£1	£2	£5	£15
*1933	£1	£2	£5	£15
1935	£1	£2	£5	£15
1937	50p	£1	£3	£10
1946	50p	£1	£3	£10
1947	50p	£1	£3	£10

ONE TWENTY-SIXTH OF A SHILLING

1841	£3	£6	£25	£60
1844	£3	£6	£20	£55
1851	£2.50	£5	£18	£55
1858	£3	£10	£40	£125
1861	£2.50	£5	£18	£50
*1866	£2	£5	£20	£60
1870	£2	£5	£15	£40
1871	£2	£5	£15	£40

ONE FORTY-EIGHTH OF A SHILLING

1877H	£5	£10	£45	£85
1877 Proof only	–	–	–	£300

ONE FIFTY-SECOND OF A SHILLING

1841	£8	£20	£50	£125
1861 Proof only	–	–	–	£500

DECIMAL COINAGE

Ordinary circulating coinage from 1986 onwards is usually available in uncirculated condition at a small premium above face value thus it is not listed here.

ONE HUNDRED POUNDS—Gold
1995 50th Anniversary of Liberation. Gold proof £500

FIFTY POUNDS—Gold
1995 50th Anniversary of Liberation. Gold proof £400

(Reduced)

TWENTY-FIVE POUNDS—Gold
1972 25th Royal Wedding anniversary. Gold	£100
1972 — Gold proof	£185
1990 50th Anniversary of Battle of Britain. Gold proof	£200
1995 50th Anniversary of Liberation. Gold proof	£185
2002 Princess Diana memorial. Gold proof	£200

TEN POUNDS—Gold
1972 25th Royal Wedding anniversary. Gold	£45
1972 — Gold proof	£55
*1990 50th Anniversary of the Battle of Britain. Gold proof	£165
1995 50th Anniversary of Liberation. Gold proof	£165

(Enlarged)

FIVE POUNDS
1972 25th Royal Wedding anniversary. Gold	£25
1972 — Gold proof	£45
*1990 50th Anniversary of the Battle of Britain. Silver Proof (5 ounces)	£100
1997 Royal Golden Wedding	£15
1997 — Silver proof	£45
*2000 Millennium. Silver proof	£35
2002 Princess Diana memorial	£10
2002 — Silver proof	£30
2002 — Gold proof	£600

TWO POUNDS FIFTY PENCE
1972 Royal Silver Wedding	£12
1972 — Silver proof	£20

DATE   UNC

TWO POUNDS
(note all modern Proof coins have frosted relief)

1972 Royal Silver Wedding	£10
1972 — Silver proof...	£15
1981 Royal Wedding, nickel silver (crown size).........................	£5
1981 — in presentation pack	£8
1981 — Silver proof...	£20
1981 — Gold proof..	£325
1985 40th Anniversary of Liberation (crown size)	£5
1985 — in presentation pack	£6
1985 — Silver proof...	£25
1985 — Gold proof..	£985
1986 Commonwealth Games..	£8
1986 — in presentation case...	£8
1986 — .500 silver..	£25
1986 — .925 silver proof	£30
1987 World Wildlife Fund 25th Anniversary	£8
1987 — Silver proof...	£28
1989 Royal Visit	£8
1989 — Silver proof...	£30
1990 Queen Mother's 90th Birthday	£8
1990 — Silver proof...	£4
1990 — Gold proof..	£425
1990 50th Anniversary of the Battle of Britain, silver proof......	£40
1993 40th Anniversary of the Coronation................................	£8
1993 — Silver proof...	£45
*1995 50th Anniversary of Liberation	£9
1995 — Silver Proof	£45
1996 HM the Queen's 70th Birthday	£8
1996 — Silver proof...	£38
1997 Bi-metal	£10
1997 — Silver proof...	£35
1997 — new portrait..	£8

ONE POUND

1972 Royal Silver Wedding	£6
1972 — Silver proof...	£12
1981...	£7
1981 Silver proof	£20
1981 Gold proof	£180
1983 New designs and specifications on presentation card (St Helier).....	£5
1983 — Silver proof...	£25
1983 — gold proof	£350
1984 Presentation wallet (St Saviour)......................................	£7
1984 — Silver proof...	£28
1984 — Gold proof..	£325
1984 Presentation wallet (St Brelade)	£7
1984 — Silver proof...	£25
1984 — Gold proof..	£350
1985 Presentation wallet (St Clement)	£58
1985 — Silver proof...	£25
1985 — Gold proof..	£350
1985 Presentation wallet (St Lawrence)	£8
1985 — Silver proof...	£25
1985 — Gold proof..	£350
1986 Presentation wallet (St Peter)	£8
1986 — Silver proof...	£25
1986 — Gold proof..	£350
1986 Presentation wallet (Grouville)	£8
1986 — Silver proof...	£25
1986 — Gold proof..	£350
1987 Presentation wallet (St Martin)	£8

DATE	UNC
1987 — Silver proof	£25
1987 — Gold proof	£350
1987 Presentation wallet (St Ouen)	£5
1987 — Silver proof	£25
1987 — Gold proof	£350
1988 Presentation wallet (Trinity)	£6
1988 — Silver proof	£26
1988 — Gold proof	£350
1988 Presentation wallet (St John)	£7
1988 — Silver proof	£25
1988 — Gold proof	£350
1989 Presentation wallet (St Mary)	£7
1989 — Silver proof	£25
1989 — Gold proof	£350

1991 Ship Building in Jersey Series

1991 "Tickler" Silver proof	£40
1991 — Gold proof	£350
1991 "Percy Douglas" Silver proof	£30
1991 — Gold proof	£350
1992 "The Hebe" Silver proof	£25
1992 — Gold proof	£350
1992 "Coat of Arms" Silver proof	£25
1992 — Gold proof	£350
1993 "The Gemini" Silver proof	£25
1993 — Gold proof	£350
1993 "The Century" Silver proof	£25
1993 — Gold proof	£350
*1994 "Resolute" Silver proof	£30
1994 — Gold proof	£350

FIFTY PENCE

1969	£3
1972 Royal Silver Wedding	£5
1972 — Silver proof	£5
1983 New design	£3
1985 40th Anniversary of Liberation	£5

TWENTY-FIVE PENCE

1977 Royal Jubilee	£3
1977 — Silver proof	£12

TWENTY PENCE

1982 Date on rocks on rev. (cased)	£3
1982 — Silver proof piedfort	£40
1983 New obv. with date, rev. no date on rocks	—

SOVEREIGN—Gold sovereign size

*1999 The Millennium	£95
1999 — Gold proof	£150

263

ALDERNEY

DATE	UNC

ONE HUNDRED POUNDS
1994 50th Anniversary of D-Day Landings. Gold proof £470

FIFTY POUNDS
1994 50th Anniversary of D–Day Landing. Gold proof................................ £260

TWENTY FIVE POUNDS
1993 40th Anniversary of Coronation. Gold proof £170
1994 50th Anniversary of D-Day Landings. Gold proof £170
1997 Royal Golden Wedding. Gold proof £170
1997 — Silver proof £20
*2000 60th Anniversary of the Battle of Britain. Gold proof £180
2002 Princess Diana memorial £225
2002 Duke of Wellington £225

TEN POUNDS
1994 50th Anniversary of D–Day Landing. Gold proof............................... £60

FIVE POUNDS
1995 Queen Mother £12
1995 — Silver proof.. £35
1995 — Silver piedfort.. £65
1995 — Gold proof... £650
1996 HM the Queen's 70th Birthday £8
1996 — Silver proof.. £40
1996 — Silver piedfort.. £65
1996 — Gold proof... £650
*1999 Eclipse of the Sun £12
1999 — Silver proof with colour centre.. £30
1999 Winston Churchill. Gold proof £650
2000 60th Anniversary of the Battle of Britain.. £10
2000 — Silver proof.. £40
2002 Golden Jubilee. Silver proof £35
2002 50 Years of Reign. Silver proof £35
2002 Diana memorial £6
2002 — Silver proof.. £30
2002 — Gold proof... £600
2002 Duke of Wellington £8
2002 — Silver proof.. £35
2002 — Gold proof... £600

TWO POUNDS
1989 Royal Visit £8
1989 — Silver proof.. £35
1989 — Silver piedfort.. £65
1989 — Gold proof... £930
*1990 Queen Mother's 90th Birthday £8
1990 — Silver proof.. £35
1990 — Silver piedfort.. £68
1990 — Gold proof... £930
*1992 40th Anniversary of Accession... £8
1992 — Silver proof.. £35
1992 — Silver piedfort.. £68
1992 — Gold proof... £930
1993 40th Anniversary of Coronation... £8
1993 — Silver proof.. £35
1993 — Silver piedfort.. £68
1994 50th Anniversary of D-Day Landings.. £8
1994 — Silver proof.. £38

DATE	UNC
1994 — Silver piedfort	£70
1995 50th Anniversary of Return of Islanders	£10
1995 — Silver proof	£35
1995 — Silver piedfort	£68
1995 — Gold proof	£750
*1997 WWF Puffin	£10
1997 — Silver proof	£35
1997 Royal Golden Wedding	£10
1997 — Silver proof	£45
1999 Eclipse of the Sun. Silver	£10
1999 — Silver proof	£35
1999 — Gold proof	£850
2000 Millennium. Silver proof	£35

ONE POUND

1993 40th Anniversary of Coronation Silver proof	£35
*1995 50th Anniversary of VE Day Silver proof	£28
1995 — Gold proof	£330

IRELAND

As in the English hammered section (q.v.) the prices given here are for the most common coins in the series. For a more specialised listing the reader is referred to *Coincraft's Standard Catalogue of Scotland, Ireland, Channel Islands & Isle of Man*, or other specialised publications. Collectors should be aware that with most of the coins of the Irish series there are many varieties struck at different mints. The coins listed are all silver unless mentioned otherwise. Another important factor to consider when collecting early Irish coins is that few examples exist in high grades.

	F	VF

HIBERNO-NORSE ISSUES (995–1155)

| Penny, imitating English silver pennies, many various types | £125 | £200 |

A typical Hiberno-Norse period example.

JOHN, Lord of Ireland (1185–99)

Halfpenny, profile		Extremely rare
Halfpenny, facing	£50	£100
Farthing	£250	£550

JOHN de COURCY, Lord of Ulster (1177–1205)

| Halfpenny | | Extremely rare |
| Farthing | £500 | £1200 |

John Lord of Ireland halfpenny.

JOHN as King of England and Lord of Ireland (c. 1199–1216)

Penny	£50	£100
Halfpenny	£100	£200
Farthing	£500	£1200

HENRY III (1216–72)

| Penny | £50 | £100 |

EDWARD I (1272–1307)

Penny	£50	£150
Halfpenny	£50	£150
Farthing	£100	£250

Henry III penny.

No Irish coins were struck for Edward II (1307–27).

EDWARD III (1327–77)

| Halfpenny | | Extremely rare |

No Irish coins were struck for Richard II (1377–99), Henry IV (1399–1413) or Henry V (1413–22).

HENRY VI (1422–61)

| Penny | | Extremely rare |

Edward III halfpenny.

	F	VF
EDWARD IV (1461–83)		
"Anonymous crown" groat	£300	£750
— penny	£750	—
"Titled crown" groat	£1000	—
— halfgroat		Extremely rare
— penny		Extremely rare
Cross on rose/Sun groat	£1250	—
Bust/Rose on sun double groat	£1500	£4000
— groat	£1750	—
— halfgroat		Extremely rare
— penny		Extremely rare
Bust/Cross & pellets groat—First issue	£75	£200
— halfgroat	£400	£750
— penny	£60	£125
— halfpenny		Extremely rare
— Second (light) issue	£75	£200
— halfgroat	£400	£750
— penny	£65	£150
— halfpenny		Extremely rare
Bust/Rose on cross groat	£350	£750
— penny	£50	£100

Edward IV groat. "Anonymous crown" issue.

Billon/Copper issues

	F	VF
Small crown/Cross farthing (1460–61)	£1000	—
— half farthing ("Patrick")	£750	—
Large crown/Cross farthing (1462)		Extremely rare
Patricius/Salvator farthing (1463–65)	£250	£1200
— half farthing		Extremely rare
Shield/Rose on sun farthing	£125	£500

Edward IV penny. "Anonymous crown" issue.

RICHARD III (1483–85)	F	VF
Bust/Rose on cross groat	£750	£2000
— halfgroat		Unique
— penny		Unique
Bust/Cross and pellets penny	£750	£1500
Shield/Three-crowns groat	£450	£1000

HENRY VII (1485–1509)	F	VF
Early issues (1483–90)		
Shield/Three crowns groat	£85	£200
— halfgroat	£150	£350
— penny	£400	£850
— halfpenny		Extremely rare
Later issues (1488–90)		
Shield/Three crowns groat	£70	£175
— halfgroat	£150	£350
— penny	£375	£750
Facing bust groat (1496–1505)	£90	£200
— halfgroat	£750	—
— penny	£650	—

Richard III bust/rose on cross groat.

Henry VII "three crowns" half groat.

LAMBERT SIMNEL
(as EDWARD VI, Pretender, 1487)

	F	VF
Shield/Three crowns groat	£750	£2000

	F	VF

HENRY VIII (1509–47)

	F	VF
"Harp" groat	£50	£125
— halfgroat	£350	£950

The "Harp" coins have crowned initials either side of the reverse harp, e.g. HR (Henricus Rex), HA (Henry and Anne Boleyn), HI (Henry and Jane Seymour), HK (Henry and Katherine Howard).

Posthumous (Portrait) issues

	F	VF
Sixpence	£100	£250
Threepence	£100	£275
Threehalfpence	£325	£850
Threefarthings	£500	£1250

Henry VIII "harp" halfgroat.

EDWARD VI (1547–53)

	F	VF
Shilling (base silver) 1552 (MDLII)	£650	£1750
Brass contemporary copy	£55	£250

MARY (1553–54)

	F	VF
Shilling 1553 (MDLIII)	£600	£2000
Shilling 1554 (MDLIIII)		Extremely rare
Groat		Extremely rare
Halfgroat		Extremely rare
Penny		Extremely rare

PHILIP & MARY (1554–58)

	F	VF
Shilling	£250	£750
Groat	£75	£200
Penny		Extremely rare

Mary Tudor shilling.

ELIZABETH I (1558–1603)

Base silver portrait coinage

	F	VF
Shilling	£250	£850
Groat	£125	£375

Fine silver, portrait coinage (1561)

	F	VF
Shilling	£175	£550
Groat	£225	£700

Third (base silver) shield coinage

	F	VF
Shilling	£150	£425
Sixpence	£100	£300

Copper

	F	VF
Threepence	£150	£450
Penny	£25	£85
Halfpenny	£75	£175

Reverse of a "fine" Elizabeth I shilling.

JAMES I (1603–25)

	F	VF
Shilling	£75	£225
Sixpence	£55	£150

Coins struck under Royal Licence from 1613

	F	VF
"Harrington" farthing (small size)	£35	£85
"Harrington" farthing (large size)	£25	£75
"Lennox" farthing	£25	£75

James I sixpence.

CHARLES I (1625–49)

During the reign of Charles I and the Great Rebellion many coins were struck under unusual circumstances, making the series a difficult but fascinating area for study. Many of the "coins" were simply made from odd-shaped pieces of plate struck with the weight or value.

Charles I "Maltravers" farthing.

Coins struck under Royal Licence from 1625

	F	VF
"Richmond" farthing	£25	£75
"Maltravers" farthing	£35	£85
"Rose" farthing	£25	£75

Siege money of the Irish Rebellion, 1642–49

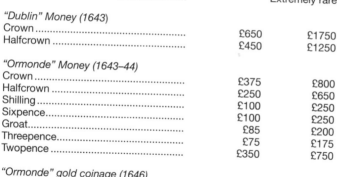

"Inchiquin" Money (1642)
	F	VF
Crown	£1500	£3250
Halfcrown	£1250	£3000
Shilling		Extremely rare
Ninepence		Extremely rare
Sixpence		Extremely rare
Groat		Extremely rare

"Dublin" Money (1643)
	F	VF
Crown	£650	£1750
Halfcrown	£450	£1250

"Ormonde" Money (1643–44)
	F	VF
Crown	£375	£800
Halfcrown	£250	£650
Shilling	£100	£250
Sixpence	£100	£250
Groat	£85	£200
Threepence	£75	£175
Twopence	£350	£750

Coinage of the Great Rebellion—a "Dublin Money" crown.

"Ormonde" gold coinage (1646)
Double pistole. 2 known (both in museums)	Extremely rare
Pistole. 10 known (only 1 in private ownership	Extremely rare

"Ormonde" Money (1649)
	F	VF
Crown		Extremely rare
Halfcrown	£850	£2500

"Ormonde" money threepence.

Dublin Money 1649
	F	VF
Crown	£2000	£5000
Halfcrown	£1500	£3000

Issues of the Confederated Catholics

Kilkenny issues (1642–43)
	F	VF
Halfpenny	£200	£550
Farthing	£300	£750

Rebel Money (1643–44)
	F	VF
Crown	£1500	£3000
Halfcrown	£2000	£3500

Kilkenny halfpenny.

	F	VF
"Blacksmith's" Money (16??) Imitation of English Tower halfcrown.....	£500	£1500

Local Town issues of "Cities of Refuge"

	F	VF
Bandon Farthing (copper)	Extremely rare	
Cork Shilling .... Sixpence.. Halfpenny (copper) .... Farthing (copper)	Extremely rare £600 Extremely rare £400	£1250 —
Kinsale Farthing (copper)	£300	—
Youghal Farthing (copper)	£350	£1000

"Cork" countermarked on a copper coin.

CHARLES II (1660–85)

	Fair	F	VF	EF
"Armstrong" coinage Farthing (1660–61)................................	£50	£175	—	—
"St Patrick's" coinage Halfpenny .... Farthing	£175 £50	£350 £125	— £375	— £750
Legg's Regal coinage Halfpennies 1680 large lettering................................ 1681 large lettering................................ 1681 small lettering .... 1682 small lettering .... 1683 small lettering .... 1684 small lettering	£25 — — £15 £25	£65 £150 £150 £25 £85	£175 £450 Extremely rare £450 £250 £350	— — — — —

"St Patrick" farthing of Charles II.

JAMES II (1685–88)

REGAL COINAGE

Halfpennies				
1685... 1686... 1687... 1688...	£10 £10 £12	£55 £45 £45	£200 £150 Extremely rare £200	£400 £300 —

	Fair	F	VF	EF

EMERGENCY COINAGE

GUN MONEY

Most of these coins were struck in gun metal but a few rare specimens are also known struck in gold and in silver

Crowns

	Fair	F	VF	EF
1690 (many varieties).....................from	£25	£45	£100	—

Large halfcrowns
Dated July 1689–May 1690

Prices from	£15	£35	£85	—

Small halfcrowns
Dated April–October1690

Prices from	£15	£35	£85	—

"Gun Money" crown.

Large shillings
Dated from July 1689–April 1690

Prices from	£10	£18	£50	£150

Small shillings
Dated from April–September 1690

Prices from	£8	£15	£50	£150

Sixpences
Dated from June 1689–October 1690

Prices from	£20	£45	£100	—

PEWTER MONEY (1689–90)

	Fair	F	VF	EF
Crown...	£450	£750	£1500	—
Groat..		Extremely rare		
Penny large bust.................................	£175	£450	—	—
— small bust	£125	£350	£750	—
Halfpenny large bust	£100	£250	£500	—
— small bust	£85	£175	£450	—

"Gun Money" shilling (large size).

LIMERICK MONEY (1690–91)

	Fair	F	VF	EF
Halfpenny, reversed N in HIBERNIA......	£15	£55	£150	—
Farthing, reversed N in HIBERNIA........	£15	£55	£150	—
— normal N	£20	£75	£175	—

WILLIAM & MARY (1688–94)

Halfpennies

	Fair	F	VF	EF
1692...	£5	£25	£75	£350
1693...	£5	£25	£70	£350
1694...	£5	£25	£85	£450

WILLIAM III (1694–1702)

	Fair	F	VF	EF
1696 Halfpenny draped bust................	£20	£50	£150	—
1696 — crude undraped bust	£30	£200	£500	—

No Irish coins were struck during the reign of Queen Anne (1706–11).

Reverse of a "Pewter Money" penny.

DATE	F	VF	EF	UNC

GEORGE I (1714–27)

Farthings

	F	VF	EF	UNC
1722 D.G. REX Harp to left (Pattern).............	£500	£1000	£1750	—
1723 D.G. REX Harp to right	£85	£175	£350	—
1723 DEI GRATIA REX Harp to right	£20	£50	£150	£300
1723 — Silver Proof	—	—	—	£1000
1724 DEI GRATIA REX Harp to right	£45	£100	£250	£500

Halfpennies

	F	VF	EF	UNC
1722 Holding Harp left	£35	£100	£250	£550
1722 Holding Harp right	£30	£85	£225	£450
1723/2 Harp right	£30	£85	£225	£500
1723 Harp right	£15	£50	£145	£300
1723 Silver Proof..	—	—	—	£2000
1723 Obv. Rs altered from Bs	£20	£75	£175	—
1723 No stop after date	£15	£60	£175	£300
1724 Rev. legend divided	£25	£75	£200	—
1724 Rev. legend continuous	£25	£85	£250	—

Farthing of George I.

GEORGE II (1727–60)

Farthings

	F	VF	EF	UNC
1737...	£20	£45	£120	£250
1737 Proof...	—	—	—	£300
1737 Silver Proof.......................................	—	—	—	£550
1738...	£20	£50	£120	£250
1744...	£20	£50	£120	£250
1760	£15	£30	£75	£175

Halfpennies

	F	VF	EF	UNC
1736...	£15	£45	£150	£275
1736 Proof...	—	—	—	£400
1736 Silver Proof.......................................	—	—	—	£750
1737...	£15	£35	£125	—
1738...	£20	£45	£150	—
1741...	£20	£45	£150	—
1742...	£20	£45	£150	—
1743...	£20	£45	£150	—
1744/3	£20	£40	£125	—
1744...	£20	£45	£175	—
1746...	£20	£45	£150	—
1747...	£20	£45	£150	—
1748...	£20	£45	£150	—
1749...	£20	£45	£150	—
1750...	£20	£45	£150	—
1751...	£20	£45	£150	—
1752...	£20	£45	£150	—
1753...	£20	£45	£150	—
1755...	£22	£75	£225	—
*1760	£15	£40	£125	—

Halfpenny of George II.

GEORGE III (1760–1820)

All copper unless otherwise stated

Pennies

	F	VF	EF	UNC
1805...	£12	£25	£125	£250
1805 Proof...	—	—	—	£300
1805 in Bronze Proof..................................	—	—	—	£300
1805 in Copper Gilt Proof............................	—	—	—	£300
1805 in Silver Proof (restrike)......................	—	—	—	£1500
1822...	£10	£20	£120	£250

DATE	F	VF	EF	UNC
1822 Proof	—	—	—	£375
1823	£8	£15	£100	£250
1823 Proof	—	—	—	£375

Halfpennies

	F	VF	EF	UNC
1766	£15	£38	£100	—
1769	£15	£38	£100	—
1769 Longer bust	£25	£55	£125	£350
1774 Pattern only Proof	—	—	—	£1000
1775	£18	£35	£115	£200
1775 Proof	—	—	—	£400
1776	£35	£100	£200	—
1781	£25	£40	£85	£200
1782	£25	£40	£85	£200
1805	£10	£25	£75	£200
1805 Copper Proof	—	—	—	£200
1805 in Bronze	—	—	—	£150
1805 in Gilt Copper	—	—	—	£250
1805 in Silver (restrike)	—	—	—	£850
1822	£10	£25	£75	£200
1822 Proof	—	—	—	£350
1823	£10	£25	£75	£200
1823 Proof	—	—	—	£350

1806 farthing.

NB Prooflike Unicirculated Pennies and Halfpennies of 1822/23 are often misdescribed as Proofs. The true Proofs are rare. Some are on heavier, thicker flans.

Farthings

	F	VF	EF	UNC
*1806	£10	£20	£50	£100
1806 Copper Proof	—	—	—	£200
1806 Bronzed Copper Proof	—	—	—	£150
1806 Copper Gilt Proof	—	—	—	£200
1806 Silver Proof (restrike)	—	—	—	£550
1822 George IV (Pattern) Proof	—	—	—	£1000

TOKEN ISSUES BY THE BANK OF IRELAND

Five Pence in Silver

	F	VF	EF	UNC
1805	£15	£30	£50	£150
1806	£20	£50	£100	£200
1806/5	£35	£100	£275	£750

Ten Pence in Silver

	F	VF	EF	UNC
1805	£12	£25	£75	£150
1806	£15	£45	£100	£175
*1813	£12	£25	£65	£135
1813 Proof	—	—	—	£300

Thirty Pence in Silver

	F	VF	EF	UNC
1808	£25	£75	£155	£350

Six Shillings

	F	VF	EF	UNC
*1804 in Silver	£75	£150	£300	£1000
1804 Proof	—	—	—	£1000
1804 in Copper (restrike)	—	—	—	£500
1804 Copper Gilt	—	—	—	£1000
1804 in Gilt Silver	—	—	—	£1750

In this series fully struck specimens, with sharp hair curls, etc., are worth appreciably more than the prices quoted.

IRISH FREE STATE/EIRE

DATE	F	VF	EF	UNC
TEN SHILLINGS				
*1966 Easter Rising	—	£5	£10	£15
1966 Cased Proof	—	—	—	£20
1966 special double case	—	—	—	£45

	F	VF	EF	UNC
HALF CROWNS				
1928	£5	£10	£30	£50
1928 Proof	—	—	—	£55
1930	£5	£20	£100	£350
1931	£5	£25	£125	£375
1933	£5	£15	£120	£300
1934	£5	£10	£40	£175
1937	£40	£100	£425	£1000
1938				Unique
*1939	£3	£8	£20	£65
1939 Proof	—	—	—	£475
1940	£3	£8	£20	£55
1941	£5	£12	£25	£60
1942	£5	£8	£20	£55
1943	£65	£150	£650	£2000
1951	£1	£2	£12	£30
1951 Proof	—	—	—	£350
1954	£1	£2	£8	£45
1954 Proof	—	—	—	£350
1955	£1	£2	£8	£25
1955	—	—	—	£450
1959	£1	£2	£8	£25
1961	£1	£2	£15	£35
1961 Obv as 1928, rev. as 1951	£15	£25	£175	—
1962	£1	£2	£5	£15
1963	£1	£2	£5	£12
1964	£1	£2	£5	£10
1966	£1	£2	£5	£10
1967	£1	£2	£5	£10

	F	VF	EF	UNC
FLORINS				
1928	£2	£4	£15	£35
1928 Proof	—	—	—	£45
1930	£3	£10	£100	£300
1930 Proof				Unique
1931	£4	£17	£125	£300
1933	£3	£15	£100	£300
1934	£5	£85	£175	£475
1934 Proof	—	—	—	£2000
1935	£2	£9	£50	£125
1937	£5	£15	£100	£275
1939	£1	£3	£20	£40
1939 Proof	—	—	—	£475
1940	£2	£4	£20	£45
1941	£2	£4	£25	£50
1941 Proof	—	—	—	£550
1942	£3	£6	£20	£45
1943	£2000	£4000	£7000	£15000
1951	50p	£1	£8	£20
1951 Proof	—	—	—	£325
1954	50p	£1	£8	£20
1954 Proof	—	—	—	£250

DATE	F	VF	EF	UNC
1955	—	£1	£4	£20
1955 Proof	—	—	—	£300
1959	35p	£1	£5	£15
1961	50p	£2	£10	£30
1962	35p	£1	£5	£15
1963	25p	£1	£4	£10
1964	25p	£1	£4	£8
1965	25p	£1	£4	£8
1966	25p	£1	£4	£6
1968	25p	£1	£4	£6

SHILLINGS

DATE	F	VF	EF	UNC
1928	£1	£3	£10	£20
1928 Proof	—	—	—	£25
1930	£2	£15	£75	£300
1930 Proof	—	—	—	£650
1931	£2	£12	£75	£300
1933	£2	£12	£75	£300
1935	£2	£8	£35	£100
1937	£5	£45	£165	£750
1939	£1	£3	£15	£35
1939 Proof	—	—	—	£475
1940	£1	£3	£12	£30
1941	£2	£5	£16	£35
1942	£2	£3	£8	£25
1951	50p	£1	£5	£14
1951 Proof	—	—	—	£300
1954	50p	£1	£4	£12
1954 Proof	—	—	—	£350
1955	50p	£1	£5	£14
1959	50p	£1	£5	£18
1962	25p	£1	£2	£7
1963	25p	£1	£2	£5
1964	25p	£1	£2	£3
1966	25p	£1	£2	£3
1968	25p	£1	£2	£3

SIXPENCES

DATE	F	VF	EF	UNC
1928	50p	£1	£5	£20
1928 Proof	—	—	—	£25
1934	50p	£2	£15	£70
1935	75p	£2	£18	£85
1939	50p	£1	£5	£35
1939 Proof	—	—	—	£450
1940	50p	£1	£5	£35
1942	50p	£1	£8	£40
1945	£1	£5	£25	£75
1946	£2	£5	£50	£250
1947	£1	£2	£20	£55
1948	50p	£2	£12	£40
1949	50p	£1	£7	£30
1950	£1	£2	£20	£70
1952	50p	£1	£3	£15
1953	50p	£1	£3	£15
1953 Proof	—	—	—	£85
1955	50p	£1	£3	£15
1956	50p	£1	£2	£12
1956 Proof	—	—	—	£100
1958	£1	£2	£10	£45
1958 Proof	—	—	—	£250
1959	25p	50p	£2	£10
1960	25p	50p	£1	£10

DATE	F	VF	EF	UNC
1961	25p	50p	£1	£10
1962	£1	£5	£25	£50
1963	50p	£2	£5	£10
1964	50p	50p	£3	£6
1966	50p	50p	£3	£6
1967	50p	50p	£1	£4
1968	50p	50p	£1	£4
1969	£1	£2	£5	£10

THREEPENCES

	F	VF	EF	UNC
1928	£1	£2	£6	£15
1928 Proof	—	—	—	£20
1933	£2	£8	£50	£250
1934	50p	£1	£8	£45
1935	£1	£3	£20	£125
1939	£2	£6	£50	£250
1939 Proof	—	—	—	£775
1940	£1	£2	£10	£45
1942	25p	£1	£5	£35
1943	£1	£2	£10	£55
1946	25p	75p	£5	£30
1946 Proof	—	—	—	£175
1948	£1	£2	£20	£55
1949	25p	£1	£5	£25
1949 Proof	—	—	—	£165
1950	25p	£1	£3	£10
1950 Proof	—	—	—	£155
1953	25p	£1	£3	£10
1956	25p	£1	£2	£5
1961	25p	50p	£1	£3
1962	25p	50p	£1	£5
1963	25p	50p	£1	£5
1964	20p	50p	£1	£3
1965	20p	50p	£1	£2
1966	20p	50p	£1	£2
1967	20p	50p	£1	£2
1968	20p	40p	£1	£2

PENNIES

	F	VF	EF	UNC
1928	£1	£2	£8	£25
1928 Proof	—	—	—	£35
1931	£1	£3	£25	£85
1931 Proof	—	—	—	£750
1933	£1	£4	£40	£150
1935	50p	£1	£20	£45
1937	75p	£1	£25	£75
1937 Proof	—	—	—	£750
1938 2 known				Unique
1940	£5	£25	£100	—
1941	50p	£1	£8	£20
1942	25p	50p	£3	£12
1943	25p	£1	£4	£18
1946	25p	£1	£3	£12
1948	25p	£1	£3	£12
1949	25p	£1	£3	£12
1949 Proof	—	—	—	£275
1950	25p	75p	£5	£18
1952	25p	50p	£3	£6
1962	30p	75p	£3	£8
1962 Proof	—	—	—	£100
1963	10p	25p	£1	£4
1963 Proof	—	—	—	£75

DATE	F	VF	EF	UNC
1964	—	25p	£1	£4
1965	—	25p	50p	£3
1966	—	25p	50p	£3
1967	—	15p	25p	£2
1968	—	15p	25p	£2
1968 Proof	—	—	—	£155

HALFPENNIES

DATE	F	VF	EF	UNC
1928	£1	£2	£8	£20
1928 Proof	—	—	—	£20
1933	£3	£12	£50	£350
1935	£2	£5	£25	£115
1937	£1	£3	£10	£45
1939	£2	£5	£25	£125
1939 Proof	—	—	—	£575
1940	£1	£2	£35	£125
1941	50p	£1	£5	£20
1942	50p	£1	£5	£20
1943	50p	£1	£6	£22
1946	£1	£2	£15	£55
1949	50p	£1	£5	£20
1953	25p	£1	£2	£8
1953 Proof	—	—	—	£350
1964	—	25p	50p	£2
1965	—	30p	75p	£3
1966	—	25p	50p	£2
1967	—	25p	50p	£2

FARTHINGS

DATE	F	VF	EF	UNC
1928	£2	£3	£6	£10
1928 Proof	—	—	—	£20
1930	£2	£3	£8	£18
1931	£3	£5	£12	£25
1931 Proof	—	—	—	£575
1932	£3	£5	£15	£30
1933	£2	£3	£8	£18
1935	£3	£5	£12	£25
1936	£3	£5	£12	£25
1937	£2	£3	£8	£18
1939	£2	£3	£5	£9
1939 Proof	—	—	—	£400
1940	£3	£4	£7	£14
1941	£2	£3	£5	£9
1943	£2	£3	£5	£9
1944	£2	£3	£5	£9
1946	£2	£3	£5	£9
1949	£3	£5	£7	£14
1949 Proof	—	—	—	£300
1953	£2	£3	£4	£5
1953 Proof	—	—	—	£200
1959	£2	£3	£4	£5
1966	£2	£3	£4	£5

For the 1928–50 coppper issues it is worth noting that UNC means UNC with some lustre. BU examples with full lustre are extremely elusive and are worth much more than the quoted prices.

Decimal issues are not included in this publication but it should be noted that many dates are virtually impossible to find in uncirculated grade. An example is the 1986 set which was sold exclusively through souvenir shops and included the only specimens of the half pence for that year.

Official and semi-official commemorative *Medals*

It is probably a strong love of history, rather than the strict disciplines of coin collecting that make collectors turn to commemorative medals. The link between the two is intertwined, and it is to be hoped that collectors will be encouraged to venture into the wider world of medallions, encouraged by this brief guide, supplied by courtesy of Daniel Fearon, acknowledged expert and author of the *Catalogue of British Commemorative Medals*.

DATE	VF	EF
JAMES I		
1603 Coronation (possibly by C. Anthony), 29mm, Silver	£350	£850
QUEEN ANNE		
1603 Coronation,29mm, AR	£375	£850
CHARLES I		
1626 Coronation (by N. Briot), 30mm, Silver	£250	£650
1633 Scottish Coronation (by N. Briot), 28mm, Silver	£175	£350
1649 Memorial (by J. Roettier). Struck after the Restoration, 50mm, Bronze	£100	£250
CHARLES II		
1651 Scottish Coronation, in exile (from design by Sir J. Balfour), 32mm, Silver	£365	£875
CROMWELL		
1651 Lord Protector (by T. Simon), 38mm, Silver	£350	£800
— Cast examples	£85	£175
CHARLES II		
1661 Coronation (by T. Simon), 29mm		
— Gold	£800	£1500
— Silver	£100	£250
1685 Death (by N. Roettier), 39mm, Bronze	£75	£175

James I Coronation, 1603

Charles II Coronation, 1661

DATE	VF	EF

JAMES II
1685 Coronation (by J. Roettier), 34mm
- Gold £850 £1650
- Silver £185 £350

MARY
1685 Coronation (by J. Roettier), 34mm
- Gold £850 £1700
- Silver £150 £350

WILLIAM & MARY
1689 Coronation (by J. Roettier), 32mm
- Gold £750 £1600
- Silver £125 £225
1689 Coronation, "Perseus" (by G. Bower),
38mm, Gold £675 £1500

MARY
1694 Death (by N. Roettier), 39mm, Bronze £85 £200

WILLIAM III
1697 "The State of Britain" (by J. Croker), 69mm,
Silver £350 £850

Charles II Coronation, 1661

ANNE
1702 Accession, "Entirely English" (by J. Croker), 34mm
- Gold £650 £1500
- Silver £85 £175
1702 Coronation (by J. Croker), 36mm
- Gold £550 £1500
- Silver £85 £175
1707 Union with Scotland (by J. Croker, rev. by S. Bull), 34mm
- Gold £500 £850
- Silver £75 £150
1713 Peace of Utrecht (by J. Croker—issued in gold to Members
of Parliament), 34mm
- Gold £450 £1000
- Silver £75 £150

GEORGE I
1714 Coronation(by J. Croker), 34mm
- Gold £650 £1650
- Silver £85 £175
1727 Death (by J. Dassier), 31mm, Silver £75 £150

GEORGE II
1727Coronation (by J. Croker), 34mm
- Gold £600 £1600
- Silver £85 £175

QUEEN CAROLINE
1727 Coronation (by J. Croker), 34mm
- Gold £600 £1650
- Silver £85 £175
1732 The Royal Family (by J. Croker), 70mm
- Silver £155 £375
- Bronze... £85 £175

George III, Coronation, 1761

279

DATE	VF	EF

GEORGE III
1761 Coronation (by L. Natter), 34mm
— Gold £650 £1800
— Silver £125 £275
— Bronze £55 £150

QUEEN CHARLOTTE
1761 Coronation (by L. Natter), 34mm
— Gold £650 £1850
— Silver £125 £275
— Bronze £55 £125
1810 Golden Jubilee, "Frogmore", 48mm, Silver £80 £175
— Bronze £55 £125

GEORGE IV
1821 Coronation (by B. Pistrucci), 35mm
— Gold £400 £750
— Silver £55 £125
— Bronze £40 £75

George IV Coronation, 1841

WILLIAM IV
1831 Coronation (by W. Wyon; rev.shows
  Queen Adelaide), 33mm
— Gold £375 £750
— Silver £55 £120
— Bronze £45 £85

QUEEN VICTORIA
1838 Coronation (by B. Pistrucci), 37mm
— Gold £385 £850
— Silver £65 £150
— Bronze £35 £85

Queen Victoria Coronation, 1838

Queen Victoria Diamond Jubilee 1897

DATE	VF	EF
1887 Golden Jubilee (by J. E. Boehm, rev. by Lord Leighton)		
— Gold, 58mm	£850	£1250
— Silver, 78mm	£85	£200
— Bronze, 78mm	£45	£120
1897 Diamond Jubilee (by T. Brock),		
— Gold, 56mm	£750	£1000
— Silver, 56mm	£45	£85
— Bronze, 56mm	£20	£35
— Gold, 21mm	£125	£165
— Silver, 21mm	£20	£35

EDWARD VII

1902 Coronation (August 9) (by G. W. de Saulles)

	VF	EF
— Gold, 56mm	£750	£1000
— Silver, 56mm	£35	£75
— Bronze, 56mm	£20	£35
— Gold, 31mm	£135	£185
— Silver, 31mm	£20	£35

Some rare examples of the official medal show the date as June 26, the original date set for the Coronation which was postponed because the King developed appendicitis.

GEORGE V

1911 Coronation (by B. Mackennal)

George V Silver Jubilee, 1937

	VF	EF
— Gold, 51mm	£750	£1000
— Silver, 51mm	£30	£75
— Bronze, 51mm	£15	£30
— Gold, 31mm	£145	£185
— Silver, 31mm	£15	£30

1935 Silver Jubilee (by P. Metcalfe)

	VF	EF
— Gold, 58mm	£750	£1000
— Silver, 58mm	£25	£65
— Gold, 32mm	£125	£175
— Silver, 32mm	£20	£35

PRINCE EDWARD

1911 Investiture as Prince of Wales (by W. Goscombe John)

	VF	EF
— Gold, 31mm	£275	£500
— Silver, 31mm	£35	£55

EDWARD VIII

1936 Abdication (by L. E. Pinches), 35mm

	VF	EF
— Gold	£375	£750
— Silver	£35	£65
— Bronze	£15	£35

GEORGE VI

1937 Coronation (by P. Metcalfe)

	VF	EF
— Gold, 58mm	£850	£1250
— Silver, 58mm	£35	£75
— Gold, 32mm	£145	£185
— Silver, 32mm	£15	£25
— Bronze, 32mm	£5	£12

Edward, Prince of Wales, 1911

DATE	VF	EF

ELIZABETH II
1953 Coronation (by Spink & Son)

	VF	EF
— Gold, 57mm	£750	£950
— Silver, 57mm	£25	£60
— Bronze, 57mm	£15	£25
— Gold, 32mm	£175	£250
— Silver, 32mm	£15	£25
— Bronze, 32mm	£10	£15

1977 Silver Jubilee (by A. Machin)

	VF	EF
— Silver, 57mm	—	£55
— Silver, 44mm	—	£35

The gold medals are priced for 18ct—they can also be found as 22ct and 9ct, and prices should be adjusted accordingly.

PRINCE CHARLES
1969 Investiture as Prince of Wales (by M. Rizello)

	EF
— Silver, 57mm	£50
— Bronze gilt, 57mm	£35
— Silver, 45mm	£35
— Gold, 32mm	£175
— Silver, 32mm	£35
— Bronze, 32mm	£15

QUEEN ELIZABETH THE QUEEN MOTHER
1980 80th Birthday (by L. Durbin)

Edward VIII Abdication, 1936

	EF
— Silver, 57mm	£50
— Silver, 38mm	£35
— Bronze, 38mm	£20

N.B.—Official Medals usually command a premium when still in their original cases of issue.

COIN
grading

CONDITION is the secret to the value of virtually anything, whether it be antiques, jewellery, horses or second-hand cars—and coins are *certainly* no exception. When collecting coins it is vital to understand the recognised standard British system of grading, i.e. accurately assessing a coin's condition or state of wear. Grading is an art which can only be learned by experience and so often it remains one person's opinion against another's, therefore it is important for the beginner or inexperienced collector to seek assistance from a reputable dealer or knowledgeable numismatist when making major purchases.

The standard grades as used in the Price Guide are as follows:

UNC — **Uncirculated**
A coin that has never been in circulation, although it may show signs of contact with other coins during the minting process.

EF — **Extremely Fine**
A coin in this grade may appear uncirculated to the naked eye but on closer examination will show signs of minor friction on the highest surface.

VF — **Very Fine**
A coin that has had very little use, but shows signs of wear on the high surfaces.

F — **Fine**
A coin that has been in circulation and shows general signs of wear, but with all legends and date clearly visible.

Other grades used in the normal grading system are:

BU — **Brilliant Uncirculated**
As the name implies, a coin retaining its mint lustre.

Fair — A coin extensively worn but still quite recognisable and legends readable.

Poor — A coin very worn and only just recognisable.

Other abbreviations used in the Price Guide are:

Obv — **Obverse**

Rev — **Reverse**

Other abbreviations, mintmarks, etc. can be identified under the appropriate section of this Yearbook.

Why not
Bank notes?

Millions of pounds worth of banknotes exchange hands every day, and yet most of us pay little attention to the coloured pieces of paper we are about to part with. To a collector however, they are to be studied and enjoyed. Sometimes they can be worth many times their face value. A historian, with careful study, can discover much about a county's history from prosperity through war, siege and its inflationary periods. Banknotes have also been used for spreading propaganda. The Gulf war is a recent example. Many banknotes still survive long after the country of issue has disappeared.

So how do you start and where can you get advice on forming a collection? The answers, together with a few interesting facts about paper money can be found here. But remember, this feature can only scratch the surface of this fascinating subject; its aim is to inspire and surprise you.

Paper money is not a modern phenomenon. Its origins can be found in China during the second century BC. Emperor Wu (140–86BC), frustrated with the time taken for heavily laden wagons of copper coins to complete their journey, used deerhide as a kind of tax money. Skins from white stags were cut into pieces each a foot square. The borders were decorated with designs of water plants and each skin was given a value of 40,000 copper coins. Around 105 AD paper, made from broken down plant fibres and old cotton textiles was invented by a Chinese minister of Agriculture. However, true paper money didn't appear in China until the Tang Dynasty somewhere between 650–800 AD. The earliest Chinese notes collectors are likely to come across are from the Ming Dynasty. Made from mulberry bark paper, these notes measure 230mm x 330mm. Although over six hundred years old, these notes can be bought for around £500. An interesting factor is that Asia was using paper money while Britain and Europe were still in the dark ages.

The first European bank to be established was in Stockholm, Sweden in July 1661. Unfortunately its banknotes were not government backed and the enterprise was forced to close within a few years.

On July 27, 1694 the Bank of England was founded by Royal Charter; the first European bank to survive to the present day. From its temporary offices at the Mercers' Hall, Cheapside, London, the Bank set to work producing its first issues. These have become known as running cash notes. At first

Notgeld, issued in Germany during the period of high inflation after World War I. The appearance of these highly colourful notes greatly stimulated the hobby of banknote collecting.

A Confederate States of America $100 note from the Montgomery issue, 1861. At the end of the American Civil War these notes had no face value but nevertheless remain interesting to collectors today.

they were written out entirely by hand on paper bought by the Bank's staff from local stationers. Forgery however, soon put a stop to this practice. Each note was made out to the bearer for the amount they had on deposit. Although there was no guarantee of conversion into gold, the notes could be cashed in for part of their original value. This led to endorsements appearing on the notes stating the date and amount paid off. The notes would change hands for payment of goods or services just as our modern banknotes do today.

During the last century many private banks were set up in towns and cities throughout Britain. The notes they issued were usually well printed and many carry a motif or vignette identifying with the place of issue. For example coats of arms often appear, so too do famous buildings. Others simply have embellished initials. It is these simple features that help to make these provincial notes popular with collectors today, coupled with the interest of owning a banknote actually issued in your town! Unfortunately most of these banks went into liquidation and many investors lost their money—it is quite common to find provincial notes with the bankruptcy court stamp or other marks on the reverse. Notes are also encountered which have been rejoined with paper strips as it was often the practice to cut notes in half—sending half by one means and the second portion at a later date, to be joined with its counterpart before it could be redeemed. This lessened the risk of the note being stolen or lost in transit.

The expression "Safe as the Bank of England" is held in high regard today. In reality the Bank has almost collapsed on at least two occasions, and in 1696 it had its first major crisis. An act passed by parliament ordered the recoinage of all metallic currency. As the notes circulated by the Bank had status of legal tender and therefore not legally convertible into gold, people naturally had more confidence in metal currency. Accounts submitted by the Bank to parliament in December of that year

showed £764,000 worth of notes in circulation. These were backed by just under £36,000 worth of gold.

The second emergency for the Bank came in 1720 after the "bursting" of the South Sea Bubble. Holding the monopoly of trade with South America, the South Sea Company offered to take on the national debt in return for further concessions. Company shares soared but when the collapse came it was found that government ministers were deeply involved and a political crisis followed. Bankruptcy was rife and people naturally wished to obtain their money. The queue of those wanting to withdraw gold from the Bank of England stretched down Ludgate Hill into Fleet Street. The Bank managed to save the situation by employing it own staff to join the queue posing as

A Mafeking siege note emergency issue from the Boer War. Highly rare and very collectable.

customers. Each would withdraw large quantities of money and then take it round to the back of the Bank where is was redeposited. This meant the tills were kept opened until the public alarm subsided.

One modern day crisis for the Bank came during World War II when Hitler's Germany decided to forge the large white Bank of England notes in current circulation at the time, in huge quantities. This operation called for around 150 prisoners, each hand picked for their skills in engraving, printing and paper making. The original idea was to drop the undetectable forgeries on the British Isles and neutral nations in an effort to destroy Britain's economy but the plan never came to fruition, although millions of pounds in face value were produced. Most of the notes were dumped into Lake Toplitz by the fleeing German forces fearing Allied retribution. However, many have since been recovered and often appear on the market today. When encountering forgeries, collectors are in a difficult position. If they hold a note, knowing it to be a forgery, they are breaking the law. If they have the note checked, they run the risk of having it confiscated!

An example of a "skit note" (a piece of paper masquerading as a banknote). George Cruikshank's famous "Bank Restriction Note" produced as a protest against counterfeiting laws.

World War II notes. From top: Japanese Invasion Money (JIM money) intended for use by the Japanese in their occupied territories; Occupation notes issued in Guernsey during the German occupation.

A banknote need not be old to be worth collecting. Many interesting notes have been issued throughout the world each with their own story to tell. In 1954 the Canadian Central Bank issued notes in which the portrait of the Queen had what appeared to be the hidden face of the Devil in the folds of her hair. The public refused to handle them and the notes were withdrawn. To this day it is not known whether the engraving was done intentionally or not.

Most countries suffer from inflation but in 1923, Germany saw one of the biggest inflationary periods of modern times. On November 1 of that year the average wage packet was 28 million marks, equivalent to 1.3 million pounds at the 1913 exchange rate. This huge sum would not have been enough to buy a newspaper, which would have cost around 3,000 million marks. This period left a legacy of hundreds of different notes for the collector today.

Unlike coins, collecting of paper money is still in its infancy. It is still possible to obtain notes from many different countries for a modest outlay. Some dealers sell starter packs that include 50 uncirculated notes from 50 different counties, all for under £30. One reason why some notes are so cheap is that many countries devalue their currency. When a new set of notes are issued, the old set after a period, become worthless. Dealers can acquire large quantities of these notes for less than the original face value.

New collectors will find many books on the subject of paper money. A good introduction to the hobby of notaphily is *The Banknote Yearbook*. Published yearly by Token Publishing Ltd *The Banknote Yearbook* includes up to date values for notes of England, Scotland, Ireland, the Channel Islands and the Isle of Man. The useful volume also features hints and tips for the collector, a review of the current market trends, a world note identifier and much more. In short it is the essential guide to the hobby of banknote collecting. (*Call 01404 44166 for more details.*)

COIN NEWS is also a useful way of keeping in touch with the every day events of the banknote world. There is a dedicated banknote section in the magazine every month often giving vital pieces of information, for example the latest auction prices realised, forthcoming events and fairs and there are also informative articles designed to be of appeal to experienced collectors as well as newcomers.

Numismatists . . .
have you written anything lately?

Do you think it would interest others?
Would you like to see it in print?
Don't know where to start?

Then look no further

TOKEN PUBLISHING LTD has a long history of publishing books and articles on coins, medals and banknotes and are always pleased to discuss projected ideas with authors. For your next move contact Managing Editor John Mussell—he will be happy to talk it over...who knows you might become a "best seller"—COIN YEARBOOK is!

TOKEN PUBLISHING LTD

**Orchard House, Duchy Road, Heathpark, Honiton, Devon EX14 1YD
Telephone: 01404 46972
email: editor@tokenpublishing.com**

Directory section

ON the following pages will be found the most useful names and addresses needed by the coin collector.

At the time of going to press with this edition of the YEARBOOK the information is correct, as far as we have been able to ascertain. However, people move and establishments change, so it is always advisable to make contact with the person or organisation listed before travelling any distance, to ensure that the journey is not wasted.

Should any of the information in this section not be correct we would very much appreciate being advised in good time for the preparation of the next edition of the COIN YEARBOOK.

Dealers who display this symbol are Members of the

BRITISH NUMISMATIC TRADE ASSOCIATION

The primary purpose of the Association is to promote and safeguard the highest standards of professionalism in dealings between its Members and the public. In official consultations it is the recognised representative of commercial numismatics in Britain.

For free a Membership Directory please send a stamped addressed envelope to:

General Secretary, BNTA
PO Box 2, Rye, East Sussex TN31 7WE
Tel/Fax: 01797 229988

The BNTA will be organising the following events:

COINEX 2004 8/9 October
at The London Marriott Hotel, Grosvenor Square, W1
COINEX 2005 30 September/01 October
at the Platinum Suite, ExCel, London Docklands, E16 1XL

The BNTA is a member of the International Numismatic Commission.

BNTA MEMBERSHIPS IN COUNTY ORDER

(Those members with a retail premises are indicated with an*)

LONDON AREA
*A.H. Baldwin & Sons Ltd.
Arsantiqva Ltd
ATS Bullion Ltd
Beaver Coin Room
*Philip Cohen Numismatics
Andre de Clermont
Michael Dickinson
*Dix Noonan Webb
Christopher Eimer
Glendining's
Harrow Coin & Stamp Centre
*Knightsbridge Coins
Lubbock & Son Ltd.
C.J. Martin (Coins) Ltd.
Morton & Eden Ltd.
*Colin Narbeth & Son Ltd.
Noble Investments
*Pavlos S Pavlou
*Seaby Coins/C.N.G. Inc.
Simmons Gallery
*Spink & Son Ltd.
Surena Ancient Art & Numismatic
AVON
Saltford Coins
BERKSHIRE
Frank Milward
CAMBRIDGESHIRE
*Lockdale Coins Ltd
DORSET
*Dorset Coin Co. Ltd.
ESSEX
E J Brooks
HAMPSHIRE
*SPM Jewellers
Studio Coins
*Victory Coins
West Essex Coin Investments
HERTFORDSHIRE
K B Coins
David Miller
KENT
C.J. Denton (Coins of Ireland)
London Coins
*Peter Morris
LANCASHIRE
*B. J. Dawson (Coins)
*Colin de Rouffignac

*Peter Ireland Ltd.
James Murphy
*R & L Coins
LINCOLNSHIRE
Grantham Coins
NORFOLK
*Roderick Richardson
Chris Rudd
NORTHAMPTONSHIRE
*Giuseppe Miceli
NORTHUMBERLAND
*Corbitt Stamps Ltd.
OXFORDSHIRE
Simon R. Porter
SHROPSHIRE
*Collectors Gallery
SUFFOLK
*Lockdale Coins Ltd
Schwer Coins
SURREY
British Notes
The Duncannon Partnership
KMCC Ltd
Graeme & Linda Monk
Mark Rasmussen Numismatist
Time Line Originals
Nigel Tooley Ltd
SUSSEX
*Brighton Coin Co.
WEST MIDLANDS
*Birmingham Coins
*Format of Birmingham Ltd.
Mint Coins Ltd
WARWICKSHIRE
*Peter Viola
*Warwick & Warwick Ltd
WORCESTERSHIRE
J. Whitmore
YORKSHIRE
Airedale Coins
Paul Clayton
Paul Davies Ltd.
*J. Smith
WALES
Lloyd Bennett
*Cardiff Coins & Medals
*North Wales Coins Ltd.
Colin Rumney

Museums and Libraries

Listed below are the Museums and Libraries in the UK which have coins or items of numismatic interest on display or available to the general public.

A

Anthropological Museum, University of Aberdeen, Broad Street, **Aberdeen,** AB9 1AS (01224 272014).

Curtis Museum (1855), High Street, **Alton,** Hants (01420 2802). *General collection of British coins.*

Ashburton Museum, 1 West Street, **Ashburton,** Devon. *Ancient British and Roman antiquities including local coin finds.*

Ashwell Village Museum (1930), Swan Street, **Ashwell,** Baldock, Herts. *Roman coins from local finds, local trade tokens, Anglo-Gallic coins and jetons.*

Buckinghamshire County Museum (1862), Church Street, **Aylesbury,** Bucks (01296 88849). *Roman and medieval English coins found locally, 17th/18th century Buckinghamshire tokens, commemorative medals.*

B

Public Library and Museum (1948), Marlborough Road, **Banbury,** Oxon (01295 259855). *Wrexlin Hoard of Roman coins.*

Museum of North Devon (1931), The Square, **Barnstaple,** EX32 8LN (01271 46747). *General coin and medal collection, including local finds. Medals of the Royal Devonshire Yeomanry.*

Roman Baths Museum, Pump Room, **Bath,** Avon (01225 461111 ext 2785). *Comprehensive collection of Roman coins from local finds.*

Bagshaw Museum and Art Gallery (1911), Wilton Park, **Batley,** West Yorkshire (01924 472514). *Roman, Scottish, Irish, English hammered, British and foreign coins, local traders' tokens, political medalets, campaign medals and decorations.*

Bedford Museum (1961), Castle Lane, **Bedford** (01234 353323). *Collections of the Bedford Library and Scientific Institute, the Beds Archaeological Society and Bedford Modern School (Pritchard Memorial) Museum.*

Ulster Museum (1928), Botanic Gardens, **Belfast** BT9 5AB (01232 381251). *Irish, English and British coins and commemorative medals.*

Berwick Borough Museum (1867), The Clock Block, Berwick Barracks, Ravensdowne, **Berwick.** TD15 1DQ (01289 330044). *Roman, Scottish and medieval coins.*

Public Library, Art Gallery and Museum (1910), Champney Road, **Beverley,** Humberside (01482 882255). *Beverley trade tokens, Roman, English, British and foreign coins.*

Bignor Roman Villa (1811), **Bignor,** nr Pulborough, West Sussex (017987 202). *Roman coins found locally.*

City Museum and Art Gallery (1861), Chamberlain Square, **Birmingham** B3 3DH (0121 235 2834). *Coins, medals and tokens, with special emphasis on the products of the Soho, Heaton, Birmingham and Watt mints.*

Blackburn Museum, Museum Street, **Blackburn,** Lancs (01254 667130). *Incorporates the Hart (5,000 Greek, Roman and early English) and Hornby (500 English coins) collections, as well as the museum's own collection of British and Commonwealth coins.*

Museum Collection, Town Hall, **Bognor Regis,** West Sussex. *Roman, English and British coins and trade tokens.*

Museum and Art Gallery,(1893), Civic Centre, **Bolton,** Lancashire (01204 22311 ext 2191). *General collection of about 3000 British and foreign coins, and over 500 British medals. Numismatic library.*

Art Gallery and Museum, Central Library, Oriel Road, **Bootle,** Lancs. *Greek, Roman, English, British and some foreign coins, local trade tokens.*

Roman Town and Museum (1949) Main Street, **Boroughbridge,** N. Yorks. YO2 3PH (01423 322768). *Roman coins.*

The Museum (1929), The Guildhall, **Boston,** Lincs (01205 365954). *Small collection of English coins.*

Natural Science Society Museum (1903), 39 Christchurch Road, **Bournemouth,** Dorset (01202 553525). *Greek, Roman and English hammered coins (including the Hengistbury Hoard), local trade tokens.*

Bolling Hall Museum (1915), Bolling Hall Road, **Bradford,** West Yorkshire BD4 7LP (01274 723057). *Some 2,000 coins and tokens, mostly 18th–20th centuries.*

Cartwright Hall Museum and Art Gallery (1904), Lister Park, **Bradford,** West Yorkshire BD9 4NS (01274 493313). *Roman coins found locally.*

Museum and Art Gallery (1932), South Street, **Bridport,** Dorset (01308 22116). *Roman coins, mainly from excavations at Claudian Fort.*

The City Museum (1820), Queen's Road, **Bristol** BS8 1RL (0117 9 27256). *Ancient British, Roman (mainly from local hoards), English hammered coins, especially from the Bristol mint, and several hundred local trade tokens.*

District Library and Museum (1891), Terrace Road, **Buxton,** Derbyshire SK17 6DU (01298 24658). *English and British coins, tokens and commemorative medals. Numismatic library.*

C

Segontium Museum (1928), Beddgelert Road, **Caernarfon,** Gwynedd (01286 675625) *Roman coins and artifacts excavated from the fort.*

Fitzwilliam Museum (1816), Department of Coins and Medals, Trumpington Street, **Cambridge** (01223 332900). *Ancient, English, medieval European, oriental coins, medals, plaques, seals and cameos.*

National Museum & Galleries of Wales, Cathays Park, **Cardiff** (029 20397951). *Greek, Celtic, Roman and British coins and tokens with the emphasis on Welsh interest. Also military, civilian and commemorative medals.*

Guildhall Museum (1979), Greenmarket, **Carlisle,** Cumbria (01228 819925). *General collection of coins and medals.*

Tullie House (1877), Castle Street, **Carlisle,** Cumbria (01228 34781). *Roman, medieval and later coins from local finds, including medieval counterfeiter's coin-moulds.*

Gough's Caves Museum (1934), The Cliffs, **Cheddar,** Somerset (01934 343). *Roman coins.*

Chelmsford and Essex Museum (1835), Oaklands Park, Moulsham Street, **Chelmsford,** Essex CM2 9AQ (01245 615100). *Ancient British, Roman, medieval and later coins mainly from local finds, local medals.*

Town Gate Museum (1949), **Chepstow,** Gwent. *Local coins and trade tokens.*

Grosvenor Museum (1886), Grosvenor Street, **Chester** (01244 21616). *Roman coins from the fortress site, Anglo-Saxon, English medieval and post-medieval coins of the Chester and Rhuddlan mints, trade tokens of Chester and Cheshire, English and British milled coins.*

Public Library (1879), Corporation Street, **Chesterfield,** Derbyshire (01246 2047). *Roman coins from local finds, Derbyshire trade tokens, medals, seals and railway passes. Numismatic library. Numismatic library and publications.*

Red House Museum (1919), Quay Road, **Christchurch,** Dorset (01202 482860). *Coins of archaeological significance from Hampshire and Dorset, notably the South Hants Hoard, ancient British, Armorican, Gallo-Belgic, Celtic and Roman coins, local trade tokens and medals.*

Corinium Museum (1856), Park Street, **Cirencester,** Glos (01285 655611). *Roman coins from archaeological excavations.*

Colchester and Essex Museum (1860), The Castle, **Colchester,** Essex (01206 712931 / 2). *Ancient British and Roman coins from local finds, medieval coins (especially the Colchester Hoard), later English coins and Essex trade tokens, commemorative medals.*

D

Public Library, Museum and Art Gallery (1921), Crown Street, **Darlington,** Co Durham (01325 463795). *General collection of coins, medals and tokens.*

Borough Museum (1908), Central Park, **Dartford,** Kent (01322 343555). *Roman, medieval and later English hammered coins, trade tokens and commemorative medals.*

Dartmouth Museum (1953), The Butterknowle, **Dartmouth,** Devon (01803 832923). *Coins and medals of a historical and maritime nature.*

Museum and Art Gallery (1878), The Strand, **Derby** (01332 255586). *Roman coins, English silver and copper regal coins, Derbyshire tradesmen's tokens, British campaign medals and decorations of the Derbyshire Yeomanry and the 9/12 Royal Lancers.*

Museum and Art Gallery (1909), Chequer Road, **Doncaster,** South Yorkshire (01302 734293). *General collection of English and foreign silver and bronze coins. Representative collection of Roman imperial silver and bronze coins, including a number from local hoards. English trade tokens, principally of local issues, medals.*

Dorset County Museum(1846), **Dorchester,** Dorset (01305 262735). *British, Roman, medieval and later coins of local interest.*

Central Museum (1884), Central Library, St James's Road, **Dudley,** West Midlands (01384 453576). *Small general collection of coins, medals and tokens.*

Burgh Museum (1835), The Observatory, Corberry Hill, **Dumfries** (01387 53374). *Greek, Roman, Anglo-Saxon, medieval English and Scottish coins, especially from local hoards. Numismatic library.*

Dundee Art Galleries and Museums (1873). Albert Square, **Dundee** DD1 1DA (01382 23141). *Coins and medals of local interest.*

The Cathedral Treasury (995 AD), The College, **Durham** (0191-384 4854). *Greek and Roman coins bequeathed by Canon Sir George Wheeler (1724), general collection of medals from the Renaissance to modern times, medieval English coins, especially those struck at the Durham ecclesiastical mint.*

Durham Heritage Centre, St Mary le Bow, North Bailey, **Durham** (0191-384 2214). *Roman, medieval and later coins, mainly from local finds.*

E

Royal Museum of Scotland (1781), Queen Street, **Edinburgh** EH1 (0131 225 7534). *Roman, Anglo-Saxon, English and Scottish coins, trade tokens, commemorative medals and communion tokens. Numismatic library. Publications.*

Royal Albert Memorial Museum (1868), Queen St, **Exeter** EX4 3RX (01392 265858). *Roman and medieval. Coins of the Exeter Mint.*

G

Hunterian Museum (1807), Glasgow University, University Avenue, **Glasgow** G12 8QQ (041 339 8855). *Greek, Roman, Byzantine, Scottish, English and Irish coins, Papal and other European medals, Indian and Oriental coins, trade and communion tokens.*

Art Gallery and Museum (1888), Kelvingrove, **Glasgow** G3 (0141 357 3929). *General collection of coins, trade tokens, communion tokens, commemorative and military medals.*

Museum of Transport (1974), Kelvin Hall, Bunhouse Road, **Glasgow** G3 (0141 357 3929). *Transport tokens and passes, commemorative medals, badges and insignia of railway companies and shipping lines.*

City Museum and Art Gallery (1859), Brunswick Road, **Gloucester** (01452 524131). *Ancient British, Roman, Anglo-Saxon (from local finds), early medieval (from local mints), Gloucestershire trade tokens.*

Guernsey Museum and Art Gallery, St Peter Port, **Guernsey** (01481 726518). *Armorican, Roman, medieval and later coins, including the coins, medals, tokens and paper money of Guernsey.*

Guildford Museum (1898), Castle Arch, **Guildford,** Surrey GU1 3SX (01483 444750). *Roman and medieval coins and later medals.*

H

Gray Museum and Art Gallery, Clarence Road, **Hartlepool,** Cleveland (01429 268916). *General collection, including coins from local finds.*

Public Museum and Art Gallery (1890), John's Place, Cambridge Road, **Hastings,** East Sussex (01424 721952). *General collection of English and British coins, collection of Anglo-Saxon coins from Sussex mints.*

City Museum (1874), Broad Street, **Hereford** (01432 268121 ext 207). *Coins from the Hereford mint and local finds, Herefordshire trade tokens, general collection of later coins and medals.*

Hertford Museum (1902), 18 Bull Plain, **Hertford** (01992 582686). *British, Roman, medieval and later English coins and medals.*

Honiton and Allhallows Public Museum (1946), High Street, **Honiton,** Devon (01404 44966). *Small general collection, including coins from local finds.*

Museum and Art Gallery (1891), 19 New Church Road, **Hove,** East Sussex (01273 779410). *English coins, Sussex trade tokens and hop tallies, campaign medals, orders and decorations, commemorative medals.*

Tolson Memorial Museum (1920), Ravensknowle Park, **Huddersfield,** West Yorkshire (01484 541455). *Representative collection of British coins and tokens, Roman and medieval coins, mainly from local finds.*

Hull and East Riding Museum (1928), 36 High Street, **Hull** (01482 593902). *Celtic, Roman and medieval coins and artifacts from local finds. Some later coins including tradesmen's tokens.*

I

The Manx Museum, Douglas, **Isle of Man** (01624 675522). *Roman, Celtic, Hiberno-Norse, Viking, medieval English and Scottish coins, mainly from local finds, Manx traders' tokens from the 17th to 19th centuries, Manx coins from 1709 to the present day.*

J

Jersey Museum, Weighbridge, St Helier, **Jersey** (01534 30511). *Armorican, Gallo-Belgic, Roman, medieval English and French coins, coins, paper money and tokens of Jersey.*

K

Dick Institute Museum and Art Gallery (1893), Elmbank Avenue, **Kilmarnock,** Ayrshire (01563 26401). *General collection of coins and medals, and the Hunter-Selkirk collection of communion tokens.*

L

City Museum (1923), Old Town Hall, Market Square, **Lancaster** (01524 64637). *Roman, Anglo-Saxon, medieval English coins, provincial trade tokens, medals of the King's Own Royal Lancashire Regiment.*

City Museum (1820), Municipal Buildings, The Headrow, **Leeds,** West Yorkshire (01532 478279). *Greek, Roman, Anglo-Saxon, English medieval, Scottish, Irish, British, Commonwealth and foreign coins. Several Roman and Saxon hoards. The Backhouse collection of Yorkshire banknotes, the Thornton collection of Yorkshire tokens, British and foreign commemorative medals.*

Leicester Museum and Art Gallery (1849), New Walk, **Leicester** (01533 554100). *Roman, medieval and later coins, mainly from local finds, tokens, commemorative medals, campaign medals and decorations.*

Pennington Hall Museum and Art Gallery, **Leigh,** Lancashire. *General collection of Roman, English and British coins and medals.*

Museum and Art Gallery (1914), Broadway, **Letchworth,** Herts (01462 685647). *Ancient British coins minted at Camulodunum, Roman, medieval and English coins, Hertfordshire trade tokens, commemorative and campaign medals.*

City Library, Art Gallery and Museum (1859), Bird Street, **Lichfield,** Staffs (01543 2177). *Roman, medieval and later English coins, Staffordshire trade tokens and commemorative medals.*

Liverpool Museum (1851), William Brown Street, **Liverpool** L3 8EN (0151 207 0001). *General collection of Roman, medieval and later British coins, tokens.*

Bank of England Museum, Threadneedle Street, **London** EC2 (020-7601 5545). *Exhibits relating to gold bullion, coins, tokens and medals, the design and manufacture of banknotes, and a comprehensive collection of bank notes dating from the 17th century to the present day.*

British Museum (1752), HSBC Coin Gallery, Great Russell Street, **London** WC1 (020-7636 1555). *Almost a million coins, medals, tokens and badges of all period from Lydia, 7th century BC to the present time. Extensive library of books and periodicals.*

British Numismatic Society (1903), Warburg Institute, Woburn Square, **London** WC1. *Library containing over 5,000 volumes, including sale catalogues, periodicals and pamphlets. Open to members only.*

Cuming Museum (1906), Walworth Road, **London** SE17 (020-7703 3324/5529). *Some 8,000 items, including Greek, Roman, medieval English and modern British coins, English tokens and commemorative medals.*

Gunnersbury Park Museum (1927), Acton, **London** W3. *Ancient British, Greek, Roman, medieval English, British and some foreign coins, tradesmen's tokens and commemorative medals, including local finds. Small numismatic library.*

Horniman Museum and Library (1890), London Road, Forest Hill, **London** SE23 (020-7699 2339). *General collection, primitive currency, some tokens.*

Imperial War Museum, Lambeth Road, **London** SE1 6HZ (020-7416 5000). *Emergency coinage of two world wars, occupation and invasion money, extensive collection of German Notgeld, commemorative, propaganda and military medals, badges and insignia.*

Sir John Soane's Museum (1833), 13 Lincoln's Inn Fields, **London** WC2 (020-7405 2107). *Napoleonic medals and medallic series of the late 18th and early 19th centuries.*

National Maritime Museum, Romney Road, Greenwich, **London** SE10 (020-8858 4422). *Commemorative medals with a nautical or maritime theme, naval medals and decorations.*

Victoria and Albert Museum (1852), South Kensington, **London** SW7 (020-7938 8441). *Byzantine gold and medieval Hispano-Mauresque coins (Department of Metalwork), large collection of Renaissance and later medals (Department of Architecture and Sculpture). Library of numismatic books.*

Ludlow Museum (1833). The Assembly Rooms. Castle Square, **Ludlow** (01584 873857). *Roman and medieval coins from local finds.*

Luton Museum and Art Gallery (1927), Wardown Park, **Luton**, Beds (01582 36941). *Coins, tokens and medals.*

M

Museum and Art Gallery (1858), **Maidstone**, Kent (01622 754497). *Ancient British, Roman, Anglo-Saxon and medieval coins found in Kent, modern British coins, Kent trade tokens, banknotes, hop tallies and tokens, primitive currency, collections of Kent Numismatic Society.*

The Manchester Museum (1868), The University, **Manchester** M13 (0161-275 2634). *Very fine collections of Greek and Roman coins, comprehensive collections of English, European and Oriental coins, over 30,000 in all.*

Margate Museum (1923), The Old Town Hall, Market Place, **Margate**, Kent (01843 225511 ext 2520). *Small collection of coins, including Roman from local finds.*

Montrose Museum and Art Gallery (1836). Panmure Place, **Montrose**, Angus DD10 8HE (01674 73232). *Scottish and British coins.*

N

Newark-on-Trent Museum (1912), Appleton Gate, **Newark**, Notts (01636 702358). *Siege pieces, trade tokens and coins from local finds and hoards.*

Newbury District Museum, The Wharf, **Newbury**, Berkshire (01635 30511). *Ancient British, Roman and medieval coins and artifacts, later coins and tokens.*

The Greek Museum, Percy Building, **Newcastle-upon-Tyne** (0191 2226000 ext 7966). *Ancient coins.*

O

Heberden Coin Room, Ashmolean Museum (1683), **Oxford** (01865 278000). *Extensive collections of all periods, notably Greek, Roman, English and Oriental coins, Renaissance portrait and later medals, tokens and paper money. Large library. Numerous publications.*

P

Peterborough Museum (1881), Priestgate, **Peterborough**, Cambs (01733 340 3329). *Roman (mainly from local hoards and finds), Anglo-Saxon, medieval English, British and modern European coins, English and British commemorative medals and tokens.*

City Museum and Art Gallery (1897), Drake Circus, **Plymouth**, Devon (01752 264878). *General collections of British and Commonwealth coins and tokens, Devon trade tokens and Plymouth tradesmen's checks, Ancient British and Roman coins from local sites.*

Waterfront Museum, 4 High Street, **Poole**, Dorset (01202 683138). *General collection of British and foreign coins, medals and tokens (view by appointment).*

City Museum (1972), Museum Road, Old **Portsmouth** PO1 (023 80827261). *Roman, medieval and later coins mainly from local finds and archaeological excavation, British coins, trade tokens of Hampshire, commemorative medals.*

Harris Museum and Art Gallery (1893), Market Square, **Preston**, Lancashire (01772 58248). *English and British coins, tokens and medals.*

R

The Museum of Reading (1883), Blagrave Street, **Reading**, Berks (0118 939 9800). *British, Roman and medieval English coins, many from local finds, tradesmen's tokens and commemorative medals.*

Rochdale Museum (1905), Sparrow Hill, **Rochdale**, Lancs (01706 41085). *Roman and medieval coins from local finds, Rochdale trade tokens, miscellaneous British and foreign coins and medals.*

Municipal Museum and Art Gallery (1893), Clifton Park, **Rotherham** (01709 382121). *Roman coins from Templeborough Forts, medieval English coins from local hoards and a general collection of British coins.*

S

Saffron Walden Museum (1832) (1939), Museum Street, **Saffron** Walden, Essex (01799 522494). *Ancient British, Roman, medieval and later coins, mainly from local finds and archaeological excavation, trade tokens and commemorative medals.*

Verulamium Museum, St Michael's, **St Albans,** Herts (01727 819339). *Coins and artifacts excavated from the Roman town.*

Salisbury and South Wiltshire Museum (1861), The Cathedral Close, **Salisbury,** Wilts (01722 332151). *Collection of coins minted or found locally, including finds of Iron Age, Roman, Saxon and medieval coins, as well as 18th and 19th century tradesmen's tokens.*

Richborough Castle Museum (1930), **Sandwich,** Kent (0304 612013). *Roman coins of 1st–5th centuries from excavations of the Richborough site.*

Scarborough Museum (1829), The Rotunda, Vernon Road, **Scarborough,** North Yorkshire (01723 374839). *Over 4,000 Roman coins, 1,500 English and 600 coins from local finds, siege pieces and trade tokens.*

Shaftesbury and Dorset Local History Museum (1946), 1 Gold Hill, **Shaftesbury,** Dorset (01747 52157). *Hoard of Saxon coins.*

City Museum (1875), Weston Park, **Sheffield** (0114 2 768588). *Over 5,000 coins of all periods, but mainly English and modern British. European coins, imperial Roman (including three hoards of about 500 coins each), Yorkshire trade tokens, British historical medals, campaign medals. Library.*

Rowley's House Museum, Barker Street, **Shrewsbury,** Salop (01743 361196). *Coins minted at Shrewsbury 925-1180, Civil War coinage of 1642, Shropshire tradesmen's tokens, English coins and medals.*

Museum of Archaeology (1951), God's House Tower, Town Quay, **Southampton,** Hants (023 8022 0007). *Main emphasis lies in Ancient British, Roman and medieval English coins from local archaeological excavations. General collection of later coins and medals.*

Atkinson Art Gallery (1878), Lord Street, **Southport,** Lancs (01704 533133). *Roman coins.*

Botanic Gardens Museum, Churchtown, **Southport,** Lancs (01704 87547). *English and British coins and medals, military medals and decorations.*

Southwold Museum (1933), St Bartholomew's Green, **Southwold,** Suffolk (01502 722375). *General collection of coins, specialised Suffolk trade tokens.*

Stamford Museum (1961), Broad Street, **Stamford,** Lincs (01780 66317). *General collection of coins, medals and tokens, including a selection from the Stamford mint.*

Municipal Museum (1860), Vernon Park, Turncroft Lane, **Stockport,** Cheshire (0161 474 4460) *Miscellaneous general collection of coins, tokens and medals.*

Stroud Museum (1899), Lansdown, **Stroud,** Glos (01453 376394). *Ancient British, Roman, Saxon, Norman, later medieval English, British coins and Gloucestershire trade tokens.*

Museum and Art Gallery (1846), Borough Road, **Sunderland,** Tyne & Wear (0191 514 1235). *Roman imperial, medieval and later English, including examples of the pennies minted at Durham, modern British and foreign coins, 17th-19th century tradesmen's tokens, local medallions and campaign medals.*

Swansea Museum (1835), Victoria Road, **Swansea,** W. Glamorgan, SA1 1SN (0792 653765). *Coins and medals of local interest.*

T

Tamworth Castle and Museum (1899), The Holloway, **Tamworth,** Staffs (01827 63563). *Anglo-Saxon coins, medieval English including coins of the Tamworth mint, later English and British coins, tokens, commemorative medallions and medals.*

Somerset County Museum, Taunton Castle, **Taunton,** Somerset (01823 255510 / 320200). *Celtic, Roman, Anglo-Saxon, early Medieval, tokens, medallions and banknotes. Strong emphasis on locally-found items.*

Thurrock Local History Museum (1956), Civic Square, **Tilbury,** Essex (01375 390000 ext 2414). *Roman coins.*

Royal Cornwall Museum (1818), River Street, **Truro,** Cornwall (01872 72205). *Coins, tokens and medals pertaining principally to the county of Cornwall.*

W

Wakefield Museum (1919), Wood Street, **Wakefield,** West Yorkshire (01924 295351). *Roman and medieval English silver and copper coins.*

Epping Forest District Museum, 39/41 Sun Street, **Waltham Abbey,** Essex EN 9. *Ancient British, Roman and medieval coins, Essex tradesmen's tokens of local interest.*

Warrington Museum and Art Gallery (1848). Bold Street, **Warrington,** Cheshire, WA1 1JG (01925 30550). *Coins, medals and tokens.*

Worcester City Museum (1833), Foregate Street, **Worcester** (01905 25371). *Roman, medieval and later coins and tokens. Coins of the Worcester mint.*

Wells Museum (18903), 8 Cathedral Green, **Wells,** Somerset (01749 3477). *Ancient and modern British and world coins, local trade tokens and medals.*

Municipal Museum and Art Gallery (1878), Station Road, **Wigan,** Lancashire. *British, Commonwealth and foreign coins from about 1660 to the present. Roman coins from local sites, commemorative medals.*

City Museum (1851), The Square, **Winchester,** Hants (01962 848269). *Roman and medieval coins chiefly from local hoards and finds. Hampshire tradesmen's tokens and commemorative medals. Small reference library.*

Wisbech and Fenland Museum (1835), Museum Square, **Wisbech,** Cambridgeshire (01945 583817), *British Roman, medieval and later coins, medals and tokens.*

Y

The Museum of South Somerset (1928), Hendford, **Yeovil,** Somerset (01935 24774). *Roman coins from local sites, medieval English, modern British coins and medals and a fine collection of tokens (particularly 17th century Somerset).*

Castle Museum (1938), **York** (01904 653611). *English and British coins, campaign medals, orders and decorations, comemorative medals.*

Jorvik Viking Centre (1984), Coppergate, **York** (01904 643211). *Coins and artefacts pertaining to the Viking occupation of York.*

The Yorkshire Museum (1823), **York** (01904 629745). *Roman imperial, medieval English and later coins, about 12,000 in all.*

Club
directory

Details given here are the names of Numismatic Clubs and Societies, their date of foundation, and their usual venues, days and times of meetings. Meetings are monthly unless otherwise stated. Finally, the telephone number of the club secretary is given; the names and addresses of club secretaries are withheld for security reasons, but full details may be obtained by writing to the Secretary of the British Association of Numismatic Societies, Philip Mernick, c/o General Services, 42 Campbell Road, London E3 4DT. Telephone 020 8980 5672. E-mail: phil@mernicks.com.

Banbury & District Numismatic Society (1967). Banbury British Rail Working Mens Club. 2nd Mon (exc Jul & Aug), 19.45. (01295 254451).

Bath & Bristol Numismatic Society (1950). Ship Inn, Temple Street, Keynsham, Bristol. 2nd Thu, 19.30. (01275 472385).

Bedford Numismatic Society (1966). RAF Association Club, 93 Ashburnham Road, Bedford MK40 1EA. 3rd Mon, 19.30. (01234 228833/358369).

Bexley Coin Club (1968). St Martin's Church Hall, Erith Road, Barnehurst, Bexleyheath, Kent. 1st Mon (exc Jan & Aug), 20.00. (020 8303 0510).

Birmingham Numismatic Society (1964). Friend's Meeting House, Linden Road, Bournville, Birmingham 30. 2nd Wed, 19.45. (0121 308 1616).

Matthew Boulton Society (1994). PO Box 395, Birmingham B31 2TB (0121 781 6558 fax 0121 781 6574).

Bradford & District Numismatic Society (1967). East Bowling Unity Club, Leicester Street, Bradford, West Yorkshire. 3rd Mon, 19.00. (01532 677151).

Brighton & Hove Coin Club (1971). Methodist Church Hall, St Patrick's Road, Hove, East Sussex. Last Wed (exc Dec), 20.00. (01273 419303).

British Cheque Collectors' Society (1980). John Purser, 71 Mile Lane, Cheylesmore, Coventry, West Midlands CV3 5GB.

British Numismatic Society (1903). Warburg Institute, Woburn Square, London WC1H 0AB. Monthly (exc Aug & Dec), 18.00.

Cambridgeshire Numismatic Society (1946). Friends' Meeting House, 12 Jesus Lane (entrance in Park Street), Cambridge, CB5 8BA. 3rd Mon, Sept–June, 19.30. (01767 312112).

Chester & North Wales Coin & Banknote Society (1996). Liver Hotel, 110 Brook Street, Chester. 4th Tue, 20.00. (0151 478 4293)

Cheltenham Numismatic Society, The Reddings & District Community Association, North Road, The Reddings, Cheltenham. 3rd Mon, 19.45 (01242 673263)

Coin Correspondence Club (1988). Postal only. A.H. Chubb, 49 White Hart Lane, Barnes, London SW13 0PP. (0181-878 0472).

Cornwall Collectors' Club (1990). The Swan Inn, 40 Bosvigo Road, Truro. 1st Wed, 20.00. (01872 73376).

Crawley Coin Club (1969). Furnace Green Community Centre, Ashburnham Road, Furnace Green, Crawley, West Sussex. 1st Tue, 20.00. (01293 548671).

Crewe & District Coin & Medal Club (1968). Memorial Hall, Church Lane, Wistaston, Crewe, 2nd Tue (exc Jan & July), 19.30. (01270 69836).

Darlington & District Numismatic Society (1968). Darlington Arts Centre, Vane Terrace, Darlington, Co Durhm. 3rd Wed, 19.30. (01609 772976).

Derbyshire Numismatic Society (1964). The Friends' Meeting House, St Helens Street, Derby. 3rd Mon (exc August), 19.45. (01283 211623).

Devon & Exeter Numismatic Society (1965). Red Cross Centre, Butts Road, Heavitree, Exeter, Devon. 3rd Tue, 19.30. (01392 461013).

Edinburgh Numismatic Society (1996). Department of History and Applied Arts, Royal Museum of Scotland, Chambers Street, Edinburgh EH1 1JF. 3rd Mon, 19.30. (0131 225 7534).

Enfield & District Numismatic Society (1969). Millfield House Arts Centre, Silver Street, Edmonton, London N18 1PJ. 3rd Mon, 20.00. (0181-340 0767).

Essex Numismatic Society (1966). Chelmsford & Essex Museum, Moulsham Street, Chelmsford, Essex. 4th Fri (exc Dec), 20.00. (01376 21846).

Glasgow & West of Scotland Numismatic Society
(1947). The College Club, University of Glasgow,
University Avenue, Glasgow G12. 2nd Thu, Oct-
May, 19.30. (0141 633 5422).

**Harrow & North West Middlesex Numismatic
Society** (1968). Harrow Arts Centre, Hatch End,
Harrow, Middlesex. 2nd and 4th Mon, 19.30. (020
8952 8765).

Havering Numismatic Society (1967). Fairkytes
Arts Centre, Billet Lane, Hornchurch, Essex. 1st Tue,
19.30. (01708 704201).

Horncastle & District Coin Club (1963). Bull Hotel,
Bull Ring, Horncastle, Lincs. 2nd Thu (exc Aug),
19.30. (01754 2706).

Huddersfield Numismatic Society (1947).
Tolson Memorial Museum, Ravensknowle Park,
Huddersfield, West Yorkshire. 1st Mon (exc Jul &
Aug), 19.30. (01484 226300).

Hull & District Numismatic Society (1967). The
Young People's Institute, George Street, Hull.
Monthly (exc Aug & Dec), 19.30. (01482 441933).

International Bank Note Society (1961). Victory
Services Club, 63–79 Seymour Street, London W1.
Last Thu (exc Dec), 18.00. (020-8969 9493).

**International Bank Note Society, Scottish
Chapter** (1995). West End Hotel, Palmerston Place,
Edinburgh. Last Sat (exc Dec), 14.30.

Ireland, Numismatic Society of (Northern Branch).
Denman International, Clandeboye Road, Bangor
or Maysfield Leisure Centre, Belfast. 1st Fri (exc Jan)
19.30. (028 9146 6743)

**Ireland, Numismatic Society of. (Southern
Branch).** Ely House, 8 Ely Place, Dublin. Last Fri,
20.00. (0035 3 283 2027).

Ipswich Numismatic Society (1966). Ipswich
Citizens Advice Bureau, 19 Tower Street, Ipswich,
Suffolk. Monthly meetings, 19.30. (01473 711158).

Kent Towns Numismatic Society (1913). Adult
Education Centre, 9 Sittingbourne Road (Maidstone)
and King's School Preparatory School, King
Edward Road (Rochester). 1st Fri of month, 19.30
alternately at Maidstone and Rochester. (01622
843881).

Kingston Numismatic Society (1966). King Athel-
stan's School, Villiers Road, Kingston-upon-Thames,
Surrey. 3rd Thu (exc Dec & Jan), 19.30. (020-8397
6944).

Lancashire & Cheshire Numismatic Society (1933).
Manchester Central Library, St Peter's Square,
Manchester M2 5PD. Monthly, Sep-June, Wed
(18.30) or Sat (14.30). (0161 445 2042).

Lincolnshire Numismatic Society (1932). Grimsby
Bridge Club, Bargate, Grimsby, South Humberside.
4th Wed (exc Aug), 19.30.

London Numismatic Club (1947). Institute of
Archaeology, 31–34 Gordon Square, London WC1H
0PY. Monthly, 18.30.

Loughborough Coin & Search Society (1964).
Wallace Humphry Room, Shelthorpe Community
Centre, Loughborough, Leics. 1st Thu, 19.30. (01509
261352).

Merseyside Numismatic Society (1947). The
Lecture Theatre, Liverpool Museum, William Brown
Street, Liverpool L3 8EN. Monthly (exc July & Aug),
19.00. (0151-929 2143).

Mid Lanark Coin Circle (1969). Hospitality Room,
The Civic Centre, Motherwell, Lanarkshire. 4th
Thu, Sep–Apr (exc Dec), 19.30. (0141-552 2083).

Morecambe & Lancaster Numismatic Society.
Monthly, 19.30. (01524 411036).

Newbury Coin & Medal Club (1971). Monthly,
20.00. (01635 41233).

Northampton Numismatic Society (1969). Old
Scouts RFC, Rushmere Road, Northampton. 1st
Thurs, 20.00.

Norwich Numismatic Society (1967). Assembly
House, Theatre Street, Norwich, Norfolk. 3rd Mon,
19.30. (01493 651577).

Nottinghamshire Numismatic Society (1948). The
Cecil Roberts Room, County Library, Angel Row,
Nottingham NG1 6HP. 2nd Tue (Sep-Apr), 18.45.
(0115 9257674).

Nuneaton & District Coin Club (1968). United
Reformed Church Room, Coton Road, opposite
Council House, Nuneaton, Warwickshire. 2nd Tue,
19.30. (01203 371556).

Orders & Medals Research Society (1942). National
Army Museum, Royal Hospital Road, Chelsea,
London SW3. Monthly, 14.30 (020-8680 2701).

Ormskirk & West Lancashire Numismatic Society
(1970).The Eagle & Child, Maltkiln Lane, Bispham
Green L40 1SN. 1st Thu, 20.15. (01704 531266).

Peterborough & District Numismatic Society
(1967). Belsize Community Centre, Celta Road
Peter-borough, Cambs. 4th Tue (exc July & Aug),
19.30. (01733 562768).

Plymouth Coin & Medal Club (1970). RAFA Club, 5
Ermington Terrace, Mutley Plain, Plymouth, Devon.
2nd Wed (exc Dec), 19.30. (01752 663803).

Preston & District Numismatic Society (1965).
Eldon Hotel, Eldon Street, Preston, Lancs. 1st and
3rd Tue, 20.00. (012572 66869).

Reading Coin Club (1964). Abbey Baptist Church,
Abbey Square, Reading. 1st Mon, 19.00. (0118
9332843).

Rochford Hundred Numismatic Society. Civic
Suite, Rayleigh Town Hall, Rayleigh, Essex. 2nd
Thu, 20.00. (01702 230950).

Romsey Numismatic Society (1969). Romsey WM
Conservative Club, Market Place, Romsey, Hants
SO5 8NA. 4th Fri (exc Dec), 19.30. (01703 253921).

Rotherham & District Coin Club (1982). Rotherham
Art Centre, Rotherham, South Yorkshire. 1st Wed,
19.00. (01709 528179).

Royal Mint Coin Club, PO Box 500, Cardiff CF1 1HA (01443 222111).

Royal Numismatic Society (1836). Society of Antiquaries, Piccadilly, London W1. Monthly (Oct-June), 17.30. Joe Cribb, Coins and Medals, British Museum, London WC1B 3DG (020-7323 8585).

Rye Coin Club (1955). Rye Further Education Centre, Lion Street, Rye, East Sussex. 2nd Thu (Oct-Dec, Feb-May), 19.30. (01424 422974).

St Albans & Hertfordshire Numismatic Society (1948). St Michael's Parish Centre, Museum Entrance, Verulamium Park, St Albans, Herts AL3 4SL. 2nd Tue (exc Aug), 19.30. (01727 824434).

Sheffield Numismatic Society. Telephone for venue. 2nd Wed, 19.00. (0114 2817129)

South East Hants Numismatic Society. Different locations. 1st Fri. Contact: Tony Matthews, 8 King George Road, Totton, Southampton SO4 3FE.

South Manchester Numismatic Society (1967). Nursery Inn, Green Lane, Heaton Mersey, Stockport. 1st & 3rd Mondays of each month (excl. Public hols), 20.00. (0161-485 7017).

South Wales & Monmouthshire Numismatic Society (1958). The W. R. Lysaght Institute, Corporation Road, Newport. 2nd Tues, 19.30. (029 20561564).

Thurrock Numismatic Society (1970). Stanley Lazell Hall, Dell Road, Grays, Essex. 3rd Wed, 19.00.

Tyneside Numismatic Society (1954). RAFA Club, Eric Nelson House, 16 Berwick Road, Gateshead, Tyne & Wear. 2nd Wed, 19.30. (0191 372 2266).

Wessex NS (1948). Hotel Bristowe, Grange Road, Southbourne, Bournemouth, Dorset. 2nd Thurs (exc Aug), 20.00. (020 7731 1702).

Wiltshire Numismatic Society (1965). Raven Inn, Poulshot, Nr Devizes, Wiltshire. 3rd Mon, Mar-Dec, 20.00. (01225 703143).

Worthing & District Numismatic Society (1967). Kingsway Hotel, Marine Parade, Worthing, West Sussex BN11 3QQ. 3rd Thu, 20.00. (01903 241503).

Yorkshire Numismatic Society (1909). Leeds Museum, The Headrow , Leeds. 1st Sat (exc Jan, Aug & Dec) (0113 286 4914).

> **Society activities are featured every month in the "Diary Section" of COIN NEWS**

> ## IMPORTANT NOTICE
>
> **Club Secretaries:**
> If your details as listed are incorrect please let us know in time for the next edition of the COIN YEARBOOK

IMPORTANT ORGANISATIONS

ADA
The Antiquities Dealers Association

Secretary: Susan Hadida, Duke's Court, 32 Duke Street, London SW1Y 6DU

ANA
The American Numismatic Association

818 North Cascade Avenue, Colorado Springs, CO 80903-3279, USA

BNTA
The British Numismatic Trade Association

Secretary: Mrs R. Cooke, General Secretary, BNTA, PO Box 2, Rye, East Sussex TN31 7WE

IAPN
International Association of Professional Numismatists

Secretary: Jean-Luc Van der Schueren, 14 Rue de la Bourse, B–1000, Brussels.

IBNS
International Bank Note Society

Membership Secretary:
Clive Rice, 25 Copse Side, Binscombe, Godalming, Surrey, GU7 3RU

RNS
Royal Numismatic Society
Ms V. Hewitt, Dept of Coins & Medals, British Museum, London WC1B 3DG. Tel: 020 7323 8228.

BAMS
British Art Medal Society
Philip Attwood, Dept of Coins & Medals, British Museum, London WC1B 3DG.

BNS
British Numismatic Society
Dr K. Clancy, The Royal Mint, Llantrisant, Pontyclun, Mid Glamorgan CF72 8YT

Directory of
Auctioneers

Listed here are the major UK auction houses which handle coins, medals, banknotes and other items of numismatic interest. Many of them hold regular public auctions, whilst others handle numismatic material infrequently. A number of coin companies also hold regular Postal Auctions—these are marked with a P.

Baldwin's Auctions Ltd
11 Adelphi Terrace, London WC2N 6BJ (020 7930 9808 fax 020 7930 9450, e-mail auctions@baldwin.sh, website: www.baldwin.sh)
Banking Memorabilia
PO Box 14, Carlisle CA3 8DZ (016974 76465).
Bloomsbury Auctions
24 Maddox Street, London, W1S 1PP (0207 495 9494)
Bonhams (incorporating Glendinings)
101 New Bond Street, London W1Y 9LG (020 7 493 2445 fax 020 7491 9181, website: www.bonhams.com).
A. F. Brock & Company
269 London Road, Hazel Grove, Stockport, Cheshire SK7 4PL (0161 456 5050 fax 0161 456 5112, website www.afbrock.co.uk, email info@afbrock.co.uk).
Christie, Manson & Wood Ltd
8 King Street, St James's, London SW1Y 6QT (020 7839 9060).
Christie's Scotland Ltd
164–166 Bath Street, Glasgow G2 4TG (0141 332 8134 fax 0141 332 5759).
Classical Numismatic Group Inc (Seaby Coins)
14 Old Bond Street, London W1X 4JL (020 7495 1888 fax 020-7499 5916, email cng@historicalcoins.com, website: www.historicalcoins.com). P
Corbitts
5 Moseley Sreet, Newcastle upon Tyne NE1 1YE (0191-232 7268 fax 0191-261 4130).
Croydon Coin Auctions
272 Melfort Road, Thornton Heath, Surrey CR7 7RR (020 8240 7924 or 020 8656 4583, website www.croydoncoinauctions.co.uk, email: croydoncoinauctions.co.uk).
Dix Noonan Webb
16 Bolton Street, Piccadilly, London. Website: www.dnw.co.uk, email: auctions@dnw.co.uk)

Edinburgh Coin Shop
11 West Crosscauseway, Edinburgh EH8 9JW 0131 668 2928 fax 0131 668 2926). P
Fellows & Sons
Augusta House, 19 Augusta Street, Hockley, Birmingham B18 6JA (0121-212 2131). www.fellows.co.uk
B. Frank & Son
3 South Avenue, Ryton, Tyne & Wear NE40 3LD (0191 413 8749 fax 0191 413 2957, email bfrankandson@aol.com).
T. Gillingham
42 Highbury Park, Warminster, Wilts BA12 9JF (01985 216486).
Gillio Coins International
1013 State Street, Santa Barbara, CA 93101, USA (805 9631345—London contact Eric Green 020-7586 3964).
Graves, Son & Pilcher Fine Arts
71 Church Road, Hove, East Sussex BN3 2GL (01273 735266 fax 01273 723813).
Hoods Postal Coin Auctions
23 High Street, Kilbirnie, Ayrshire KA25 7EX (fax/tel 01505 682157). P
Kleeford Coin Auctions
19 Craythorns Crescent, Dishforth, Thirsk YO7 3LY. (tel/fax 01845 577977). P
W. H. Lane & Son
65 Morrab Road, Penzance, Cornwall TR18 2QT (01736 61447 fax 01736 50097) also: Trafalgar House, Malpas Road, Truro, Cornwall TR1 1QH (01872 223379).
Lawrence Fine Art Auctioneers
South Street, Crewkerne, Somerset TA18 8AB (01460 73041).
Lockdale Coins
Shops at: 37 Upper Orwell Street, Ipswich IP4 1BR.(01473 218588), 168 London Road South, Lowestoft NR33 0BB (01473 218588) & 23 Magdalene Street, Cambridge, CB3 0AF (01223 361163) website: www.lockdales.co.uk

London Coin Auctions
12, Redhill Wood, New Ash Green, Kent DA3 8QH (01474 871464 , email: Slockcoin@aol.com www.londoncoins.co.uk)

Moreton & Eden Ltd
45 Maddox Street, London W1S 2PE (020 7493 5344 fax 020 7495 6325, email info@mortonand eden.com, www.mortonandeden.com)

Neales
192–194 Mansfield Road, Nottingham NG1 3HU (0115 9624141 fax 0115 9856890).

R & W Coin Auctions
307 Bretch Hill, Banbury, Oxon OX16 0JD (01295 275128).

Sheffield Coin Auctions
7 Beacon Close, Sheffield S9 1AA (0114 249 0442).

Simmons Gallery
PO Box 104, Leytonstone, London. Tel: 0207 8989 8097. www.simmonsgallery.co.uk email: info@simmonsgallery.co.uk

Spink & Son Ltd
69 Southampton Row, Bloomsbury, London. WC1B 4ET (020 7563 4055, fax 020 7563 4068, website www.spink-online.com, email: info@spinkandson.com).

St James's Auctions
43 Duke Street, St James's, London, SW1Y 6DD (020 7930 7597/7888)

Sussex Auction Galleries
59 Perrymount Road, Haywards Heath, West Sussex RH16 3DS (01444 414935 fax 01444 450402).

Warwick & Warwick
Chalon House, Scarbank, Millers Road, Warwick CV34 5DB (01926 499031 fax 01926 491906, email: info@warwickandwarwick.com, website: www.warwickandwarwick.com

Information correct at time of going to press

directory of Fairs

Listed below are the names of the fair organisers, their venue details where known along with contact telephone numbers. Please call the organisers direct for information on dates etc.

Aberdeen
Jarvis Amatola Hotel, Great Western Road, also venues in **Glenrothes** and **Glasgow**. *Cornucopia Collectors Fairs. (01382 224946)*

Birmingham
National Motor Cycle Museum, Bickenhill, Birmingham. *Midland Stamp & Coin Fair. (024 7671 6587)*

Bristol
Jury's Hotel, Prince Street. *AMP Fairs. (01952 597 587).*

Cardiff
City Hall. *AMP Fairs. (01952 597 587)*

Cheltenham
Town Hall or White House Hotel. *AMP Fairs. (01952 597 587)*

Exeter
Priory High School, Earl Richards Road, off Topsham Road. *Phoenix Fairs. (01761 414304)*

Leeds-Morley
Cedar Court Hotel, Denby Dale Road, Calder Grove, Wakefield WF4 3QZ. *N. C. S. Promotions. (01552 684681).*

Lichfield
Civic Hall, Castle Dyke, City Centre. *C. S. Fairs. (01562 710424)*

London
Holiday Inn, Coram St., Bloomsbury, London WC1. *London Coin Fair. (020 8989 8097)*

London
The Bonnington Hotel, 92 Southampton Row, London WC1. *West Promotions. (020 8641 3224).*

London
Jury's Hotel, 16-22 Great Russell Street, London WC1 3NN. *Davidson Monk Fairs. (020 8656 4583 or 020 8651 3890)*

Malvern
Lyttleton Rooms. *AMP Fairs. (01952 597 587)*

Plymouth
Lower Guildhall. *Bruce Stamps. (01749 813324)*

Sutton Coldfield
Fellowship Hall, South Parade. *C. S. Fairs. (01562 710424)*

Newcastle upon Tyne
The Royal Station Hotel. B. Frank & Son. (0191 413 8749)

West Bromwich
Town Hall, High Street. *C. S. Fairs. (01562 710424)*

York
The Grandstand, York Racecourse. *York Coin Fair (01793 513431 or 020 8946 4489)*

Annual events
The B.N.T.A. (Coinex)
Tel: 01797 229 988 for details
The I.B.N.S. (World Paper Money Fair)
Tel: 020 8868 5582 for details

Directory of **Dealers**

The dealers listed below have comprehensive stocks of coins and medals, unless otherwise stated. Specialities, where known, are noted. Many of those listed are postal dealers only, so to avoid disappointment always make contact by telephone or mail in the first instance, particularly before travelling any distance.

Abbreviations:
ADA—Antiquities Dealers Association
ANA—American Numismatic Association
BADA—British Antique Dealers Association
BNTA—British Numismatic Trade Association
IAPN—International Association of Professional Numismatists
IBNS—International Bank Note Society
P—Postal only
L—Publishes regular lists

ABC Coins & Tokens
PO Box 52, Alnwick, Northumberland NE66 1YE (01665 603851, email: d-stuart@d-stuart.demon. co.uk, www.abccoinsandtokens.com)

A. Ackroyd (IBNS)
62 Albert Road, Parkstone, Poole, Dorset BH12 2DB (tel/fax 01202 739039, website www.AAnotes.com). *P. L. Banknotes and cheques*

Afribilia Ltd
16 Bury Place, London WC1A 2JL (020 7404 7134, fax: 020 7404 7138, email: info@afribilia.com, www.afribilia.com). *Medals, coins, banknotes etc*

Airedale Coins (ANA, BNTA)
PO Box 7, Bingley, West Yorkshire, BD16 1XU (01535 272754 fax 01535 275727, website www.airedalecoins.com, email info@airedalecoins.com).
P. L. British and modern coins of the world.

All Gold of Sevenoaks
Email: goldsovereigns@aol.com. (01732 462255)
Quality Sovereigns

David Allen Coins and Collectables
PO Box 125, Pinner, Middlesex HA5 2TX (020 866 6796). *P. L. British and world coins, tokens, banknotes.*

Joan Allen Electronics Ltd
190 Main Road, Biggin Hill, Kent TN16 3BB (01959 71255). Mon-Sat 09.00–17.00. *Metal detectors.*

Ancient & Gothic (ADA)
PO Box 5390, Bournemouth, BH7 6XR (01202 431721). *P. L. Greek, Roman & Medieval antiquities with coin section.*

Ancient World
16 High Petergate, York, YO1 2EH (01904 624062) 10.30–17.00 weekdays. *Greek, Roman, Celtic and medieval coins, also antiquities.*

Antiquestall.com
On line numismatic market place. *Coins, medals, banknotes etc*

Keith Austin (IBNS)
PO Box 89, Carlisle, Cumbria CA3 0GH (01228 819149, fax 01228 521176, email kaustin@kabc.freeserve.co.uk). *L. Banknotes.*

Mark Bailey
120 Sterte Court, Sterte Close, Poole, Dorset BH15 2AY (01202 674936). *P. L. Ancient, modern, world coins and antiquities.*

A. H. Baldwin & Sons Ltd (ANA, BADA, BNTA, IAPN)
11 Adelphi Terrace, London WC2N 6BJ.
09.00–17.00 weekdays. (email coins@baldwin.sh)
Coins, tokens, commemorative medals, war medals and decorations, numismatic books.

Banking Memorabilia (IBNS)
PO Box 14, Carlisle, Cumbria (016974 76465).
09.00– 18.00 (not Sun). *Cheques, banknotes, related ephemera.*

Banknotes 4 U
Roger and Liz Outing, PO Box 123, Huddersfield HD8 9WY www.banknotes4u.co.uk e mail rogerouting@aol.com (01484 860415). *World banknotes*

Banknotes of Auld Scotland
Sconser, Isle of Skye IV48 8TD. (01478 650459, website www.scottish-banknotes.com, email johnaunc@aol.com).

G. Barrington Smith
Cross Street, Oadby, Leicestershire LE2 4DD (01533 712114). 08.30–17.15 weekdays. *Albums, catalogues and accessories.*

Bath Stamp and Coin Shop
Pulteney Bridge, Bath, Avon BA2 4AY (01225 463073). Mon-Sat 09.30–17.30. *British*

Michael Beaumont
PO Box 8, Carlton, Notts NG4 4QZ (0115 9878361).
P. Coins, medals and tokens of the world.

Beaver Coin Room (BNTA)
57 Philbeach Gardens, LondonSW5 9ED (020 7373 4553). *P. European coins and medals.*

R. P. & P. J. Beckett
Maesyderw, Capel Dewi, Llandyssul, Dyfed SA44 4PJ. (Fax only 01559 395631, email rppjbeckett@btinternet.com) *P. coin sets and banknotes.*

Lloyd Bennett (BNTA)
PO Box 2, Monmouth, Gwent NP5 3YE (01600 890634). Abergavenny Market (Tue), Monmouth Market (Fri–Sat) 09.00–16.00. *English hammered, milled and coins of the world.*

Berkshire Coin Centre
35 Castle Street, Reading, Berkshire RG1 7SB (01734 575593). 10.00–16.00 weekdays, half-day Sat. *British and world coins.*

Beron Coins
64 Rosewood Close, Glascote, Tamworth, Staffs B77 3PD (01827 54541). *P. L. British & world coins.*

Stephen J. Betts
4 Victoria Street, Narborough, Leics LE9 5DP (0116 2864434). *P. L. Medieval and modern coins, counters, jetons and tokens, countermarks and medals.*

Bigbury Mint
River Park, Ermington Mill, Ivybridge, Devon PL21 9NT (01548 830717. *Specialists in reproduction hammered coins*

Birchin Lane Gold Coin Company
6 Castle Court, St Michael's Alley (off Cornhill), London EC3V 9DS (020 7621 0370 and 020 7263 3981). Mon-Fri 10.00–16.30. *Gold and bullion coins.*

Barry Boswell
24 Townsend Lane, Upper Boddington, Daventry, Northants NN11 6DR (01327 261877, fax 01327 261391, email Barry.Boswell@btinternet.com). *P. L. British and world banknotes.*

James & C. Brett
17 Dale Road, Lewes, East Sussex BN7 1LH. *P. L. British and world coins.*

J. Bridgeman Coins
129a Blackburn Road, Accrington, Lancs (01254 384757). 09.30–17.00 (closed Wednesday). *British & World coins.*

Brighton Coin Company (ANA, BNTA)
The Hove Coin Shop, Church Road, Hove, (01278 737537) Mon-Fri 9.45–17.30, Sat 9.45–15.30 (closed alternate Wednesdays and Saturdays). *World coins.*

Britannia Jewellery Co
234 Yorkshire Street, Rochdale, Lancs OL16 2DP (01706 341046/55507. Mon-Sat 10.00–17.00.

BRM Coins
3 Minshull Street, Knutsford, Cheshire WA16 6HG (01565) 651480 and 0606 74522). Mon-Fri 11.00–15.00, Sat 11.00–1.00 or by appt. *British coins.*

Peter F. Broadbelt
10 Dragon Road, Harrogate, North Yorkshire HG1 5DF (01423 562037). Mon-Sat 11–18.00. *Specialist in Foreign coins.*

A. F. Brock & Company
269 London Road, Hazel Grove, Stockport, Cheshire SK7 4PL (0161 456 5050/5112, email info@afbrock.co.uk, www.afbrock.co.uk). Mon-Sat 09.30–17.30. *Auctioneers and valuers.*

E. J. & C. A. Brooks (BNTA, IBNS)
44 Kiln Road, Thundersley, Essex SS7 1TB (01268 753835). Any time up to 23.00. *L. British*

Iain Burn
2 Compton Gardens, 53 Park Road, Camberley, Surrey GU15 2SP (01276 23304). *Bank of England & Treasury notes*

BBM Coins
8–9 Lion Street, Kidderminster, Hereford & Worcester, DY10 1PT (01562 744118). Wed-Sat 10.00–17.00. *World coins.*

Cambridge Stamp Centre Ltd
9 Sussex Street, Cambridge CB4 4HU (01223 63980). Mon-Sat 09.00–17.30. *British coins.*

Castle Curios
165 Wellgate, Rotherham, South Yorkshire S60 4DT. Wed-Sat 11.00–17.00. *English coins.*

Castle Galleries
81 Castle Street, Salisbury, Wiltshire SP1 3SP (01722 333734). Tue, Thu Fri 09.00–17.00, Sat 09.30–16.00. *British coins, medals and tokens.*

Cathedral Coins
23 Kirkgate, Ripon, North Yorkshire HG4 1PB (01765 701400). Mon-Sat 10.00–17.00.

David L. Cavanagh
49 Cockburn Street, Edinburgh EH1 1PB (0131 226 3391). Mon-Sat 10.30–17.00. *British coins.*

Cavendish Coins
14 Longfields, Ongar, Essex CM5 9BZ. *P. Modern crown-sized coins.*

Central Bank of Ireland
Currency Centre, Sandyford Road, Dublin 16, Ireland. *New coin and banknote issues of Ireland.*

Lance Chaplin
17 Wanstead Lane, Ilford, Essex IG1 3SB (020 8554 7154). *P. L. Roman, Greek, Celtic, hammered coins and antiquities.*

Chard (BNTA)
521 Lytham Road, Blackpool, Lancs FY4 1RJ (01253 343081). Mon-Sat 09.00–17.00. www.chards.co.uk. *British, Commonwealth and European coins.*

Chelsea Coins Ltd (BNTA)
PO Box 2, Fulham Road, London SW10 9PQ. (020 8870 5501 Fax 020 8875 1459). *P. World coins.*

Nigel A. Clark
28 Ulundi Road, Blackheath, London SE3 7UG (020 8858 4020). *P. L. Mainly 17th century tokens.*

Classical Numismatic Group
14 Old Bond Street, London W1X 4JL. (020 7495 1888 Fax 020 7499 5916, Email cng@historicalcoins.com). *P. Ancient and world coins. Publishers of the Classical Numismatic Review.*

Paul Clayton (BNTA)
PO Box 21, Wetherby, West Yorkshire LS22 5JY. (01937 72441). *Modern gold coins.*

André de Clermont (BNTA)
PO Box 3615, London, SW10 0YD. (020 7351 5727, Fax 020 7352 8127). *World coins, especially Islamic & Oriental coins, Latin America.*

M. Coeshaw
PO Box 115, Leicester LE3 8JJ (0116 287 3808). *P. Coins, banknotes, coin albums and cases*

Philip Cohen Numismatics (ANA, BNTA)
20 Cecil Court, Charing Cross Road, London WC2N 4HE (020 7379 0615). Mon-Sat 10.30–17.30 (half-days Mon and Sat).

Coin & Collectors Centre
PO Box 22, Pontefract, West Yorkshire WF8 1YT (01977 704112, website www.coincentre.co.uk, email sales@coincentre.co.uk). *P. British coins.*

Coincraft (ANA, IBNS)
44/45 Great Russell Street, London WC1B 3LU
(020 7636 1188 and 020 7637 8785 fax 020 7323 2860,
Website www.coincraft.com Email
info@coincraft.com). Mon-Fri 09.30–17.00, Sat
10.00–14.30. *L (newspaper format). Coins and
banknotes.*

Coinote Services Ltd
PO Box 53, Sorting Office, Clarke Street,
Hartlepool TS26 NYL (01429 890894). Shop at 74
Elwick Road, Hartlepool, TS26 9AP *P. L. Coins
and banknotes 1615 todate. Accessories and books.*

Coins of Beeston
PO Box 19, Beeston, Notts BG9 2NE. *P. L. Tokens,
medals and paranumismatics.*

Coins of Canterbury
PO Box 47, Faversham, Kent ME13 7HX (01795
531980). *P. English coins.*

Collecta Coins Limited
PO Box 101, Northampton NN1 3LT (01604
766607/27076). Mon-Sat 09.00–21.00. *World coins.*

The Collector
242 High Street, Orpington, Kent BR6 0LZ (01689
890045). Mon-Sat 09.45–17.30 (closed Tue). *Coins,
medals, banknotes, badges, militaria, cigarette cards etc*

Collectors' Corner
Watford Market (off High Street), Watford, Herts
(020 8904 0552). Tue, Fri, Sat 09.00-17.00. *World
coins.*

Collectors Gallery (BNTA, IBNS)
24 The Parade, St Mary's Place, Shrewsbury SY1
1DL (01743 272140 fax 01743 366041). Mon-Fri
09.00–18.00, half-day Sat. www.collectors-
gallery.co.uk. *Coins and banknotes, accessories and
related books. Agents for the Abafil range of coin cases.*

Collectors' World
188 Wollaton Road, Wollaton, Nottingham NG8
1HJ. (01159 280347). *Coins, Tokens, Banknotes,
Accessories.*

Constantia CB
15 Church Road, Northwood, Middlesex HA6
1AR. *P. Roman and medieval hammered coins.*

Colin Cooke
257 Brooklands Road, Manchester M23 9HF (0161
973 2395 fax 0161 962 2864, email
coins@colincooke.com). *L. British coins.*

Corbitts (BNTA)
5 Mosley Street, Newcastle Upon Tyne NE1 1YE
(0191 232 7268 fax: 0191 261 4130). *Dealers and
auctioneers of all coins and medals.*

G. D. Courtenay
58 New Peachey Lane, Uxbridge, Middlesex UB8
3SX. *P. L. Coins, medals, tokens and banknotes.*

David Craddock
PO Box 3785, Camp Hill, Birmingham B11 2NF.
(0121 733 2259) *L. Crown to farthings. Copper and
bronze specialist. Some foreign.*

Mark Davidson
PO Box 197, South Croydon, Surrey CR3 0ZD (020
8651 3890). *Ancient, hammered coinage.*

Davidson Monk Fairs
PO Box 201, Croydon, Surrey CR9 7AQ (020 8656
4583). *Organiser of monthly fairs at the Jury's Hotel,
16–22 Great Russell Street, London, WC1 3NN.*

Paul Davies Ltd (ANA, BNTA, IAPN)
PO Box 17, Ilkley, West Yorkshire LS29 8TZ (01943
603116 fax 01943 816326). *P. World coins.*

Ian Davison
PO Box 256, Durham DH1 2GW (0191 3750808. *L.
English hammered and milled coins 1066–1910.*

DD Coins of Windsor
24–28 St Leonards Road, Suite 100, Windsor, Berks
SL4 3BB. (01753 739487). *L. GB milled list.*

B. J. Dawson (Coins) (BNTA)
52 St Helens Road, Lancs BL3 3NH (01204 63732).
Mon Tue Sat 09.30–16.00, Thu Fri 09.30–17.30, Wed
09.30–13.00. *L. Ancient, hammered and milled coins,
tokens and banknotes.*

Decus Coins
The Haven, Brockweir, Chepstow, Gwent NP6
7NN (01291 689216). *P.*

Dei Gratia
PO Box 3568, Buckingham MK18 4ZS (01280
848000). *P. L. Pre-Roman to modern coins,
antiquities, banknotes.*

Clive Dennett (BNTA)
66 St Benedicts Street, Norwich, Norfolk NR2 4AR
(01603 624315). Mon-Fri 09.00–17.30, Sat 09.00–
16.00 (closed 1.00–2.00 & Thu). *L. Paper money.*

C. J. Denton (ANA, BNTA, FRNS)
PO Box 25, Orpington, Kent BR6 8PU (01689
873690). *P. Irish coins.*

Detecnicks
3 Orchard Crescent, Arundel Road, Fontwell. West
Sussex BN18 0SA (01243 545060 fax 01243 545922)
Retail shop. Wide range of detectors and accessories.

Michael Dickinson (ANA, BNTA)
Ramsay House, 825 High Road Finchley, London
N12 8UB (0181 441 7175). *P. British and world coins.*

Dolphin Coins (ANA)
22 High Street, Leighton Buzzard, Beds. LU7 7EB.
(01525 383822 fax 01525 383872)
Mon-Fri 09.30– 17.00. Sat appt only. *L. British and
world coins.*

Dorset Coin Co Ltd (BNTA)
193 Ashley Road, Parkstone, Poole, Dorset BH14
9DL (01202 739606, fax 01202 739230). *P. L.
Separate coin and banknote lists.*

Drizen Coins
1 Hawthorns, Leigh-on-Sea, Essex SS9 4JT (01702
521094). *P. L. British and world coins.*

Dyas Coins & Medals
30 Shaftmoor Lane, Acocks Green, Birmingham
B27 7RS (0121 707 2808). Fri 10.30–18.30, Sun
10.30–13.00. *World coins and medals.*

Eagle Coins
Winterhaven, Mourneabbey, Mallow, Co. Cork,
Ireland (010 35322 29385). *P. L. Irish coins.*

Eden Coins
PO Box 77, Brierley Hill, West Midlands DY5
2GS (01384 834648). *P. English coins, tokens and
medals.*

Edinburgh Coin Shop (ANA)
11 West Crosscauseway, Edinburgh EH8 9JW
(0131 668 2928 fax 0131 668 2926). Mon-Sat
10.00–17.30. *L. World coins and medals. Postal auctions.*

Christopher Eimer (ANA, BNTA)
PO Box 352 London NW11 7RF (020 8458 9933 fax
020 8455 3535, email art@christophereimer.co.uk). *P.
Commemorative medals.*

Elm Hill Stamps & Coins
27 Elm Hill, Norwich, Norfolk NR3 1HN (01603 627413). Mon. 09.00–17.00, Tues-Wed. 09.00–17.00, Thur. 0900–13.00, Sat. 09.30–15.00 *Mainly stamps, occasionally coins*

Europa Numismatics (ANA, BNTA)
PO Box 119, High Wycombe, Bucks HP11 1QL (01494 437307). *P. European coins.*

Evesham Stamp & Coin Centre
Magpie Antiques, Paris House, 61 High Street, Evesham, Worcs WR11 4DA (01386 41631). Mon-Sat 09.00–17.30. *British coins.*

Michael E. Ewins
Meyrick Heights, 20 Meyrick Park Crescent, Bournemouth, Dorset BH3 7AQ (01202 290674). *P. World coins.*

I. Fine & Son Ltd
Victoria House, 93 Manor Farm Road, Wembley, Middlesex HA10 1XB (020 8997 5055). *P. British & World coins.*

Robin Finnegan Stamp Shop
83 Skinnergate, Darlington, Co Durham DL3 7LX (01325 489820/357674). Mon-Sat 10.00–17.30 (closed Wed). *World coins.*

Richard N. Flashman
54 Ebbsfleet Walk, Gravesend, Kent, DA11 9EW. *L. P. British banknotes.*

David Fletcher (Mint Coins) (ANA, BNTA)
PO Box 64, Coventry, Warwickshire CV5 6SN (024 7671 5425, Fax 024 7667 7985). *P. World new issues*

Folley Island Coins
PO Box 361, Dunstable, Bedfordshire LU5 4YU. (01582 667734). *World and English coins.*

Format of Birmingham Ltd (ANA, BNTA, IAPN, IBNS)
18 Bennetts Hill, Birmingham B2 5QJ (0121 643 2058 fax 0121 643 2210). Mon-Fri 09.30-7.00. *L. Coins, tokens and medals.*

B. Frank & Son (ANA, IBNS)
3 South Avenue, Ryton, Tyne & Wear NE40 3LD (0191 413 8749). *P. L. Banknotes and cheques, coins of the world. Organiser of the North of England fair.*

Frank Milward (BNTA)
2 Ravensworth Road, Mortimer, Berks, RG7 3UU (01734 332843). Mon-Sat 09.00-18.00. *British and World coins.*

Dennis Fudge Coins
127 Hadrian Road, Jarrow, Tyne & Wear NE32 3TS (0191 421 6221). *P. L. Ancient coins.*

Galata Coins Ltd (ANA)
The Old White Lion, Market Street, Llanfylin, Powys SY22 5BX (01691 648 765). *P. British and world coins.*

G. Gant
Glazenwood, 37 Augustus Way, Witham, Essex CM8 1HH. *P. British and Commonwealth coins.*

James Garriock
38 Hazel Close Bemerton Heath, Salisbury, Wiltshire SP2 977 (01722 500590). *P. L. Mainly hammered coins.*

John Gaunt
21 Harvey Road, Bedford MK41 9LF (01234 217685). By appointment. *Numismatic books.*

Alistair Gibb (IBNS)
5 West Albert Road, Kirkcaldy, Fife KY1 1DL (01592 269045). *P. L. Banknotes and books on banking.*

A. & S. Gillis
59 Roykilner Way, Wombwell, Barnsley, South Yorkshire S73 8DY. (01226 750371, website www.gilliscoins.com, email: catalogues@gilliscoins.com) *P. L. Ancient and medieval coins.*

Richard Gladdle
9 Cork Street, London W1X 1P9. (01327 858511). *Tokens. P. L.*

Glance Back Books
17 Upper Street, Chepstow, Gwent NP6 5EX (01291 626562). 10.30–17.30. *World coins, medals, banknotes.*

Glendining's (Bonhams) (ANA, BNTA)
101 New Bond Street, London W1Y 9LG (020 7493 2445). Mon-Fri 08.30-17.00, Sat 08.30–13.00. *Auctioneers.*

GM Coins
www.onlinecoins.co.uk/gmcoins, email: gmcoins@cleeve95.freeserve.co.uk, (01242 701144) *Hammered and milled coins*

Phil Goodwin (ANA)
PO Box 69, Portsmouth, Hants PO1 5SH (02392 423267 or 02392 752006 incl. fax). *P or by appointment. L. Ancient coins and antiquities.*

Ian Gradon
PO Box 359, Durham DH7 6WZ (0191 3719 700, email: ian@worldnotes.co.uk, www.worldnotes.co.uk). *L. World banknotes.*

Grantham Coins (BNTA)
PO Box 60, Grantham, Lincs (01476 870565). *P. L. English coins and banknotes.*

Eric Green—Agent in UK for Ronald J. Gillio Inc,
1013 State Street, Santa Barbara, California, USA 93101 (020 8907 0015, Mobile 0468 454948). *Gold coins, medals and paper money of the world.*

R. I. Groves
8 Catherine Street, Dumfries DG1 1JA (01387 266617, email: richard@i-groves.demon.co.uk). *P. British & world coins.*
PO Box 45, Hereford, HR2 7YP (01432 268178). *P. L. British and foreign coins and banknotes.*

Anthony Halse
The Headlands, Chepstow Road, Langstone, Newport, Gwent NP6 2JN (01633 413238). *P. L. English and foreign coins and tokens.*

A. D. Hamilton & Co (ANA)
7 St Vincent Place, Glasgow G1 5JA (0141 221 5423, fax 0141 248 6019, website www.antiquesglasgow, email jeffrey@hamiltons.junglelink.co.uk). Mon-Sat 10.00-17.00. *British and World coins.*

Peter Hancock
40–41 West Street, Chichester, West Sussex PO19 1RP (01243 786173). Tues-Sat. *World coins, medals & banknotes.*

P. Hanson
160 Princess Road, Buckhurst Hill, Essex IG9 5DJ. *P. L. Inexpensive world coins.*

Munthandel G. Henzen
PO Box 42, NL - 3958ZT, Amerogngen, Netherlands. (0031 343 430564 fax 0031 343 430542, email henzen.coins@tiscali.nl *Ancients, Dutch & foreign coins. L*

History In Coins.com
www.historyincoins.com (01949 836988) *World Coins*

Craig Holmes
6 Marlborough Drive, Bangor, Co Down BT19 1HB. *P. L. Low cost banknotes of the world.*

R. G. Holmes
11 Cross Park, Ilfracombe, Devon EX34 8BJ (01271 864474). *P. L. Coins, world crowns and banknotes.*

John L. Homan
Oxford Grange, Marsh Lane, Barrow Haven, Barrow-on-Humber, South Humberside DN19 7ER (01469 32109). *P. Greek, Roman and Byzantine coins.*

Homeland Holding Ltd (IBNS)
Homeland, St John, Jersey, Channel Islands
JE3 4AB (01534 65339). Mon-Fri 09.00-2.00. *World coins.*
HTSM Coins
26 Dosk Avenue, Glasgow G13 4LQ. *P. L. British and foreign coins and banknotes.*
T. A. Hull
15 Tangmere Crescent, Hornchurch, Essex RM12 5PL. *P. L. British coins, farthings to crowns, tokens.*
Humber Coins (BNTA)
PO Box 16, Scunthorpe Humberside DN15 7AA (01724 763990) *P. British Coins*
J. Hume
107 Halsbury Road East, Northolt, Middlesex UB5 4PY (020 8864 1731). *P. L. Chinese coins.*
D. A. Hunter
www.dahunter.co.uk/coins, email coins@dahunter.co.uk. *P., L. UK and world coin*
D. D. & A. Ingle
380 Carlton Hill, Nottingham (0115 9873325). Mon-Sat 09.30–17.00. *World coins.*
R. Ingram Coins
206 Honeysuckle Road, Bassett, Southampton, Hants SO16 3BU. (023 8032 4258, website: www.ringramcoins.com, email: ybu36@dial.pipex.com. *P. L. Dealers in UK coins*
Intercol London (ANA, IBNS)
43 Templars Cresent, London N3 3QR (020 7349 2207) *P Paper money of the world*
Peter Ireland Ltd (BNTA, IBNS)
31 Clifton Street, Blackpool, Lancs FY1 1JQ (01253 621588 fax 01253 621589). Mon-Sat 09.00-17.30. *British and world coins, medals and tokens.*
JAK (IBNS)
31 Vapron Road, Mannamead, Plymouth, Devon PL3 5NJ (01752 665405). *P. L. GB and Commonwealth banknotes.*
F. J. Jeffery & Son Ltd
Haines Croft, Corsham Road, Whitley, Melksham, Wilts SN12 8QF. (01225 703143). *P. British, Commonwealth and foreign coins.*
Richard W. Jeffery
Trebehor, Porthcurno, Penzance, Cornwall TR19 6LS (01736 871263). *P. British and world coins.*
Jersey Coin Co Ltd
26 Halkett Street, St Helier, Jersey, Channel Islands (01534 25743). Mon-Sat 09.00–17.00. *World coins.*
J. G. Coins
PO Box 206, Southshore, Blackpool FY1 6GZ. (01253 349138). *P. L British Coins.*
Ian Johnson
PO Box 28, Swinton, Manchester M27 3FR (01204 393944). *P. L. Ancient European and Oriental coins.*
I. L. Johnson
63, Sedley Close, Parkwood, Kent ME8 9QZ. (01634 261037) *P. L. English coins 1672–1967*
Robert Johnson Coin Co
PO Box 181, Stamford, Lincs PE9 4XA (01778 561520). *British and world coins.*
Jumbo Coins
22 Woodend Lane, Stalybridge, Cheshire SK15 2SR (0161 338 5741). Fri-Sat 14.00-19.00. *World coins, medals and tokens.*
Kates Paper Money
Kate Gibson,PO Box 819, Camerley, Surrey, GU16 6ZU. www.katespapermoney.co.uk (01276 24954) *Banknotes*

KB Coins (BNTA)
50 Lingfield Road, Martins Wood, Stevenage, Herts SG1 5SL (01438 312661, fax 01438 311990). 09.00–18.00 by appointment only. *L. Mainly British coins.*
K&M Coins
PO Box 3662, Wolverhampton WV10 6ZW (0771 2381880/079719 50246, email: M_Bagguley@hotmail. com). *English milled coin*
Knightsbridge Coins (ANA, BNTA, IAPN, PNG)
43 Duke Street, St James's, London SW1Y 6DD (020 7930 8215/7597 Fax 020 7930 8214). Mon-Fri 10.00–17.30. *Quality coins of the world.*
Lancashire Coin & Medal Co
31 Adelaide Street, Fleetwood, Lancs FY7 6AD (01253 779308). *P. British coins and medals.*
Lennox Gallery Ltd
K12/13, 4 Davies Mews, London, W1Y 1AR. (020 7629 9119 fax 020 7629 9119). *Ancient coins.*
Peter Licence
31 Reigate Way, Wallington, Surrey SM6 8NU (020 8688 5297). *P. British and world coins.*
Lighthouse Publications (UK BNTA)
4 Beaufort Road, Reigate, Surrey RH2 9DJ (01737 244222 Fax 0737 24743). *L. Manufacturers and stockists of coin albums, cabinets and numismatic accessories.*
Lindner Publications Ltd
3a Hayle Industrial Park, Hayle, Cornwall TR27 5JR (01736 751914 fax: 01736 751911, email lindneruk@cs.com). Mon–Fri 09.00–13.00. *L. Manufacturers of coin albums, cabinets and accessories.*
Jan Lis (BNTA)
Beaver Coin Room, 57 Philbeach Gardens, London SW5 9ED (020 7373 4553 fax 020 7373 4555). *By appointment only. European coins.*
Keith Lloyd
45 Bramblewood, The Beeches, Ipswich, Suffolk IP8 3RS (01473 603067). *P. L. Greek, Roman coins.*
Lockdale Coins (BNTA)
Shops at: 37 Upper Orwell Street, Ipswich IP4 1BR.(01473 218588), 168 London Road South, Lowestoft NR33 0BB (01502 568468) & 23 Magdalene Street, Cambridge, CB3 OAF. (01223 361163). *L.* (Shops open 9.30–4.30 Mon–Sat). *World coins, medals, banknotes and accessories.*
Stephen Lockett (BNTA)
12, Redhill Wood, New Ash Green, Kent DA3 8QH (01474 871464). *British and world coins.*
Lodge Antiquities (John & Margaret Cummings)
PO Box 38, Grantham, Lincs NG31 6AA (01476 593833, email: lodgeantiquities.com). *Ancient coins and artefacts.*
Mike Longfield Detectors
83 Station Road, Balsall Common, nr Coventry, Warwickshire CV7 7FN (01676 533274). Mon-Sat 09.30-17.00. *Metal detectors.*
Richard M. Lubbock (ANA, BNTA, IAPN, IBNS)
PO Box 352, London E14 7WB (020 7790 5115 fax 020 7790 5445). *World coins and medals.*
Don MacRae Coins
PO Box 233, Uxbridge, Middlesex UB9 4HY (01895 832625). *P. British and world coins.*
David Magnay
11 Lake Hill Drive, Cowbridge, Vale of Glamorgan, Wales UK CF71 7HR. (01446 774335) *Toy and Model Coins, Imitation Spade Guineas.*

Mannin Collections Ltd
5 Castle Street, Peel, Isle of Man, IM5 1AN (01624 843897, email: manncoll@advsys.co.uk). Mon-Sat 10.00-16.00. Closed Thu. *IOM coins, tokens, etc*

Manston Coins of Bath
Bartletts St. Antique Centre, Bath (01761 416133. *Coins, tokens, medals.*

I. Markovits
1-3 Cobbold Mews, London W12 9LB (020 8749 3000). *Enamelled coins.*

Marron Coins
7 Beacon Close, Sheffield, South Yorkshire S9 1AA (0114 2433500, website www.marroncoins.free-online.co.uk, email marronsca@aol.com). *P. English coins.*

C. J. Martin (Coins) Ltd (BNTA)
85 The Vale, Southgate, London N14 6AT (020 8882 1509, www.ancientart.co.uk). P. L. Bi-monthly catalogue. *Greek, Roman & English hammered coins.*

M. G. Coins & Antiquities
12 Mansfield, High Wych, Herts cm21 0JT. (01279 721719). *L. Ancient and hammered coins, antiquities.*

Giuseppe Micelli
204 Bants Lane, Duston, Northampton NN5 6AH (01604 581533). *P.L. British coins and medals.*

Michael Coins
6 Hillgate Street, London W8 7SR (020 7727 1518). Mon-Fri 10.00-17.00. *World coins and banknotes.*

David Miller Coins & Antiquities (ANA, BNTA)
PO Box 711, Hemel Hempstead, HP2 4UH (tel/fax 01442 251492). *Ancient and hammered English coins.*

Timothy Millett
PO Box 20851, London SE22 0YN (tel: 020 8693 1111, fax: 020 8299 3733). *L. Historical medals.*

Frank Milward (ANA, BNTA)
2 Ravensworth Road, Mortimer, Berkshire RG7 3UU (01734 322843). *P. European coins.*

Graeme & Linda Monk (ANA, BNTA)
PO Box 201, Croydon, Surrey, CR9 7AQ (020 8656 4583 fax 020 8656 4583). *P. Fair organisers.*

Mike Morey
9 Elmtrees, Long Crendon, Bucks HP18 9DG. *P. L. British coins, halfcrowns to farthings.*

Peter Morris (BNTA, IBNS)
1 Station Concourse, Bromley North Station, Bromley, BR1 1NN or PO Box 223, Bromley, BR1 4EQ (020 8313 3410 fax 020 8466 8502, website www.petermorris.co.uk, email info@petermorris.co.uk). Mon-Fri 10.00-18.00, Sat 0900-14.00 or by appointment. *L. British and world coins, proof sets and numismatic books.*

James Murphy
PO Box 122, Chorley, Lancashire PR7 2GE. (01257 274 381). *P. L. Ancient coins and antiquities.*

Colin Narbeth & Son Ltd (ANA, IBNS)
20 Cecil Court, Leicester Square, London WC2N 4HE (020 7379 6975 fax 01727 811 244, website http://www.colin-narbeth.com). Mon-Sat 10.30-17.00. *World banknotes.*

New Forest Leaves
Bisterne Close, Burley, Ringwood, Hants BH24 4BA (014253 3315). *Publishers of numismatic books.*

Peter Nichols
2 Norman Road, St Leonards on Sea, East Sussex TN37 6NH. (01424 436682, website www.coincabinets.com, email coincabinets@freezone.co.uk).

Wayne Nicholls
PO Box 44, Bilston, West Midlands. (01543 45476) *L. Choice English coins*

Noble Investments (UK) plc (BNTA)
Barton Hall, Hardy Street, Eccles, Manchester M30 7WJ. London Office (by appointment 0207 581 0240, email: igoldbart@aol.com). *Ancient Greek, Roman, hammered, milled and world coins*

North Wales Coins Ltd (BNTA)
1b Penrhyn Road, Colwyn Bay, Clwyd (01492 533023/532129). Mon-Sat (closed Wed) 09.30-17.30. *British coins.*

Notability (IBNS)
'Mallards', Chirton, Devizes, Wilts SN10 3QX (01380 723961, website www.notability-banknotes.com, email: banknotes@ukdealers.com. *P. L. Banknotes of the world.*

NP Collectables
9 Main Street, Gedney Dyke, Spalding, Lincs PE12 0AJ (01406 365211Ireland (010 35322 29385). *P. L. English Hammered and Milled coins.*

Glenn S. Ogden
Duncraig, Canada Hill, Ogwell, Newton Abbot, Devon TQ12 6AF. (01626 331663) *P. L. English milled.*

John Ogden Coins
Hodge Clough Cottage, Moorside, Oldham OL1 4JW (0161 678 0709) *P. L. Ancient and hammered coins.*

Michael O'Grady (IBNS)
PO Box 307, Pinner, Middlesex HA5 4XT (020 8868 5582). *P. British and world paper money.*

Colin James O'Keefe
5 Pettits Place, Dagenham, Essex RM10 8NL. *P. British and European coins.*

Don Oliver Gold Coins
Stanford House, 23 Market Street, Stourbridge, West Midlands DY8 1AB (01384 877901). Mon-Fri 10.00-17.00. *British gold coins.*

Ongar Coins
14 Longfields, Marden Ash, Ongar, Essex IG7 6DS. *P.World coins.*

Tim Owen Coins
63 Allerton Grange Rise, Leeds 17, West Yorkshire (0113 2688015). *P. L. Quality hammered coins.*

Oxford Coins
25, Weldon Road, New Marston, Oxford OX3 0HP (01865 726939). *British coins.*

P&D Medallions
PO Box 269, Berkhampstead, Herts HP4 3FT. (01442 865127, email P&D@medallions.freeserve.co.uk). *Historical and Commemorative medals of the world. P.*

Pavlos S. Pavlou
Stand L17, Grays Antique Market, 1-7 Davies Mews, Mayfair, London W1Y 2LP (020 7629 9449) email: pspavlou@hotmail.com. *Ancient, Medieval & Modern Coins*

Penrith Coin & Stamp Centre
37 King Street, Penrith, Cumbria CA11 7AY (01768 64185). Mon-Sat 09.00-17.30. *World coins.*

Pentland Coins (IBNS)
Pentland House, 92 High Street, Wick, Caithness KW14 L5. *P. British and world coins and world banknotes.*

Gary Phelps
PO Box 136, Benfleet, Essex SS7 4WG (garyph@bluyonder.co.uk, www.garyphelps.co.uk) *Modern patterns and crowns*

John Phillimore
The Old Post Office, Northwood, Shropshire SY4 5NN. *L. Foreign coins 1600–1950.*

Phil Phipps
PO Box 31, Emsworth, Hants PO10 7WE (tel/fax 01243 376086, email philip@worldcurrency.cc). *P. L. World and German banknotes*

David C. Pinder
20 Princess Road West, Leicester LE1 6TP (0116 2702439). *P. Greek, Roman and Byzantine coins.*

Pobjoy Mint Ltd (ANA)
Millennium House, Kingswood Park, Bonsor Drive, Kingswood, Surrey KT20 6AY (01737 818181 fax 01737 818199). Mon–Fri 09.00–17.00. *Europe's largest private mint. New issues.*

S. R. Porter (BNTA)
18 Trinity Road, Headington Quarry, Oxford OX3 8LQ (01865 766851). *P. L. Ancient and British coins, some foreign, tokens, banknotes and accessories.*

David Pratchett
Trafalgar Square Collectors Centre, 7 Whitcombe Street, London WC2H 7HA. (020 7930 1979, fax 020 7930 1152, website www.coinsonline.co.uk, email info@coinsonline.co.uk). Mon–Fri 10.00–7.30. *Specialist in gold and silverworld coins.*

Predecimal.com
Hauptstr. 33, Burkhardsdorf, 09235, Germany. (+491741 477182) www.predecimal.com. *British coins*

Irfan Raja
67 Stamford Street, Bradford BD4 8SD (07731 841264, email: irygfg@lycos.co.uk). *World coins.*

George Rankin Coin Co Ltd (ANA)
325 Bethnal Green Road, London E2 6AH (020 7729 1280 fax 020 7729 5023). Mon–Sat 10.00-18.00 (half-day Thu). *World coins.*

Mark Rasmussen (BNTA)
PO Box 42, Betchworth RH3 7YR (01737 84100, email mark.rasmussen@btinternet.com). *Hammered and milled coins. L*

Mark T. Ray (formerly MTR Coins)
22a Kingsnorth Close, Newark, Notts NG24 1PS. (01636 703152). *P. British coins.* 2379). Mon-Sat

Rhyl Coin Shop
12 Sussex Street, Rhyl, Clwyd (01745 338112). Mon-Sat 10.00-17.30. *World coins and banknotes.*

Chris Rigby
PO Box 181, Worcester WR1 1YE (01905 28028). *P. L. Modern British coins.*

Roderick Richardson (BNTA)
The Old Granary Antiques Centre, King's Staithe Lane, King's Lynn, Norfolk. (01553 670833) *L. English, Hammered and early milled coins.*

F. J. Rist
PO Box 4, Ibstock, Leics LE67 6ZJ (01530 264278). *P. L. Ancient and medieval coins, British coins and antiquities.*

Robin-on-Acle Coins
Parkeston House, Parkeston Quay, Harwich, Essex CO12 4PJ (01255 554440, email: enquiries@robin-on-acle-coins.co.uk). *Ancient to modern coins and paper money.*

Ian Robinson
PO Box 929, Burgess Hill, West Sussex RH15 9FN (01444 242215, website www.iamcoins.co.uk, email ian@iamcoins.co.uk). *P. L. Quality English milled coins.*

S. J. Rood & Co Ltd
52–53 Burlington Arcade, London W1V 9AE (0171 493 0739). Mon-Sat 09.30-17.00. *World gold coins.*

Royal Gold
PO Box 123, Saxonwold, 2132, South Africa, e-mail royalg@iafrica.com (+27 11 483 0161, email: royalg@iafrica.com) *Gold Coins*

Royal Mint Coin Club
PO Box 500, Cardiff CF1 1YY (01443 623456). *P. New issues struck by the Royal Mint.*

Colin de Rouffignac (BNTA)
57, Wigan Lane, Wigan, Lancs WN1 2LF (01942 237927) *P. English and Scottish hammered.*

Chris A. Rudd (IAPN, BNTA)
PO Box 222, Aylsham, Norfolk, NR11 6TY (01263 735007 fax 01263 731777, website www.celticcoins.com). *P. L. Celtic coins.*

Colin Rumney (BNTA)
26 Caer Felin, Llanrheadr, Denbigh, Clwyd LL16 4PR (074 578621). *All world including ancients.*

R & J Coins
21b Alexandra Street, Southend-on-Sea, Essex SS1 1DA (01702 345995). Mon-Sat 10.00–16.00 (closed Wed). *World coins.*

Safe Albums (UK) Ltd
16 Falcon Business Park, 38 Ivanhoe Road, Finchampstead, Berkshire RG40 4QQ. (0118 932 8976 fax 0118 932 8612).

Saltford Coins
Harcourt, Bath Road, Saltford, Bristol, Avon BS31 3DQ (01225 873512). *P. British, Commonwealth and world coins.*

Satin
PO Box 63, Stockport, Cheshire SK4 5BU. (07940 393583 answer machine)

Schwer Coins (ANA, BNTA)
6 South Hill, Felixstowe, Suffolk, IP11 8AA (01394 278580 fax 0394 271348). *P. World coins.*

David Seaman
PO Box 449, Waltham Cross EN9 3WZ. (01992 719723, email davidseamancoins@lineone.net). *P. L. Hammered, Milled, Maundy.*

Patrick Semmens
3 Hospital Road, Half Key, Malvern, Worcs WR14 1UZ (0886 33123). *P. European and British coins.*

Mark Senior
553 Falmer Road, Woodingdean, Brighton, Sussex (01273 309359). By appointment only. *P. L. Saxon, Norman and English hammered coins.*

S. E. Sewell
PO Box 104, Ipswich, Suffolk IP5 7QL (01473 626 950). *Mainly British milled coins.*

Robert Sharman Numismatist (ANA)
36 Dairsie Road, Eltham, London SE9 1XH (020 8850 6450). *P. British coins.*

Shepshed Coins & Jewellery
24 Charnwood Road, Shepshed, Leics LE12 9QF (01509 502511). Mon, Wed-Sat 09.15-16.30. *British coins.*

Simmons Gallery (ANA, BNTA, IBNS)
PO Box 104, Leytonstone, London E11 1ND (020 8989 8097, email info@simmonsgallery.co.uk, www.simmonsgallery.co.uk). *Organisers of the London Coin Fair, Holiday Inn, Bloomsbury, London W1. L. Coins, tokens and medals.*

Raymond J. Sleet
11 Seagull Close, Kempshott, Basingstoke, Hants RG22 5QR (01256 53256 fax 01256 63525) *General world coins and tokens.*

J. Smith (BNTA)
47 The Shambles, York YO1 2LX (01904 654769).
Mon-Sat 09.30–17.00. *World coins.*

Neil Smith
PO Box 348, Lincoln LN6 0TX (01522 684681 fax
01522 689528). *GB and World Gold coins 1816 to date,
including modern proof issues.*

Jim Smythe
PO Box 6970, Birmingham B23 7WD (e-mail
Jimdens@aol.com). *P. L. 19th/20th century British
and world coins.*

S & B Coins
Suite 313, St Loyes House, 20 Loyes Street, Bedford
MK40 1ZL (01234 270260). *P. L. British coins and
medallions.*

George Sowden
Coins Galore, The Lizard, nr Helston, Cornwall
TR12 7NU (01326 290300). *P. World coins.*

Spink & Son Ltd (ANA, BNTA, IAPN, IBNS)
69 Southampton Row, Bloomsbury, London.
WC1B 4ET (020 7563 2820, fax 020 7563 4066,
website www.spink-online.com, email
info@spinkandson.com). *Ancient to modern world
coins, orders, medals and decorations, banknotes and
numismatic books*

SPM Jewellers (BNTA)
112 East Street, Southampton, Hants SO14 3HD
(023 80 223255/020 80 227923, fax 023 80 335634,
wwbsite www.spmgoldcoins.co.uk, email
user@spm.in2home.co.uk).
Tue-Sat 09.15–17.00, Sat 09.15–16.00. *World coins
and medals.*

Stamp & Collectors Centre
404 York Town Road, College Town, Camberley,
Surrey GU15 4PR (01276 32587 fax 01276 32505).
Mon, Tue, Thu, Sat 09.00–17.00, Wed, Fri 09.00–
1900. *World coins and medals.*

St Edmunds Coins & Banknotes
PO Box 118, Bury St Edmunds IP33 2NE. (01284
761894)

Sterling Coins & Medals
2 Somerset Road, Boscombe, Bournemouth, Dorset
BH7 6JH (01202 423881). Mon-Sat 09.30–16.30
(closed Wed). *World coins and medals.*

Strawbridge
Tanglewood, Ivy Tree Hill, Stokeinteignhead,
Newton Abbott, Devon TQ12 4QH (01626 873783,
emailjim@strawbridge.co.uk).
P. L. Coins, tokens, medals, banknotes.

Studio Coins (ANA, BNTA)
16 Kilham Lane, Winchester, Hants SO22 5PT
(01962 853156 fax 01962 624246). *P. English coins.*

Surena Numismatics (BNTA)
PO Box 2194, London NW8 6QQ (0831 220010). *P.
Parthian, Sassanian, Islamic coins.*

The Collector
PO Box 335, Tiptree, Colchester, Essex CO5 9WP
(01376 572755 fax 01376 573883, email
collector@btinternet.com). *Collectable items.*

The Coin Exchange
www.the-coin-exchange.com Email: info@the-
coin-exchange.com. Phone 01340 881422. *British
coins*

Time Line Originals
PO Box 193, Upminster, RM14 3WH Tel: (01708)
222384. Mobile 07775 651218, Email: sales@time-
line.co.uk

Stuart J. Timmins
Smallwood Lodge Bookshop, Newport, Salop
(01952 813232). Mon-Sat 09.30–17.00. *Numismatic
literature.*

R. Tims
39 Villiers Road, Watford, Herts WD1 4AL. *P. L.
Uncirculated world banknotes.*

Trafalgar Square Collectors' Centre (ANA, LM,
OMRS)
7 Whitcomb Street, Trafalgar Square, London
WC2H 7HA (020 7930 1979). Mon-Fri 10.00–17.30.
*World coins and commemorative medals. War medals
and decorations.*

D. A. Travis
8 Cookridge Drive, Leeds LS16 7LT. *P. L. US
coins.*

Michael Trenerry Ltd
PO Box 55, Truro, Cornwall TR1 2YQ (01872
277977 fax 01872 225565). By appointment only. *L.
Roman, Celtic and English hammered coins, tokens.*

Vera Trinder Ltd
38 Bedford Street, Strand, London WC2E 9EU (020
7836 2365/6). Mon-Fri 08.30–17.30. *L. Coin
catalogues and books, albums, envelopes, cases etc*

Robert Tye
Poll Toran, Loch Eynort, South Uist PA81 5SJ. *P.
European and Oriental hammered coins.*

Valda Coins
80 Aberfan Road, Aberfan, Mid Glamorgan CF48
4QJ. (01443 690452). *P. L.*

Vale (ADA BNTA)
21 Tranquil Vale, Blackheath, London SE3 0BU
(020 8852 9817). Mon-Sat 10.00–17.30 (closed Thu).
British coins and medals.

Valued History
9 Market Place, Ely, Cambs CB7 4NP. (01353
654080, www.historyforsale.co.uk). *Coins and
antiquities.*

Tony Vaughan Collectables
PO Box 364, Wolverhampton, WV3 9PW (01902
27351). *P. L. World coins and medals.*

Victory Coins (BNTA)
184 Chichester Road, North End, Portsmouth,
Hants PO2 0AX (023 92 751908/663450). Thurs-Sat
09.00–17.00. *British and world coins.*

Viking Metal Detectors
1 angela Street, Mill Hill, Blacburn, Lancashire BB2
4DJ (01254 55887 fax 01254 676901, email
viking@metaldetectors.co.uk)). *Metal detectors and
accessories*

Mark J. Vincenzi (BNTA)
Rylands, Earls Colne, Essex. CO6 2LE (01787
222555). *P. Greek, Roman, Hammered.*

Vista World Banknotes
5 Greenfields Way, Burley-in-Wharfedale, Ilkley,
W. Yorks LS29 7RB. (Email
vistabanknotes@barclays.net).

Mike Vosper
PO Box 32, Hockwold, Brandon IP26 4HX (01842
828292, website www.vosper4coins.co.uk, email
mikevosper@vosper4coins.co.uk).

B. M. & S. A. Weeks
PO Box 1447, Salisbury, Wilts SP5 2YG (01725
510311). *L. British coins, world crowns and medals.*

Weighton Coin Wonders
E-shop www.weightoncoin.com (01430 879060)
Modern gold, silver proofs and sets.

John Welsh
PO Box 150, Burton-on-Trent, Staffs DE13 7LB
(01543 73073 fax 0543 473234). *P. L. British coins.*

Pam West (IBNS, BNTA)
PO Box 257, Sutton, Surrey SM3 9WW (020 8641
3224, website west-banknotes.co.uk, email
pamwestbritnotes@compuserve.com). *P. L.
English banknotes.*

West Essex Coin Investments (BNTA, IBNS)
Croft Cottage, Station Road, Alderholt,
Fordingbridge, Hants SP6 3AZ (01425 656 459).
British and World coins and paper money.

R & J White (IBNS)
29 Shortacre, Basildon, Essex SS14 2LR (01268
522923). *P. L. Banknotes and world ephemera.*

Whites Electronics (UK) Ltd
35 Harbour Road, Inverness IV1 1UA (01463
223456 , email sales@whelects.demon.co.uk) *Metal
detectors*

Whitmore (BNTA)
Teynham Lodge, Chase Road, Upper Colwall,
Malvern, Worcs WR13 6DT (01684 40651). *P.
World coins, tokens and medals.*

Gary R. Williams
PO Box 2929, Eastbourne BN20 9WE (01323 486044).
*British coins from Roman to modern (some foreign),
specialist in crowns and farthings.*

World Coins
35–36 Broad Street, Canterbury, Kent CT1 2LR
(01227 768887). Mon-Sat 09.30–17.30 (half-day
Thu). *World & British coins, tokens & banknotes.*

Worldwide Coins (IBNS)
PO Box 11, Wavertree, Liverpool L15 0FG. email:
sales@worldwidecoins.co.uk,
www.worldwidecoins.co.uk. *World coins and paper
money.*

World Treasure Books
PO Box 5, Newport, Isle of Wight PO30 5QE (01983
740712). *L. Coins, books, metal detectors*

Barry Wright,
54 Dooley Drive, Bootle, Merseyside. L30 8RT. *P.
L. World banknotes.*

I. S. Wright (Australia Numismatic Co)
208 Sturt Street, Ballarat, Vic. Australia 3350 (0061
3 5332 3856 fax 0061 3 5331 6426, email
ausnumis@netconnect.comau. *P. Coins, banknotes,
medallions, tokens.*

B. N. Yarwood (ANA)
Yarwood Hall, Luttongate Road, Sutton St
Edmund, Spalding, Lincs PE12 0LH.
P. British and US coins.

York Coins
P.M.B #387 7211 Austin Street, Forest Street, New
York. Tel/fax: (718) 544 0120 email:
antony@yorkcoins.com

Banks, Mints and Numismatic *Bureaux* of the world

Many national banks and mints operate numismatic bureaux and sales agencies from which coins, medals and other numismatic products may be obtained direct. The conditions under which purchases may be made vary considerably. In many cases at the present time bureaux will accept orders from overseas customers quoting their credit card number and its expiry date; but in others payment can only be made by certified bank cheque, or international money order, or by girobank. Cash is seldom, if ever, acceptable. It is best to write in the first instance to enquire about methods of payment.

A

National Mint, Baghe Arg, Kabul, Afghanistan

Bank Mille Afghan, Kabul, Afghanistan

Banque d'Algerie, Sucursale d'Alger, 8 Boulevard Carnot, Alger, Algeria

Banco de Angola, Luanda, Daroal, Angola

Casa de Moneda de la Nacion, Avenida Antartica, Buenos Aires, BA, Argentina

Royal Australian Mint, Department of the Treasury, Canberra, ACT, Australia

GoldCorp Australia, Perth Mint Buildings, GPO Box M924, Perth, Western Australia 6001

Oesterreichsiches Hauptmunzamt, Am Heumarkt 1, A-1031 Wien, Postfach 225, Austria

Oesterreichische Nationalbank, A-1090 Wien, Otto Wagner-platz 3, Austria

B

Treasury Department, PO Box 557, Nassau, Bahamas (*coins*)

Ministry of Finance, PO Box 300, Nassau, Bahamas (*banknotes*)

Bank of Bahrain, PO Box 106, Manama, Bahrain

Eastern Bank, PO Box 29, Manama, Bahrain

Monnaie Royale de Belgique, Avenue de Pacheco 32, B-1000 Bruxelles, Belgium

Banque Nationale de Belgique SA, Caisse Centrale, Bruxelles, Belgium

Banque de Bruxelles SA, 2 Rue de la Regence, Bruxelles 1, Belgium

Casa de la Moneda, Potosi, Bolivia

Banco Central de Bolivia, La Paz, Bolivia

Casa da Moeda, Praca da Republica 173, Rio de Janeiro, Brazil

Hemus FTO, 7 Vasil Levski Street, Sofia C-1, Bulgaria

Banque de la Republique, Bujumbura, Burundi

C

Banque Centrale, Douala, Boite Postale 5.445, Cameroun

Royal Canadian Mint, 320 Sussex Drive, Ottawa 2, Ontario, Canada K1A 0G8

Casa de Moneda, Quinta Normal, Santiago, Chile

Casa de Moneda, Calle 11 no 4-93, Bogota, Colombia

Numismatic Section, The Treasury, Avarua, Rarotonga, Cook Islands

Banco Centrale de Costa Rica, Departamento de Contabilidad, San Jose, Costa Rica, CA

Central Bank of Cyprus, PO Box 1087, Nicosia, Cyprus

Artia, Ve Smekach 30, PO Box 790, Praha 1, Czech Republic

D

Den Kongelige Mønt, Amager Boulevard 115, København S, Denmark

Danmarks Nationalbank, Holmens Kanal 17, 1060 København K, Denmark

Banco Central de Santo Domingo, Santo Domingo, Dominican Republic

E

Banco Central, Quito, Ecuador

Mint House, Abbassia, Cairo, Egyptian Arab Republic

Exchange Control Department, National Bank of Egypt, Cairo, Egyptian Arab Republic

Banco Central de la Republica, Santa Isabel, Equatorial Guinea

Commercial Bank of Ethiopia, Foreign Branch, PO Box 255, Addis Ababa, Ethiopia

F

Currency Board, Victoria Parade, Suva, Fiji

Suomen Rahapaja, Katajanokanlaituri 3, Helsinki 16, Finland

Suomen Pankki, PO Box 10160, Helsinki 10, Finland

Hotel de Monnaie, 11 Quai de Conti, 75-Paris 6e, France

G

Banque Centrale Libreville, Boite Postale 112, Gabon

Verkaufstelle fur Sammlermunzen, D-638 Bad Homburg vdH, Bahnhofstrasse 16–18, Germany

Staatliche Munze Karlsruhe, Stephanienstrasse 28a, 75 Karlsruhe, Germany

Staatliche Munze Cannstatt, Taubenheimerstrasse 77, 7 Stuttgart-Bad, Germany

Bayerisches Hauptmunzamt, Hofgraben 4, 8 Munich, Germany

Hamburgische Munze, Norderstrasse 66, 2 Hamburg 1, Germany

Bank of Ghana, PO Box 2674, Accra, Ghana

Pobjoy Mint, Millennia House, Kingswood Park, Bonsor Drive, Kingswood, Surrey KT20 6AY

Royal Mint, Llantrisant, Mid Glamorgan, Wales, CF7 8YT

Royal Mint Coin Club, PO Box 500, Cardiff, CF1 1HA

Bank of Greece, Treasury Department, Cash, Delivery & Despatch Division, PO Box 105, Athens, Greece

Casa Nacional de Moneda, 6a Calle 4-28, Zona 1, Ciudad Guatemala, Republica de Guatemala CA

States Treasury, St Peter Port, Guernsey, Channel Islands

Bank of Guyana, PO Box 658, Georgetown, Guyana

H

Banque Nationale de la Republique d'Haiti, Rue Americaine et Rue Fereu, Port-au-Prince, Haiti

Banco Central de Honduras, Tegucigalpa DC, Honduras CA

State Mint, Ulloi utca 102, Budapest VIII, Hungary

Artex, PO Box 167, Budapest 62, Hungary

Magyar Nemzeti Bank, Board of Exchange, Budapest 54, Hungary

I

Sedlabanki Islands, Reykjavik, Iceland

Indian Government Mint, Bombay 1, India

Arthie Vasa, Keabajoran Baru, Djakarta, Indonesia

Perum Peruri, Djakarta, Indonesia

National Mint, Tehran, Iran

Bank Markazi Iran, Tehran, IranCentral Bank of Iraq, PO Box 64, Baghdad, Iraq

Central Bank of Ireland, Dublin 2, Republic of Ireland

The Treasury, Government Buildings, Prospect Hill, Douglas, Isle of Man

Israel Stamp and Coin Gallery, 4 Maze Street, Tel Aviv, Israel

Istituto Poligraphico e Zecca dello Stato, Via Principe Umberto, Roma, Italy

J

Decimal Currency Board, PO Box 8000, Kingston, Jamaica

Mint Bureau, 1 Shinkawasakicho, Kita-ku, Osaka 530, Japan

Numismatic Section, Treasury Department, St Helier, Jersey

Central Bank of Jordan, Amman, Jordan

Banque Nationale du Liban, Rue Masraf Loubnan, Beirut, Lebanon

K

Central Bank, PO Box 526, Kuwait

L

Bank of Lithuania, Cash Department, Gedimino av. 6, 2001 Vilius, Lithuania

Caisse Generale de l'Etat, 5 Rue Goethe, Luxembourg-Ville, Grande Duche de Luxembourg

M

Institut d'Emission Malgache, Boite Postale 205, Tananarive, Madagascar

Central Bank of Malta, Valletta 1, Malta

Casa de Moneda, Calle del Apartado no 13, Mexico 1, DF, Mexico

Le Tresorier General des Finances, Monte Carlo, Principaute de Monaco

Banque de l'Etat du Maroc, Rabat, Morocco

Banco Nacional Ultramarino, Maputo, Republica de Mocambique

British Bank of the Middle East, Muscat

N

Royal Mint, Dharahara, Katmandu, Nepal

Nepal Rastra Bank, Katmandu, Nepal

Rijks Munt, Leidseweg 90, Utrecht, Netherlands

Hollandsche Bank-Unie NV, Willemstad, Breedestraat 1, Curacao, Netherlands Antilles

Central Bank of Curacao, Willemstad, Curacao, Netherlands Antilles

The Treasury, Private Bag, Lambton Quay, Wellington, New Zealand

Banco de Nicaragua, Departamento de Emison, La Tresoria, Apartada 2252, Managua, Nicaragua

Nigerian Security Printing and Minting Corporation, Ahmadu Bello Road, Victoria Island, Lagos, Nigeria

Central Bank of Nigeria, Tinubu Square LB, Lagos, Nigeria

Norges Bank, Oslo, Norway

Den Kongelige Mynt, Hyttegaten, Konigsberg, Norway

P

Pakistan State Mint, Baghban Pura, Lahore 9, Pakistan

National Development Bank, Asuncion, Paraguay

Casa Nacional de Moneda, Calle Junin 791, Lima, Peru

Central Bank of the Philippines, Manila, Philippines

Bank Handlowy w Warszawie, Ul. Romuald Traugutta 7, Warsaw, Poland

Desa Foreign Trade Department, Al. Jerozolimskie 2, Warszawa, Poland

Casa da Moeda, Avenida Dr Antonio Jose de Almeida, Lisbon 1, Portugal

R

Cartimex, 14-18 Aristide Briand St, PO Box 134-135, Bucharest, Roumania

Bank of Foreign Trade, Commercial Department, Moscow K 16, Neglinnaja 12, Russian Federation

Banque Nationale du Rwanda, Boite Postale 351, Kigali, Republique Rwandaise

S

Numismatic Section, Box 194, GPO, Apia, Samoa

Azienda Autonoma di Stato Filatelica-Numismatica, Casalla Postale 1, 47031 Repubblica di San Marino

Banque Internationale pour le Commerce, 2 Avenue Roume, Dakar, Senegal

Bank of Yugoslavia, PO Box 1010, Belgrade, Serbia

The Treasury, PO Box 59, Victoria, Seychelles

Bank of Sierra Leone, PO Box 30, Freetown, Sierra Leone

The Singapore Mint, 249 Jalan Boon Lay, Jurong, Singapore

South African Mint, PO Box 464, Pretoria, South Africa

Government Printing Agency, 93 Bukchang Dong, Chungku, Seoul, Republic of South Korea

Fabrica Nacional de Moneda y Timbre, Jorge Juan 106, Madrid 9, Spain

Bank of Sri Lanka, PO Box 241, Colombo, Sri Lanka

Hong Kong and Shanghai Banking Corporation, PO Box 73, Colombo 1, Sri Lanka

Sudan Mint, PO Box 43, Khartoum, Sudan

Bank of Sudan, PO Box 313, Khartoum, Sudan

Bank of Paramaribo, Paramaribo, Suriname

Kungelige Mynt och Justeringsverket, Box 22055, Stockholm 22, Sweden

Eidgenossische Staatskasse, Bundesgasse 14, CH-3003, Berne, Switzerland

Central Bank of Syria, Damascus, Syrian Arab Republic

T

Central Mint of China, 44 Chiu Chuan Street, Taipei, Taiwan, ROC

Royal Thai Mint, 4 Chao Fah Road, Bangkok, Thailand

Numismatic Section, The Treasury, Nuku'alofa, Tonga

Central Bank of Trinidad and Tobago, PO Box 1250, Port of Spain, Trinidad

Banque Centrale de Tunisie, Tunis, Tunisia

State Mint, Maliye Bakanligi Darphane Mudurlugu, Istanbul, Turkey

U

Bank of Uganda, PO Box 7120, Kampala, Uganda

Numismatic Service, US Assay Office, 350 Duboce Avenue, San Francisco, CA, 94102, USA

Office of the Director of the Mint, Treasury Department, Washington, DC, 20220, USA

Philadelphia Mint, 16th and Spring Garden Streets, Philadelphia, PA, 19130, USA

Franklin Mint, Franklin Center, Pennsylvania, 19063, USA

Banco Central del Uruguay, Cerrito 351, Montevideo, RO del Uruguay

V

Ufficio Numismatico, Governatorato dello Stato della Citta de Vaticano, Italy

Banco Central de Venezuela, Caracas, Venezuela

Y

Yemen Bank, Sana'a, Yemen.

Z

Bank of Zambia, PO Box 80, Lusaka, Zambia

Chief Cashier, Reserve Bank, PO Box 1283, Harare, Zimbabwe

Numismatics and
The Law

Counterfeit Currency

A counterfeit is a forgery or imitation of a coin or banknote produced with the intention of defrauding the revenue of the State or deceiving members of the public. By the Coinage Offences Act (1861) it was a felony to counterfeit gold or silver coins. Lesser offences included the gilding of farthings and sixpences to pass them off as half-sovereigns, the possession of moulds, machines or tools clandestinely removed from the Royal Mint, the impairment or diminution of gold or silver coins by filing or clipping (or even the possession of such filings and clippings).

The Coinage Act of 1870 made provision for the counterfeiting of base-metal coins, or the stamping of letters or words on coins of any kind, or the forging of colonial coinage. The most celebrated prosecution under this Act occurred in 1930 when Martin Coles Harman was convicted and fined £5 for issuing bronze coins resembling the British penny and halfpenny for the island of Lundy of which he was then the proprietor. Interestingly, no attempt was made to prosecute the Birmingham Mint which actually struck the coins (prudently omitting the H mintmark).

The making of medals or coins resembling current coin became a misdemeanour under the Counterfeit Medal Act of 1883.This Act is invoked from time to time against manufacturers or distributors of medallic pieces or coin jewellery. Such pieces, often struck in 9 carat gold, are deemed to infringe the Act if, for example, they have a figure even vaguely resembling St George and the Dragon on one side. The use of the royal effigy, however, without due authorisation, is regarded as a misdemeanour punishable by an unlimited fine and the confiscation of tools, dies and instruments. At the present time it is a serious offence to make a counterfeit of a currency note or coin with the intention of passing it off or tendering it as genuine. This offence carries a maximum penalty of ten years' imprisonment or an unlimited fine, or both. Making a counterfeit of a currency note or coin without lawful authority incurs a penalty up to two years'

imprisonment or an unlimited fine, or both.

Passing or tendering as genuine anything which is known or believed to be a counterfeit of a currency note or coin renders the criminal on conviction to a term of ten years' imprisonment or an unlimited fine, or both. The mere possession of any forged note or coin is itself a criminal offence. Possessing countertfeits without authority or permission so to do, and doing so knowingly, renders the possessor liable to two years' imprisonment or an unlimited fine, or both. The Act also stipulates that the reproduction of a current banknote—of the Bank of England or of the Scottish and Northern Irish banks is a serious offence. This clause covers even such apparently innocent acts as making a photocopy (whether in black and white or full colour) of a current banknote, the photography of such a note or the illustration of such a note in any book, magazine or newspaper. Strict regulations are laid down concerning the legitimate illustration of notes, whether current or not, in books and periodicals; such illustrations must be either greatly reduced or enlarged *and* must bear a prominent defacement, such as SPECIMEN or CANCELLED. It is also a serious offence to utilise a reproduction of a current British banknote in any medium. Theoretically this includes such things as tea-towels, T-shirts, mugs, plates and other souvenirs in glass or ceramics, but in practice the law seems to turn a blind eye to such practices. Imitations and parodies of notes and coins are also regarded as infringements of the law, but in these instances prosecution of the offender seldom proceeds; a warning is generally regarded as sufficient, provided that the offending article or articles are withdrawn and suppressed.

The advent of high-definition colour photo-copying in recent years has brought the offence of reproduction into prominence once more. The regulations have been tightened considerably and there have been several cases of successful prosecution. In each case, however, the intent deliberately to deceive the public by uttering a colour photocopy as a genuine note was proved. Technically the offence takes places as soon as the photocopy is made, for whatever purpose, but as a rule only those cases in which an element of fraudulent deception subsequently arose are pursued with the full rigour of the law. The law is quite clear, however, and it is a criminal offence to make a photocopy or photograph of any current British note unless permission to do so has been obtained from the Treasury. The maximum penalty on conviction is an unlimited fine.

The note-issuing banks have, of course, taken steps in recent years to incorporate further security devices into their notes, notably the use of latent images and underprints in colours which are difficult, if not impossible to photocopy accurately. At the same time, the adoption of metal strips and more complex watermark devices has theoretically made the task of the forger much more difficult. If, by some unlucky chance, someone passes a dud note on to you, you must make no attempt to pass it in turn. To do so renders you liable to prosecution for uttering a forgery. Forged notes must be handed over to the police as soon as possible. If you receive a forged note in payment for goods or services you are entitled to claim its face value from the person who gave it to you. Even if the person giving you the note did not realise that it was counterfeit, it is assumed in law that he or she represented to you that the note was worth its face value at the time the note was passed. If the tenderer knew that the note was forged, he can be prosecuted; but at the end of the day he is still liable to you for the fraud and can be sued in the civil courts for the recovery of the sum involved. If, on the other hand, you received the money as a gift, you have no legal claim against the person who gave it to you. If you pay someone with a counterfeit note or coin unknowingly, you have committed no offence, but you must pay again. The degree of culpability is often difficult to prove or disprove, but it is unlikely that a prosecution would be initiated on the basis of a single note or coin.

It is also a serious offence to manufacture blanks, discs or washers which are intended to defraud the proprietors of vending machines, or to possess tools and equipment for the dishonest manufacture or alteration of such blanks for this purpose. Under the Gold and Silver Export Control Act (1920) melting down gold or silver coins to extract their precious metal content is an offence punishable by a fine of £100 or two years' imprisonment, or both.

Legal Tender

The dictionary defines this as currency which a creditor is bound by law to accept as payment of a money debt. Debts and purchases must be paid for in cash of legal tender unless the creditor or seller is willing to accept payment in another form, such as a postal order, money order, cheque or, nowadays, credit card. Bank of England notes of any denomination are legal tender in England and Wales. Formerly Bank of England pound notes (but no other) were legal tender in Scotland. Technically, since the demise of the pound note, no Bank of England notes are legal tender in Scotland, although in practice they circulate freely north of the Border. Even more surprisingly, Scottish banknotes are not legal tender anywhere, not even in Scotland! The subtle difference is reflected in the actual wording of the promise on English and Scottish banknotes. Thus English notes are inscribed *"I promise to pay the bearer on demand the sum of . . ."* without stipulating any specific place, the promise being made by the Chief Cashier. Scottish notes, on the other hand, have the promise in the third person. It is the bank itself which makes the promise *"to pay the bearer on demand . . . pounds sterling at their head office here in Edinburgh, by order of the Board"*. In practice, however, Scottish banknotes are accepted without question, not only throughout Scotland but also in parts of England, and are generally accepted in London, although there is no obligation on the part of a creditor so to do.

Apart from gold coins, the base-metal pound coin is legal tender for payment of any amounts. So, too, presumably, are the various two-pound and five-pound base-metal coins of recent years, even though they have been struck as commemoratives and not intended for general circulation in the ordinary sense. Smaller denominations are only legal tender up to a maximum value in each case. In the case of 50p coins, 25p crowns and 20p coins, they may be used alone, or in combination with each other, in payment of amounts up to £10. 10p and 5p coins, alone or in combination, may be used for sums up to £5. Bronze 1p and 2p coins, however, can only be used for payment of amounts up to 20p. In practice, of course, you can probably get away with making payment in larger quantities (within reason!) although strictly speaking there is no obligation on the part of your creditor to accept them.

An Offence to Possess Legal Tender Coins

From the foregoing it will be seen that gold coins are, and always have been, legal tender. Since 1817 the legal tender gold coin of the United Kingdom has been the sovereign (with its sub-division and multiples). Yet there have been times when actual possession of these legal tender coins has been, *per se*, an illegal act. The first attempt to regulate the movement and possession of gold coins arose in 1947 with the passage of the Exchange Control Act which made it illegal to buy, borrow, lend or sell any gold or foreign currency, unless authorised to deal in gold. Moreover it was stipulated that *"any person possessing gold should offer it for sale to an authorised dealer at a price not exceeding the authorised price, unless the Treasury consented to this retention of the gold"*.

The serious implications of this Act were mitigated in the case of numismatists by the Exchange Control (Collectors' Pieces Exemption) Order 1947, which allowed collectors to hold on to *"any gold coin which was minted in 1816 or earlier, and any gold coin which was minted after 1816 and which has a numismatic value greater than the value of the gold content which would have been received if the coin had been sold to an authorised (bullion) dealer"*. In effect this meant that numismatists and coin dealers were not hindered from buying and selling gold coins as long as the coins were in collectable condition and possessed numismatic interest. This loophole was brazenly breached in the 1960s and led to the Exchange Control (Gold Coins Exemption) Order of 1966 which aimed to prevent the loss of currency reserves caused by the import of gold coins from abroad, and to eliminate the hoarding of gold by speculators. By the terms of this Order no one was permitted to hold more than four gold coins minted after 1837 unless they had received express permission from the Treasury. The maximum was set at four coins so that people who had one or two sovereigns as mementoes could keep them without breaking the law. Numismatists who possessed more than four post-1837 gold coins on April 27, 1966 had to apply to the Treasury for permission to retain them. To do so they had to prove that they were *bona fide* collectors by completing form GC 1, providing a detailed list of the coins in their possession—not only in gold, but also in silver (pre-1816, 1816–1919 and post-1919) and base metals (before and after 1860). Several individuals were successfully prosecuted under this draconian legislation and their holdings of gold sovereigns confiscated, although no one was imprisoned or heavily fined as the legislation provided. The 1966 order was rescinded in 1970, re-imposed in a modified form in 1975, and finally revoked in 1979. Since that date numismatists and speculators alike have been free to collect (or hoard) gold to their hearts' content.

Value Added Tax

This is a matter which primarily concerns dealers, but it also applies to those who dabble in coins on a part-time basis, and has implications for collectors at all levels. Briefly, anyone conducting a business, or in self-employment, who has a turnover in excess of £43,000 per annum, must register

with HM Customs and Excise for the collection and payment of Value Added Tax. Anyone whose turnover is less than £43,000 is exempt from the obligation to register, but is at liberty to register if he or she feels that this would be advantageous. It is nice to think that there is an element of choice in this, although one would be hard pressed to think why anyone would voluntarily register for VAT unless they absolutely had to! Incidentally, the government raised the VAT registration level by 40 per cent to £35,000 in March 1991 with the avowed intention of relieving a large number of businesses from this burden, at a time when the rate of tax was increased from 15 per cent to 17.5 per cent. Assuming that you are a dealer with a turnover above the magic limit, then you are committing a serious offence if you fail to register. Registration then lays you open to the full machinery of the system. You have to charge VAT on all goods and services, issuing VAT invoices and receipts and keeping detailed accounts which are liable to snap inspection at any time. You have to make quarterly returns to Customs and Excise of the amount of tax you have collected. From this you are allowed to deduct the VAT which you yourself have paid out in the course of your business, and you then have to remit the difference to the VAT collector. Of course, should the amount you have paid exceed the tax you have collected, you receive a repayment in due course. This arises in businesses which handle zero-rated goods and services, but coins and medals do not come within that category.

For dealers in gold bullion, coins or medals, there is a special VAT leaflet which covers regulations specific to such matters. Since January 2000 investment gold has been exempt from VAT. A coin is classified as investment gold if it satisfies the following conditions: 1. Minted after 1800; 2. At least .900 fine; 3. Is or has been legal tender of its country of origin; 4. Is of a description of coin that is normally sold at a price that does not exceed 180% of the open market value of the gold contained in the coin. This is a complicated issue and further advice can be obtained from Customs & Excise Public Notice 701/21/99. A list of coins qualifying as investment gold is published in Public Notice 701/21A/99. When VAT is applicable of course it needs to be accounted for on the profit margin. It is vital therefore to maintain accurate records of all buying and selling, and which coins and medals are subject to VAT and which are exempt. Furthermore, the onus is on you to ensure that the source of the gold you bring into the country is impeccable. There are extremely heavy penalties for smuggling gold, and ignorance of the law, or apparently innocent handling of smuggled gold subsequently, are no defence.

From January 1, 1995 the special margin scheme of accounting for VAT currently available for certain second-hand goods, such as cars, was extended to almost all second-hand goods. The scheme allows businesses buying and selling eligible goods to account for VAT only on the difference between the buying and selling prices of these items.

A special system of accounting exists which enables some dealers to account for VAT without the need to keep a detailed record of every transaction. Certain works of art, antiques and collector's items, including "secondhand" coins, defined in Notice 712 *Second-hand goods*, were exempt from VAT at import. From January 1, 1996 these items became subject to VAT at import at an effective rate of 2.5 per cent.

Export and Import

Some coins do require an export licence before they can be taken out of the country and unfortunately these controls have been extended during the past year. Following the lifting of the export regulations relating to gold coins in 1979, then prior to April 1, 1993 the only coins which required any export licence were those with a value in excess of £35,000. However the agreement by the UK to implement an EC directive on the removal of cultural goods has resulted in a fresh interpretation of previous UK legislation on these coins which are on the market as a result of an archaeological find. Therefore as from April 1, 1993, any coin *whatever its value* which has come from an archaeological source within the UK will require an export licence even to take it to another EC country. Certain other coins of EC provenance other than the UK will now require an EC export licence. The value limit for non-archaeological source coins has been increased to £39,600 (Ecu 50,000). Both types of licence are issued by the Department of National Heritage, 2–4 Cockspur Street, Trafalgar Square, London SW1Y 5DH who can also supply a handy flow-chart to enable you to tell at a glance whether a licence is needed and what type. These new regulations are imposing an enormous additional burden on the trade and the British Numismatic Trade Association has held numerous meetings with the authorities in an attempt to reduce to a minimum the number of licence applications needed. Hopefully, by next year's edition there will be better news.

The restrictions applied to the importation of gold coins were removed in 1979, as previously mentioned. Coins of any kind are now permitted under Open General Import licence from any country and a specific or individual licence is no longer required. Details of any duties which may be payable on imported coins can be obtained from HM Customs and Excise, King's Beam House, Southwark, London SE1 or any local Customs and Excise office. Until recently, the only gold coins under embargo were Krugerrands. This was a political decision, aimed at tightening sanctions against South Africa, and applied to the importation of new gold coins from that country, but not to Krugerrands which had been brought into the United Kingdom, or any of the countries of the European Community, prior to the imposition of sanctions. In practice, it was very difficult to regulate the movement, let alone the importation, of Krugerrands, and with the relaxation of Apartheid this regulation has been lifted.

Importing Coins by Mail

Elsewhere in this volume will be found the names and addresses of mints, banks and numismatic bureaux around the world from whom it may be possible to obtain currency direct. It is a wise precaution to write to these bodies in the first instance for details of their sales and distribution. In some cases they appoint a dealer in Britain as an agent and this is a method of purchase that removes a great deal of the hassle and red tape. Nowadays, however, many mints and banks are quite happy to use the credit card system to make it easy to part you from your money. The problem arises, however, when the coins are despatched. As a rule, banks and mints stipulate quite clearly that they will not accept orders prepaid in cash, and it is an offence to send coins or banknotes out of the country as payment, except through banks authorised for this purpose. Cheques drawn on British banks should not be used. Indeed, this may be actively discouraged by the imposition of heavy clearance and handling charges at the other end. The converse is also true, although Americans seem to think that dollar cheques drawn on some obscure mid-West bank will be eagerly accepted here, and are consequently aggrieved when it is tactfully pointed out to them that this creates enormous problems—to say nothing of the swingeing bank charges incurred in converting such cheques to sterling. Other than credit cards, the Girobank system is probably the best method of remitting currency from one country to another; full details may be obtained from any post office. Details on the preferred method of sending remittances, or transferring cash to another country, as well as the transmission of coins by post to different countries, will be found in the *Royal Mail International Service Guide*. This also lists, among the prohibitions pertaining to each country, which countries accept gold or silver, and which ban the transmission of precious metals by post.

The receipt of postal packets containing coins from abroad makes you liable for Value Added Tax on their importation. As a rule, the despatching mint or bank will have affixed a Customs declaration to the packet, listing the contents, their weight and value, and it is on that basis that VAT will be calculated. The position regarding the import and export of coins by post is more complicated, and applies also to goods sent on approval. In such cases you must consult your Customs and Excise office who will advise you on the correct procedure and what your liabilities will be to tax in either case. This also applies to dealers taking stock out of the country to a coin show and then re-importing the unsold stock afterwards, or importing material purchased at the show.

Buying and Selling

When goods are sold, the seller and the buyer enter into a contract which confers rights and imposes obligations on both parties. The contract need not be in writing. There is no law governing the quality of goods sold by a private individual. If you purchase a coin from a fellow-collector as a result of an informal meeting at the local numismatic society it is incumbent on you to ensure that what you buy is what you think you are buying. If you purchase something from a dealer or shopkeeper, however, you are entitled under the Sale of Goods Act to goods of "merchantable quality" which means that they must be reasonably fit for their purpose. Items sold under a specific description, on the other hand, must correspond exactly with that description. If they do not, the seller *even a private individual* can be sued under the Sale of Goods Act. This is an important distinction because there is an erroneous notion that the Act does not apply to transactions between private individuals.

If A sells a coin to B, purporting it to be a rare date, and B subsequently discovers that the date has been deliberately altered, then B can sue A. Even if A claims that he made the sale in good faith, believing the coin to be a genuine rare date, he will still be liable for restitution (giving B his money back) and may also face a claim for damages. The Sale of Goods Act thus overturns the traditional adage *caveat emptor* which, in its full formula, translates as "let the buyer beware for he ought not to be ignorant of the nature of the property which he is buying from another party". Traditionally this was the maxim applicable at auctions. Once the auctioneer's gavel had dropped, the successful bidder had, in effect, made a contract with the vendor and was bound to pay for the lot, even if he subsequently discovered that what he had purchased was not what he had imagined. The view was that it was

up to the purchaser to ensure beforehand that what he purchased was genuine and answered the description in the sale catalogue.

Because of vexatious disputes arising from questions of authenticity, and with the Sale of Goods Act breathing down their necks, many auctioneers now have a safety net, in the form of extensions. These enable successful bidders to delay payment for two or three weeks while they seek expertisation of doubtful material. In other words, the law allows a cooling-off period, but only for he legitimate purpose of verifying the authenticity of items over which there may be some doubt. This is only operative in cases where a coin or medal is sold as genuine, and described and estimated in value accordingly. In many doubtful cases, however, an auctioneer will cover himself by adding the crucial words "as is" to the description of a lot. Then, indeed, it is a case of *caveat emptor*. The auctioneer has done everything humanly possible to draw attention to the controversial nature of the item, and it must then rest on the judgment of the purchaser.

On the subject of auctions there are legal aspects which are not always apparent, as well as subtle differences in law and practice between England and Scotland. These tend to arise in cases where coins and medals come up for sale at provincial general mixed auctions, rather than in the sales conducted by numismatic auctioneers. Goods up for auction may be subject to an upset price which is made public as the price at which the bidding will start. A reserve price, on the other hand, is known only to the auctioneer, and if it is not reached the goods will not be sold. Upset prices are common in Scotland, reserve prices in England. If no upset price is specified and the goods are not subject to a reserve price then the highest bid secures them, even though it may not be as high as the vendor hoped for. If a seller notifies other bidders that he is bidding for his own goods, or that he has employed an agent to bid for him, the bidding is legal. If he does not give notice and bids himself, or gets someone to bid for him, thus forcing up the price, the sale is fraudulent, and the buyer can purchase the goods for the amount of the last bid he made before fraudulent bidding started.

One frequently hears dark, but usually apocryphal, tales of "the ring" in action to depress the bidding and secure items below the price commensurate with their actual value. This is a fraudulent practice and in law is regarded as a criminal conspiracy. In practice, however, it would be very difficult for a group of dealers or other individuals to keep the bidding down merely by sitting on their hands. This practice could only operate successfully in sales which were largely, if not entirely, frequented by dealers. But coin sales, like other specialist collector-orientated auctions, are characterised by a high proportion of private bidders in attendance. Any conspiracy by a ring would merely allow some private bidder to step in and secure the lot at a bargain price. Rings are illegal, but in practice prosecutions are very rare as it is extremely difficult to obtain proof of their operations. What is more likely to happen is that dealers have been known to act in concert to force up the bidding to frighten off some unwelcome interloper. Here again, such tales are legion, but astonishingly lacking in specific details. The golden rule in attending auctions is to know what you are going after, and to have a pretty precise idea of how much you are prepared to pay. Do not be stampeded in the heat of the moment into going way beyond your limit.

Taxation of Profits on Disposal

The Inland Revenue define an asset as "any form of property (other than sterling) wherever situated". A disposal includes a sale, exchange or gift of an asset, or the receipt of a capital sum in respect of them. In layman's terms you dispose of an asset when you sell it, give it away, exchange it or lose it. A transfer of assets between husband and wife doesn't count (unless they are legally separated), nor does the transfer of an asset you leave when you die. If a disposal results in a profit you could be liable to tax. Any profit made on the sale of certain assets, including coins, medals and other collectables, constitutes a capital gain and is subject to Capital Gains Tax (CGT) which is now charged at the same 25% and 40% rates as income tax. However the government allows you to make a total capital gain in the current tax year of £5,500 before tax becomes chargeable. If this is the case, and the total proceeds from disposal do not exceed £10,000, then a simple declaration to this effect is all you need to make in the relevant section of your annual tax return.

Computing the actual capital gain is a complicated matter. Suppose you purchased a coin in 1960 for £5,000 and sold it in 1993 for £12,000. On the face of it, you've made a capital gain of £7,000 and you might think that you were liable to CGT because the gain was over £5,500. However, the

length of time you've held the asset also has to be taken into consideration. From April 6, 1988 the law was altered so that only gains made after March 31, 1982 are now taxable. In effect, you are taxed as if you acquired the coin on March 31, 1982. The initial value of the coin is deemed to be its market value at that date. If the gain from March 1982 to the time of disposal is greater than the overall gain from acquisition in 1960 to disposal in 1993, you take the lesser of the two figures. If this produces a gain, whereas the old method of working it out would have produced a loss, you will be regarded, for tax purposes, as having made neither a gain nor a loss on disposal. You have a choice of opting for computing from the time of actual acquisition or from March 1982, whichever seems the more advantageous; but once you've made your choice you cannot subsequently change your mind.

How do you establish what the coin was worth in March 1982? The Inland Revenue tend to regard Seaby, Krause or other relevant catalogues as their yardstick. The difference between the nominal or catalogue value in 1982 and what you eventually got for the coin *assuming that the latter was greater*, might be regarded as the capital gain, but even then the position is complicated by inflation in the intervening years eroding the real value of the coin.

At this stage things get really complicated as you have to work out the indexation allowance. This is determined by the Retail Prices Index (RPI), and you need to know the RPI for (a) the month of disposal, and (b) the month in which you acquired the asset, or March 1982, if later. The RPI is announced each month by the Departmenrt of Employment and is published in its *Employment Gazette* which ought to be available in your local public library. Take the RPI for the month of the disposal and subtract the RPI for the month when indexation commenced. Then divide the result by the RPI for the month when indexation began, and work out this figure to the nearest third decimal place. This is known as the indexation factor, which you then multiply by the initial value of your coin. Simple isn't it? In most cases, however, I expect you will have made a capital loss in real terms, so these sums, though necessary to satisfy the Inland Revenue, are largely academic.

Treasure
and the Law

Until the introduction of the new Treasure Act, the legal position regarding articles of value, found long after they were hidden or abandoned, was not as simple and straight-forward as it might be supposed. Furthermore, this was a case where the law in England and Wales differed fundamentally from that in Scotland.

Treasure Trove was one of the most ancient rights of the Crown, deriving from the age-old right of the monarch to grave treasure. In England and Wales, the law applied only to objects made of, or containing, gold or silver, whether in the form of coin, jewellery, plate or bullion. Moreover, the object had to be shown to have been deliberately hidden and the owner could not be readily found. The English law therefore excluded precious stones and jewels set in base metals or alloys such as bronze or pewter. It also took no account of artifacts in pottery, stone, bone, wood or glass which might be of immense antiquarian value.

In recent years, as a result of the rise in metal-detecting as a hobby, the archaeological lobby brought pressure to bear on Parliament to change the law and bring it into line with Scotland where the rules on Treasure Trove were far more rigor-ously interpreted. In Scotland the Crown is entitled to *all* abandoned property, even if it has not been hidden and is of little value. This applies even to objects dumped in skips on the pavement. Strictly speaking you would be committing a criminal offence if you removed an old chair from a skip without the owner's permission, although in practice such helping oneself rarely proceeds to a prosecution. In 1958 an archaeological expedition from Aberdeen University found several valu-able artifacts on St Ninian's Isle, Shetland. These included silver vessels and ornaments, as well as

Metal detecting can be fun—but be sure you know the rules!

a porpoise bone which had incised decoration on it. The archaeologists challenged the rights of the Crown to this treasure, arguing that the Crown would have to prove that the articles had been deliberately hidden, and that a porpoise bone was in any case not valuable enough to count as treasure. The High Court, however, decided that as long as the property had been abandoned, it belonged automatically to the Crown. Its value, intrinsic or otherwise, or whether or not it was hidden, did not make any difference. Since then, as a result of this decision in case law, the criteria for Treasure Trove have been very strictly applied in Scotland. It would have only required a similar test case in England or Wales to result in a similar tightening of the rules. This has been resisted, mainly by the detectorist lobby, but inevitably the government considered legislation to control the use of metal detectors, if not to ban them altogether.

In England and Wales a find of gold or silver coins, artifacts or ornaments, or objects which contain some of these metals, which appears to have been concealed by the original owner, was deemed to be Treasure Trove. It was not even necessary for the articles to be buried in the ground; objects concealed in thatched roofs or under the floorboards of buildings have been judged to be Treasure Trove. Such finds had to be notified immediately to the police who then informed the district coroner. He then convened an inquest which decided whether all or part of the find was Treasure Trove. Establishing the gold or silver content was straightforward, but the coroner's inquest had to decide whether the material was hidden deliberately and not just lost or abandoned, and that the owner could not be located. A gold coin found on or near a country footpath might reasonably have been dropped by the original possessor through a hole in pocket or purse and in such cases it was very unlikely that it would be deemed Treasure Trove, even if the coin turned out to be very rare. In this instance the coroner would then have had to determine who was the lawful owner of the find: the actual finder, the owner of the land where it was found or even the tenant of the land. As a rule, however, it was left to the finder and landowner to decide between them who the owner of the coin should be, and in some cases the matter could only be resolved by referring to a civil court. For this reason it was vital that metal detectorists should secure permission *in writing* from landowners before going on to their land, defining rights and obligations on both sides, in order to determine the disposal or share-out of any finds or proceeds from the sale of finds, *beforehand*.

If the coroner decided that the articles were deliberately concealed, and declared them to be Treasure

The Snettisham torcs—one of our country's greatest finds.

Trove, the find automatically reverted to the Crown. In practice the find was considered by the Treasure Trove Reviewing Committee of the Treasury. They might decide that although the articles *invariably coins* were gold or silver, they were so common that they were not required by the British Museum or one of the other great national collections, and would return them to the finder to dispose of at his discretion. If some or all of the coins were deemed vital for inclusion in a national collection the finder was recompensed with the full market value of the material. On the other hand, if someone found gold or silver which might be Treasure Trove and failed to declare it at the time, that person was liable to prosecution under the Theft Act should the find subsequently come to light. Not only could he face a heavy fine but the articles would be forfeit to the Crown, and of course no reward or recompense was then payable either.

The anomalies and inconsistencies of existing law on Treasure Trove were eliminated and the position considerably tightened up by the passage, on July 5, 1996, of the Treasure Act.

Announcing that the Treasure Act had received the Royal Assent, Lord Inglewood, National Heritage Minister, said, "This represents the first legislation on treasure trove to be passed in England and Wales and will replace common law precedents and practices dating back to the Middle Ages. The Act, which offers a clearer definition of treasure and simplified procedures for dealing with finds, will come into force after a code of practice has been drawn up and agreed by both Houses of Parliament". The Act came into force in England,

Wales and Northern Ireland on September 24, 1997, replacing the common law of treasure trove.

The act was introduced as a Private Member's Bill by Sir Anthony Grant, after the failure of an earlier attempt by Lord Perth. For the first time, it would be a criminal offence to fail to report within 14 days the discovery of an item which would be declared Treasure Trove. Finders will continue to be rewarded for reporting their discoveries promptly, while landowners and occupiers will also be eligible for rewards for the first time.

The Treasure Act covers man-made objects and defines treasure as objects other than coins which are at least 300 years old and contain at least 10 per cent by weight of gold or silver; coins more than 300 years old which are found in hoards (a minimum of two coins if the precious metal content is more than 10 per cent, and a minimum of 10 coins if the precious metal content is below 10 per cent). The act also embraces all objects found in clear archaeological association with items which are treasure under the above definitions. It also covers any object which would have been Treasure Trove under the previous definitions (e.g. hoards of 19th century gold or silver coins).

The maximum penalty for failing to report the discovery of treasure within 14 days will be a fine of £50,000 or three months imprisonment, or both.

In Scotland the police pass the goods on to the procurator fiscal who acts as the local representative of the Queen's and Lord Treasurer's Remembrancer. If the articles are of little value, historically or intrinsically, the finder will usually be allowed to keep them. If they are retained for the appropriate national collection then a reward equal to the market value is payable.

A favourite haunt of metal-detectorists these days is the beach, and many hobbyists make quite a lucrative living by sweeping the beaches especially just after a Bank Holiday. It's surprising how much loose change gets lost from pockets and handbags over a holiday weekend. Technically the coins recovered from the beach are lost property, in which case they ought to be surrendered to the police, otherwise the finder may be guilty of theft. In practice, however, the law turns a blind eye to coins, on the sensible grounds that it would be impossible to prove ownership. On the other hand, banknotes are treated as lost property since

someone could in theory at least identify a note as his by citing the serial number.

In the case of other objects, such as watches and jewellery, of course the law governing lost property is enforced, and the old adage of "finders keepers" does not apply. Any object of value, identifiable as belonging to someone, that is washed up on the foreshore or found in territorial waters is known technically as "wreck". This includes not just a wrecked ship, but any cargo that was being carried by a ship.

If wreck is not claimed by its owner, it falls to the Crown. In this case it is not necessary to prove deliberate concealment, as in the case of Treasure Trove. This law has a specific numismatic application in the case of the gold and silver coins washed up after storms around our shores, from Shetland to the Scillies. Such coins, emanating from wrecks of Spanish treasure ships and Dutch East Indiamen in particular, are well documented, and any such finds ought to be reported immediately to the police.

Stray finds of coins, as well as other objects of value, on public places, such as the street, a public park or a sports ground, are also subject to law. In this case the finder must take all reasonable steps to locate the owner. Anyone who keeps a coin without making reasonable effort to find the owner could be prosecuted for theft. As with the beach, however, such "reasonable effort" would clearly be impractical. Finding coins on private premises is another matter. In this case large bodies, such as the Post Office, British Rail, the British Airports Authority, bus companies, municipal authorities, hospitals, the owners of department stores, theatre and cinema proprietors and the like, may have bye-laws, rules and regulations for dealing with lost property found within their precincts, or in their vehicles. If you found a purse or wallet on a bus or train, or in a telephone kiosk or a shop, common sense (and your conscience) would tell you to hand it over to the driver, conductor, shopkeeper or official in charge. As a rule, unclaimed lost property reverts eventually to the finder, but not always; British Rail and some other organisations have a rule that in such cases the property reverts to the organisation. In any event, failure to disclose the find immediately might render you liable to prosecution for stealing by finding.

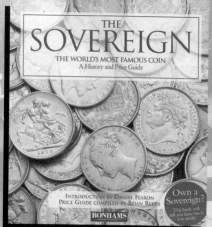

Treasure Act
Code of
Practice
—a summary

For easy reference a summary of the main points of the new law is reproduced here*. Further information will be found in the *Code of Practice on the Treasure Act*, which can be obtained free of charge from the Department for Culture, Media and Sport (formerly the Department of National Heritage) (telephone: 020 7211 6200). Metal detectorists are strongly advised to obtain a copy of the Code of Practice which, among other things, contains guidance for detectorists, sets out guidelines on rewards, gives advice on the care of finds and has lists of useful addresses.

What is the definition of treasure?

The following finds are treasure under the Act (*more detailed guidance is given in the Code of Practice*):

1. *Objects other than coins:* any object other than a coin provided that it contains at least 10 per cent of gold or silver and is a least 300 years old when found (objects with gold or silver plating normally have less than 10 per cent of precious metal).

2. *Coins:* all coins from the same find provided they are at least 300 years old when found (but if the coins contain less than 10 per cent of gold or silver there must be at least 10 of them; there is a list of these coins in the Code of Practice).

An object or coin is part of the same find as another object or coin if it is found in the same place as, or had previously been left together with, the other object. Finds may have become scattered since they were originally deposited in the ground.

Only the following groups of coins will normally be regarded as coming from the "same find":

(a) hoards that have been deliberately hidden;

(b) smaller groups of coins, such as the contents   of purses, that may have been dropped or lost   and

(c) votive or ritual deposits.

Single coins found on their own are not treasure and groups of coins lost one by one over a period of time (for example those found on settlement sites or on fair sites) will not normally be treasure.

3. *Associated objects:* any object, whatever it is made of, that is found in the same place as, or that had previously been together with, another object that is treasure.

4. *Objects that would have been treasure trove:* any object that would previously have been treasure trove, but does not fall within the specific categories given above. These objects have to be made substantially of gold or silver; they have to have been buried with the intention of recovery and their owner or his/her heirs cannot be traced.

The following types of find are not treasure:

(a) objects whose owners can be traced;

(b) unworked natural objects, including human and animal remains, even if they are found in association with treasure;

(c) objects from the foreshore, which are wreck.

If you are in any doubt, it will probably be safest to report your find.

What about objects found before the Act came into force?

You should report objects that come into any of the four categories just described (if found after September 23, 1997). There is no need to report any objects found before that date unless they may be treasure trove (see 4 above).

What should I do if I find something that may be treasure?

You must report all finds of treasure to the coroner for the district in which they are found *either* within 14 days after the date on which you made the find *or* within 14 days after the day on which you realised that the find might be treasure (for example, as a result of having it identified). The obligation to report finds applies to everyone, including archaeologists.

How do I report a find of treasure?

Very simply. You may report your find to the coroner in person, by letter, telephone or fax. The coroner or his officer will send you an acknowledgement and tell you where you should deliver your find. The Code of Practice has a list of all coroners' addresses, telephone and fax numbers.

There are special procedure for objects from a few areas for which treasure franchises exist, but they should be reported to the coroner in the usual way. The main franchise-holders (the Duchies of Lancaster and Cornwall, the Corporation of London and the City of Bristol) have confirmed that they will pay rewards for finds of treasure from their franchises in the normal way.

Where will I have to take my find?

You will normally be asked to take your find to a local museum or archaeological body. Local agreements have been drawn up for each coroner's district in England and Wales to provide the coroner with a list of such museums and archaeological organisations. The Department is publishing a series of leaflets, roughly one for each country of England and one for Wales, listing the relevant coroners, museums and archaeological services in each area.

The body which receives the find on behalf of the coroner will give you a receipt. Although they will need to know where you made the find, they will keep this information confidential if you or the landowner wish—and you should do so too.

The body receiving the find will notify the Sites and Monuments Record as soon as possible (if that has not already happened), so that the site where the find was made can be investigated by archaeologists if necessary. A list of Sites and Monuments Records is in Appendix 3 of the Code of Practice.

What if I do not report a find of treasure?

If you fail to report a find that you believe or have reasonable grounds for believing to be treasure without a reasonable excuse you may be imprisoned for up to three months or receive a fine of up to level 5 on the standard scale (currently £5,000) or both. You will not be breaking the law if you do not report a find because you do not initially recognise that it may be treasure, but you should report it once you do.

What happens if the find is not treasure?

If the object is clearly not treasure, the museum or archeological body will inform the coroner, who may then decide to give directions that the find should be returned without holding an inquest.

What happens if the find is treasure?

If the museum curator or archaeologist believes the find may be treasure, they will inform the British Museum or the National Museums & Galleries of Wales. The museums will then decide whether they or any other museum may wish to acquire it.

If no museum wishes to acquire the find, the Secretary of State will be able to disclaim it. When this happens, the coroner will notify the occupier and landowner that he intends to return the object to the finder after 28 days unless he receives an objection. If the coroner receives an objection, the find will be retained until the dispute is settled.

What if a museum wants to acquire my find?

If a museum wants to acquire part or all of a find, then the coroner will hold an inquest to decide whether it is treasure. The coroner will inform the finder, occupier and landowner and they will be able

to question witnesses at the inquest. Treasure inquest will not normally be held with a jury.

If the find is declared to be treasure, then it will be taken to the British Museum or the National Museums & Galleries of Wales, so that it can be valued by the Treasure Valuation Committee.

How do I know I will receive a fair price for my find?

Any find of treasure that a museum wishes to acquire must be valued by the Treasure Valuation Committee, which consists of independent experts. The Committee will commission a valuation from one or more experts drawn from the trade. You, together with the museum that wishes to acquire the find and any other interested party, will have an opportunity to comment on the valuation and to send in a separate valuation of your own, before the Committee makes its recommendation. If you are dissatisfied you can appeal to the Secretary of State.

What if the coroner or museum loses or damages my find?

They are required to take reasonable steps to ensure that this does not happen; but, if it does, you should nonetheless be compensated.

Who will receive the reward?

This is set out in detail in the Code of Practice. To summarise:

— where the finder has permission to be on the land, rewards should continue to be paid in full to him or her (the burden of proof as to whether he or she has permission will rest with the finder). If the finder makes an agreement with the occupier/landowner to share a reward, the Secretary of State will normally follow it;

— if the finder does not remove the whole of a find from the ground but allows archaeologists to excavate the remainder of the find, the original finder will normally be eligible for a reward for the whole find;

— rewards will not normally be payable when the find is made by an archaeologist;

— where the finder has committed an offence in relation to a find, or has trespassed, or has not followed best practice as set out in the Code of Practice, he or she may expect no reward at all or a reduced reward. Landowners and occupiers will be eligible for rewards in such cases.

How long will it take before I receive my reward?

The Code of Practice states that you should receive a reward within one year of you having delivered your find, although this may take longer in the case of very large finds or those that present special difficulties. If no museum wants to acquire the find it should be disclaimed within six months or within three months if it is a single object.

Reproduced from "The Treasure Act, Information for Finders of Treasure (England and Wales)" leaflet DCMSJ0229NJ, published by the Department for Culture, Media and Sport.

Coin News

Britain's Best-Selling Coin Magazine

Subscribe to
COIN NEWS today
from just £30.00

Call 01404 44166

visit www.tokenpublishing.com

or e-mail info@tokenpublishing.com

Index
to COIN NEWS

This index of persons, places, events, articles and reviews, as well as new issued detailed to COIN NEWS, covers the period from September 2003 to August 2004. Entries are indicated by numbers signifying the month (e.g. 9-12 relate to September to December 2003 and 1-8 refer to January to August 2004) followed by the page number.

Seleucid Coins 2/8
Standard Catalog of World Coins
    6/47, 7/10
Standard Catalog of World Gold
    Coins 6/10
Standard Catalog of World Paper
    Money 9/47
A Thousand Guineas 12/45
Tokens and Tallies through the Ages
    3/62
US Paper Money Errors 10/50
World Paper Money General Issues
    4/45

NEW ISSUES
Armenia 11/46
Australia 9/14, 1-/14, 11/14, 12/16,
    2/16, 5/14, 6/14, 7/14, 8/14
Austria 9/14, 11/14, 12/16, 1/14,
    3/14, 4/14, 5/14, 6/14, 7/14
Bermuda 6/15
British Virgin Islands 10/14, 1/14,
    2/16, 3/14
Canada 11/8, 19, 5/10, 6/14, 7/15
China 5/14
Cook Islands 12/16
Cuba 11/46
Czech Republic 11/14, 8/14
Faroe Islands 3/50
France 2/14
Germany 2/14
Gibraltar 12/16, 1/14, 3/14
Greece 2/14, 7/12
Guernsey 7/14
Hong Kong 5/58
Hungary 2/14
Iraq 12/49, 1/46, 2/49, 3/49
Ireland 12/12
Isle of Man 10/14, 11/14
Israel 9/14, 5/14
Jordan 2/50
Kenya 11/45, 6/15
Laos 12/16
Latvia 4/14
Liberia 6/8
Lithuania 9/14, 10/14, 1/14, 6/14
Mongolia 8/14
New Zealand 10/16, 2/12
Nicaragua 9/48

Norway 2/8
Poland 9/14, 10/14, 11/14, 12/16,
    1/14, 6/14, 7/14
Portugal 1/14
Qatar 12/50
Romania 2/50
Rwanda 11/46
Serbia 7/15
Sierra Leone 9/14, 12/16, 2/16
Singapore 7/15
Slovakia 1/14, 4/14, 7/14
Solomon Islands 2/16
South Georgia 10/14
Spain 4/14
Surinam 8/15
Switzerland 4/14, 8/14
Taiwan 4/14
Tonga 7/14
Turkey 4/12
Uganda 6/15
Ukraine 3/50
USA 11/13, 45, 6/8
Vatican 11/14, 12/16, 5/14
Vietnam 10/14

CONTRIBUTORS
Ackroyd, Alan 9/52, 10/56, 11/52,
    12/55, 1/50
Allen, Leslie L. 8/36-7
Andrew, John 9/18-20, 10/19-20,
    11/30-1, 12/21-3, 1/19-21, 2/21-
    3, 3/19-21, 4/19, 73, 5/19-20,
    6/8, 18-20, 7/19-20, 8/18-20, 30
Baker, Paul 10/31-2, 12/32, 1/334-5,
    3/31-2
Beaney, Walter 11/55, 2/67, 5/73,
    7/73
Bennett, Graham 12/25-6
Blair, Dennis G. 10/45-6, 2/37,
    5/35-6
Box, Roger 9/27-8, 10/25-7, 11/23-5
Dales, John S. 12/45
Derriman, Mary 1/37
Dracott, I.W.P. 4/29-41, 5/44-6,
    7/30-1
Falkiner, Richard 4/20
Fogg, Nicholas J. 10/73
Forrest, Bob 7/39-40, 8/43-4

Grant, Jim 7/44-5
Groves, Richard I. 7/10
Hammond, P. 10/43
Horwood, Mike 1/31-2, 7/33-4
Jewell, Brian 3/62
Keogh, Steve 1/67
Landon, Graham 4/50
Lanyon, Angela 10/41, 12/34-5,
    5/49-50
Leighton, Phil 8/50-1
McCreath, William 11/19-20, 7/23-4
McGroarty, Derick 4/31-2
Mackay, James 9/50-1, 10/53-4,
    11/49-50, 12/ 52-3, 1/48-9, 2/54-
    5, 3/53-4, 4/47-8, 63, 5/61-2,
    6/59-60, 7/57-8, 8/47-9, 59-60
Makarov, Alexei 5/23-4, 6/31-2
Matthews, David, 11/32-3, 8/35
Matthews, Robert 8/27-8
Morgans, Geraint 6/49-50
Morris, Eric 12/71
Murray, Ron 6/73
Muslish, N. 6/35-6
Palermo, Raymond 9/30-2, 10, 28-9,
    11/27, 2/29-30, 3/42-3, 4/27-8,
    5/27-9, 6/27-8. 7/27-8, 8/31-3
Petts, William 2/25-7
Plant, Richard 9/45, 10/49, 11/41,
    12/43, 1/60, 2/42, 4/62, 5/65,
    6/63m 7/62, 8/64
Pottinger, David 9/41-2, 3/57-8,
    7/47-8
Rodgers, Dr Kerry 4/52-4, 7/60
Rubin, Norman A. 2/52-3
Rudd, Chris 10/22-3, 1/43, 3/24-5
Selby, Peter 4/65-6
Skellern, Steven 2/33-5, 3/34-6
Sly, John 11/34-6, 12/37-8, 3/39-40,
    4/35-6, 5/31-2, 6/44-5, 7/36-7
Stevens, William 9/22-4, 1/27-9,
    6/23-5
Webb, Christopher 3/75
Webb, Denzil 9/35, 10/34, 11/39,
    1/39-40, 2/41-2, 5/39-40,
    6/3940, 8/39-40
Webster, Mish 12/40-2
Wilkin, Trevor 6/15
Wilson, L.M. 3/27-8, 4/23-4